'...an original, insightful, and innovative contribution to the literature on terrorism.'

– Jeffrey M. Bale, Monterey Institute of International Studies

'...among the most original and sweeping theoretical works to come from the terrorism studies genre in the last decade.'

– Jeffrey B. Cozzens, White Mountain Research LLC

'It is rare to find a work of such originality in a field like terrorism studies, which is dominated either by journalistic cliches or a crudely logistical analysis. Griffin locates terrorism in a richly conceived context that is ethical and epistemological as much as it is political.'

– Dr. Faisal Devji, University of Oxford

'In an analysis that is at once philosophical, psychological, political, and historical, Roger Griffin brings to the study of modern terrorism the same breadth of knowledge, aquaintance with specialized literature, and empathic insight he brought to his study of Modernism and Fascism. This new book builds upon the foundation of Griffin's study of modernism and the responses to it which determined the epochal nature of the twentieth century. For him, "terrorism" is a product of a fear of loss of meaning in the world combined with the conviction that the world must be remade if meaning is to be saved. Thus, terror is a response to a historical situation that regularly recurs, but modern terrorism can be understood only within the context of the threats to meaning posed by modernism itself. The book has a practical aspect as well as a theoretical one. It tries to provide insight into the "inside" of modern terrorism – what motivates, sustains, and reproduces "the terrorist."'

– Hayden White, Professor Emeritus of Historical Studies,
University of California

'...both innovative and original...'

– The Bookseller

'Since 9/11 there have been any number of detailed studies of terrorist groups, many of them by counter-terrorism professionals or reporters specialising in a particular region. Meanwhile, a small band of academics have tried to step back from the present so as to metaphysically locate what all or most terrorists are seeking to achieve, whether they realise it or not. Roger Griffin is a well-known expert on political violence and European Fascism. He brings a great deal of conceptual clarity and prodigious learning to a subject where emotion and prejudice are often uppermost. This is a valuable contribution to understanding the terrorism phenomenon."'

– Michael Burleigh, author of Blood and Rage: A Cultural History of Terrorism

Terrorist's Creed

Fanatical Violence and the Human Need for Meaning

Roger Griffin
Professor in Modern History, Oxford Brookes University

First published 2012 by
PALGRAVE MACMILLAN

Palgrave Macmillan in the UK is an imprint of Macmillan Publishers Limited, registered in England, company number 785998, of Houndmills, Basingstoke, Hampshire RG21 6XS.

Palgrave Macmillan in the US is a division of St Martin's Press LLC, 175 Fifth Avenue, New York, NY 10010.

Palgrave Macmillan is the global academic imprint of the above companies and has companies and representatives throughout the world.

Palgrave® and Macmillan® are registered trademarks in the United States, the United Kingdom, Europe and other countries.

ISBN 978–0–230–24129–9

This book is printed on paper suitable for recycling and made from fully managed and sustained forest sources. Logging, pulping and manufacturing processes are expected to conform to the environmental regulations of the country of origin.

A catalogue record for this book is available from the British Library.

A catalog record for this book is available from the Library of Congress.

10   9   8   7   6   5   4   3   2   1
21   20   19   18   17   16   15   14   13   12

Printed and bound in Great Britain by
CPI Antony Rowe, Chippenham and Eastbourne

To Mariella and Vincent,
my antidotes to terror

Of war and peace the truth just twists,
Its curfew gull just glides.
Upon four-legged forest clouds
The cowboy angel rides,
With his candle lit into the sun,
Though its glow is waxed in black —
All except when 'neath the trees of Eden

The savage soldier sticks his head in sand
And then complains
Unto the shoeless hunter who's gone deaf
But still remains
Upon the beach where hound dogs bay
At ships with tattooed sails
Heading for the Gates of Eden

With a time-rusted compass blade,
Aladdin and his lamp
Sits with Utopian hermit monks
Side-saddle on the Golden Calf,
And in their promises of paradise
You will not hear a laugh —
All except inside the Gates of Eden

Contents

Acknowledgements

Writing acknowledgements for a new book reminds me (at least in my case) of preparing a speech for an awards ceremony when you have not even been short-listed for a prize, and which will in any case not be covered by the media. Who will read these lines other than a few intimate friends and family who will probably not read the book, or a few students who peruse them as a displacement activity when they should be studying the text? But I welcome the convention as an opportunity to thank in writing those who made this book possible.

And that is where the problems start. Those of us working in the human sciences are all dwarfs standing on the backs of giants, or stage-divers borne aloft by many pairs of hands. In writing a book so far beyond my habitual comfort zone of comparative fascist studies, I feel particularly puny and assisted. Its completion has been reliant on the wonderful academic resources and institutions which have formed coral-like over the centuries as a vast barrier reef, teeming with the weirdest life-forms of independent intellectual and spiritual life, protecting society against the storm-waves of collective fanaticism and charismatic politics, and the predatory deep-sea Krakens of ignorance, superstition, and despotism. They are organisms worth preserving against all totalitarianisms, secular or religious, who are prepared to destroy them entirely by dynamite fishing for non-existent shoals of 'new men' or new believers.

The staff of the Bodleian and Brookes libraries, the many editors, publishers, and translators who have made it possible for hundreds of specialists, some of them of extraordinary multi-lingual talent and culture, to make their knowledge available in print or in cyberspace on which I have drawn so extensively in researching for this project, the gifted novelists and film-makers who have fashioned bathyscaphes plunging far deeper and more creatively into the recesses of the human psyche than I ever could: all their work is subsumed in this book. It is a book which is, as a study of generic patterns of phenomena within an extremely broad remit, far more lightweight and superficial than much of the material I have devoured to write it. I am also deeply appreciative of the algorithmic and communication miracles conjured up by IT geniuses in the last 40 years, and Google in particular, whose search engine has allowed me to carry on writing much of this book many miles away from the nearest library by supplementing my own considerable paper archive of books, photocopies, and notes.

As for specific debts, I am grateful to the five cohorts of MA students at Oxford Brookes University taking my special subject on terrorism who were exposed to my theories before they had fully matured. I am grateful to my supportive colleagues in the History Department and to the sabbatical scheme that allowed me to write the book. I thank Michael Strang, formerly of Palgrave Macmillan, for helping me launch the 'Modernism and' series, the tight format for which this volume soon outgrew and thus developed into a 'real' monograph. I thank his colleagues Ruth Ireland and Alison Howe, for their encouragement and flexibility over word-length, and Jenny McCall for piloting the boat into the harbour as Palgrave Macmillan's new History Editor.

I owe a special debt to Jeffrey Bale and Jeffrey Cozzens, both outstanding 'terrorologists' of formidable expertise, who generously made time to read the manuscript despite onerous commitments and suggested some vital amendments to the first draft, and who deserve considerable credit if the final result is worth reading. Of particular help was the input of James Clarke, a promising postgraduate student from Oxford Brookes, who conscientiously proofread it chapter by chapter as it came off the production line (in two versions!) and then compiled the bibliography. I am also grateful to the MD, comedian, and documentary-maker, Phil Hammond, who in the last stages of writing 'interviewed' me about terrorism for another project with an intelligence and enthusiasm that inspired me to complete the book with a certain gusto. Once the manuscript was complete three eminent academics, Faisal Devji, Hayden White, and Michael Burleigh, showed generosity of spirit and time in reading it. Their enthusiastic endorsements have encouraged me to hope that I may have made a serious contribution not just to terrorist studies but to understanding better the extraordinary episodes of violence and calculated inhumanity which have characterized modern history. It was also deeply satisfying that Bob Dylan's closest associates have so generously allowed me to use three verses from his *Gates of Eden* as the epigraph to this book because they recognized that my underlying approach to human violence and fanaticism is consonant with his, even if it sadly lacks the poetic concision and transformative power of his language.

I thank my wife Mariella, as always my most severe but most inspiring critic, who can take credit for the final title when the first was deemed unsuitable. A special acknowledgment goes to my son Vincent, who has now reached an age where he understands that citing other people's books in an academic text is not 'cheating'. He took a real interest in how the book was going from the outset, and is responsible for the concept and initial sketches for the cover design. I thank my wife's mother, Rosalba, for the delicious *tortellini* and *polpettoni* which kept me going while I was finishing the book in Italy. I thank my English family Paul, Maggi, Gill, and Peter, for their unswerving faith in my academic ability, however unintelligible to them my publications may be. I thank my mother, Joan Harbour, whom I hope would have been enthralled by this book, despite the disturbing nature of its contents. To examine the extremist fruits of modern anomy and existential terror requires a degree of emotional security and physical wellbeing, which is what my wider Anglo-Italian family has always given me. If this book can deepen humanistic understanding of and encourage intelligent responses to terrorism and all forms of fanatical violence in readers from any walk of life (even among violent fanatics themselves!), I dedicate it to them too.

OXFORD AND CAMPOMORONE

1
Forethoughts: The Liquid Fear of Terrorism

Apocalypse in the subway

MIT astrophysicist John Koestler drives at top speed from Lexington, Massachusetts to a subway station in Manhattan determined to avert a major catastrophe. Two days earlier he witnessed a horrendous plane crash right next to the motorway where he was gridlocked. This, he is now convinced, in a bizarre episode of premonition, was predicted along with all the major calamities to occur on earth since 1959 in a list of continuous numbers which encrypted the precise location, date and number of victims. The next disaster is due to occur today at Lafayette Station, near New York's Little Italy. Despite telling the FBI to seal off the area in a phone tip-off the night before, Koestler is disconcerted to find the station still open, so he pushes his way onto the crowded platform to see what he can do. There his eyes alight on a man – in his twenties with a generically foreign complexion and an incongruous woollen hat – lurking behind a column and behaving suspiciously, his jacket bulging with some object he is keen to conceal.

Convinced the man is a suicide bomber and is about to wreak carnage, Koestler gives chase through the dense throng of commuters and pursues him into a crowded carriage, closely followed by armed police who initially treat him as the suspect instead. Finally persuaded to turn their attention to the man he has cornered in front of the locked interconnecting door of the last carriage, a cop orders him to put his hands up. A bunch of stolen DVDs fall on the floor. It has been a false alarm. But the fulfilment of the prophecy announced in the coordinates and death toll for that date on his list of major disasters immediately ensues with chilling inevitability. An electrical malfunction in the track-switching mechanism (due, we will learn, to the same solar flare activity which caused the plane to crash and which will soon consume planet Earth entirely) forces a train on the other track to career off the rails and mount the platform out of control, cutting a gruesome swathe of death through the thronged commuters, a catastrophe recreated in graphically realistic CGI detail. The final crane shot from outside the station, with an American flag fluttering forlornly in the foreground, reveals a scene of urban death and destruction unmistakably designed to trigger painful memories of 9/11 in the US psyche.

Alex Proyas' *Knowing* (2009) is a science fiction film starring Nicholas Cage. Commentators have seen encoded within the narrative apocalyptic echoes of the *Final Destination* film series, the best-selling Christian fundamentalist *Left Behind* novel and DVD series (over 65 million book sales by 2010), and even the salvationist doctrine of Scientology (*scientia* means knowledge, or knowing) with its guardian angels and higher forces directing human destiny. What concerns us here, though, is what the airplane and subway disaster scenes in the film tell us about the way terrorism has entered the collective imagination of the West in (late? high?) modernity. And when I say 'us' I am not referring to the many thousands living daily in a tragic life-or-death situation in which they are exposed to a statistically high risk of terrorist outrage and political or religious murder – for whom reading a book like this would generally be an absurd cultural luxury far removed from their minute-to-minute concerns of survival. I have in mind the countless millions who are objectively more likely to win the national lottery than become victims of a terrorist outrage, yet whose lives are gnawed at by the subliminal fear of terrorism and by apocalyptic presentiments about the end of the world (perhaps a cosmic projection of the end of *their* world?) given such powerful allegorical expression in *Knowing*.

The trauma of 9/11, which within minutes had become one of the most important global media events ever generated by the 'society of the spectacle',[1] left such a powerful subconscious state of alert in New York that in 2005, when a Cirrus SR20 crashed into Manhattan's Belair Building through pilot error, the city 'went through it all again', witnessing a wave of panic during which 'the mobile phone networks jammed as people rushed to telephone their loved ones', and causing the Pentagon 'to scramble jets over several US cities including New York, Washington, Los Angeles and Seattle'.[2] Three years later, on 27 April 2009, when a low-flying VC-25 (the iconic plane used for the presidential Air Force One) circled low over New York City for a photo opportunity, it unleashed enough mayhem on the streets below to lead to the resignation of Louis Caldera, director of the White House Military Office.[3]

September 11th 2001 was the day when terrorism mutated as a fact of modern life, first for US citizens and then in an emotional pandemic spreading throughout what used to be called 'the First World', most of which had been for decades habituated to living at a safe distance from political hotspots. It was no longer something remote that happens elsewhere and to other people, like famines or revolution. Instead it could potentially occur whenever an individual passed over the invisible threshold from private into public space. As headline-grabbing terrorist attacks in the haunts of First World citizens proliferated along with their choice of civilian targets – airport lounges, theatres, night-clubs, pubs, restaurants, rush-hour traffic, shopping malls, sporting stadia, beach-resorts – metropolises acquired a shadowy aura of nameless menace. It was seared into adult consciousness that any public space could become the site for anyone to become the victim of someone else's utopian cause, the banal furniture of urban existence – a supermarket, a railway station, a disco, a bus – suddenly turning out to be the last things a commuter, shopper, tourist, or school-girl might ever see on their way to a destination they would never reach because it happened to intersect with the itinerary of someone's private war on society. A decade on, the insecurity bred by this momentous event, simultaneously real and mythic, more ontological than concrete when contrasted with the risks of death by heart attack, traffic accidents, or muggings to which the average Westerner is exposed, had subtly altered the experience and texture of modern life for millions.[4]

The absent towers now cast a long shadow. In 2001 42,196 US citizens died in road accidents, a figure that remains stubbornly constant year on year, yet the threat of dying in a car has never wormed its way into the day-to-day sense of security of the inhabitants of modernity. Less than 3,000 died in the 9/11 attacks, but since that day there are millions in the modern world for whom, however secure their material circumstances, a permanent subjective threat of terrorist violence now lurks, spasmodically waiting to pop out of the back of the mind in the bustle of urban routine like a phantom tooth-ache. In an important essay on the need for academics to get a historical 'grip' on terrorism to restore a sense of proportion, Isabelle Duyvesteyn compares the modern psychosis about terrorism to the late nineteenth century in Europe when sporadic anarchist violence had, thanks to its sensationalist coverage in the press, succeeded in creating 'an all-pervasive fear that gripped whole societies'. The collapse of scenery in a Parisian theatre unleashed pandemonium as people rushed in terror to the exits to avoid the imminent explosions.[5] In this context the subway scene in *Knowing* could be cited as evidence to support the striking thesis explored in five monographs[6] by the world's most influential expert on the sociology of modernity, Zygmunt Bauman, namely that under its impact reality is becoming 'liquid'. He highlights the paradoxical feature of being a citizen in a 'materialistic' civilization which has on average, at least in the First World, objectively extended longevity and maximized consumption while minimizing threats to physical well-being and the risk of violent or avoidable death: modern life is pervaded by a state of groundless anxiety bordering on paranoia.

Certainly there is an increasingly conspicuous nexus of collective, global threats to the future of our planet or species to be worried about – the demographic explosion, ecological depredation and disasters, irreversible climate change, the depletion of food and energy resources to name but a few. Then there are culture-specific dangers – the shift of the hubs of economic and productive domination from the Europeanized and Americanized world to Asia, unpredictable migratory pressures and mass immigration, the loss of the paradoxical Cold War securities, the unforeseeable evolution of Islamic societies, the running sores and open wounds of trouble spots such as Israel and her immediate neighbours, as well as Iraq, Iran, Afghanistan, and North Korea, and the descent into anarchy and guerrilla warfare in some central African states. Such concrete problems are given a particular resonance in the context of the social, experiential and technological forces and factors that ever since the nineteenth century have been progressively 'disenchanting' or 'disembedding' reality to produce a sociological and psychological quicksand under even the well-heeled feet of the earth's fully 'modernized' inhabitants. Modernity may look solid materially, but it provides no foothold, no ground, no existential or psychological *terra firma*. We are all at sea, even if some of us are more temperamentally predisposed to notice it or admit it to ourselves than others, and more prone to ontological sea-sickness than our companions in the temporary life-boat chance has thrown us into.

In the context of the 'liquid fear' identified by Bauman, one reason why terrorism especially since 9/11 has had such a profound resonance in the modern (i.e. Western) psyche is arguably because it crystallizes and renders palpable the liquefying impact of modernity on reality and the anxiety this induces. Not just each successful act of terrorism, but every foiled plot and trial relating to it that hits the headlines confirms one of the ongoing subplots of contemporary history, the story that it could all be snuffed out in a moment, at least from the solipsistic vantage point of our own lives. To quote car accident statistics is irrelevant, because we have learned to live subjectively with that risk. But the terrorist threat is of a different order. If an unknown sociopath had once sabotaged your car by cutting the hydraulic pipe to the brakes, even if you got out of the ensuing accident unscathed, the terrifying memory of hurtling towards a road junction impotent to slow down would undermine the subliminal sense of security with which you had always driven. Even the slightest unresponsiveness of the brakes might induce in you involuntary panic. You no longer trust the car. Driving precipitates liquid fear.

The Titanic syndrome

9/11 and its sequels in Bali, Madrid, and London and numerous near-sequels have had a similar effect, undermining the sense of security and the taken-for-granted solidity of reality which once underlay the lives of millions in the urbanized democracies of the West. It has triggered what Bauman calls 'the Titanic syndrome', namely 'the horror of falling through the wafer-thin crust of civilization into that nothingness stripped of the elementary staples of organized, civilized life'. It is a nothingness akin to death itself within the limits of the human *imaginaire*, or the closest our mortal minds can get to grasping emotionally the inconceivable prospect of personal non-being. For Bauman the true horror of the *Titanic* disaster was not embodied in the iceberg, but in what went on in the bowels of the ship between the moment when it was struck and the moment when it sank, 'something all the more horrifying for staying concealed most of the time (perhaps all of the time) and so taking its victims by surprise whenever it crawls out of its lair, always catching them unprepared and inept to respond'. The sinking of a luxury liner on its maiden voyage became a living metaphor for the return to the surface of the repressed awareness that 'civilization is vulnerable: it stays but one shock away from inferno'.[7] The sense of civilization's fragility and imminent destruction (dramatized in such graphic CGI detail in Roland Emmerich's 2009 disaster movie *2012* and its kin) is, at least on one level, an unconscious displaced metaphor for the fact that one day our own all too solid flesh shall melt.

It would be insensitive to trivialize, intellectualize, or spirit away through a preoccupation with symbolism the horrendous human and material destruction of that day and the immense physical suffering and emotional pain it caused to the immediate victims and their loved ones. Yet, on one level the Twin Towers can be seen not just as a pair of functional skyscrapers, but as the static, vertical *Titanic* of a triumphalist post-Cold War liberal (capitalist? Western?) civilization, some of whose doomed passengers fell into the thin air of a radiant blue September morning instead of the black, freezing waters of the Atlantic. The irresistibly haunting quality emanating from Richard Drew's photographs of one of the approximately 200 victims who jumped from the towers that morning to escape the lethal flames and smoke turned 'The Falling Man' into an iconic image of the disaster,[8] inspiring Don Delillo's novel *Falling Man* (2007) exploring the psychological and symbolic aspect of terrorism, and prompting an American theologian to declare that 'perhaps the most powerful image of despair at the beginning of the twenty-first century is not found in art, or literature, or even popular music. It is found in a single photograph'.[9] Certainly, the instant of static, geometric perfection distilled from the obscene kinetic event of a man plunging head-first to his death in a yoga-like pose framed by the vertical lines of the North Tower is deceptive and artificial, since he was actually tumbling grotesquely as he fell. Living horror has been effaced by abstract form. Moreover, the man was eventually identified with some measure of certainty as 43-year-old Jonathan Briley, who worked in the top-floor restaurant. However, the aesthetic perfection of the image of a single, and still nameless victim of 9/11 who is about to be smashed to unrecognizable pulp on the street below turned him into the equivalent of the 'unknown warrior' of a war, permitting the empathetic imagination to come as close as it ever may to the experiential horror of that morning for those trapped in the building, a synecdoche of the entire tragedy that had struck the US 'out of the blue'.

Within the context of Bauman's study of the modern liquefaction of fear, the image's powerful resonance is comparable to the morbid fascination with the experiences of the passengers between the moment the ocean-liner struck the iceberg and when it finally broke apart and sank, a fascination demonstrated in a stream of eyewitness accounts which filled the newspapers of the day and 85 years later helped make James Cameron's film one of the most viewed films of all time. Bauman suggests the enduring fixation with the fate of the *Titanic* is not just with the event itself but with what it symbolizes *existentially*: 'This single momentous, obsessing act flung to the surface the suppressed recognition of the acute fragility not just of the Western project of progress but of our own existential insecurity and mortality. It brought forward the deferred confrontation with our day of reckoning juggled away in routine existence, like a ghastly drowned victim bobbing up on the surface of the lake to confront in a nightmare its murderer who for years thinks he or she has "got away with it".'[10] In a directly analogous way, we (even a female 'we') can recognize in the 'falling man' a presentiment of ourselves in a future moment when we (are forced to) execute our own *salto mortale* into the void from the false security temporally found in the Iron Cage of rational existence, even if the bars are decked with computer screens, games consoles, and flat-screen TVs. *Hypocrite voyeur. Mon semblable, mon frère.*[11]

The implication of this lengthy train of thought is this: beyond any immediate strategic objectives, the aim of terrorism is to disseminate terror, and the virtual resonance chamber which dramatically amplifies the impact of terrorist strikes in the heartlands of stable First World societies, thereby helping to realize the goals of the terrorists, is the liquid fear that is endemic to societies under a Western modernity which has destroyed communal existential certainties. It is a fear sometimes raised to fever pitch by a media-dominated society addicted to rolling news and images of catastrophe small and great. A 'safe' distance from the war zones, functioning modernity has created a bizarre situation in which both potential terrorists and the demonized Others ('the Enemy'), a handful of whom may one day by a freak of chance be their immediate victims, and the countless more who are the real targets of the attacks, namely the spectators who find the spectacle of terrorism so compelling and are duly terrorized, cohabit the same social space, even if they experience them through utterly different lenses. Commenting on the 7/7 London suicide bombings, Bauman remarks that:

> A dozen or so Islamic plotters, ready to kill, proved to be enough to create the atmosphere of a besieged fortress and raise a wave of 'generalized insecurity'. Insecure people tend to seek feverishly for a target on which to unload their gathering anxiety and to restore their lost self-confidence by placating their offensive, frightening and humiliating sentiment of helplessness. The besieged multi-ethnic and multicultural cities are turning into habitations shared by both the terrorists and their victims. Each side confirms the worst fears of the other and adds substance to their prejudices and hatreds. Between themselves, locked into a sort of liquid modern version of the *dance macabre*, the two sides won't allow the phantom of a siege ever to rest.[12]

Such reflections cast light on one of the principal purposes of this book. It is written to call a unilateral halt to the macabre dance of mutual incomprehension and demonization between terrorists and their targets, not, of course, the victims, but the spectators who survive to have their sense of security further eroded and their achievements in life relativized. It sets out to do this by making terrorists more comprehensible, less alien, less demonized, and certainly more human to the vast majority who live outside the charmed but cursed orbit of their fanaticism. It aims to dispel some of the irrational anxieties which surround violent events whose 'rational', objective threat to society is amplified by a particular constellation of apparently irrational but on closer inspection intelligible social and historical factors. These factors have in the past impeded the academic understanding of such phenomena as the witch-craze, the French Revolution, 'la Grande Peur', the Terror, Bolshevism, revolutionary nationalism, fascism, and the Holocaust.

The aim of this book, then, is to demystify terrorism. If it cannot fully allay the liquid, irrational fears which exacerbate the perfectly *rational* anxiety provoked by the threat of terrorism along with myriad other daily threats to our security and our well-being, then it hopes at least to turn it into something more solid, less disturbing. The last chapter will suggest that fear can even be channelled into something more humanly productive altogether. This book presents the murderous commitment to a terrorist cause as primarily neither pathological nor criminal, but as an intelligible, analysable, reconstructible response, however pervaded with utopian, mythic thinking, to a particular *objective* cultural threat or existential dilemma, or combination of the two. It intends to lay the spectre of fear and dissipate the atmosphere of nebulous *angst* that still envelops the subject in some quarters of the media, state security, government, and even academia, prompting reductive categories of analysis, simplistic diagnoses, and xenophobic misperceptions of 'alien' cultures and religions, not to mention the impulsive urge to wage wars against demonized enemies who in some notable cases, once killed, prove subsequently to have had no link to terrorism as such. At the same time it wants to underscore the legitimacy and solid empirical basis of certain fears by throwing into stark relief the ideological mainsprings of terrorist threat to peaceful civic coexistence.These, as we will show, may lie deep within the visceral urge to defend a culture and whole way of life against destruction, to regain a lost (and often mythically reconfigured) homeland, or to ensure that certain scripturally based interpretatations of established religions will prevail over 'heresy' and decadence, or that a 'new religious movement' takes history by storm.

Clearly this is an investigation that does not propose to discuss the strategic, instrumental, military, or political aspects of terrorist objectives, or even the biographies or testimonies of terrorists themselves. Instead, the focus will be on bringing the subject more firmly within the orbit of humanistic understanding by considering the *non*-instrumental rationales, the symbolic, existential, *metapolitical* motivations of terrorist acts. One of the world's best-selling videogames is the series *Assassins Creed*, which has sold 31 million units since its launch in November 2007. As a form of ritualized vicarious violence dramatized through a blend of history with science fiction it is only loosely based on one of the most famous premodern terrorist organizations, the Assassins, and shows no interest whatsoever in the highly elaborate 'creed' which sustained the orginal murderers. By contrast, this book is precisely concerned with the *creed* of terrorists, their credo, what they believe, what *they* have convinced themselves they are doing when they commit an act of terrorism. Christians, Jews, and Muslims have had creeds to commit to memory (known in Western Christianity as part of the catechism and order of service). They are formulaic statements of the articles of their faith, their morality, the essential truths in their path or struggle for salvation. Apart from the ten or so versions of the Christian creed, there have been secular creeds as well, most famously the 'American's Creed', while under Mussolini impressionable youths were taught 'the Fascist catechism'. In the context of this book, the creed will not be the sort written down as a ritualized verbal formula. Instead, even when not published as a manifesto, it will invisibly inform calculated, premeditated acts of violence which often appear unintelligible, pathological, or plain 'mad' to outsiders.

My principal sources for undertaking this investigation are four-fold. Fortunately, a number of social and political scientists have offered insightful analyses of the motivation of terrorists, though since 9/11 explorations of the religious drivers of fanatical violence, especially Islamist ones, have been considerably overrepresented in comparison with work on secular extremism. Second, supplementing the abundant specialist literature on terrorism itself, there is a wealth of literature originating in a variety of disciplines which help illuminate the processes by which human beings create cultures and total world-views by which to live, explain how they react to threats to their culture, trace the devastating impact of modernity on identity and beliefs, and provide causal explanations for ideologically motivated extremism, violence, and fanaticism, all of which can be enlisted for their explanatory power in confronting terrorism. My third source is less orthodox. There have been occasional attempts to consider how terrorism is portrayed in narrative[13] and cinematic[14] fiction, but to my knowledge there have been no sustained attempts to use the insights drawn from fiction to complement the Human Sciences in identifying the metapolitical, non-instrumental dimension of the terrorist radicalization process.

Fourthly, this book draws on two decades of specialist research into fascism, and in particular my extensive investigation in *Modernism and Fascism* (2007)[15] into the complex relationship of Fascism and Nazism to modernity (defined as a force which breaks down cultural cohesion) and modernism (conceived as a general term for all attempts to restore a sense of meaning and purpose to existence, aesthetically, socially or politically). On the basis of this previous work I will propose for simplicity's sake two distinct ideal types of terrorism, Zealotic and Modernist. What distinguishes them is the nature of the creed or metapolitical cause for which their protagonists risk their lives and commit extreme acts of violence. Are they fighting to preserve a (mythically conceived and idealized) traditional community from destruction at the hands of military, political, religious or cultural enemies (inner or outer) in the spirit of fanaticism associated with the Zealots under the Romans, and the assassinations carried out by their lethal terrorists, the Sicarii? Or are they setting out to purge existing society of decadence and create the space for a (utopian) new society freed of the injustices and evils of the present, a goal which I will argue is related to the modernist revolt against Western modernity in various spheres of society. It will become clear in the later chapters that in particular circumstances, these two species of terrorism lend themselves to a hybridization process in which the violence is aimed simultaneously at preserving or restoring a tradition and at bringing about its utopian metamorphosis into a new society, a hybrid devastatingly exemplified by Islamism.

It is by concentrating almost exclusively in this book on the *creed* of terrorists, and on the metapolitical dimension of terrorism, that I hope to identify a distinct pattern in the socio-psychological process of radicalization which can produce such extreme acts of apparently absurd, gratuitous violence. In particular, I am exploring the link between the fanaticism that enables an individual to carry out an act of terroristic violence (something far more personal than combat in a modern army) and the human need for meaning that makes some either prepared to risk their lives to defend the culture or religion that is their reservoir of meaning, or to search desperately to create something transcendental to believe in and live for when their world has slipped into absurdity. Radicalization is thus portrayed in these pages as a psychodynamic process of extraordinary intensity, transforming someone who initially feels powerless and irrelevant in the face of an alien culture or a tyrannical state, or else hopelessly adrift on the boundless ocean of absurdity or decadence, into a fanatical devotee of a cause. It is a cause which, even if not religious, is sufficiently 'sacred' for him or her to shatter social and religious taboos and so be prepared to kill and even be killed to fulfil the mission that is demanded.

Another claim of this book is that the 'radicalization syndrome', which underlies the upsurge in terrorism that has changed the entire climate of contemporary politics, makes considerably more sense when its historical roots are traced to cases of violence committed by small groups of dedicated killers against an enemy culture long before the onset of modernity. By the last chapter, after a broad sample of terrorist episodes have been examined in the light of the two species of terrorist radicalization, Zealotic and Modernist or their hybrid, the liquid, the irrational, and the nebulous elements should have largely drained out of the topic, shrinking it to one of manageable proportions fully accessible to humanistic understanding. By the time the fundamental pattern has been exposed which links the creed of the Sicarii asserting the need to resist Judea's Hellenization to the cyber-manifesto of Breivik declaring a future war on Europe's Islamization, terrorism may hopefully have yielded up some of its mysteries as a form of human activity, an activity which imbues existence with total meaning for the agent.

Liquid meanings: The need for definition

However, before we can proceed, another element of 'flux' in investigating the nature of terrorism as an object of study has to be 'fixed', namely the definition of the term itself. Certainly 'terrorism' is unusual in the political sciences because what it combines with the suffix 'ism' is not a noun, proper name, or adjective which distinguishes its ideology or delimits its context, but a powerful emotional affect, or, to be more precise, the psychological *effect* of 'terror', of a debilitating fear which deliberate acts of violence (or the threat they pose) are designed to have not on those directly caught up in them but on their target audience (rulers, politicians, the military, the public whose opinion and 'mood' is to be changed). But its ambiguous, 'polysemic' nature has little to do with its unusual formation or the nature of terrorist violence as such. Instead, as Max Weber showed in his theory of the *ideal type* and subsequent generations of methodologists and philosophers of science have confirmed, it has more to do with the semantic problems posed whenever the inquiring mind selects a single term as the focus for studying a segment of reality (Weber gives the example of 'capitalism').[16]

Like any generic 'ism' that captures the interest of the human sciences – fascism, modernism, ideology and all their kin – terrorism is a deeply heterogeneous[17] and also multicausal[18] phenomenon which frustrates the analytical requirement for a neat, uncontentious, self-contained object of study. Instead, the more it is studied the more connotations it spawns.

By 1988 it already admitted '109 definitions of terrorism that covered a total of 22 different definitional elements',[19] and doubtless the protean quality of the term has been on steroids since 9/11. In 2004 Walter Laqueur, one of the most well-known and prolific authorities on terrorism in the Anglophone world, had reached the conclusion that trying to define it was pointless since 'the only general characteristic of terrorism generally agreed upon is that terrorism involves violence and the threat of violence',[20] (and there is already a world of difference between just these two components). Three years later one of the authors of the seminal *Mapping Terrorism Research* lamented the continuing failure to achieve 'a consensual definition of terrorism' which was hindering progress in its transdisciplinary study.[21] Another expert in the same volume cites the result of a survey of literature on terrorism by a National Research Council which concluded that it remained 'an essentially contested concept', with 'a multiplicity of overlapping efforts' to define it, 'some more satisfactory than others, but none analytically sufficient'.[22]

As Weberians would stress, equivalent observations could be made about any intensely studied generic term in the human sciences, but there are two additional complicating factors that make this fish particularly slippery for conceptual nets. The first is the prevalence of implicit victim or 'law and order' perspectives and the resulting moral and legal condemnation that flows from the emphasis on the negative experience of 'terror' in the context of attacks on civil society, the state, and the status quo. Terrorism is certainly morally indefensible for the 'target' audience in terms of most value systems and doctrines of human rights, religious or secular. Yet to make the devastating impact of terrorism on its victims and hence its moral iniquity the starting point for its investigation can lead to blind spots about its dynamics and deeper socio-psychological causes in the same way that Nazism remained largely unintelligible to two generations of historians until it started to be understood (but certainly not justified except by revisionists) in terms of its *own* goals and values. As for the 'state' perspective, it is worth remembering that both Nazis and Stalinists referred to resistance movements as terroristic,[23] just as the Indian government still dismisses as terrorism 'Maoist' attempts to mobilize politically those millions dispossessed by their country's 'democratic' drive for industrial progress.[24] The profoundly pejorative, not to say demonizing, connotations of the term accounts for the reluctance of most terrorists to adopt the label, preferring to give their movements ones that evoke 'resistance' or 'defence' or 'militancy' against oppression, or an ideological or religious idealism, such as The People's Will in Tsarist Russia, Mujahideen (People struggling or performing jihad for Allah), Lohamei Herut Israel (Fighters for the Freedom of Israel), Hezbollah (Party of God), Euskadi Ta Askatasuna or ETA (Basque Homeland and Freedom), Red Army Faction (dissenting warriors for socialism), Third Position (the struggle for a world neither capitalist nor communist).[25]

The second 'awkward' fact that hinders the formulation of neat definitions is that when 'terrorism' first entered political discourse over two centuries ago it was not to describe violence directed *against* the state, but violence inflicted *by* the state on its own citizens (often in the name of crushing what authoritarian states now routinely refer to as 'terrorism'). On 30 January 1795, when the heads of those alleged to have betrayed the Revolution were plopping bloodily into overflowing baskets in Paris, London's *The Times* reported, 'There exists more than one system to overthrow our liberty. Fanaticism has raised every passion; Royalism has not yet given up its hopes, and Terrorism feels bolder than ever.' Thus terrorism originally referred exclusively to what is now called 'state terror'.

This is, of course, an entirely legitimate and pressing field of enquiry – especially given the readiness of the US and its allies to have recourse to techniques of coercion and terror on occasion in the pursuit of their own 'war on terror' – and has already been the subject of much illuminating research.[26] It has also given rise to some formidable exposures of the systemic inhumanity of some democracies which make difficult reading for those who harbour naive assumptions about the respect for universal human rights that prevails in the citadels of power of democratic states.[27] However, state terror lies outside the scope of this book, as does the use of terrorism by organized crime (which some anarchists would have thought was a pretty good definition of the state).[28]

In penetrating beyond the shrouds of fear, misunderstanding, and incomprehension still wafting around terrorism and exploring its metapolitical dimension, this book will thus focus exclusively on violent attacks *against* the status quo which broadly conform to the following ideal-typical (and hence heuristic, non-definitive, and *non-essentialist*) definition:

Terrorism is a generic term for extremely heterogeneous acts of violence originating from an asymmetrical relationship of force with the perceived source of oppression or decadence, and carried out within civic space (or at least outside the traditional contexts/spaces of military conflict), generally targeting non-combatants. The violence has a direct object, the human or material targets of the attack which are typically destroyed, and an indirect object, the third parties for whom the violence is a 'message', a performative, semiotic act conceived to force them to change their behaviour, policies, actions, or way of thinking by undermining their sense of security and disseminating fear of further outrages. Terrorist acts thus have a purpose beyond their immediate destructiveness as part of a campaign to exploit the particular psychological impact of unpredictable attacks by an invisible 'enemy', namely a diffuse sense of anxiety, insecurity, and terror, so as to achieve pragmatic, instrumental goals. At the same time they have for the terrorists themselves utopian/metapolitical objectives invisible to outsiders, and their enactment thus fulfils a particular transcendent 'mission' or suprapersonal goal to which the terrorist feels fanatically committed.

A more discursive definition in the context of this book would highlight the idea that terrorism is identified here with:

The deliberate use by a movement, group, or individual of extreme violence against either human or symbolically significant material targets associated by the perpetrators with a demonized 'Other'. This (frequently highly mythicized) 'enemy' can assume a variety of forms: e.g. a foreign army of occupation, an imperialist civilization perceived to be destroying the militant's culture and society, a domestic regime perceived as a coercive, unrepresentative and 'alien' state, the human symbols or material emblems of an 'evil', 'filthy', and morally indefensible institution (e.g. an administration, a social movement, a commercial corporation, an academic institution, or an entire system, society, state, or civilization), or an 'out-group' (representatives of a particular ethnic, religious, linguistic minority, sexual orientation, gender, etc.) whose culture or values are considered 'decadent' (i.e. subversive of the ideal moral or social order) or threatening to the hegemonic 'home' culture .

The purpose of terrorist violence is to inflict personal suffering or strategic damage on the enemy, institution, or regime in a spectacular way that disseminates profound anxiety and exacerbates a generalized subjective sense of instability and crisis. In contrast to most violence in conventional warfare, the immediate casualties and damage caused are thus not the prime objective of terrorist attacks, which is to inflict psychological pressure on a third party who have become the 'audience' or 'spectators' of the outrage (religious sect, ethnic community, section of civic society, academic community, business, state authority, military force, etc.) to make it prepared to change its behaviour, policies, or values to put an end to the attacks. The tactical purposes of such a strategy are highly varied: to defend the purity or integrity of a way of life, tradition, ethnicity, culture or religion from destruction (whether by 'purging' it of enemy forces or by creating a new homeland); to undermine the unquestioned sense of security and legitimacy enjoyed by the 'ordinary' citizens of a hated 'system' so as to allow an alternative society (sometimes utopian and ill-defined) eventually to be established in its place; to force a regime to change a particular policy which is symptomatic of a wider change in values; or to terrorize a particular outgroup and force it to become socially invisible or move away so as to restore a mythic national integrity or racial purity. In one way or another, terrorism aims to disrupt the (perceived) historical continuum, and force a segment of society, a regime, or even the entire world to enter a new era, thereby changing the course of history.

Simultaneously, terrorist violence has non-instrumental, expressive ends. It is conceived deliberately to achieve a symbolic blow or victory against a demonized Other in a subjective ideological, metaphysical, cosmic war or struggle between good and evil, decadence and renewal invisible to outsiders. This symbolic, non-instrumental aspect of terrorism is inseparable from its significance to the terrorists themselves not just as a tactical or instrumental event, but as a performative act of resistance or defiance against a perceived evil which has demanded (especially in cases of martyrdom for the sake of the cause) a profound existential commitment. As such, terrorist acts usually contain a hidden symbolic or psychological meaning within the subjective inner world and cosmology of the terrorists themselves over and above any pragmatic function they may have within the campaign against the targeted outgroup, institution, or regime. This 'metapolitical' dimension of terrorism emanating from the world-view or creed of the terrorist may remain largely impenetrable and incomprehensible to an outsider, but provides an essential ingredient to the rationale and 'logic' of terrorist acts and campaigns to their protagonists.

The place of this book within terrorism studies

Like all definitions in an academic context, the two offered above are tentative and tendentious, and especially so in this case since they have been consciously conceived to help establish the dual rationale of this book. This is firstly to contribute to the demystification and 'cutting down to size' of terrorism as a topic fully capable of investigation by the empirical, rational methodologies of the Human Sciences – and so contribute through this approach to the 'solidification', and hence reduction, of the liquid fear still emanating in public space from terrorism as an inexplicable source of violence and threat, some of which continues to seep into academic discourse. This I propose to do by concentrating exclusively and

hence one-sidedly on the utopian, metapolitical, and existential dimension of terrorism's causation seen from the terrorist's own perspective which is deliberately
alluded to in both definitions. Secondly, it is to propose a schematic model on
the basis of this approach of the subjective process of radicalization that turns an
'ordinary' human being with no overt criminal or psychopathological predisposition into a person willing to kill and even be killed for a 'higher', *suprapersonal*
cause.[29] The premise behind both these objectives is that it is only when the subjective, symbolic, existential dimension of terrorism for the *terrorist*, when his or
her world-view, cosmology and creed, is taken into account and given due weight
in investigations that the topic opens itself up fully to academic attempts to make
it humanly intelligible and causally explicable in terms of its intrinsic meaning
and purpose for the protagonist. As Jean Rosenfeld put it in an important essay on
'the Religion of Osama bin Laden':

> Whether a terrorist movement is secular or religious, it acts purposively to fur-
> ther goals that are symbolically constructed and understood by its intended
> audience. The point I wish to emphasize is that it is the symbolic world of ter-
> rorist movements that must be rationally understood if we are to understand
> and rationally assess a group's motives, goals and actions.[30]

In *Waging War without Warriors* Christopher Coker makes a parallel point. The
West's almost exclusive preoccupation with 'utilitarian, rational' aspects of violence has, he claims, created a blind spot about what violence 'signifies', or
'expresses', and 'what the warrior is': 'Expressive violence is not only aimed at
an enemy but also expresses a way of life.'[31]

It should be stressed at the outset that this book is exploratory and 'heuristic' in
its purpose. It has no intention of reducing terrorism to some mythic 'essence' or
suggest the *primacy* of the subjective or expressive dimension of terrorism over its
external features as a political, social, military, instrumental, strategic, or historical phenomenon, or over in-depth reconstructions of individual terrorist episodes
or movements, all of which are perfectly legitimate scholarly tasks.[32] Nor has it
any cryptic revisionist or *apologetic* intent in focusing on the inner 'cosmological'
world of the terrorist and the private existential issues his or her commitment
resolves, any more than taking the ideology of a Nazi or religious fundamentalist seriously means justifying the acts carried out in the name of their 'faith'.
The aim is 'simply' to complement the already abundant literature on the political, strategic, and instrumental aspects of individual specimens of terrorism and
the numerous surveys of its 'external' history as a socio-political and paramilitary
phenomenon, while also contributing in a more direct manner to the far less prolific literature on terrorism's deeper historical, social and psychological dynamics.
In doing so it attempts to go some way towards meeting the need in terrorist
research flagged up three years after the physical dust of 9/11 had settled, namely
'for a better understanding of the motivations, thought processes, mindsets and
historical consciousness of terrorists' without which 'insightful and thoughtful
analysis' in this area is impossible.[33]

The timeliness of such an investigation is further underscored by the authoritative survey of the 'state of the art, gaps, and future direction' of the discipline published two years after 9/11 in *Mapping Terrorism Research*. In his seminally important chapter on Al Qaeda, Jeffrey Cozzens, one of the world's foremost experts on jihadism, criticizes the excessive concentration, typical of a functionalist approach to politics,[34] on the immediate strategic goals and tactics of the paramilitary 'war' terrorists are engaged in while ignoring their 'grand strategy'.[35] This in turn can only be understood, he claims, by taking account of the 'non-instrumental' component of the conflict, or the 'big picture' of what they are fighting for,[36] and hence the 'ideological framework' which determines their actions. This is the world-view of 'Global Salafi Jihad' (GSJ), also known as Salafism or 'Global Jihad', 'a world-wide revivalist movement' of which Al Qaeda 'is only the most high-profile manifestation'. To make sense of Al Qaeda means taking *seriously* the 'apocalyptic beliefs, the idea of salvation through conflict, dualism, and the notion of a persecuted elite' that motivates its most fanatical followers. It is a principle which applies not only to GSJ, but to all warfare against states or societies, since 'the grand strategic level of warfare – whether that of state or non-state actors – cannot be fully understood apart from the protagonist's culture, or the ideologies that express them'.[37]

To correct the distortion of a predominantly 'instrumentalist' and 'functionalist' understanding of terrorism, Cozzens advocates the *complementary* use of an approach based on 'culturalism'[38] which in the case of Al Qaeda reveals 'a less apparent and more personally relevant "Al-Qaeda" that is reflected in nearly every stratum of operative... that embraces its world view and seeks to implement it through violent jihad'. Beneath the surface of overtly political and military externalizations of its ideology, 'its underlying religious framework and intertwined culture of jihad [the 'expressive dimension' of their struggle] compels its operatives to fight as "rational true believers"'.[39] Nor does Cozzens see the value of a theoretical framework based on 'culturalism' as restricted to the study of Islamism. He suggests 'it could be useful in generating new lines of academic enquiry as well as directing Western anti- and counter-terrorism efforts onto what is arguably a comprehensive [and I would add *comprehensible*] representation of the threat they face'.[40]

Joshua Sinai's essay in the same volume also stresses the need to give more weight to the subjective realm of values and beliefs in studies of terrorism, stating that '[i]deas, and, in the contemporary period, especially radical religious ideologies, are among the major drivers that mobilize individuals and groups into committing acts of terrorism and provide them with cultural and religious underpinning and guide for action.' He goes on to highlight two major gaps in current understanding:

> However, there are problems in the terrorism discipline in understanding why individuals and groups turn to religious fundamentalism for their ideological solutions, especially when progress in so many areas is made possible through the modern, secular, pluralistic, and democratic paths. Because this process is

not clearly understood, the analytical literature *does not place religiously fundamentalist radicalization within the context of modernization theory*, which is necessary to understand such phenomena.[41]

In adopting its own resolutely 'culturalist' approach to terrorism, one of the main features of the present volume is that it seeks to show how insights drawn from the study of radical 'modernist' responses to modernity can be used effectively to locate terrorism within modernization theory, and in particular to explain why terrorists so violently reject the vision of progress which Sinai imagines to be achievable through 'modern, secular, pluralistic and democratic paths'.

In this context it is intriguing that he leaves an important thought incomplete in the passage we have cited. He refers to those who turn their back on democracy and secular modernity for 'their ideological solutions', without specifying what the *problems* are that they are trying to solve ideologically, thereby cutting off in its prime a fruitful line of inquiry. Clearly in extreme situations of civil strife, state persecution, or enemy oppression these can be primarily political and social, but the culturalist approach emphasizes that they can be *simultaneously* existential, and in the absence of objective conflict and suffering they may even be *primarily* existential. It is precisely by focusing in generic terms on the role played by 'ontological', essentially *metapolitical* problems of identity and transcendent purpose in the genesis of fanatical creeds and the violence that flows from them, and by reflecting on how modernity may be experienced as the root cause of such problems rather than their solution, that this book hopes to add a new dimension to 'explaining terrorism' in terms of the creeds of the terrorists' themselves. What Jeffrey Bale states about the pattern of Al Qaeda attacks is also true of all terrorism, namely that they 'must be viewed from the enemy's own point of view',[42] which demands the deployment of the faculty of 'methodological empathy' with the agents of atrocities. In adopting this approach, this book highlights the need for a historical contextualization of terrorism that reaches far beyond the nineteenth century, which is where the one scholar in the 'mapping' exercise who rightly underlines the neglected 'role of history and continuity in terrorism research' starts her narrative.[43] It is by considering the ancient, premodern prototypes of modern terrorism that emerged in the last two millennia that the existence of two very distinct terrorist relationships to modernization is thrown into relief: one which seeks to ward off the culture-cidal threat it poses to an existing cultural tradition, and another which seeks to transform a particular aspect of existing modernity or even create an entirely new society. As will become clear, a third relationship exists in which 'conservative' and 'revolutionary' terrorist projects are hybridized into goals which simultaneously preserve and renew a cultural, national, or religious 'essence'.

The terrorist's creed

It should be clear from what has been said that, while it explores single-mindedly the world-view that underpins and rationalizes acts of terrorism, this book does not commit the simplistic fallacy of reducing the causes of terrorism to metapolitical creeds. No matter how much emphasis there is on ideology and cosmology, and on the human need for overarching meaningful ideology, it should be taken as read that a unique constellation of concrete, and often highly material social, economic, political, religious, cultural, or ethnic factors – or a blend of several of these – shape each historic context which engenders any one of its specific manifestations. There is thus no intention to suggest that such factors are secondary, forming mere 'epiphenomena' or background to some basic psycho-cosmological syndrome or state of mind which is the *real* cause of terrorism. By starting with a consideration of the terrorism of antiquity, this book deliberately avoids the trap of treating Al Qaeda as if it were the template for all terrorism (indeed it will become obvious that it is a hybrid of two distinct, far older species of the genus). There is a hint of both these fallacies in Michael Ignatieff's impassioned reaction to George Bush's declaration of a 'war on terror' made even before the air had cleared over Ground Zero:

> What we are up against is apocalyptic nihilism. The nihilism of their means – the indifference to human costs – takes their actions not only out of the realm of politics, but even out of the realm of war itself. The apocalyptic nature of their goals makes it absurd to believe they are making political demands at all. They are seeking the violent transformation of an irremediably sinful and unjust world. Terror does not express a politics, but a metaphysics, a desire to give ultimate meaning to time and history through ever-escalating acts of violence which culminate in a final battle between good and evil.[44]

Instead, consistent with Cozzens' approach, the position adopted in this volume is that 'terror' expresses *both* a politics and a metapolitics. It articulates political demands, provoked by what for the terrorists themselves are far from apocalyptic or nihilistic, but concrete empirical threats, injustices, or aspirations. Yet *simultaneously* terrorism also seeks to 'give ultimate meaning to time and history'. It certainly can take the form of an 'apocalyptic nihilism' which invokes Manichaean fantasies of cosmic good pitted against cosmic evil, but can also assume much more down-to-earth, realizable, restrained goals shaped by the terrorist's hunger for freedom, as is the case of many 'liberation struggles' for an independent homeland against occupation by what is perceived as an enemy culture. Where my analysis agrees with both Ignatieff and Cozzens, is that the immediate demands and actions not just of Al Qaeda but of all the terrorist movements in history cannot be understood simply in military, functionalist, or 'counter-insurgency' terms. They need to be related to their 'cause', the 'grand strategy', that drives them. This in turn can only be understood fully in the context of beliefs, whether religious or secular, that have assumed in the mind of the 'operatives' themselves a 'fanatical' quality. This term has long been used by social scientists as a heuristic device in the exploration of the subjective world of the extremist.[45] However, in the present context it retains echoes of the original Latin word *fanaticus*, derived from *fanum* meaning temple, to connote 'inspired by a God',[46] and by extension the suprapersonal – and even suprahuman – sacrality with which terrorists tend to endow their mission.

The militant fanatic can be imagined as self-enclosed in a sacred cognitive and moral space, his or her own inner temple, from which the 'profane', and hence threatening or decadent, world is observed. Taken to extremes this absolutist outlook, purged of ambivalence, doubt, and tolerance, has the effect of dehumanizing the inhabitants of the profane world to the point where their murder becomes abstracted as 'collateral damage' or even as a necessary 'sacrifice' in the fight to realize a higher cause. As Cozzens' essay in *Mapping Terrorism Research* argues so forcefully, the neglect of this inner space, and hence of the 'non-instrumental' dimension of terrorism, leaves unexplored the subjective, phenomenological aspect of engagement in violence, with especially serious consequences for understanding the dynamics of suicidal (or rather, from the terrorist perspective, 'martyr') violence. Such an ultimate act of self-immolation for the sake of a creed demands an exceptional, transcendental, almost mystic, state of self-sacrificial idealism, commitment, and *belief*, qualities intimately bound up with the way the terrorist cause and the murder it so often demands is *sacralized* in the mind of its agents,[47] something that holds true for much ultranationalist, guerrilla and partisan warfare as well. (When pronouncements by terrorists are approached simply as 'propaganda', it is worth reminding ourselves that it originated as the Vatican's term for the dissemination of the Catholic *faith*.) Closely linked to the recurrent tunnel vision in academic research concerning terrorism's 'non-instrumental' causes, is the failure of many mainstream 'terrorologists' to appreciate the potential contribution that approaches drawing on social psychology[48] can make to understanding the appeal of a terrorist cause to particularly vulnerable or idealistic individuals.[49] A similar blind spot prevails concerning the need for more incisive transdisciplinary research involving elements of sociology, cultural anthropology, and social anthropology[50,51] to encourage what Cozzens calls 'out of the box thinking'.

The book's structure

The structure of this book grows out of its aim to illuminate terrorism's extensive but frequently neglected non-instrumental dimension. This chapter has been devoted to establishing the peculiar vantage point from which it is written, and the interpretive strategy it has adopted, which may certainly seem to some readers 'out of the box', and even 'off the wall', but at least the title should by now have lost the cryptic aura of pseudo-profundity or pretentiousness it may have had for some. The 'terrorist's creed' of the title, apart from its obvious allusion to the highly popular computer game *Assassin's Creed*, refers to recurrent metapolitical patterns and subliminal psychological constants within the extraordinarily variegated belief-systems and conscious motivations of individual terrorists down the centuries. 'Metapolitics' has acquired some highly technical meanings within the political sciences remote from our own concerns, for example in the eponymous work of Alain Badiou,[52] but here it is being used in a way which corresponds closely to what Cozzens refers to as the 'culture' of terrorism. The Greek prefix 'meta-' means simply 'beyond', and in the context of this investigation refers to the non-political, non-strategic, non-instrumental goals being fulfilled by a terrorist campaign from the perspective of the terrorists themselves, such as the defence or purification of a culture, religion, or ethnicity, the creation of a new type of society, or the precipitation of a cataclysmic event in fulfilment of some abstruse apocalyptic scheme of history, religious or secular, according to which a new era is about to dawn.

On one level both 'creed' and 'the metapolitics' of terrorism thus refer to the 'ideological framework' and 'grand strategy' which Cozzens highlighted as an under-researched area of motivation and rationale for terrorist actions. While creed is saturated with the connotations of religious faith, 'metapolitics' is a term extensively used by the European New Right's (ENR) use of the term in its attack on the hegemony of the pluralistic, democratic values of secular humanism, with the important difference that, with the exception of Anders Breivik's killing rampage in Norway in July 2011, most proponents of the ENR's celebration of cultural difference disdain violence to achieve their ends. Instead they see metapolitics as the *precondition* for a new totalizing form of cultural politics needed to secure the threatened patchwork of unique ethnic identities being eroded by modernity. It is a usage, paradoxically influenced by the notion of 'cultural hegemony' promoted by the Marxist theorist Antonio Gramsci, and its right-wing use is illustrated by this declaration of a major ideologue of the German 'New Right' (*Neue Rechte*), Pierre Krebs:

> It is impossible to overthrow a political apparatus without previously having gained control of cultural power. The assent of the people must be won first: their ideas, ethos, ways of thinking, the value-system, art, education have to be worked on and modified. Only when people feel the need for change as a self-evident necessity will the existing political power, now detached from the general consensus, start crumbling and be overthrown. Metapolitics can be seen as the revolutionary war fought out on the level of world-views, ways of thinking and culture. It is precisely the metapolitical level which is our starting point. We want to take over the laboratories of thinking.[53]

From such observations it should already be self-evident that the 'culturalism' that results from our focus on terrorism's metapolitical creeds has nothing to do with the reduction of the multiple historical realities subsumed under the term terrorism to mere 'culture', and hence to an ultimately diaphanous and chimerical 'discourse' which drains material historical realities and events of all substance. This error arises when theoretical insights drawn from the 'cultural turn' which occurred within the human sciences in the last decades of the twentieth century are applied in the most crudely reductive, fundamentalist spirit of post-structuralism in a way that dissolves rather than illuminates empirical realities.[54] 'Culturalism' in this sense has on occasion been attributed with pejorative and offensive connotations, whether out of prejudice or ignorance, to scholars such as Emilio Gentile and myself who take ideology and political religion seriously in interpreting fascism. It must thus be emphasized, therefore, that in this volume on terrorism its connotations are entirely consistent with Cozzens' claim that the 'grand strategy' of any terrorist cause 'cannot be fully conceptualized apart from looking at [its] culture and related ideology', and must be used to *complement* academic concern with the instrumental dimension of terrorism, and not to replace it (an undertaking beyond the scope of this volume).[55]

At the same time it should be stressed that in this book 'creed' has a second level of meaning, referring to another precondition for political action not captured in Cozzens' analysis, but extensively reviewed in two other chapters in *Mapping Terrorism Research.*[56] This is the substratum of personal, largely subliminal, psychological, human, and metaphysical needs being fulfilled for the terrorists themselves through their conversion to a world-view, devotion to a cause, and joining a community (even an exclusively virtual one), leading to the readiness to commit violence for the sake of a 'mission' which has in some cases become literally more important even than their own lives, and certainly of greater value than the lives of their victims. There will be frequent reference to the term 'fanatic', and it is important that this is not read simply as a pejorative term to write off all terrorist acts as 'crazy'. As we have already explained, fanaticism here, rather than connoting the pathology suggested in the word field where any thesaurus locates it, making it the bedfellow of terms such as 'addict', 'crank', 'meschugge', 'freak', 'maniac', 'monomaniac', 'nut', 'demon', 'fiend', or 'fool', is being used in a way that emphasizes unshakeable belief, thus placing it in the company of 'radical', 'ultraist', 'visionary', 'zealot', 'bigot', 'devotee', 'enthusiast', 'extremist', 'militant'. In other words, 'fanaticism' refers to a state of total commitment (not necessarily hot-headed, fervent, or passionate but rather calculating, single-minded, and 'rational') which allows no self-doubt, is intolerant of pluralism, moderation, and 'deviant' opinions. It thus places the religious believer or secular ideologue in a mental state where he or she is capable of acts which transgress conventional civic or moral laws in the name of a higher principle which is (in Nietzschean terms) 'beyond good and evil'. This extreme state of mind is arrived at through a complex process of acculturation and psychological transformation in which a particular cause comes to be experienced as a 'higher cause' which assumes transcendental significance. This 'grand ideal' thus, at least within the symbolic world and psyche of the fanatic, is 'hallowed' and 'sacralized' into an ultimate purpose, even if it is to be fulfilled through the human agency of terrorist acts committed in secular ('profane') time and even when the ideological framework specifically rejects any traditional form of religious metaphysics.

Within this methodological framework, which stresses the key role played in the terrorist mindset by the primal human need for a 'higher' meaning to live by and the mythopoeic and ritual resources to create it from within society, terrorism is treated not as having a fibrous root-system which spreads laterally throughout the surface layers of (partially) Westernized modern societies. Instead it proves to have a taproot of enormous strength and depth that stretches down to the most ancient strata of cultural creation when human societies first coalesced around a shared material culture and habitat, a shared language, a shared cosmological myth, and shared ritual which they were prepared to defend to the death. These cultures held otherwise isolated, atomized, desperate individuals together by a shared narration of the tribe's or people's 'story' which explained and imparted sacred significance to birth, change, and death, fixed and delimited its members' place in the infinite cosmos, and secured their access to magic time and the numinous which enabled them to partake in some form of eternal or immortal dimension to existence. This book thus deliberately creates a diachronic historical framework for looking at terrorism *de longue durée*, stretching right back to the earliest well-recorded incidence of using terror tactics to change the status quo, the Sicarii militants of the Jewish Zealots of the first-century AD (by the Christian reckoning of historical time which for convenience will be used throughout)[57] Judea, some of the first partisans. It concludes with the horrific twin attack by self-styled 'Knights Templar', Anders Breivik, on Norwegian government buildings and a summer camp for young Labour Party activists in July 2011. I can only hope that by the time this book is published other major terrorist attacks have not occurred to grab momentarily the media attention, but there will doubtless have been a steady trickle of them in places where they have become established weapons in an asymmetrical war against a perceived force of occupation.

To fulfil the goal of providing a diachronic and synchronic account of terrorism's non-instrumental dimension, Chapter 2 will explore the metapolitics of one ideal-typical category of terrorism, namely the Zealotic. This is the violent expression of resistance and retrenchment (in the military, not the economic sense) undertaken in defence of a tradition which is under threat from a more powerful culture, and thus becomes fanatically intolerant not just of 'the enemy', but of any form of moderation, liberalization, reform, pluralism, or perceived deviation from orthodoxy within the domestic culture. These are seen as 'the thin end of the wedge', as weak spots within the cultural fortifications which could lead to enemy infiltration or incursion and hence to the culture's eventual destruction. Having refined this ideal type by drawing on a wide range of existing scholarship, and established the concept of 'nomos' which is so central to our analysis of what terrorists of all ages are fighting for, it is applied to two contemporary examples of Zealotic terrorism: first, the Chechens' resort to terrorism to defend their Caucasian culture from extermination at the hands of a 'liberalized' Russia, the latest bloody episode in over 200 years of having to repel Russification and cultural genocide (culturecide); second, the doomed struggle of the Tamil Tigers to preserve their culture within Tamil Eelam, their sacred homeland.

Chapter 3 introduces a contrasting category of terrorism in which the fundamentalist mindset is applied not to defending an established culture under siege (nomos), but to creating a new culture, a new nomos. It is thus a tactic deployed in a revolutionary assault on the status quo carried out not through mass mobilization or popular insurgency, or even a paramilitary vanguard, but by the violent actions of a minute number of 'urban warriors'. It will be argued that in the shift from a rear-guard conservative mission of cultural conservation to a futural, avant-garde one the Zealotic terrorist becomes a *Modernist*, expressing a modernism of violent political and metapolitical deeds rather than of experimental sculptures, utopian architectural projects, or visionary manifestos. Modernist terrorism produces the fanatic of a future creed, of a faith which in some cases has not even been formulated but which nevertheless demands the destruction of the existing order in order to take shape. It seeks to establish an alternative modernity purged of the iniquities of the present, or to reinstate values and norms which can only be conserved by going *forward* in time to an entirely new age. Drawing on theories of modernism as a socio-political as well as an aesthetic phenomenon, this type will be illustrated by considering the anarchism embraced by the Russian nihilists in the late nineteenth century.

In what may seem at first a detour, Chapter 4 will consider the insights into the metaphysics and psychological dynamics of terrorism that can be gleaned from its portrayal by five very different novelists: Fyodor Dostoevsky, Joseph Conrad, André Malraux, Tom Robbins, and Sunjeev Sahota. Taken together they refine the ideal type of both Zealotic and Modernist fanaticism, and highlight the common denominator between them by featuring a subjective level, invisible to outsiders, at which the terrorist resolves existential needs for a meaning-giving 'narrative' as a prophylactic (literally an 'advance-guard') against nihilistic despair induced either by the imminent loss of a culture or the lack of a satisfying communal identity under the conditions of modernity. Their six novels thus provide an introduction to Chapter 5 which proposes an ideal type of the key stages in the process of terrorist radicalization, further illuminated first by secondary sources in the human sciences and then by two key films which probe into the inner, 'phenomenological' dynamics of fanatical violence. The result is a schematic model 'the metapolitical syndrome of terrorist radicalization'. Astute political scientists will be conscious of the lack of concrete case studies drawn from the history of terrorism to illustrate this schematic account of the main stages in the formation of a homocidal and even suicidal terrorist from the raw material of a 'normal' human being. It is thus important to note that the accounts of individual cases of terrorism encountered in the last four chapters, for example those of Timothy McVeigh or Bobby Sands, implicitly offer specific case studies in the abstract syndrome we have postulated, or at least their behaviour should become considerably more intelligible in the light of the processes we have identified.

Chapters 6 and 7 are thus devoted to deepening our understanding of Zealotic and Modernist terrorism in the light of the syndrome we have established in Chapters 4 and 5, nuancing and humanizing our initial accounts of them. Chapter 8 then focuses on what has since 9/11 become the most important form of terrorism within both Western and Asian consciousness, that inspired by forms of what is generally referred to as 'religious fundamentalism'. The term 'fundamentalism' is a highly contested one outside the narrow context of Christianity and it should be emphasized that in this book it acquires two different sets of connotations. In a narrowly theological context 'fundamentalism' will refer to the way the most zealous representatives of revealed, scripture-based faiths react to the threats posed to their very existence by the secularization, materialism, or pluralism of modernity. Unless it is clear from the context, this will usually be referred to as 'religious fundamentalism' to distinguish it from the second way the term is used in this book, and will already have been encountered in this sense in Chapters 2 and 6. Following well-established usage in the human sciences, 'fundamentalism' will also refer to a particular type of mindset closely associated with 'fanaticism'. It rejects with hostility and aggression to pluralism, ambivalence, and the erosion of transcendent meaning by postulating a single set of truths which must be upheld against the decadence of a world which ignores them. In due course the underlying link between these two usages in the terrorist context will become clear.

Chapter 8 will show that the conditions of modernity encourage a particular type of fundamentalist mindset in the second sense in which fundamentalist interpretations of religion in the first sense can come to be blended with elements alien to traditional religious faith to produce a hybrid of the Zealotic and Modernist. It is an analysis which applies to the form of terrorist creed that has come to dominate the modern media while still being widely misunderstood even by terrorist experts, the Islamism of Al Qaeda, and helps account for some of its paradoxical features as a revolutionary creed.

The implications of our study for terrorism studies and counter-terrorism will be addressed in the 'afterthoughts' of Chapter 9. The conclusions return to the premise of this book, namely that terrorism cannot be combated by applying military and counter-insurgency intelligence alone. It requires the application of a different type of intelligence, one steeped in the spirit of 'methodological empathy', informed by the most relevant scholarship in the Human Sciences relating to belief systems and social and psychological needs they satisfy in the modern world, and enriched by the most sensitive treatments of the topic in the hands of novelists and film-makers. It hopes to humanize a phenomenon which, like Nazism before it, lends itself to demonization even by liberals and academics as long as liquid fear gushes out of the deep gashes it makes in our collective sense of security and in our traditions of humanistic understanding and tolerance. The tide of literature produced on Hitler and the Third Reich in the aftermath of the Second World War was not just a quest for objective historiographical understanding, but also had the subliminal function of exorcizing the collective trauma in European history the Nazis had inflicted on liberal civilization. It allowed the heirs of the Enlightenment, liberal and Marxist traditions symbolically to regain intellectual hegemony over the narrative of the Second World War, the tide of unimaginable atrocities it had unleashed, and the unfolding historical process of modernity itself.

Perhaps the recent spate of academic books on terrorism is subliminally also an attempt to exorcise through analytical reason the collective trauma of 9/11 and regain control of the narrative of history which had been temporarily wrested from the Westernized mind that limpid September morning. Certainly this book is consciously conceived as a gesture towards regaining the primacy of Enlightenment humanism (and for that matter all humanisms) over the apparently irrational forces driving fanatical violence by exploring the deeper historical and psychological factors shaping the ideological rationales for calculated inhumanity encountered in the study of terrorist radicalization. Of course, liquids can turn to gas as well as solids. It is for the reader to judge whether my analysis, once applied by others to concrete episodes, succeeds in 'grounding' terrorist phenomena in empirically robust facts about actual cases of terrorism, or perversely envelops the topic in even denser shrouds of mystifying jargon and conceptual obfuscation.

2
Terrorism as Zealotry: Defending the Nomos

The human need for a 'sacred canopy'

To begin at the beginning, the premise of the argument to be unfolded in the following chapters is that the sustaining creeds and the metapolitics of contemporary terrorism have their deepest historical tap-root in a psycho-social drive which is constitutive of our humanity. This is the drive to orient our lives towards the fulfilment of a higher cause or purpose whose significance transcends that of our own brief existence. There is a measure of convergence between at least some notable scholars working in different disciplines that for their mental or spiritual survival in a hostile or, worse still, indifferent universe, human beings have, alongside their many material requirements for physical survival, an in-built longing, hunger even, to belong to a particular community. This is not just a physical community, but one bound together by unquestioned cosmological assumptions, beliefs, and especially in premodern times also 'ancient' rituals, norms, customs, and traditions which together form their 'culture'. Thus, in the absence of communal identity defined by ethno-linguistic distinctiveness, habitat, or beliefs, human beings will tend naturally to forge a new community, and in the absence of a source of transcendent meaning in world-view or activity they are predisposed to create one.

One of the most influential of these scholars is the sociologist and cultural anthropologist Peter Berger, whose seminal text, *The Sacred Canopy* (1967)[1] identified the myriad, highly contrasting cultures that have thrived and perished in the (within geological time) brief history of our species as different manifestations of a basic structure he termed the 'nomos' in the original sense of the Greek meaning not just 'the law', but the mythic spirit of the law personified in the God Nomos. One of the Orphic Hymns to Nomos (number 64) refers to:

> The holy king of gods and men I call, heavenly Nomos, the righteous seal of all: the seal which stamps whatever the earth contains, and all concealed within the liquid plains: stable, and starry, of harmonious frame, preserving laws eternally the same. Thy all-composing power in heaven appears, connects its frame, and props the starry spheres.[2]

From this mythicized concept Berger derives his idiosyncratic usage of nomos as an ideal type for the 'meaningful order', cosmological and social, into which most humans are born and which they subsequently perpetuate, modify, and transmit to the next generation. In premodern societies each nomos is taken for granted as 'reality', the subliminal precondition for the illusion of solidity and permanence, for the intrinsic purposefulness and orderliness of life, and for the belief in a suprahuman structure inherent to the universe (often a mysterious, magical, numinous, and even, to humans, cruel and unforgiving cosmic order). Such an order or 'law' banishes ambivalence and absurdity from the world and serves as the premise of a viable, self-evidently purposful individual existence not wracked by the 'modern' plague of isolation, angst, and despair. Thus Berger asserts that '[T]he anthropological presupposition [for the nomos] is a human craving for meaning that appears to have the force of instinct'. In other words, human beings are congenitally compelled to impose a meaningful order upon reality'.[3] He portrays this instinct as bound up with the innate human drive towards self-preservation. Human beings construct a social world not just for practical considerations of economic cooperation, but so as to impose order and self-transcending significance on the 'discrete experiences and meanings of individuals'.

The resulting nomos acts as 'a shield against terror', protecting human beings – who have been uniquely blessed and cursed in contrast with all other living creatures with reflexive self-consciousness and a post-Edenic awareness of mortality – from 'the danger of meaninglessness', from 'being submerged in a world of disorder, senselessness and madness' when confronted by 'the potent and alien forces of chaos'. Most of all, the nomos protects them from the direct, unmediated and hence potentially shattering personal confrontation with the prospect of an ineluctable, absurd personal death, a realization which 'must be kept at bay at all cost'. Thus 'every nomos is an area of meaning carved out of a vast mass of meaninglessness, a small clearing of lucidity in a formless, dark, always ominous jungle'.[4] So profound is the terror of nothingness in the human psyche that, according to Berger, it produces a paradox which assumes considerable significance in understanding the radicalization process that leads to terrorism, especially 'martyr terrorism': 'Anomy is unbearable to the point where *the individual may seek death in preference to it*. Conversely, existence within a nomic world may be sought at the cost of all sorts of sacrifice and suffering and *even at the cost of life itself*, if the individual believes that this sacrifice has nomic significance.'[5]

It is arguably the terror of death which provides the ultimate metaphysical reason for human beings to remain in existing communities and their corresponding *nomoi* or create new ones, over and above their considerable practical, material, 'instrumental', and social advantages for survival. The attraction of communal coexistence is powerfully reinforced by the fear of being exiled from the living, sacral experience of the suprapersonal nomos and condemned to exist in a state of psychological isolation generally accompanied by mental suffering (which in a religious context is generally interpreted as the outward manifestation of 'sin', 'evil', or 'illusion'). The resulting despair is familiar from the descriptions of

'anomie' in the writings of Émile Durkheim, but is spelt 'anomy' by Berger to designate an absence of the nomos as he has defined it rather than in the sense given
the term by the French sociologist. Thus he writes of anomy as 'radical separation
from the social world' in which individuals or entire social groups 'lose moral and
cognitive bearings' with 'disastrous psychological consequences'.[6] Within Berger's
perspective all societies and civilizations can be imagined as existing under their
unique 'sacred canopy', which protects their inhabitants from the abyss of absurdity and existential isolation thanks to the anti-anomic power of a communal,
totalizing, metaphysical world-view.

However much a tradition may insist on its derivation from divine revelation
recorded in oral or written culture, the nomos is – from the secular humanistic perspective operated by the Western human sciences (and fiercely rejected
by all religious fundamentalists) – the product of a dynamic process of collective mythopoeia. This process postulated in all its legion permutations (until the
secularizing forces of Western modernity began to exert its devastating impact
on traditional world views) some form of suprahuman metaphysical order established *in illo tempore* (in a primordial time)[7] before human beings were created.
Each of the countless cultures, great and small, imparted to their inhabitants
the sense of living under the laws of a preordained cosmic system, their everyday life shaped by the invisible spiritual principles underlying 'creation', even in
the absence of the personal God or the other-worldly heavenly realm encountered in dualistic Middle Eastern and Christian religions. The nomos was sacred.
In the modern era when the dominant Western nomic canopy is officially based
on secular ideals, earthly utopias or a mythicized 'science', prevailing *nomoi* still
serve the function of 'totalizing', and what Berger calls 'cosmizing', reality for
their believers into something ordered, suprapersonally meaningful, and of transcendent value. A powerful dynamic in the modern world is for those who feel
threatened by secularization's erosion of 'higher' meanings to life to find ways to
re-sacralize their world, leading to the phenomenon of 're-enchantment' or 'desecularization' that is increasingly recognized as a major feature of a post-secular
society.[8]

In his groundbreaking studies of the psychoanalytic dynamics of religion, Ernest
Becker came to similar conclusions to Berger on the existential needs fulfilled by
cultural myths. In order to resist the terror of an absurd death, human beings
must create a heroic, gigantized image of their role and value in the cosmos,
thereby locating their ephemeral, finite lives within an 'immortal' suprapersonal
order:

> It does not matter whether the cultural hero-system is frankly magical, reli-
> gious, and primitive or secular, scientific, and civilized. It is still a mythical
> hero-system in which people serve in order to earn a feeling of primary
> value, of cosmic specialness, of ultimate usefulness to creation, of unshake-
> able meaning.... The hope and belief is that the things that man [and woman,
> a/n] creates in society are of lasting worth and meaning, that they outlive or
> outshine death and decay.[9]

On the basis of this analysis, all religions and mystery cults reveal themselves as driven by the same psychological mechanism: the innate need to create mythic heroes who face and overcome mortality for us or in us, thereby providing an 'immunity bath' to protect devotees from the greatest 'evil': 'death and the dread of it'. The 'organismic' fear of annihilation drives human cultural production.[10] In an earlier book Becker portrayed history as a 'succession of ideologies that console for death', from outside patently dismissable as mystifications and lies, but to the believer a source of immortality and self-perpetuation which endows life with 'the only abiding significance it can have'. It thus becomes understandable that believers 'go into a rage over the fine points of belief' since 'if your adversary wins the argument about truth *you die*': hence the sectarian violence that can break out periodically over the core doctrines of a religion, metaphysical or secular, all of whose theological or ideological tenets are equally nonsensical to an outsider.[11] It is through cosmizing, nomizing ideologies that the eternal human struggle with nihilism can be transposed into a heroic battle against 'wickedness', so that the earth becomes 'a theatre for heroism', and life 'a vehicle for heroic acts which aim precisely to transcend evil', and to 'triumph over disease, want, death'. For Becker this innate urge to heroize one's own existence as a barrier against the confrontation with an absurd death, an urge which stems from our species' unique capacity for reflexivity and self-awareness, might be simply comic or trivial if it did not tend to combine fatally with our predisposition to 'splitting' and demonization of the Other. At this point it 'produces a formula that is no longer pathetic but terrifying. It explains almost all by itself why man, of all animals, has caused the most devastation on earth.'[12]

Like Berger, Becker thus offers an ontological analysis of the function of cultural production and the mechanisms of self-heroization as a way of symbolically transcending death. For both scholars, culture acts as a shield against a state of angst-ridden morbidity and a chronic, life-sapping sense of futility. In fact Becker's works have been made the basis of a school of psychology called Terror Management Theory (TMT) which holds that:

> all cultural worldviews serve an important anxiety-reducing function by providing a sense of meaning and a recipe for attaining either symbolic or literal immortality.... Psychologically, then, the function of culture is not to illuminate the truth, but rather to obscure the horrifying possibility [realization?] that death entails the permanent annihilation of the self.[13]

As a result any feeling that reality is intrinsically purposeful is a culturally maintained illusion:

> By providing a view of reality as stable, orderly, meaningful, and permanent, cultural worldviews allow us to deny that we are merely transient material organisms, clinging to a clump of dirt in a purposeless universe fated only to die and decay. Instead, we live out our time on earth believing we are eternally significant contributors to a meaningful reality.[14]

For TMT therapists, the illusion of belonging to a community of shared meaning and hence participating in a totalizing vision of the cosmic order (Berger's 'nomos') is essential to a vitalistic, life-affirming, angst-free sense of self, saving otherwise anomic individuals from 'existential terror': 'Cultures provide ways to view the world – world-views – that "solve" the existential crisis engendered by the awareness of death'. The 'humanly constructed beliefs about the nature of reality that are shared by individuals in a group...mitigate the horror and blunt the dread caused by the reality of the human condition, that we all die'.[15] They quote in support of this approach the anthropologist David Maclagan who states in his study of creation myths that 'Death is the obverse of the self-preserving, appetitive drive or "desire" of all living organisms: It can therefore be seen as the hidden mainspring of the created world'.[16] Translated into the discourse of Freudian psychoanalysis (which is not part of the conceptual framework of this book), human culture is thus the collective mechanism of mythopoeia through which the life-asserting Eros principle defeats the death principle, Thanatos. One of the tenets of the New Age 'Atman Project, Eros Thanatos' is that 'Culture's purpose is to manufacture surplus Eros and reduce Thanatos'.[17]

If the vitalistic, death-conquering rituals and transcendence-sustaining visions provided by traditional cultures ultimately stem from a subliminal fear of the void, it suggests a paradox encapsulated in a metaphor taken from outer space: the black hole. Once only a mathematical possibility, and then detected in just a handful of star systems, there is a growing consensus among cosmologists that black holes exist at the centre of most if not all galaxies (including our own). Far from performing solely the awesome feats of swallowing up anything from spaceships to entire solar systems dramatized in sci-fi films, it is becoming increasingly accepted within astrophysics that they play a crucial role in triggering the formation of stars and even entire galaxies, in an extraordinary process of literally cosmic creative destruction. As one science writer puts it, black holes have a 'Jeckyll and Hyde' character,[18] or more precisely are reminiscent of Shiva, the supreme Hindu God who destroys the world in order for a new world to be born. Ultimately (obviously from a non-creationist perspective) we, along with all life on Earth, may owe our physical existence to a primordial black hole at the heart of our galaxy which crushes everything it sucks into it with gravitational forces powerful enough to change the atomic structure of matter itself, while simultaneously precipitating the changes within amorphous interstellar matter necessary for stars and eventually planets to take shape. One of these, Earth, cooled sufficiently and eventually had just the right atmospheric and geological conditions for carbon-based life-forms to appear.

According to the speculations of Berger, Becker, and TMT, the role of human reflexivity and the consequent awareness of death has had a similarly ambivalent evolutionary function, making *homo sapiens* and *homo faber* simultaneously cursed and blessed with the awareness of death which makes 'him' (which will be used to refer to all genders of human being) behave simultaneously as *homo symbolicus*, *homo religiosus*, and *homo aestheticus* capable of creating transcendent beliefs and art of stupendous sublimity and beauty. As Charles Strozier puts it in a major collection of essays on the recurrence of apocalyptic fantasies in history,

'It is knowledge of our own death that distinguishes humanity and is an important part of the process in the creation of culture'.[19] It is the terror of finality that sends totem poles, *axes mundi*, ziggurats, temples, pyramids, mosques, and cathedrals soaring into the sky in defiance of mortality and in celebration of a mythic immortality. It is the fear of absurdity that creates the human need to locate each individual's life within an epic story, a metanarrative[20] of loss and rebirth, death and life, despair and hope, pain and joy which is infused with suprapersonal meaning and value. In his bestselling *Black Mass. Apocalyptic Religion and the End of Utopia* John Gray writes in a passage on the common ground between Marxism, Nazism, and the liberal theory of progress that 'in all these accounts history is told as a coherent narrative, and nothing is more threatening than the idea that it is a meandering flux without purpose or direction'.[21]

In premodern societies the 'narrative arc' necessary to human life is provided by the traditional nomos and cultural hero-system, which serves what the military and business strategist John Boyd called 'a grand ideal, overarching theme or noble philosophy that represents a coherent paradigm within which individuals as well as societies can shape and adapt to unfolding circumstances'.[22] Such a paradigm enables human beings to satisfy their basic existential needs, and corresponds to what Eric Fromm in such groundbreaking works as *The Sane Society* and *The Anatomy of Human Destructiveness* called a 'frame of reference and devotion' or a 'frame of orientation'. Thus he writes in *The Revolution of Hope*:

> Man is born as a freak of nature, being within nature and yet transcending it. He has to find principles of action and decision-making which replace the principles of instincts. He has to have a frame of orientation which permits him to organize a consistent picture of the world as a condition for consistent actions. He has to fight not only against the dangers of dying, starving, and being hurt, but also against another danger which is specifically human: that of becoming insane. In other words, he has to protect himself not only against the danger of losing his life but also against the danger of losing his mind.[23]

Before the rise of Western modernity, myriad traditional (but never static) cultures allowed human beings to live out their lives beneath an illusory 'sheltering sky'[24] of bustling, deep-hued cosmic significance that concealed the black 'silence of infinite spaces'[25] beyond. The spreading and deepening of Western secularization and materialism has not resolved the human need for a nomos and a heroic narrative arc to imbue life with significance. If anything it has intensified it.

The former Romanian Iron Guard sympathizer and postwar existentialist, Émile Cioran, composed his work of unrelenting, elegantly rhetorical pessimism about the human condition, *A Short History of Decay*, in 1945 when the obscene crimes committed in the name of racial purity by the Nazis had just been branded in everyone's consciousness and conscience. In it he depicted with a caustic sarcasm, in direct contrast to Fromm's qualified optimism, the catastrophic practical consequences of human need for a frame of reference, devotion, and orientation, presenting it as the key to the 'genealogy' of the fanaticism which has littered history with battle fields, torture chambers, killing fields, and charnel houses. Human beings, it seemed to him, have a perverse capacity to worship the products of their own religious mythopoeia and kill in the defence of the sacral realities which they cannot afford to realize have been invented not revealed. The need to ward off this shattering insight may help account for the repeated episodes of cruelty committed and the vast quantities of blood shed in the name of a higher cosmological principle, religious or secular. He wrote, with a vitriol more bitter than Nietzsche's Zarathustra ever produced, that:

> History is nothing but a procession of false Absolutes, a series of temples raised to pretexts, a degradation of the mind before the Improbable. Even when he turns from religion, man remains subject to it; depleting himself to create fake gods, he then feverishly adopts them: his need for fiction, for mythology triumphs over evidence and absurdity alike. His power to adore is responsible for all his crimes: a man who loves a god unduly forces other men to love his god, eager to exterminate them if they refuse. There is no form of intolerance, of proselytism, or ideological intransigence which fails to reveal the bestial substratum of enthusiasm.... We kill only in the name of a god or his counterfeits.[26]

Defending a beleaguered tradition: The Zealotic response

What follows from the innate human need for a 'sacred canopy' as the premise for spiritual and cognitive survival is the vital *nomic*, life ordering and redeeming function performed at an individual level by the innumerable diverse cultures that have existed in the history of humankind. But what also follows is the deeply ambivalent capacity of this primordial need to function as a cause both of cultural creativity, and of extreme violence towards perceived threats to the strength or integrity of what has been created. As generators and custodians of suprapersonal meaning, cultures thus offer prophylactics to nihilism and despair for their own inhabitants, whatever the blood-chilling scale of the destruction of the human life and cultural artefacts of other societies they may commit in the defence or assertion of their nomos as the only truly sacred *reality*. The primordial role in maintaining sanity and normality played by culture in an infinitely absurd cosmos helps account for the *desperate, fanatical, and violent* way some groups react once it is threatened with disintegration or erosion by 'culture-cidal' ('nomocidal') forces perceived to be at work from within or without.

In their study of 'political paranoia', Robert Robins and Jerrold Post confirm the fruitfulness of this line argument when they attribute the origins of several examples of terroristic violence committed by religious believers not to their dogmatism or fervour as such, but to their drive to defend the integrity of their 'belief systems' (their nomos) from external attack:

> Their actions were defensive aggression against the enemy without. Strong beliefs may serve as a protection against psychological stress [anomy], especially

for the fanatical believer, whose sense of self rests upon the integrity of his [sic] belief system.... For the passionate believer, it is not the beliefs that generate the passion. To the contrary, the rigid beliefs provide a sense-making container for powerful feelings. Because attacks upon those beliefs threaten the believer's control and risk his [sic] being overwhelmed by the feelings, such attacks provoke a passionate, even violent response.[27]

Obviously when the belief system under threat is not just that of small groups of individuals but of an entire people, then the psychological turbulence and resulting violence can take place on a vaster scale altogether, even to the point of bringing about historical watersheds. In a talk given as part of the BBC's 1999 Reith Lectures on the theme 'Runaway World', Anthony Giddens, the world's leading expert on modernization, defined modern religious fundamentalism as the self-defensive strategy of a 'beleaguered tradition', the 'religious, ethnic, nationalist, or directly political' response of a culture to the threat to its survival posed by globalization. He emphasized that such a response was 'edged with the possibility of violence'.[28] The Serb superstar of post-communist social and cultural criticism, Slavoj Žižek, sums up the situation with his usual incisiveness in a passage of his study of contemporary extremism and social unrest called simply *Violence*. On the subject of the disastrous impact of secularizing modernity on religious tradition he writes:

In Europe, where modernisation took place over several centuries, there was time to adjust to this break, to soften its shattering impact, through *Kulturarbeit*, the work of culture. New social narratives and myths slowly came into being. Some other societies – notably the Muslim ones – were exposed to this impact directly, without a protective screen or temporal delay, so their symbolic universe was perturbed much more brutally. They lost their (symbolic) ground with no time left to establish a new (symbolic) balance. No wonder then, that the only way for some of these societies to avoid total breakdown was to erect in panic the shield of 'fundamentalism', that psychotic-delirious-incestuous reassertion of religion as direct insight into the divine Real, with all the terrifying consequences that such a reassertion entails, and including the return with a vengeance of the obscene superego divinity demanding sacrifices.[29]

As we shall see, it is entirely consistent with the theoretical framework implicit in such passages that what is widely treated by Western scholars as the first documented example of a terrorist movement, the Sicarii of first-century AD Judea, emerged as part of a fundamentalist response of a religious culture (nomos) threatened with destruction by hostile military and cultural forces from without and within.

With the onset of modernity, traditional cultural and religious certainties in the West lost their self-evidence and solidity gradually enough for the terror of anomy to be offset by the emergence of various secular utopian creeds. These underwrote a faith in historical progress while retaining the force of a religious creed for their most fervent supporters. In some cases new compensatory religions or metaphysical systems of belief were generated, whether in the form of new religious sects or new religious movements (NRMs). Both reactions provided a replacement sacred canopy to ward off the looming existential terror. As we shall see in the next chapter, the revolutionary mindset associated with the emergence of particularly radical new world-views creates the preconditions for other forms of terrorism directed not to preserving an existing nomos, but to establishing a new one, or at least creating the *tabula rasa* needed for it to be erected as the basis of a new order.

To understand the significance of the drive to defend through fanatical violence an *existing* traditional nomos, which is the subject of this chapter, it is helpful to consider the model of cultural dynamics devised by a historian who devoted his long academic life to studying the flowering, death and renewal of civilizations and cultures. Though this phrase might be taken to allude to Oswald Spengler's *Decline of the West*, it is in fact a reference to Arnold Toynbee's *The Study of History*, the monumental 12 volume 'catalogue raisonné' of all the major world civilizations, a central theme of which is how cultures respond successfully or unsuccessfully to the threat posed by competing, stronger civilizations. Though the explanatory patterns he postulated in his work have been widely criticized for their excessive speculative and pseudo-empirical nature, the value of one pair of contrasting concepts he devised, 'Herodian' and 'Zealotic' responses to cultural aggression, has withstood the test of time. In particular, its direct bearing on understanding the mainsprings of political fanaticism and violence in the modern world has been already highlighted in Luciano Pellicani's neglected masterpiece, *Revolutionary Apocalypse. Ideological Roots of Terrorism*.[30]

Toynbee introduces these twin concepts in a section of volume eight of his *magnum opus* entitled *Heroic Ages. Contacts between Civilizations in Space (Encounters between Contemporaries)*.[31] The template for 'Herodization' is the voluntary Hellenization of Judaism under King Herod as a pragmatic response to Roman occupation. The king's strategy for 'coping with Hellenism was, first to take the objective measure of this alien social force's irresistibly superior power with a sober eye, and then to learn and borrow from Hellenism every Hellenic accomplishment' that served the purpose of 'equipping themselves for...contriving to lead a more or less comfortable life, in the Hellenizing World that was their inescapable new social environment'.[32] 'Herodianism' thus becomes in Toynbee's analysis a generic category for those who adopt the collaborative strategy of 'sleeping with the enemy'. They resist enforced colonization through voluntary acculturation to and alignment with the alien culture asserting its hegemony in a process amounting to self-colonization. A modern parallel would be the appearance of powerful collaborationist factions and strata in all the countries occupied by the Nazis and Soviets in the twentieth century. Some were motivated solely by the imperative to survive at all costs, but others by the idealistic choice (no matter how perverse or cynical it may seem in hindsight) to incorporate their nation or ethnic group into the Third Reich's 'New European Order' or the emerging 'Socialist World

Order'. These collaborationists, whether they were idealistic or merely oppor-
tunistic, could for a time seem to have history on their sides and thus held out
the prospect of safeguarding and eventually revitalizing their threatened culture,
albeit in compromised form. Similarly Toynbee's 'Herodians' convince themselves
that their threatened culture can be invigorated and regenerated by harnessing it
to the superior energy and creativity of the invaders. He cites the modernization
of Japan under the Meiji revolution (*ishin*) in the nineteenth century in response
to Westernization as an outstanding example of Herodization.[33]

However, the second ideal-typical response to the prospect of being absorbed,
subjugated, or annihilated by a superior (or at least more powerful) alien culture he
calls the 'Zealotic' one, after the sect of Zealots who formed under the Romans. It
was a faction 'recruited from people whose impulse, in face of attacks delivered by
a stronger and more energetic aggressive alien civilization, was to take the mani-
festly negative line of trying to fend off the formidable aggressor'. Their method to
avoid contamination from Hellenism 'and all its works, ways, feelings, and ideas'
was 'to retreat into the spiritual fastness of their own Jewish heritage, lock themselves within this psychic *donjon*, close their ranks ... and find their inspiration,
their ideal, and their acid test in the loyalty and sincerity of their observance of
every jot and tittle of a traditional Jewish law'.[34] Toynbee compares the Zealots'
stance of militant religious fundamentalism faced with the destruction of their
sacred nomos to a tortoise withdrawn into his shell or a hedgehog rolled into a
prickly ball with spines pointing outwards. He does not point out that Zealots
can also use their spines to inflict wounds on the enemy, despite his crushing
superiority of force, in individual acts of terrorism.

Zealots naturally see Herodians as traitors and heretics, a 'fifth column' or
'enemy within' which through their compromise with the foe, instead of safeguarding their culture, are colluding with, and hence accelerating, the process of
its disintegration. Europe's anti-Nazi resistance and partisan movements during
the Second World War can be seen as the modern equivalent of an aggressive
Zealotic reaction to foreign invasion and occupation. The term 'Zealot' comes
from the Greek for someone following a leader or pursuing a cause with 'zeal', an
ardent enthusiasm born of a jealous (a word derived from the French deformation
of the Latin *zelosus*) possessiveness of the sole truth which cannot be understood
by or shared with others. It was the Zealots of Judea who bequeathed the term
'zealotry' for a state of blind, fanatical religious belief which leads to the condemnation of any perceived betrayal of the true faith as a sinful heresy, a belief that can
lead not just to words but to violent punitive action (often in the form of barbaric
tortures and executions) against God's enemies. According to our analysis, what
Toynbee's 'Zealots' are defending themselves against is not just the religious and
cultural pollution they consciously fear, but the tsunami of subliminal existential
terror that will engulf them if the cultural defences are breached by a mortal assault
on their nomos. Zealots are fighting for their spiritual lives, a struggle which even
in ancient history has led to terroristic violence, starting within the ranks of the
Judaic Zealots themselves.

Zealotic terrorism in the ancient world: The Sicarii

The rise of political and paramilitary violence committed by a terrorist faction within the Zealot sect to resist both Roman occupation and the Herodian policy of Hellenization and Romanization must be placed in the context of a more general rise of religious fundamentalism, millennarianism, messianism, and sectarian militancy in defence of the Judaic sacred canopy in the world of classical antiquity. In this context a particularly relevant book is Albert Baumgarten's study of the millennarian sects which flourished in the Maccabean Era (164 BC to 63 BC), after a successful guerrilla war against the Seleucid Empire had enabled the Jews to regain political and cultural control of their own homeland.[35] Baumgarten suggests that such 'apocalyptic' movements arise as a source of relief from the 'cognitive dissonance' (the painful clash between world-view and reality) caused by social and political upheavals. They are able to do this through their ability to offer 'a new or transformed set of fundamental images of the world and relationships'.[36] In other words, a mortal threat to the sacred canopy, a collective nomic crisis, is overcome by an explosion of religious mythopoeia which projects contemporary manifestations of anarchy into a cosmic narrative which interprets them as a symptom of the imminent turning point in history from decadence to a new era, from decay to rebirth.

Baumgarten depicts the confluence of a number of factors in this period which together caused the distressing experience of the 'liquefaction' of a culture which had previously seemed solid: the profound threat which had been posed to Jewish culture once Judea became a client state of the Hellenistic Seleucid Empire before the Maccabean revolt had established the Hasmonean dynasty (under which scholars believe the Jewish Biblical canon was fixed); the success of that revolt which encouraged beliefs that further eschatological expectations would be fulfilled; the expansion of the Roman Empire now bent on extending its hegemony throughout the ancient world including the Middle East and (which eventually overthrew the Hasmonean dynasty in 63 BC); the rise of literacy; the rural exodus. Baumgarten argues that thousands who no longer found a secure spiritual home in a phase of history whose outcome was so unpredictable would naturally 'be receptive to symbols of the world as itself out of joint and on the brink of radical transformation' and so 'be attracted to a group that undertook to model its own life on that new picture of reality'.[37] The vision of 'imminent redemption' was thus an expression of 'anguish with the contemporary situation'.[38]

It is within a Messianic and millennarian climate supercharged by the annexation of Judea into the Roman Empire in 6 AD and the overpowering influence of Hellenism – precisely the period into which Jesus was born, according to Christian scripture, in fulfilment of Judaic Messianic prophecies – that the Zealots first emerged as a fundamentalist sect. In his *Jewish Antiquities*, Josephus – a first-century Romano-Jewish historian who embodies the 'Herodization' of Judaic culture in his fusion of Judaic Orthodoxy with Graeco-Roman thought and culture – calls the Zealots the 'fourth sect' alongside Pharisees, Essenes, and Saduccees. He observed that while in religious beliefs they were close to the

ultraorthodox Pharisees (who accommodated Roman rule), they had 'an inviolable attachment to liberty' and would not recognize the Romans as their rulers
at any cost. Pursuing this liberty meant initially protesting against the burden on
the Jews of Quirinius' tax reform, but the Zealots soon developed into what would
now be seen either as a partisan or resistance movement against foreign occupation. Precluded from fighting a guerrilla war as the Maccabeans had done, they
turned to the archetypal resource of fanatics engaged in an asymmetrical conflict
with state power: terrorism. It would be carried out by the Zealots' own terrorist
wing, the Sicarii, the 'dagger-men'.

Their mission was to drive from their sacred homeland, Judea, the occupying Romans and their sympathizers – notably Herodians and Jews profiting from
Roman rule. It was a mission formulated within an apocalyptic millennarian,[39]
eschatological,[40] and soteriological[41] narrative of history. As two leading experts
on Jewish terrorism put it:

> The Sicarians aspired towards the autonomous existence of the Jewish people
> and unreservedly opposed foreign rule. For them this was a religious principle
> of the highest degree. Their basic guideline was that non-capitulation to a for-
> eign ruler was one of the three cardinal *yehareg ubal yaavor* commandments,
> that is a person must be willing to sacrifice his or her life rather than violate
> one of these directives. They also believed the redemption of the Jewish peo-
> ple was approaching, and as long as the Romans continued to rule, its coming
> would be delayed.[42]

What is significant here is that the nomos for the Sicarii constituted an inextricable blend of the struggle to preserve territorial integrity and autonomy
with the struggle to maintain 'pure' Judaic religious and cultural traditions
free from foreign contamination. It is a complex principle of a renewed order
that can be summed up in the mind of the terrorist in the simple concept
of 'freedom', the purest form of which for a religious believer is found within
the normative constraints of a divinely ordained Law (nomos) believed to be
revealed in scripture and literally primordial in the fullest sense: namely preceding
humanity itself.

In the defence of their unique sacred canopy, the Zealot militants carried out
a number of assassinations literally using cloak and dagger tactics to obtain
maximum proximity to the victim in a crowd, both to enable them to escape
undetected, and, most significantly, to disseminate fear and anxiety in civic society among the occupiers and their 'collaborators', their target audience. One of
their highest profile victims was Jonathan the High Priest. Another was Eleazar,
the governor of the Temple precincts, who was successfully kidnapped but released
for an exchange of Sicarii imprisoned by the Romans.

It is suggested by some scholars who see the Gospels as documenting historical fact that both Barabbas and Judas Iscariot (whose name may allude to his
identity as a 'Sicarius') were members of the movement, as allegedly was one of
Jesus' disciples, Simon Zelotes.[43] In his history of the Jewish liberation struggle,

The Jewish War (75 AD), Josephus documented the key role played by the Sicarii in the Jewish Revolt of 66–73. The fanaticism of their bid to force the Roman occupation forces to withdraw by fomenting a general uprising led them to commit atrocities and (according to the Talmud) destroy Jerusalem's food supply in order to prevent a negotiated settlement with the 'enemy'. It was Sicarii who wrested the rock fortress of Masada from its Roman garrison in 66 AD to use as a base for terrorist operations. It was Sicarii who died, many in a collective suicide, along with their leader Eleazar ben Ya'ir in the fortress in 73 AD in a last act of defiance against what they experienced as the desecration of Jewish civilization, the subjugation of God's chosen people, and the postponement of the new millennium.

The recognition of the Sicarii as the first Jewish terrorists is no mere flight of the scholarly imagination. In 1931, some 19 centuries after their defeat, a new generation of Zionist militants fighting for a Jewish homeland in Palestine formed the League of Sicarii in a conscious act of 'recovering roots'.[44] It was set up by the Achimeir circle of radicalized Zionist youth, a group dedicated to 'direct' (i.e. terrorist) action in the pursuit of their cause. This terrorist strain in Zionism was perpetuated after 1945 in the ruthless attacks carried out by Lohamei Herut Israel (the Stern Gang) to force the British out of Palestine, a campaign that played a key role in the creation of the State of Israel. There is no doubting the fanaticism of the original Sicarii. Josephus reports even the mass suicide at Masada could not quench their fanaticism:

> Some of the faction of the *Sicarion* ... not content with having saved themselves, again embarked on new revolutionary scheming, persuading those that received them there to assert their freedom, to esteem the Romans as no better than themselves and to look upon God as their only Lord and Master.[45]

It is a passage that bears vivid testimony to the determination of the 'Zealotic' reaction to the very real threat to their sacred nomos posed by the inexorable geopolitical forces of Hellenist cultural imperialism and Roman militarism they sought to overcome through isolated acts of violence.

The Judaic nomos was represented by an ancient and almost unique monotheistic religion consolidated by a rich ritual, social, cultural and scriptural tradition. It was observed by a people which had been forged by shared sufferings and persecutions into a 'community of destiny' with a powerful ethnic identity and sense of history. Under external pressures it had become torn apart by sectarianism between 'modernizers' and 'fundamentalists' as its cultural homogeneity and state power were eroded. But while the violence of the Sicarii and their allies in the great revolts of 70 and 135 AD failed to re-establish Jewish autonomy, the cultural nomos survived sufficiently intact during the ensuing Diaspora, despite the loss of a physical homeland, to contribute to the foundation of the State of Israel in 1948, and to the extraordinary renaissance of Judaic orthodoxy and Hebrew culture conserved in 'exile' for nearly two millennia. As we shall see, the Zealotic violence of the Sicarii can be seen as a prototype of the many acts still being committed today both by 'religious terrorists' and nationalist ones in defence of their nomos from new forms of imperialism and geopolitical or globalizing pressures. Before we consider a contemporary example it is worth examining another sect of pre-modern terrorists which resonates far more within modern consciousness, especially among the young: the Assassins.

The Assassins' defence of their nomos

In the twelfth century AD Hassan as-Sabbah, the leader of the Nizari Ismailis, an ancient, and today the second largest, branch of Shi'ite Islam, created an independent state for them governed from the Alamut Fortress set in the mountainous region bordering the Southern Caspian Sea in present-day Iran. He did so at a time of intense sectarian conflict between Shi'ite and Sunni Muslims. The profound religious, political, and cultural instability of the times was heightened further by the threat to Islam itself posed by the Crusades further west. It was thus in a period of acute cultural crisis that Sabbah not only reformed the Nizari sect militarily and administratively, but also set about turning it into a fortress of spiritual power by building on the mystic and eschatological dimension of belief bound up with the Shi'ite cult of the 'Hidden Imam' or Mahdi, and expectations of his reappearance in the 'end days' (*eschatos*), a tradition that has always distinguished Shi'ite from Sunni forms of Islam. He thus founded not just a state, but a hierarchical monastic order to serve as the guardians of its secret doctrinal core. The order's cultic structure of progressive initiation may have been partly modelled on another mystic Shi'ite sect, the tenth-century 'Brethren of Purity' and its compendium of esoteric teachings, the *Encyclopedia of the Brethren of Purity*.[46] As a result the Alamut castle soon resembled one of the medieval Ordensburgen (Castle of the Order) of the Teutonic Knights in Europe which the Nazis sought to emulate in the Third Reich, and whose originals may even have been influenced by the Alamut itself.

The new Nizari state found itself immediately in a situation of deeply asymmetrical power with the Great Seljuq Empire which had been created by a branch of the Oghuz Turks in the early eleventh century, and by 1100 stretched from the Hindu Kush to Eastern Anatolia and from Central Asia to the Persian Gulf. As upholders of Sunni Islam, the geopolitical ambitions of the Seljuq armies threatened the Ismailis with extermination, not just military and political, but cultural and religious. With no 'Herodian' response to the threat of ethnocide and even genocide conceivable, Sabbah's instinctive transformation of Nizari Islam into a deeply fundamentalist, politicized, and militarized variant of the Muslim faith can be seen as a classic example of the Zealotic reaction to a cultural threat identified by Toynbee. Furthermore, the highly syncretic variant of traditional Shi'ite Islam constructed as the nomos of the Nizari Ismailis by Sabbah and his successors, widely regarded by fellow Muslims as a heretical version of it,[47] can be seen as an outstanding example of the process of nomic renewal that will be considered in the next chapter. The same process can be shown to play an important role in the modern religious terrorism to be considered in Chapter 8. The major scholarly expert on the sect, Farhad Daftary, found nothing to endorse the elaborate New Age speculations about the order offered by the likes of Richard Shand.[48] Yet he does confirm that the Ismailis in the Alamut period cultivated an elaborate metaphysical doctrine about the progressive levels of metaphysical understanding which culminated in the final union of the elite with full truth (*kulli*). They also developed a conception of the Imam which imagined him as 'a single cosmic individual who summed up in his position the entire cosmos'.[49]

It is thus against the background of a beleaguered, fundamentalized, and fanaticized tradition engaged in a sustained attempt to make itself militarily and theologically impossible to eradicate that the Nizari sect created a caste of warrior-priests analogous to the far better known Hindu social order (*varna*), the *Kshatriya*. To defend the nomos from Sunni attack they were specially trained in a technique for achieving military aims well established in Muslim history: assassination. The Fida'is or 'devotees' (cognate with the modern Arabic term for anti-Israeli terrorists, Fedayeen, meaning 'those who redeem themselves through self-sacrifice') were young men physically and mentally prepared to carry out martyr missions against enemies of their religion, notably eminent representatives of Muslim Abbasid, Seljuq, and Christian Crusader élites, often going undercover for months to carry out their mission. The term 'Assassin' with which they are now identified in popular folklore and the world of video-gaming derives from the pejorative term for them connoting 'hashish-junkies', but the notion that they were drugged as part of their initiation into the caste or preparation for murder seems to be pure fantasy. One scholar raises the intriguing possibility instead that *Hashāshīn* is a deformation or misunderstanding of the term '*Asasiyun*, meaning people who are faithful to the *Asās*, meaning "foundation" of the faith'.[50] Such an etymology would be especially significant since Al Qaeda means 'the base' or 'foundation'.

In short, the terrorism of both the Sicarii and the Assassins can be seen as being deeply embedded in Zealotic reactions to the very real threat of assimilation or extinction at the hands of aggressive imperial forces superior not just in numbers but military and cultural strength. Rejecting any sort of capitulation or Herodian compromise with the enemies, both groups represent the 'spiritual warrior', zealously dedicated to saving a homeland both physical and metaphysical. Their coldly fanatical acts of violence point to the fact that the nomos can in conditions of extreme subjective anomy or objective cultural crisis become, at least for a small percentage of those who feel threatened in their very being by the assault on their nomos, something literally more important than life itself. The historical Sicarii were eventually destroyed, and their doomed bid to resist through uncompromising orthodoxy and murderous violence is commemorated today in negative terms in the calls of liberal Israelis to put an end to 'Sicarii Zionism' so as to assure the nation's future.[51] By contrast, Nizari Ismailism survived the destruction of the Alamut and the Nizari state to be perpetuated in less esoteric and more moderate forms to this day, while travesties of its original cultic, terroristic embodiments continue to be re-enacted in the millions of violent combats played out in the heads of the zealots of Xbox fantasy games.

Chechen terrorists as modern Zealots

Although 'religious terrorism' is one of the main manifestations of fanatical violence in the modern age, it will become clear in the last three chapters of this book that much of it is actually a mixture of traditional religious and fundamentalist rejections of the 'denomizing' impact of modernity with palingenetic schemes of renewal imbued with the secular utopianism of modernity itself. They are thus hybrids rather than the relatively unadulterated modern equivalents of the Zealotic mobilization of militant factions of first-century Jews or twelfth-century Shi'ites in defence of their sacred canopy and the territory beneath it. However, there are several examples of contemporary religious causes whose terroristic expressions display a deep kinship with the structural conditions which led to the fanatical violence of the Sicarii and the Assassins.

One, Chechen terrorism, was put on the map of the global media by its series of spectacular attacks on the Russian civilian population; notably the seizure of Moscow's Dubrovka Theatre in October 2002 when more than 120 hostages were killed by Russian Special Forces in the course of their liberation; the occupation of a school in North Ossetia in September 2004 which led to the deaths of over 300, mostly children; the derailing in November 2009 of the Nevsky Express used by the Russian business and political elite; and the detonation of two bombs by female suicide bombers in a Moscow metro station in March 2010 killing 39. It is natural, given the international preoccupation with the globalization of Islamism since 2001, for the Chechen Muslims to be viewed as just another battle front in the 'war against terror', an assumption that it suits the Russian government to perpetuate. Yet historically speaking the spate of Chechen terrorist violence over the last decade is to be seen as just the latest stage in a struggle for liberation from Russian domination and for self-preservation from the repeated episodes of savage repression and cultural genocide against the indigenous Chechens that has been taking place for over 200 under Tsarist, Soviet, and post-Soviet regimes.[52]

The ultimate origins of the Chechens are lost in the proverbial mists of time when their cultural, somatic, and linguistic ancestors first colonized the area of the Caucasus around present-day Chechnya between 10,000 and 3,000 years ago, possibly as a result of migration from the Fertile Crescent of Mesopotamia. The mountainous area was subject to invasion and incursions from various tribes, including the Cimmerians and Scythians, and having fended off the threat of Arabian occupation, in the thirteenth and fourteenth centuries, came under sustained attack by the Mongols in the same wave of imperial expansion that had destroyed the Nizari Ismailis. The Caucasian people, who by then were now a distinct ethnic group recognizable as proto-Chechens, resisted the Mongols successfully, but at terrible human cost. It was a presage of even greater national disasters.

The event which forged a homogeneous 'community of identity' with an unbroken continuity to modern Chechens was the brutal conquest of the Caucasus mountain region and the surrounding plains by Russian Cossacks in the second half of the eighteenth century. It precipitated the national embrace of an Islam blended with ancient indigenous religious cults as an outward symbol of resistance to 'Christian' Russification in the area, and to the declaration of a Holy War or jihad against Russia in 1785 by the Chechen leader Sheikh Mansur. The Russian war to 'pacify' (state doublespeak for 'ruthlessly crush') and colonize the 'savage' mountain peoples was, on the behest of the Tsar, fought by the Cossack and Russian troops with a singular barbarity. Under the imperial general Aleksey Yermolov, commander-in-chief of the Russian forces in Georgia between 1816 and 1827, the suppression of Chechen resistance attained a genocidal ferocity consistent with his frank declaration in a letter to the Tsar Alexander I that 'I desire that the terror of my name shall guard our frontiers more potently than chains or fortresses'.[53]

Thanks to this explicit policy of state terrorism reminiscent of the systemic war-crimes committed in the Nazi occupation of Poland and during Operation Barbarossa, the Chechen population fell drastically in the nineteenth century owing to emigration, expulsion, slaughter, and terrible privation. Having been annexed by the Russian empire, the Chechens rose once more in 1877 against the brutality of what they still regarded as the barbaric colonization of their nation. The insurgency was ruthlessly crushed. By then the spread of modern national consciousness had helped crystallize the Chechen sense of unique cultural and historical identity, one which was further challenged when the discovery of major oil deposits caused an influx of Russian and Ukrainian workers and Armenian bankers, as well as the appearance of a 'Herodified' Chechen elite profiting from the country's incorporation into the Russian empire and the exploitation of their fellow Chechens.

The Russian Revolution briefly raised hopes that Bolshevik victory promised liberation from the yoke of Russian imperialism, some Chechen Sufis actually joining the Communist Party, but Lenin's regime soon proved no less imperialist and liberticidal than the Tsarist one. The Chechen Autonomous Oblast formed in 1922 was in reality a subjugated Soviet province and in 1934 was merged with the neighbouring Ingush Autonomous Oblast to further dilute ethnic identities. However, the successful outcome of the Finnish–Russian War of 1939–1940 inspired the organization of a Chechen guerrilla movement to fight for the liberation of Chechnya from the Soviet yoke. Alhough the ensuing nationalist independence movement attempted to take advantage of the Nazi invasion, it refused to ally itself with the Nazis and so compromise Chechen freedom by becoming subject to another imperialist force. Nevertheless Stalin regarded the Chechens as Nazi collaborators, and in the course of the enforced mass deportations of the entire population which took place in February 1944, those civilians who resisted or who were deemed 'untransportable' suffered atrocities on a par with those committed by the Nazis in their 'resettlement' of Jews.

Between 1944 and 1948 over 350,000 Chechens were transported, approximately 170,000 of whom died in the process, about half the total population. At the same time Chechen culture was entirely 'disappeared' from Russian history books, encyclopedias and maps. As part of Stalin's policy of ethnic eradication, a library of historical texts written in Chechen and Georgian and using both Arabic and Georgian script was destroyed, and along with it invaluable information about the Chechens' unique culture. 'Ethnic biblioclasm'[54] is perhaps the ultimate act of 'nomocide' that can be committed against a people, one which erases not just its living representatives, but the collective memory of its history. Such acts were committed, for example, by Catholics against the Mayans, the Chinese Red Guards against Tibetans, Pol Pot against Cambodians, and the Serbs against Bosnians. The deportation of the Chechens was officially recognized as an act of genocide by the European Parliament in 2004. By then all the surviving deportees had been allowed to return in 1957 by Khrushchev. Although they still found themselves firmly shackled to the Soviet Union politically and economically, brutal policies of Russification and deliberate culturecide had failed. The Chechens succeeded against the odds in preserving their unique language, their cultural identity, and their national variant of the Sunni Muslim faith with its admixture of paganism, tribalism, and Sufism.

Predictably, even the collapse of the Soviet empire did not mean the end to Russian colonialism in the Caucasus. The Chechens now found themselves ruled from Moscow within the framework of the Russian Federation Republic of Chechnya. Equally predictably palingenetic expectations rose dramatically among Chechen separatists now that Soviet communism had ended, leading to the rise of a powerful independence movement which took shape in the Chechen All-National Congress founded in 1991. Boris Yeltsin's response to the spectre of Chechen independence was, of course, to impose brutal military repression, leading to the First Chechen War against Chechen guerrillas in which tens of thousands of civilians died before the ceasefire in 1996. By this time a significant change in the sacred canopy under which the Chechens were carrying out their struggle had come about: it was being not just Islamized but Islamicized.

Dzodhar Dudayev, the first president of the breakaway state, the Chechen Republic of Ichkeria, made no reference to Islam in his pre-election programme of 1991, but from 1994 he started using the symbolism and rhetoric of Islam to rally the forces of Chechen resistance to Russia. By 1996 resistance leaders were switching allegiance from traditional variants of Sufism to a form of Salafi Islamism which portrayed the Chechen conflict in the Caucuses as another front of a global war between Islam and 'the West', and which even more intransigently than its predecessor 'celebrate[d] death, suicide and mass murder as weapons against the infidel'.[55] The Islamicization of Chechen terrorism is an example of the universal phenomenon of an established religion being radicalized and politicized when a traditional nomos is beleaguered so as to provide the heightened sense of communal identity, purpose, heroism and spirit of self-sacrifice needed to motivate fighters to the point of being prepared to die for their nation's freedom. What is fascinating is that an idiosyncratic national form of Islam associated with Sufi mysticism was within a few years largely replaced by an explicitly fundamentalist, Islamist form of Sunni faith, a process paralleled and influenced by the rise of Islamicism among the Mujahideen who had been fighting the Russians in Afghanistan a decade earlier. As a result the most militant Chechens could feel that their cause was no longer a local fight for liberation but an integral part of

Global Salafi Jihad.[56] It was a development that contributed to the success of the Chechens in forcing a Russian withdrawal in 1996. In April 1997 the first public execution imposed by an Islamic court in Chechnya was televised and in the same year the country was declared an Islamic Repubic.

But the newly Islamicized Chechen militants were not content with their hard won independence. Their support for a separatist movement in Dagestan in 1999 triggered the second Chechen War which killed 30,000 to 40,000 civilians, crushed the guerrillas, and led to the re-imposition of Russian military rule, as well as the extensive destruction of the centre of the capital, Grozny. Since 2000 the emphasis of the Chechens' deeply asymmetrical struggle against Russia's military might has shifted to a terrorist campaign fought not just within Chechnya (which saw nearly 1000 incidents of violence in 2008), but also elsewhere in the Caucasus and, most dramatically of all, in Russia, sometimes with spectacular results.

Chechen terrorism, however Islamicized since the 1990s, provides an illuminating modern case study in Zealotic terrorism. It originated in the physical struggle to defend the nomos of land, tradition, culture and faith from destruction at the hands of invaders and colonizers. It radicalized and politicized the indigenous religion of the homeland (itself a foreign import originally) because it served as a marker of ethnic distinctiveness with respect to both 'Christian', communist, and post-communist Russians. It also illustrates how a local resistance movement may transform its ideology, in this case its religion, to create a sense of global struggle even if this paradoxically means a loss of cultural uniqueness. By the late 1990s foreign Islamists affiliated to Al Qaeda, including veterans from the Mujahideen war against Russia, were fighting in Chechnya and splits were growing up between traditional Chechen and Salafi factions within the resistance movement. What all the indigenous Chechen fighters share, however, is the same fanatical commitment to defend to the death the unique Chechen nomos that had enabled earlier generations of their nation to survive during the Soviet-imposed diaspora.

It is not land, or possessions, or religion, or even physical survival that the hard core of the Chechen independence movement has always fought for. Nor is it even now the 'global Caliphate' dreamed of by international Islamists, at least in the first instance. Rather it is for the totality of Chechenness as a suprapersonal, suprahistorical, holy reality, the sacred canopy which protects ethnic Chechens from existential extinction. It is this nomos that some Chechen women and men are prepared to kill and die for, just as the Sicarii and Assassins before them, in their life and death struggle against Hellenization and Sunnification. A month before the Chechen attack on the Russian metro in March 2010 which he directed, the self-styled Emir of the Caucasian Mujahideen, Dokka Abu Usman, issued a statement, expressed in a typical blend of ultranationalism and Islamism, condemning the Russian declaration of the Krasnodar Territory to be no longer part of the Caucasus, and reinforcing the idea of defence of the homeland in primordial Zealotic terms as a *sacred duty*:

The Krasnodar Territory, as infidels call it, is in fact the land of our brothers, the best brothers and the best Muslims in this world. This is the land of Adygs, the land of Abazins, the land of Circassians. So I want to state with full responsibility and I bequeath it to the Mujahideen who will come after us, God willing. They will come. There is no doubt about it, that this is the land of our brothers. And it is our sacred duty to liberate these lands from infidelity. And, God willing, we will do it, we will achieve this goal. Therefore, we will never exclude a Caucasian land from the Caucasus. Moreover, after we liberate the land of our brothers, coreligionists and Caucasian Muslims, we will, God willing, liberate other lands that are now occupied by Russia. They are Astrakhan and the Volga lands that are now under the heel of Russian infidels.[57]

The Tamil Tigers' defence of their sacred canopy

One of the historic events which links the roots of Chechen terrorism to the rise of the Tamil Tigers is another act of 'ethnic biblioclasm', namely the burning of the Jaffna library in 1981. This caused the destruction of over 97,000 books, including the only existing copy of *Yalpanam Vaipavama*, a history of Jaffna, and countless other irreplaceable documents of Tamil culture. Before ceding independence to Ceylon in 1948, the British had granted the Tamil Hindus in the north, one-fifth of the population, with a history, language and culture distinct from the Sinhalese majority, privileged nationality status and parliamentary representation, as well as legal recognition of Tamil and Sinhalese as national languages. (The collective act of vandalism committed on the restored library by a large group of Sinhalese 'tourists' in October 2010 points to the continued mythic power which the building retains as a symbol of the Tamils' nomos even after the defeat of their independence movement.) The burning of the library was the culmination of growing ethnic tensions resulting from the Sinhalese attempt to impose their distinctive language and social traditions based on Theravada Buddhism as the sole legitimate culture in the newly independent Sri Lanka. This policy involved not just the removal of the Tamils from positions of political, social and cultural influence, but deliberate attacks on their cultural nomos as a force contaminating the purity of a Sinhalese island nation.[58]

It is in the context of the Sinhalese government's sustained assault on their cultural identity that the announcement in 1958 that Sinhala was henceforth the only official language of the country served as a 'delegitimizing event', one which 'propels ... towards violence those who feel victimized'.[59] It sparked off not a Tamil but an anti-Tamil riot reminiscent of the anti-Jewish pogroms of nineteenth-century Eastern Europe, leaving hundreds dead and thousands homeless. Elections in 1977 led to another wave of anti-Tamil violence, convincing many that the leader of the Federal Party had been right to abandon the prospect of negotiating a peaceful federal solution to the deepening ethnic and territorial crisis as a pipe-dream, and that they should call instead for the creation of an independent homeland, Tamil Eelam (Eelam is the Tamil for Sri Lanka). Even in lulls in active hostility, Tamils were being increasingly discriminated against in public life as inferior aliens unassimilable into official Sri Lankan society. The country had descended rapidly into an Asian equivalent of apartheid South Africa or the early years of post-Soviet Balkan democracy, where your quality of life was determined by what ethnicity you belonged to, and the police and military were regularly used to crush and not defend human rights. This situation inevitably caused a backlash among broad sections of the Tamils, especially within a younger generation who felt they were being brutally excluded from any future in the new nation. After many centuries of continuous Tamil occupation of substantial areas of the North accompanied by the flowering of a rich indigenous culture which gave them a separate identity from the Tamils on the Indian mainland, they naturally considered Sri Lanka their birthright, and so resisted Sinhalese calls for them to 'go home'. They were there already.

An expression of the increasing frustration and militancy was the formation in the early 1970s of national secessionist movements, the most radical of which was the Liberation Tigers of Tamil Eelam. The LTTE underwent considerable expansion and radicalization in the wake of the Jaffna library atrocity of 1981, closely followed by government-orchestrated anti-Tamil riots in 1983 which the rebels took as further proof that all chances of a peaceful settlement were long gone and that guerilla war was the only option. The breakdown of the fragile 'accord' arrived at between the Sinhalese government and the Tamils in 1987 (only under Indian military pressure) marked the start of a full-scale war between the Sinhalese army and the Tigers. The LTTE soon grew into one of the most sophisticated, fanatical, and deadly guerrilla and terrorist organizations in the world, forcing the officially 'Buddhist' Sinhalese to adopt draconian measures to end the stalemate. In May 2009, under the cover of tight reporting restrictions to keep the world's media from documenting what was happening, the Tigers' militia was finally encircled and annihilated by the Sinhalese army using overwhelming force in an action which cost some 40,000 Tamil Hindu and Christian lives and was accompanied by the terrible atrocities recorded in a British TV documentary on LTTE fighters and civilians, thousands of whom died in a military operation of genocidal intensity.[60] By this time the 50-year civil war had cost the lives of more than 135,000 Tamil men, women and children, and 1.1 million Tamils had fled the country. An ancient, unique cultural tradition, way of life and source of identity had been destroyed for ever, leaving Tamil Eelam to be perpetuated only in the imagination of expatriates and the dispossessed.

Until the annihilation of the LTTE's militia in 2009 (it survives as a virtual force on websites and within diaspora communities but is no longer an active force in Sri Lankan politics),[61] the LTTE had the reputation of being one of the most ruthless, and in military if not political terms, effective terrorist movements in the world. From 1987 they started to use martyr bombers, male and female[62] (known as Black Tigers) to devastating effect, killing major symbols of Sinhalese state and military power such as the Defence Minister, the Minister for Industrial Development, the Chief of the Sri Lankan Navy, and several top army officers. The most high-profile victim was Sri Lanka's President, Ranasinghe Premadasa, by a bicycle-riding 'suicide' assassin at a May Day rally in Colombo, in 1993. The LTTE also used a woman martyr bomber to assassinate former Indian Prime Minister Rajiv Gandhi, no friend of the Tamils, to stop him becoming Prime Minister once again. Perhaps more significant was the killing of a moderate Tamil leader of the Tamil United Liberation Front (TULF), symptomatic of the rejection of any 'Herodian' compromise with the enemy. The 'Zealotic' elimination of moderate rivals reached a peak in May 1986 with the 'full-scale massacre of members of Tamil Eelam Liberation Organization and their leader Sri Sabaratnam'.[63] The LTTE also ruthlessly applied the tactics of 'suicide terrorism' so extensively that they generated a mood of national tension and anxiety for over a quarter of a century, and proved that they could be used effectively against naval targets, a lesson not lost on Al Qaeda.[64] It perfected a blend of guerilla and terrorist warfare.[65] In the course of their doomed 20-year 'holy' struggle to create Tamil Eelam so as to conserve their culture, they killed many hundreds of innocent Sinhalese citizens in the war-crimes now documented on government websites, although unbiased statistics are impossible to obtain for the atrocities committed by either side. What is clear is that the state terror against Tamil separatism and the terrorism against the state were both waged with utter disregard for human life, a betrayal of both Buddhist and Tamil religious values.

So what drove LTTE fanaticism? While most Tamils remain Hindu, a small number have long since embraced Islam or Christianity, and the Tigers were generally careful to present themselves as protectors of Tamil religion *'whatever it may be'*[66] against the onslaught of Sinhalese Buddhism, so that it never explicitly took the form of 'religious terrorism'. The Tigers were also accused of revolutionary Marxism by the Sinhalese and celebrated as Marxists–Leninists by International Socialists.[67] However, it is clear from scholarly accounts of the LTTE[68] that, like the Sicarii, the Assassins, and the Chechens before them, it was the defence of the nomos, identified in this case with the creation of Tamil Eelam as a separate homeland, that motivated them. A Tamil school teacher who organized a cricket match between his pupils and the armed forces was killed because no collaboration or compromise was to be contemplated in a situation where the Sri Lankan Tamils' tradition was not merely 'beleaguered': its sacred canopy was being systematically annihilated:

> Our houses become our graves . . . our villages become cremation grounds. The Sinhalese racist demons slowly take over our ancient land. On our own soil, the soil where we were born and lived since time immemorial, our people are turned into refugees, into slaves, they are being destroyed.[69]

The new recruits were put through a three month training to ensure their utter dedication to the sacred cause of the Motherland reviving 'ancient traditions of hero warriors following their chieftain into the field and death', and celebrating the myth of a mother who willingly sends her little son into battle once all the men in the family have been killed in war. Their readiness to die was symbolized by carrying a cyanide capsule in case of capture, prompting one Black Tiger to write 'Yes, our death lives with us. It sleeps with us. . .That makes us clear-headed and purposeful'. The Tamil motherland was evoked in its writings as a divine entity,[70] and before a mission the terrorists enjoyed a ritual 'last supper' with the LTTE chief

Prabhakaran before setting out, pointing to a sacralization both of the mythicized homeland and of the fight to preserve 'Her'. The most brutal and effective episode of ethnic cleansing by a state (officially, a democratic Buddhist state!) since the Second World War has reduced Tamil Eelam to no more than a utopian fantasy.[71] But there is another form of terrorism whose projects do not finish, but actually start out as a figment of the utopian imagination. This will be the subject of the next chapter.

3
Modernist Terrorism: Creating the Nomos

The dynamics of cultural renewal

In the last chapter we considered the terrorist violence that has on occasion been engendered both in the distant past and in contemporary history by the communal need to physically defend the nomos from destruction at the hands of hostile alien forces. But throughout human history defensive strategies to conserve a 'beleaguered tradition' have often failed owing to inner processes of dissolution or external pressures, a fact documented with overwhelming erudition in the many volumes of Toynbee's *The Study of History* and its Germanic role model, Oswald Spengler's *The Decline of the West*. As a result the world's museums are littered with the flotsam and jetsam of bygone civilizations, failed cultures, forgotten religions, and dead languages, the fossils of extinct nomoi. Each bust of a ruler whose earthly empire has long since turned to dust conjures up the ghost of the Pharaoh Ramesses the Great, immortalized, ironically enough, not through his own 'works' as he had arrogantly assumed, but in Percy Shelley's poem *Ozymandias* which ends with the famous lines:

> Nothing beside remains. Round the decay
> Of that colossal wreck, boundless and bare
> The lone and level sands stretch far away.

In contrast to the focus in the last chapter on preserving a threatened nomos from the fate of Ozymandias, this one considers the fanatical violence that can arise long after attempts to resolve the nomic crisis that occurs once the sacred canopy is beyond restoration by the mobilization of militant fundamentalist or millennarian mythic energies in its defence. At this point cultural innovation not conservation becomes necessary, a revolution to create a new nomos in order to 'cosmize' the world once more, and thereby restore a sense of higher communal purpose which keeps the terror of nihilism at bay. The desperate bid to stave off the void is one that will in particular circumstances produce terrorist violence which appears nihilistic to the outsider, but to the protagonist is a creative gesture, the signal that the nomic world is about to change, or at the very least demands

47

transformation. The crucial point to note is that, as we saw implicitly with the Sicarii and Assassins and explicitly with the Chechens and Tamil Tigers, the nomos is not necessarily a religious, suprahistorical, metaphysical reality as such, but the total culture which one particular belief system (and, in the case of the Sri Lankan Tamils, *a plurality of belief systems*) helped bind together beneath a single creed, a single nomic sky. Especially under the modern conditions of secularization there is no reason why the new metapolitical nomos should be rooted in a supranatural, *suprahuman* reality, as long as it is a supra-individual, *suprapersonal* cause whose intrinsic value, and hence the mission to realize it, can be felt to transcend that of the believer's own life.

In this context a passage in Peter Berger's *The Sacred Canopy* assumes a particular resonance:

> Every human society is an edifice of externalized and objectivated meanings, always intending a meaningful totality. Every society is engaged in the never completed enterprise of building a humanly meaningful world. Cosmization implies the identification of this humanly meaningful world with the world as such, the former now being grounded in the latter, reflecting it or being derived from it in its fundamental structures. Such a cosmos, as the ultimate ground and validation of human nomoi, need not necessarily be sacred. Particularly in modern times there have been thoroughly secular attempts at cosmization, among which modern science is by far the most important. It is safe to say, however, that originally all cosmization had a sacred character.[1]

Two important points are implicit in this statement. Firstly, human cultures are not static but in a constant state of dynamic evolution as generation after generation of human beings attempts to 'build a humanly meaningful world' to ward off potentially shattering intimations of life's futility and absurdity which plunge them into the abyss of anomy. This is a never-ending enterprise, especially since historical conditions are in permanent flux, and each culture is exposed to possibly destructive contacts with other cultures from without while exposed to the risk of new factions and sects arising to breed pluralism and anarchy from within, often as a response to objective socio-political or economic developments, wars or natural disasters. In this context it is clear that the repeated crises of legitimacy accompanying so many episodes of contested monarchical or imperial succession throughout human history have an underlying existential dimension, since legitimate succession was crucial to the renewed recosmization of the community and yet smooth political transitions were constantly thwarted by the vagaries of reproduction and health and the constant tendency to factionalization. This helps explain the extreme violence which has often characterized such *rites de passage* to a new reign, since the desperate communal drive to 'cosmization' can be more powerful than the lust for personal power or wealth.

Second, it is implied in Berger's statement that 'modern times' – i.e. the secularizing, denomizing conditions of modernity – have created the possibility that the quest for higher meaning may lead to the emergence of a new genus of nomoi which are not derived from tradition and are not religious or metaphysical in the traditional sense. Instead they relate to *human-made* metapolitical values and utopian projects which are *temporalized* and hence are to be lived out, fought for, and realized within secular historical time.[2] The rich literature on ultranationalism, Nazism and Bolshevism as 'political religions'[3] corroborate this point, while also underlining how even new nomoi, such as communism, however secular in theory, tend to acquire their own suprapersonal and hence sacral value for those who become 'fanatically' attached to them. Such numinous 'isms' are the product of the unique historical situation created by what Nietzsche called 'the death of God' in Western civilization, and which inspired a famous convert to Anglo-Catholicism, T.S. Eliot, to write in *Choruses from the Rock* (1934):

But it seems that something has happened that has never happened before: though we know not just when, or why, or how, or where.
Men have left GOD not for other gods, they say, but for no God; and this has never happened before
That men both deny gods and worship gods, professing first Reason,
And then Money, and Power, and what they call Life, or Race, or Dialectic.

Carl Jung put it more succinctly: 'Our fearsome gods have only changed their name: they now rhyme with ism'.

This chapter sets out to investigate the fanatical violence that can be inspired by belief in such modern 'Gods' or 'isms' and the struggle to establish them as the new nomos. Such a struggle is born of a palingenetic process in which human societies create and institute new nomoi when the traditional ones have failed, but which now can take the form of a higher, transcendent but *secular*, 'man-made' ideal society. Instituting a new value system is an undertaking which, to use Anthony Giddens' words, can also 'be edged with the possibility of violence' just as much as defending a 'beleaguered tradition'. In order to understand the cultural dynamics at work in the creation of a this-worldly nomos, it is helpful to understand the process by which new metahistorical nomoi emerged in premodern societies. This, of course, involves mechanisms of enormous complexity, but a conceptual 'handle' on it is offered by what has been established by the research of social anthropologists into 'revitalization movements'.

One heuristically powerful model of how new cultural nomoi emerge was offered by the pioneering anthropologist Victor Turner when he turned his attention to cultural situations in which the mechanisms for coping with change and death through the power of ritual and myth are no longer adequate. Arnold van Gennep had carried out pioneering work on the significance of *rites de passage* in ensuring the individual or collective experience of progressing from one stable state to another (e.g. puberty to adulthood, life to death) via a 'liminal', or transitional, in-between stage which is always resolved in a new phase. Turner refined this model by postulating a 'liminoid' phase in which the liminal stage remains unresolved and there is no third stage of stability to be accessed. Within Berger's framework it is at this point that anomy sets in. Turner analysed the recurrent link between the social experience of the liminoid and the emergence of a revitalization movement striving to establish a new regenerative nomos. Under the leadership of a *propheta* (a charismatic leader) a secessionist *communitas* forms, pursuing a regenerative vision of a new society. It is a vision which is essentially heretical in terms of the pre-crisis tradition, but which is received as the revelation of a holy new order to the 'heretics' who follow him or her, even when it is presented as the fulfilment of the original pristine vision that has been lost. This new nomic community will, if the secession is successful, form the core of a new culture under a new sacred canopy.[4]

Some years earlier, another anthropologist, Anthony Wallace, had anticipated Turner's model of how nomic renewal and *reinvention* resolves liminoid situations in a seminal essay[5] which pointed to the important role played in the formulation of the new nomos by *syncretism*. The metaphysical view of the world promulgated by the leader of the sect (*propheta*) is generally made up of a blend of tradition with elements often adapted from neighbouring *nomoi* or invented through a mythopoeia supercharged in visionary intensity by the existentially urgent need for a solution to the nomic crisis. As a result it will often be shot through with millennarian or apocalyptic visions of a new dawn or a new era following the collapse of the old society, an archetypically palingenetic response of human consciousness to times of suffering and crisis. Wallace called such a process of renomization 'a mazeway resynthesis', since the synthesizing of nomic elements has the subliminal purpose of leading the *propheta's* followers out of the labyrinth of anomy and anarchy. The Native American 'Ghost Dance', through which an indigenous population sought to resist nomocide at the hands of White settlers in the late nineteenth century during the internal colonization of the US, is widely seen as a paradigmatic revitalization movement. It was a ritual of recosmization based on intensive ideological and ritual syncretism which transformed fear of destruction into millennial hope based on a new creed mutating despair into hope.[6]

It is consistent with this model of cultural renewal that the syncretic formation of new religious *nomoi* played a major role in China's history after the decay of its imperial traditions set in under the impact of an already globalizing modernity spreading from Europe. This ushered in a period of profound liminoidality for the Chinese which could not be repelled or resolved by the forces of tradition. The nineteenth century hosted two notable examples of mass revitalization movement, the Taiping Rebellion and Boxer Rebellion, each of which contained strong elements of millennarianism (one a native variant of imported Christianity the other a home-grown New Religious Movement with strong esoteric elements). Both unleashed violent palingenetic energies, thereby fomenting murderous civil war conditions which led to the deaths of millions.[7]

The way liminoid social conditions can become a laboratory for the production of competing revitalization movements is further illuminated by Colin Campbell's concept of the 'cultic milieu'[8] which describes an 'underground region' that opens up within a dominant culture in times of crisis 'where true seekers test hidden, forgotten, and forbidden knowledge. Ideas and allegiances within the milieu change as individuals move between loosely organized groups, but the larger milieu persists in opposition to the dominant culture'.[9] Illustrations of this principle at work are the emergence of 'cultic milieux' hosting syncretic religions in the late Hellenic and Roman worlds trapped in slow but terminal decline. Syncretic religions have also been the features of other cultures existing in liminoid conditions, such as the revivalist cults that emerged in the Caribbean and Latin America in circumstances of extreme multiculturalism and despair during the period of colonization and slavery.

Another example of this pattern is the bizarre creed forged by the Barghawata Berbers on what is now the coast of Morocco. The Barghawata kingdom (744–1058 AD) was consolidated by a unique synthesis of elements taken from Sunni, Shi'a and Kharijite Islam, Judaism, plus an admixture of astrological and heathen traditions. The formation of new nomoi through 'mazeway resynthesis' assumes particular importance when it is realized that it has not only produced outlandish cults and curious sects. It played a pivotal role in the founding of 'minor' religious communities such as the Bahai and Druze. This process of mazeway resynthesis can also be shown (at least to the satisfaction of non-believers) to have contributed decisively to the genesis of several of the world's major religions, namely Hinduism, Buddhism,[10] Jainism, Sikhism, Judaism, Christianity, and Islam, all of which resolved liminoid situations which had emerged through historical processes.[11]

Modernism as a revolt against anomy

The reader will already have noticed several vague allusions in this text to 'premodern' and 'traditional' in contrast to 'modern' societies, and 'modernity'. The connotations and periodization of these highly value-laden and problematic terms vary considerably according to the society under examination and the expert consulted. They have also deeply ingrained imperialist connotations when 'traditional' implies 'primitive', and so subliminally legitimates the imposition of an 'advanced' (normally connoting Western) civilization on an indigenous population, either through aggressive or simply insensitive colonization, often with culturecidal consequences, as the histories of the Americas, Africa, Indonesia, Asia, and Australia amply testify.[12] Clearly they are equally misleading terms if they imply a basic dichotomy between timeless, static communal systems preserved in the aspic of established religion, and a homogeneously 'globalized' dynamic modern world which threatens to engulf them, a spinning vortex of secularization, materialism, and individualism. History is in constant flux, however much the Platonic imagination would like to imagine otherwise.

In practice the elements of continuity or symbiosis between tradition and 'Western' or 'globalizing' modernity, and the capacity of many decaying traditional societies to reinvent and modernize themselves in a seamless process of evolutionary adaptation is extraordinary, producing a rich biodiversity of unique 'modernities' shot through with traditional elements.[13] Yet despite its shortcomings and ambiguities as a term, there is a widespread usage of 'modernity' in

the human sciences[14] to make it synonymous with Westernization and secularization and thus endow it with particular value in the present context. Used in
this way 'modernity' refers to a nexus of forces that 'disenchant', 'disembed',
'decentre' societies, which introduces pluralism and relativism where once there
was a 'whole' culture, and which replaces organic 'community' with an extensively atomized 'society'. As the quotations from Eliot and Jung have suggested,
modernization in this sense has had a devastating impact on traditional religious
nomoi. In the West, where it stretched over centuries as a process arising from
within, and hence 'endogenic' to, social and intellectual developments in Europe,
there has been time for a vast array of utopian myths and projects to arise offering overarching responses to the erosion of the Christian nomoi, many of them
proposing a scheme of secular, linear progress. Some of the more radical of these
have assumed millennarian form at a time of profound societal upheaval and thus
promised a new type of society altogether, an imminent new era, an *alternative*
modernity offering the existential protection of a traditional sacred canopy, but
erected through human agency to fulfil a fully human 'higher purpose'.[15] Nazism
and Bolshevism leap to mind as examples.

The most devastating nomocidal impacts of modernization have been experienced when it has been 'exogenic', arriving as a by-product of imperial expansion
or globalization imposed from without to impact cultures whose traditional religious nomoi were naturally evolving but intact. The effect of rapid modernization
on such societies can lead to wholesale destruction in the form of a thorough-
going acculturation to it, a modern equivalent of 'Herodization'. Or else it can
provoke a defensive retrenchment and radicalization of the religion, an insistence on the immutable and inviolable truths inferred from a particular reading
of scripture or tradition that is familiar as 'religious fundamentalism', terroristic
examples of which we considered in the last chapter in the account of the more
recent Islamist current within Chechen resistance to the threat of nomocide. Even
where modernization is not resisted because it is an endogenic, home-grown force
of change, contemporary modernity tends to erode the possibility of commu-
nally held nomoi while dissolving any prospect of metaphysical certainty, so that
(to cite *The Communist Manifesto*) 'all that is solid melts into air'.[16] Michael Mazarr,
in his study of terrorism as a revolt against modernity, claims that it is a force that
'ploughs under traditional social norms and values and at least potentially generates vast alienation.... Beloved cultural values, so essential to furnishing human
beings with a stable concept of reality, are torn apart.'[17] It 'poses an often mortal
threat to those established habits of the group in which people have invested their
identity',[18] and 'shreds old cultural narratives directly'.[19]

But the less conspicuous and perhaps more devastating impact of Western
modernity on societies – whether they host it or suffer it, welcome it or
reject it – is that it gradually brings about an existential situation of irre-
solvable ambivalence[20] and liquefaction,[21] a sense of permanent transition or
liminoidality[22] that demands the birth of something qualitatively that will bring
closure while simultaneously denying closure.[23] It is thus melodramatic and misleading to suggest nomic certainties always collapse suddenly under the impact of

modernity. Its impact may be experienced less as a hurricane and more as a change of climate, a prolonged drought. Traditional cultural structures may, on contact with globalizing modernity, remain outwardly intact but be subject to a gradual erosion of substance which hollows them out, desiccating their once abundant sap. Experientially this creates the feeling that absolute truths are melting away like a Salvador Dali clock, that heaven is receding ever further from the earth, that the divine has become a 'deus absconditus' playing a comic or cruel game of hide and seek with human beings. In a Western society, or one which becomes Westernized (Herodized?) rather than fundamentalized, individuals, at least those of a demanding metaphysical temperament, may find that numinous truths are elusive, intermittent, able to be glimpsed only sporadically if at all and in a way that is irreducibly ambiguous.

Meanwhile the foundations of existence become shallow and soft, and language itself seems to lose its power to capture an ever more evanescent reality. The result is less a nomic crisis than a nomic *disturbance*, existential disquiet, a *malaise*, the 'Unbehagen' alluded to in the German title of Freud's *Civilization and its Discontent*, or the unsettling experience of a character in Woody Allen's *Deconstructing Harry* (1997) who wakes up one day to find he is 'out of focus' to all who see him. Modernity breeds ontological fuzziness. Or else it spawns idiosyncratic searches for a more intense, pristine reality, providing not just the hidden psychological mainspring of all extreme sports, but the quest for the epiphanies of the every day. Such a quest is documented in Jack Kerouac's *On the Road* or reconstructed in Jon Krakauer's *Into the Wild*, based on the life of Christopher McCandless who gave up the prospect of a glittering career to penetrate ever deeper into inner and outer solitude with tragic consequences.

By the second half of the nineteenth century, the Enlightenment human-ist, liberal, technological, positivist, and socialist visions of progress as well as the radical Romantic utopian alternatives to them had failed to fill the grow-ing nomic pit being excavated by the accelerating impact of modernity on the Europeanized world. It is at that point that some of its most gifted artists per-formed the 'prophylactic' mission implicit in the term 'avant-garde', namely to register the spiritual (i.e. *nomic*) crisis threatening society from within, and find ways to draw attention to, or even transcend and repel, the mounting tide of 'deca-dence'. A vast number of artists working in every medium deliberately abandoned traditional aesthetics. Instead they experimented with new forms, techniques, and themes to articulate a reality that had slipped into the inchoate and incompre-hensible and, where possible, express fleeting glimpses or sustained visions of a primordial but now transfigured transcendent reality, neither expressible in tra-ditional iconography nor with conventional techniques. Aesthetic modernism was born.

Modernism's recurrent expressions of concern with decadence, the loss of roots, of 'soul', of beauty, of higher meaning, can all be seen as registering the rising tide of the liminoid under the impact of modernity. Meanwhile the myriad expres-sions of the search for re-enchantment and re-embedding, for renewed access to the sacral and the numinous, the longing for transcendent ('kairotic') time, for moral redemption, for secular salvation through art, for rebirth and spiritual palingenesis are the modern manifestation of the eternal, primordial human response to anomy. Just as nature abhors a vacuum, so human nature abhors a nomic void. What artists of 'high modernism' as disparate as Dostoevsky, Tolstoy, Ibsen, Strindberg, Munch, Kafka, Klimt, Wilde, Wagner, Musil, D'Annunzio, Joyce, Woolf, Marinetti, and Svevo have in common is that they all register, in different modes and moods, the loss of traditional, stable sources of transcendental, cosmic meaning. They assert, even if only through the power of art to transcend absurdity, a new nomos which, sometimes, as in the case of Italian Futurism, Russian Constructivism and Ernst Jünger's utopian vision of a new type of Worker, was paradoxically based on the celebration of an aspect of technical modernity itself, a prime source of disenchantment. Each modernist artist or intellectual can be seen as engaged in creating his or her own 'mazeway resynthesis' to break through to an art form and aesthetic that enables anomy to be overcome and the world (at least the artist's own inner world) to be 'renomized' and re-'cosmized'. However, modernist attempts at the revitalization of an increasingly anomic European society since the mid-nineteenth century have not been confined to art. They have also taken place in the spheres of social and political transformation, of militant action, of revolutionary bids to change the status quo.

Terrorism as a form of programmatic modernism

While cultural historians have generally equated modernism with artistic innovation and formal experimentation, there are good grounds for the compass of this term to be extended far beyond the sphere of aesthetics. It is a small step from understanding the metaphysical dynamic of modernist aesthetics to recognizing a fundamentally modernist component in the preoccupation of such major philosophers as Friedrich Nietzsche,[24] Martin Heidegger, Giovanni Gentile, Albert Camus, and Jean-Paul Sartre with the crisis of humanity, with decadence and renewal, with the death and regeneration of ultimate values and meaning, with 'renomizing' the world. From this vantage point it then becomes self-evident to see the hallmarks of modernism in the drive towards the 'secular cosmization' referred to by Peter Berger which expressed itself in the explosion of visionary projects for radical transformation through a process of scientific, social, political, or ethical renewal which characterized the culture of late nineteenth and early twentieth century.

Theosophy, anthroposophy, the architectural schemes of the Bauhaus and Le Corbusier, the rise of ritualistic displays of ultra-nationalism, youth movements, the body reform movement, the cult of sport and health, the social hygiene movement and eugenics, Freudianism, Jungianism, totalitarian fascist and communist schemes for a new society and a 'New Man', and all their kin, arose against the background of the revolt of *fin-de-siècle* artists and thinkers against decadence. Originally little more than a pessimistic 'mood' during the *fin-de-siècle*, the West's decline was objectified and made manifest for millions by the slaughtering fields and secular hecatombs of the Great War and the ensuing breakdown in the socio-political structures of many European societies, unleashing a wave of liminoidality and anomy that triggered widespread longings for regeneration and salvation from the chaos. All these initiatives display a basic affinity in their rejection of 'actually existing modernity' for a new, deeply palingenetic, vision of a regenerated society. All can be seen as forms of modernism, rebellions against anomy undertaken outside the sphere of culture in the narrow, 'artistic' sense.

A seminal essay to endorse this deliberate expansion of modernism's remit to embrace some of the most violent attempts to change the world is Peter Fritzsche's 'Nazi Modern', which argues that:

> The most spectacular displays of modernism are not to be found in a museum of expressionist art or a collection of prose poetry, but in the avant-garde political collaborations that sought to come to terms with a brand-new world regarded as unstable and dangerous. With every step, the political adventurer as much as the modernist poet or painter revealed ground that was tremulous, breaking apart, unclear. Liberal certainties that proposed to reveal the coherence of the world appeared completely inadequate. But whereas the latter made manifest the disenchantment that had been revealed, the former proposed more fearsome designs to overcome it.[25]

A sophisticated theoretical underpinning to Fritzsche's groundbreaking assertion is Peter Osborne's investigation into the politics born of the peculiar quality of the experience of time and corresponding vision of history under the impact of modernity. He pays particular attention to discussing the rival 'temporalities' that have arisen promising meaning and closure so as to overcome the sense of permanent flux and transition, or what we have termed 'the liminoid'. What emerges from his analysis is that all modern species of radical politics can be interpreted as offering solutions to the dilemma of anomic temporality, the revolutionaries of Marxism and fascism equally committed to forcing historical closure, inaugurating a new beginning, and resacralizing or recosmizing time itself. As such they seek, just as much as artists, though using the medium of politics, to realize a *modernist* project which 'affirms the temporality of the new'.[26]

A vindication of the fruitfulness of Fritzsche's and Osborne's approach was the magnificent exhibition *Modernism1914–1939. Designing a New World* staged at the Victoria and Albert Museum in London in 2006. Together the artifacts, taken from a breathtaking range of countries and areas of cultural production in the widest sense, and the essays in the catalogue provided an articulate endorsement of the contention that aesthetic modernism, far from being modernism *tout court*, was just one facet of a tidal wave of optimism starting in the mid-nineteenth century and peaking in the inter-war period that modernity itself, despite its catastrophic consequences, was on the cusp of a metamorphosis to a healthier, more beautiful, more communal, more spiritually grounded era which would supersede the age of anomy, disease, urban anarchy, national conflict and war.

The organizer of the exhibition, Christopher Wilk, states in his introductory essay for the catalogue that modernism was 'a loose collection of ideas' covering a range of movements and styles in many countries, especially within the avant-garde of key cities in Germany and Holland, as well as in Paris, Prague, and later New York. He goes on:

> All these sites were stages for an espousal of the new and, often an equally vocif-erous rejection of history and tradition; a utopian desire to create a better world, to reinvent the world from scratch; an almost messianic belief in the power and potential of the machine and industrial technology. . . . All these principles were frequently combined with social and political beliefs (largely left-leaning) which held that art and design could, and should, transform society.[27]

Such reflections lead to an important ideal-typical distinction to be made within the now vastly extended kinship system of modernisms. Whereas a modernist artist such as Baudelaire is driven by the quest to express the anomic state of modernity and wrest moments of sublime beauty from it in his cycle of poems, *Le Fleurs du Mal*, thus symbolically transcending decadence (the liminoid) in his art, a social theorist such as Georges Sorel expressed in his *Réflexions sur la violence* the belief in the need for myth-inspired campaigns of violence against 'bourgeois' society in order to regenerate society through political change. These contrasting modes of modernism I have termed 'epiphanic' and 'programmatic',[28] since many modernist artists are concerned with capturing ephemeral experiences of a higher, numinous realm of reality (what Virginia Woolf called 'moments of Being' and James Joyce termed 'epiphanies'). Meanwhile the belief of social, technocratic, and political revolutionaries, and also some modernist artists,[29] in the possibility of establishing a new order on the basis of a new nomos lends itself to mani-festos and programmatic statements announcing utopian schemes to overcome the prevailing anomy.[30] Within this perspective it becomes possible to recognize that some kinds of terrorism, rather than defend an existing nomos from destruc-tion as we saw in the last chapter, are violent expressions of the drive to, in the words of Peter Berger, 'carve out a small clearing of lucidity in a vast mass of mean-inglessness' and so renomize society. They thus represent a form of *programmatic modernism*. On closer examination modernist, nomos-*creating* forms of terrorism exhibit entirely different metapolitical dynamics from the nomos-*defending* ones considered in the last chapter.

The modernist dynamic in Russian nihilism

A case study in the species of terrorism that pursues the modernist utopia of renomizing a degenerate society through violent strikes against the established order is provided by the militants of the counter-cultural, anti-Tsarist movement known as 'Russian nihilism'. Its activists first burst into notoriety in the late 1870s when they carried out the assassination of the Governor of Kharkov and then used the recently invented 'dynamite' to blow up part of the Winter Palace. Mem-bers of nihilism's most notorious terrorist cell, Narodnaya Volya (People's Will), succeeded in killing Tsar Alexander II in a gruesomely executed bomb attack in

March 1881 as he travelled by open carriage through the streets of St Petersburg, the third attempt on his life.

Nihilist activists were strongly influenced by Sergey Nechayev, a student agitator in St Petersburg who had himself plotted to assassinate the Tsar, and is still famous in international anarchist circles for his *Catechism of a Revolutionary* published in 1869, a creed of total and ruthless dedication to political struggle which was reissued by Black Panther Party on the centenary of its publication and influenced the formation of the terrorist Red Brigades in Italy the same year. The catechism set forth 26 principles which would enable revolutionaries to 'weld the people into one single unconquerable and all-destructive force' in order to carry out the 'terrible, total, universal, and merciless destruction' of the state. It also gave a penetrating insight into the fanatical mindset needed to carry out such destruction. In the second paragraph we read:

> The revolutionary is a doomed man. He has no private interests, no affairs, sentiments, ties, property nor even a name of his own. His entire being is devoured by one purpose, one thought, one passion – the revolution. Heart and soul, not merely by word but by deed, he has severed every link with the social order and with the entire civilized world; with the laws, good manners, conventions, and morality of that world. He is its merciless enemy and continues to inhabit it with only one purpose – to destroy it.[31]

This ascetic renunciation of the world highlights an important aspect of the terrorist creed: the attempt to resolve a nomic malaise by intensifying it to crisis point and cultivating complete social isolation, whether alone or in a small cell of militants. However, rather than remaining trapped within what Berger calls the 'unbearableness' of this exclusion from society's normality, this voluntary withdrawal into a world of total anomy becomes the precondition for the fanatic to find within the self-imposed darkness the light of a portal which provides access to a higher state of morality and purpose. It is a light invisible in 'normal' states of consciousness, and only granted to the fanatic who has renounced the world as it is. The paradox of 'losing the world to find it' is deeply familiar to students of any ascetic or mystic disciplines which demand that initiates 'empty themselves' or 'renounce the world' to be filled by the Spirit, the power of a transcendent nomos. The difference is that in this case the cause is an entirely secular one of political revolution, and withdrawal is not the liminal stage of a triadic rite passed down by a religious tradition to be resolved when the initiate rejoins the community. Instead, it has been transformed into an extreme technique through which a liminoid crisis of extreme alienation from society (experienced as putrefaction, corruption, 'filth') is resolved through the catharsis of violent symbolic action against it. Hence Nechayev declares:

> The revolutionist despises all doctrines and refuses to accept the mundane sciences, leaving them for future generations. He knows only one science: the science of destruction. For this reason, but only for this reason, he will study

mechanics, physics, chemistry, and perhaps medicine. But all day and all night he studies the vital science of human beings, their characteristics and circumstances, at every possible level of social existence. The object is perpetually the same: the surest and quickest way of destroying the whole filthy order.[32]

The modernist dynamic behind this impulse to destroy the 'whole filthy order' is thrown into relief if we take into account the formative influence on him exerted by Mikhail Bakunin. Bakunin was part of a generation of the European intelligentsia who lived through the intellectual aftershocks of the seismic events of the French Revolution and its ensuing political and social chaos. While the old feudal order of Europe seemed doomed to extinction in the long term, the European Restoration of the *ancien régime* dashed hopes of absolutism's imminent collapse, while the French experiments with constitutional monarchy, the totalitarian democracy of the Jacobins, charismatic republicanism, and liberal (or 'bourgeois') monarchy had all failed to deliver either stability or social justice. In the acute liminoidality which resulted, cosmopolitan cities in Europe became hot-houses of deeply utopian schemes for a new society, as the contrasting ideas of such highly idiosyncratic thinkers as Kant, Hegel, Babeuf, Blanqui, Saint-Simon, De Bonald, Ballanche, Fourier, Cabet, Proudhon, Bentham, Owen, Marx and Comte circulated. All can be seen as early forms of programmatic modernism in which the modernizing, nomocidal effects of the 'dual revolution' (French and Industrial) on traditional nomoi in politics provoked totalizing futural solutions through the establishment of a new nomos, whether it was based on the reign of the executioner (de Maistre), the principle of the happiness of the greatest number (Bentham), the transcending of capitalism (Marx), or the abolition of the state (Proudhon).

In Russia, the slow economic progress under the Tsar and the Western education of largely unemployed upper-class males created a particular intellectual and artistic climate. Various permutations of Hegelian and Romantic liberalism, populism (the Narodnik movement), the Slavophile movement, utopian socialism, and communism circulated within St Petersburg, Moscow, and among Russian exiles fleeing a regime increasingly prepared to deploy a secret police (even abroad) to suppress 'sedition'. The lives of Alexander Herzen, Peter Kropotkin, Ivan Turgenev, Leo Tolstoy, Fyodor Dostoevsky, and Anton Chekhov provide windows into this period of intense intellectual and ideological ferment which formed the essential background to Lenin's 'voluntarist' adaptation of Marxism to the 'backward', feudal circumstances of Russia that was to have such a profound effect on the course of history.[33]

From 1830 till 1849 Mikhail Bakunin led a peripatetic existence in Europe absorbing the most radical political influences of the period. Eventually he was in a position to forge his own 'mazeway resynthesis', a syncretic revolutionary vision of the ideal society that could be created once not just the Russians, but all the oppressed peoples of Europe were released from the thrall of state oppression. He advocated a collectivist form of anarchism based on a radical communalization of labour and wealth and the sharing of mutual responsibility for the welfare of the whole of society, a project deeply influenced by Proudhon. The stateless *communitas* of the future would secure happiness for all in communal harmony. The corollary of this project was to wage a clandestine war on feudalism, capitalism and the Tsarist state. True to his convictions, he led the popular revolt in Dresden in 1849, an important episode in what are now known as the '1848 Revolutions'. Arrested, imprisoned, and handed over to the Russian authorities, he was exiled to Siberia. Having ingeniously escaped (via Japan!), he immersed himself in the Italian unification wars and Europe's thriving underground of sedition and revolution, which in Geneva brought him into contact with Nechayev, who wrote his *Catechism of a Revolutionary* of 1869 directly under Bakunin's ideological and personal influence. In the same year Bakunin wrote his own *Catechism of a Revolutionary* which preached the absolute rejection of all state authority in less ascetic, more collectivist terms. Comparing these texts with the manifestos and creeds of modern artists collected by Alex Danchev[34] leaves no doubt about their credentials as texts of programmatic modernism, announcing imminent social and metaphysical palingenesis. This insight has led Peter Osborne to analyse Marx's *Communist Manifesto* of 1848 as a major text of European modernism.[35]

The active nihilism of God's orphans

By the time Nechayev met Bakunin their call for the utter destruction of the state by force was identified with 'nihilism'. In Russia, the home of revolutionary expressions of nihilism, its activists, drawn mostly from the ranks of a privileged but disaffected younger generation, saw themselves engaged in a total but clandestine (and hence terrorist) war against Tsarist Russia, as well as an intense ideological struggle with advocates of 'reactionary' Slavophile, Conservative, or Orthodox solutions to Russia's problems. The term had gained currency and notoriety when it was used in Ivan Turgenev's *Fathers and Sons* (1862) to describe the negative attitude to life of the fictional character Eugene Barazov who rejected as naively optimistic the Enlightenment faith in progress of an earlier generation of liberals.[36] The label was worn as a badge of pride by the literary and social critic Dmitry Pisarev who ensured its further circulation by associating it with a sardonically expressed revulsion for everything that Tsarist Russia and its optimistic 'modernizers' stood for.

As Alfred Evans points out in his article on the subject, 'the term "nihilism" was a misnomer from the start. Though the nihilists were often described as people who no longer believed in anything, *in actuality they believed in their own ideas with passionate and indeed fanatical intensity*'. 'Sentimental idealism' had to be replaced by 'scientific rigor and realism' embodied in 'an exceptional minority' as the only means 'of leading the way to a new society'.[37] Once we explore the paradox of nihilism not as an annihilating, but as a regenerative, *palingenetic* force we arrive at the heart of programmatic modernism and the way it can manifest itself in terrorist violence. It is a paradox we encountered in the last chapter which introduced the metaphor of the black hole for the way the terrifying intimation of total absurdity and personal finitude can act paradoxically as the driving force behind the human mythopoeic urge to create a sacred canopy. Every modern exercise in forging a new nomos to live by, either at an intensely private level of mystic contemplation or as part of a mobilized mass seeking revolutionary change, thus partakes of the primordial culture-forming energy that once built the Pyramids and Angkor Wat, though usually with a creative charge in the ratio of a spark to a blazing furnace.

One work which explores the ideological mechanisms at work when an act of apparently wanton destruction is conceived by its perpetrator as the prelude to regeneration is Shane Weller's *Modernism and Nihilism*. In it he attaches particular significance to the crucial distinction which Nietzsche draws between 'passive' and 'active' nihilism.[38] Whereas passive nihilism simply leads to withdrawal from the world in a state of despair, to stoically enduring the mental anguish induced by the absence of a higher moral order, the active nihilist rebels against meaninglessness. More precisely, he or she 'overcomes' the certitude of eternal nothingness in a deliberate act of life affirmation which defiantly creates its *own* moral system ('beyond good and evil'), one which corresponds to no *objective* metaphysical or sacred order in the cosmos. What results is a resolute mood of 'creative destruction', a defiantly arbitrary 'will' to create subjective meaning through myth in the total absence of any objective meaning. The intensification of this mood can lead to a deeply utopian mindset in which acts of violent destruction undertaken against the status quo can assume a higher moral significance to the perpetrators as gestures towards achieving the *tabula rasa* necessary to bring about the radical reordering of reality, thereby creating the preconditions for what Berger terms the renomizing and recosmizing of the world in an eventual process of rebirth, of total *palingenesis*. It is a concept that Weller sees exemplified not only in Dada's 'anti-art',[39] but in the 'political modernism' of the French Revolution, the first revolution based on the notion that History could begin anew after a period of radical destruction. It was a logic externalized not only in the invention of a new calendar and new rituals,[40] but in the mass executions and spontaneous pogroms of the Terror which cost as many as 40,000 lives and was accompanied by countless apparently gratuitous, but ritually cathartic, atrocities alongside the 'rational' functioning of Madame Guillotine.[41]

This perspective on nihilism as a *regenerative* principle central to the creativity displayed in modernist art, modern social philosophy, and totalitarian politics is the subject of a remarkable trilogy in the history of ideas by the Israeli scholar, David Ohana, *The Nihilist Order*. Deeply convergent with Weller's analysis, the first volume, *The Dawn of Political Nihilism*, explores in forensic detail the 'nihilist-totalitarian syndrome', the rise of the anomic nihilism of 'inertia' under the impact of modernity and the 'dynamic nihilism' pioneered by Nietzsche. Dynamic or positive nihilism, a modern permutation of the archetypal human myth of palingenesis symbolized in the phoenix, reacts against the collapse of meaning under the impact of modernity by interpreting it as the harbinger of new meaning, a new nomos. Instead of fleeing the abyss of absurdity, Nietzsche tells his readers to be *more* modern, to live dangerously, to build their cities on the slopes of Vesuvius.[42] In defiance of the disenchantment of the world, positive nihilism, according to Ohana, asserts the primacy of an entirely human-made 'aesthetic absolute' expressed in the 'totalitarian mentality', the paradoxical 'wish to destroy, coupled with a strong desire to create imposing structures'. What resulted in the early twentieth century was an 'explosive combination of nihilist leanings' with 'a craving for totalitarianism' which 'became the ideal of philosophers, cultural critics, political theorists, engineers, architects and aesthetes long before it materialized in flesh and blood, not only in technology, but also in Fascism, Nazism, Bolshevism and radical European political movements'.[43] And, we could add, in certain forms of terrorism.

Alain Badiou is another major thinker who lends his weight to the thesis that the extreme violence of modern history is partly explicable as the result of the rebellion of 'active nihilists' against the collapse of the sacred canopy in the West. Like Weller, he identifies a 'Nietzschean' dimension to the twentieth century, the will to overcome the growing crisis of (passive) nihilism by precipitating a caesura in history, 'a radical commencement that would bear within it the foundation of a reconciled humanity'.[44] Badiou argues that the previous century was characterized by the 'disjunction' between (mass) resignation to anomy (identified by Nietzsche with the 'last men') and the bid of small, self-appointed elites to induce social rebirth through regenerative acts of destruction, 'legitimated by the creation of the new man'. This aspiration 'only makes sense within the horizon of the death of God. A Godless humanity must be recreated, so as to replace the humanity that was subject to the gods'.[45] In this sense, the violence of Nazis, Bolsheviks and Maoists can be seen as heirs of Nietzsche's 'Dionysian modernism'.[46]

Thus, from Badiou's perspective, the genocidal violence that characterized many episodes of politics in the twentieth century was not 'nihilistic' in the sense of wanton destruction for destruction's sake, or the manifestation of sheer sadism and hatred (or in premodern terms of 'evil'). It was the product of 'active', cathartic nihilism. As such he presents it as *cosmogonic*, literally creating *ex nihilo* a new nomic universe, a new order in the absence of any objective, pre-existing nomos. Using this conceptual framework, the attempts of modernist terrorists to renomize the world, in contrast to the struggle of Zealotic terrorists to defend and restore a religion or homeland under physical and cultural attack, are not just revolutionary in the socio-political sense. On a metapolitical level they are 'cosmogonic'.

It is consistent with this analysis that an examination of the affective core of the anarchist assault on the state, whether absolutist or liberal, discloses the myth of creative destruction. Thus Bakunin declared in 1842 (before his atheism had ripened): 'Let us therefore trust the eternal Spirit which destroys and annihilates only because it is the unfathomable and eternal source of all life. The *passion for destruction is a creative passion*, too!'[47] It is a sentiment echoed by the Godfather of anarchism, Pierre-Joseph Proudhon, who chose as the epigraph of volume one of *The Philosophy of Misery* (1847) *Destruam et ædificabo*, 'I shall destroy and build', citing not Bakunin but the Book of Deuteronomy in the Old Testament. It was a direct allusion to Bakunin's dictum, however, when the peripatetic German anarchist, Johann Most, an ardent evangelist of the use of dynamite in attacks against the state (which earned him the nickname 'Dynamost') declared in his highly

influential anarchist journal *Freiheit* (1879–1910), 'Let us rely upon the unquench-
able spirit of destruction and annihilation which is the perpetual spring of new
life. The joy of destruction is a creative joy!'[48] It is the utopian vision that assumes
destruction, even of civilian populations, will magically bring about palingenesis that informs one of his most famous declarations: 'The existing system will
be quickest and most radically overthrown by the annihilation of its exponents.
Therefore, massacres of the enemies of the people must be set in motion.'[49]

Luciano Pellicani's analysis of Russian nihilism adds another important component to our understanding of the metapolitics of the type of terrorism that
is born of the desperate impulse to counteract the denomizing of the impact of
modernity through acts of destruction conceived as inaugurating a new social
order. He portrays the rise in the second half of the nineteenth century of a new
class, an educated (and largely unemployable) elite who felt too Russian to identify totally with the European intelligentsia, while being utterly alienated from
the Orthodoxy of Tsarist Russia or the feudal traditions of its rural society. They
formed not just a privileged caste of social outcasts. They were also prime victims
of the general erosion of the sacred canopy in the West which meant that 'the
disillusioned individual was now alone, abandoned and powerless, and forced to
wander in a universe deprived of an immanent *telos* [or intrinsic metaphysical
purpose and nomos] and seemingly senseless and amoral', making reality 'absurd
and intolerable'.[50] In 1885 Nietzsche wrote of 'the most disconcerting' or 'freaky'
('der unheimlichste') of all guests standing at society's door: nihilism.[51] Pellicani
claims that its unwelcome tour throughout the Europeanized world produced a
new type of human being described by Max Horkheimer as, 'the orphan of God',
who, though exiled from the existential security of traditional Christian culture,
was still obsessed by the 'nostalgia for the absolute Other', for a 'higher reality'. Pellicani argues that when Marx rejected Hegel's attempt to identify a *telos*
within the historical process and set about using dialectics as the basis of a revolutionary programme for changing history, it marked the metamorphosis in the
nature of human knowledge from contemplative understanding to 'an absolute
transforming faculty':

> With Marx's dialectic, gnosis [liberating, revelatory knowledge] changes from
> contemplative to activist and for this reason becomes a belligerent and rev-
> olutionary call, directed to all 'God's orphans', allowing them to become
> Promethean builders of the millennarian Kingdom of Liberty.[52]

The proliferation of utopian schemes of social renewal that we referred to earlier,
some of the most famous of which actually predated *The Communist Manifesto* of
1848, are thus to be seen as early examples of what Berger calls 'thoroughly secular
attempts at cosmization'. They were produced by the first generation of European
'orphans of God' desperately seeking to resolve the nomic crisis of modernity they
had been born into through revolutionary programmes of 'creative destruction'.
Marx's promise that communism would put an end to 'alienation' (Entfremdung),
though on one level a socio-economic project, at the same has an important

subliminal *existential* dimension, promising converts to Marxism an end to anomy. The utopias of a new society promulgated by the likes of Proudhon, Fourier, Marx, Bakunin, and Nechayev, from which alienation had been banished and in which the human species had finally created a total physical, social and *metapolitical* home, could not fail to exert an irresistible appeal to those caught in the vice-like grip of acute anomy. In Pellicani's words, God's orphans were predisposed to have 'the prophetical-messianic calling of permanent revolution' to solve their personal nomic crisis. As a result, a socio-political vision based on the active nihilism of creative destruction, the spectacular annihilation of the system followed by its total reordering, represented to this new breed of activist ideologue:

> an exciting prospect for all the intellectuals who were experiencing God's death as a tragedy: it gave them a redeeming mission; it bestowed a meaning upon existence and provided an escape from the desert of nihilism.[53]

Pellicani's diagnosis is confirmed by Aileen Kelly in her introduction to Isaiah Berlin's seminal essays on the Russia's intelligentsia under the Tsar. She portrays it as gripped by 'a yearning for a lost wholeness', and 'eager in an age of fears and neuroses to trade the doubts and agonies of moral responsibility for determinist visions, conservative or radical'.[54]

Fin-de-siècle anarchism and 'modernism of the deed'

Once this line of analysis is accepted, it follows that *socio-political* modernism, with its characteristic redemptive or 'soteriological' formulas for saving contemporary society from injustice, decadence, anarchy, or the loss of the spirit, can be seen to have *preceded* by some 20 years the radical artistic experimentation and innovation associated with the pioneering phase of *aesthetic* modernism which emerged in the 1850s (epitomized in the work of Baudelaire), and which is still widely identified with modernism as such. Anarchism is to be located within the explosion of utopian schemes to inaugurate a new modernity and a new temporality provoked by the impact of the dual revolution on the European nomoi of Christianity and rational progress. It sits alongside not just the spread of international socialism and communism, but the rise of ultra-nationalism with its sacralization of 'the people',[55] and the appearance of eugenic schemes for scientifically imposing racial health.[56] All can be seen as expressions of the countervailing forces of re-enchantment and resacralization at work to avert the looming nomic catastrophe of a secularized, desacralized human society.

Such an analysis highlights the *metapolitical* substratum of anarchist terrorism. Once the new Gnosis, redemptive knowledge of the nomos, became identified for God's orphans with uncompromising revolutionary violence rather than analysis, the way was opened for new type of *activist* modernism. The sentiment is summed up in Bakunin's *Letters to a Frenchman on the Present Crisis* (1870) when he stated that 'we must spread our principles, not with words but with deeds, for this is the most popular, the most potent, and the most irresistible form of propaganda'. The phrase 'propaganda by the deed' was then popularized by the French anarchist Paul Brousse who argued that the 1871 Paris Commune and the uprising in Benevento demonstrated the principle in action. The most persistent advocate of the principle was the dynamitist Johann Most, who claimed violence against reactionaries was to be publicized since anarchists 'preach not only action in and for itself, but also action as propaganda'. It was a principle which legimitized a number of attacks carried out on important personalities for the symbolic rather than strategic value of their death. (One which dominated the headlines of US newspapers in 1892 was the attempted assassination of industrialist Henry Clay Frick by Alexander Berkman. He was inspired and aided in the attack by his lover, the anarchist activist Emma Goldman. They were bent on avenging the lives of several workers killed by Frick's henchmen during a lockout and precipitating an armed uprising by a symbolic attack on the capitalist system.) This line of thought leads to the conclusion that there is a category of terrorism that could be called 'modernism of the deed', when individuals commit an act of violence as a symbolic gesture *against* the 'filth' of the present 'system' and *for* a new society and a new nomos.

This approach is at loggerheads with the central thesis of David Weir's *Anarchy and Culture*. In it Weir argues that it was 'the failure of anarchism' as a revolutionary movement which 'assured the success of [aesthetic] modernism', because 'the politics of anarchism was transformed into the culture of [aesthetic] modernism by a number of artists who gave aesthetic expression to [its] political principles'.[57] Rather it suggests that political anarchism and avant-garde aesthetic modernism are to be pictured as trees of different species, anarchism the older, aestheticism eventually the more prolific and resistant, growing out of the same soil, their canopies interlacing and interleaving. Given anarchism's stress on releasing human creativity and emancipating humanity from the shackles of deadening traditions and state oppression, it is only natural that an 'elective affinity' was felt with them by some innovative *fin-de-siècle* artists, in the same way that many highly creative minds would later feel drawn to the liberating theories of Nietzsche and Freud, or to the revolutionary politics of Bolshevism,[58] Fascism,[59] and even Nazism.[60]

When it comes to examples of affinities felt by artistic modernism and anarchist terrorism, the complexity of the topic demands that we tread carefully. Anarchism is an extremely broad, ill-defined, and multifaceted phenomenon which spawned a vast amount of theory and campaigning but relatively little practice, or, as the Italians say, lots of smoke but not much roast. From early on there was a polarization between the arch-individualism promoted by readings of Max Stirner, Friedrich Nietzsche, and Sergei Nechayev and the communitarian politics of solidarity advocated by Mikhail Bakunin and Peter Kropotkin. Furthermore, the activism it did spawn changed, particularly after the First World War, from individual acts of spectacular violence carried out by loners or small cells to attempts to use collective proletarian power to disrupt the workings of capitalism through large-scale communal actions, such as a general strike, carried out within the ideological framework of anarcho-syndicalism. It was a change of tactic encouraged by the spread of Sorelian theories of the essential role played by myth and violence in mobilizing the masses as the precondition of successful revolutions. Such ambiguities mean that when scholars document the profound appeal exerted by anarchism as an exhilaratingly liberating world-view on Picasso,[61] Futurists,[62] the late nineteenth-century Parisian avant-garde,[63] or surrealism,[64] this is no indication of artistic modernism's association with or approval of *terrorism* as such. In fact the precise sub-genus of anarchism that attracted them and the particular socio-political context of its attraction have to be identified carefully before the relationship can be understood.

However, there are some fascinating cases of individuals living in artistic milieux finding enough affinity with the clandestine subculture that gave rise to 'propaganda of the deed' for anarchism to become *chic*. One notable case was the explicit approval which Helena and Olivia Rossetti, daughters of the Pre-Raphaelite painter William Rossetti, gave in their political journal *The Torch* to Émile Henry's infamous bombing of the Café Terminus in 1894.[65] Another was the association of the Spanish anarchist Francesco Ferrer, founder of the 'Modern School' in Barcelona, with terrorists that led to his execution in 1909.[66] After his death the 'Modern School' movement he inspired in the United States fostered links between avant-garde artists and anarchists, though not all of them violent. One product of this subversive art scene was Carl Zigrosser, who went on to become a major figure in the history of American modernist painting, but in his early days provided rhetorical endorsement of anarchist violence.[67] Before the First World War several incidents of 'propaganda of the deed' against the Parisian police, who were widely despised in artistic circles as embodiments of an oppressive system, were the responsibility of shadowy anarchists known by the Romanticized name 'les apaches'. The Vorticist Henri Gaudier-Brzeska identified with their strikes against 'the system' to the point where it influenced both his own art and led to a famous portrait of him as an 'apache' by Alfred Wolmark.[68]

However, occasional direct links between aesthetic and political modernism are less important than the realization that, as well as the Zealotic type of terrorism that defends an existing nomos, there is also a Modernist variant which seeks to create a new one. Whereas the redemptive Gnosis of the Zealot has been handed down (according to myth) by a sacred tradition, the Gnosis of the Modernist, expressed in a secular revolutionary creed, is constitutive of a new secular reality which is about to be established in the new era destined to follow the 'eschatos', the destruction of the old order by human agency.

Once again Pellicani is useful here. He sees the 'secular millennarianism' of the Nihilists and of the early Bolsheviks as 'a modern version of apocalyptic Gnosticism'. By 'Gnosticism' he is not referring to the cluster of pre-Christian mystic traditions that, according to Eric Voegelin, survived in travestied form in modern 'political religions' such as liberalism and Nazism.[69] He uses the term to evoke a particular 'existential predisposition' dominated by a 'veritable *horror of the existing*' that fills [the revolutionary] with concern, nausea and anguish.... The world he sees is *radically* evil'. He is 'dominated by a desperate *nostalgia* for a *totally different* world, which he has never seen, but from which he feels unjustly exiled.'

Life therefore becomes for the modern Gnostic, religious or secular, 'a state of *permanent* waiting for radical renewal, which is both *resurrection* and *restoration*'. As a result history is experienced as 'a *soteriological drama of fall and redemption*'. After the final battle 'the whole cosmos will be overturned and reordered, and Great Universal Harmony will reign forever'.[70]

Following this analysis, revolutionary violence and anarchist terrorism can be seen, in Berger's terminology, as an act of recosmizing and renomizing the world, and in my terminology a Modernist act. Modern revolutionary ideologies are thus simultaneously political and *metapolitical*, products of the same powerful mythopoeic energies which enabled the earliest human beings to carve 'an area of meaning' out of 'a vast mass of meaninglessness', and make 'a small clearing of lucidity in a formless, dark, always ominous jungle'. There is thus a deep-seated historical continuity between the communal creation of the first cultures and first religions as metaphysical 'shields against terror', and the secular ideologies that have taken their place. There is also a deep-seated affinity between renomizing terrorism and all other modernist projects whose effect is to erect a new suprapersonal, transcendent and hence sacred canopy to provide a refuge from the subjective collapse of the cosmos into primordial meaninglessness.

Modernist terrorists are thus the Zealots of a *futural* nomos. For them the umbilical cord with any meaningful period of history has been irrevocably cut, and there can be no 'Herodian' accommodation with a modernity which drains life of meaning and hope. They do not defend their nomos against the invasion of an alien force such as Hellenization, Sunniization, Russification or Sinhalization, but against the nomocidal impact of *modernization* itself. In the last four chapters of this book we will encounter a number of ways the Zealotic and Modernist species of terrorism can in practice form complex hybrids accompanied by correspondingly complex metapolitical creeds. But before that the psychodynamic process involved in an individual's conversion to a radical version of a traditional nomos or a Gnostic vision of a new one demands closer scrutiny. For this we shall turn not to the abstract models of social scientists or external reconstructions of historians, but to the forensic fictions of novelists and film-makers.

4
The Metapolitics of Terrorism in Fiction

Fyodor Dostoevsky: The terrorist as 'devil'

Our inquiry into the historical roots of extreme violence has revealed two contrasting species of terrorism: Zealotic and Modernist. Outside the artificially tidy world of idealizing abstraction, in the so-called 'real world', fuzzy boundaries and porous membranes naturally exist between these two types. The last three chapters will use specific case studies to illustrate the hybridization that tends to arise as complex 'mazeway resyntheses' come into being which identify new causes to kill and die for so as to save, regenerate, or create the nomos. Each offers to the convert a way of overcoming one of the unique configurations of anomic, 'soul-destroying' forces constantly arising in the modern world as political situations emerge which threaten established cultures with rapid physical or cultural extinction, or traditional nomoi are degraded and eroded by globalizing 'disenchantment' and its concomitant processes of rapid or gradual culturecide. To prepare the ground further for the unusual 'reading' of terrorism offered in this book we will turn for deeper insights into the underlying metapolitical dimension and 'creed' of fanatical violence to those non-academic explorers of human spirituality and motiovation: novelists and film-makers.

Just as 'one good picture is worth a thousand words' in journalism, so in the Human Sciences one good novel, poem or film can be worth a whole shelf of impenetrable theory (and this is, of course, a piece of 'self-criticism'). There is nothing original about this insight. Towards the end of John Gray's *Black Mass*, a savage indictment of the persistence of archaic utopian and religious myths under the guise of ultra-modern rational politics and economics, he refers to the lasting value that Dostoevsky's *The Devils* has retained 'as an account of the psychology of the revolutionary mind'.[1] He also draws attention to the irony that the journalist David Brooks, whom Gray claims to be victim of his own Bushian and Neo-conservative – and hence apocalyptic – delusions about the unfolding of history, declared in a column of the *New York Times* in 2004 that for real intelligence about the threat of terrorism he would not trust the assessments of 'game theorists or risk assessment officers'. Instead he would place his trust in 'Mafia bosses, studio heads and anybody who has read a Dostoyevsky novel during the past five years'.[2] Intellectuals and journalists who invoke his fiction as a source of illumination about terrorism are implicitly recognizing that it has a *metapolitical* dimension that the Human Sciences are ill-equipped to address.

If we start with Dostoevsky, it is not just because several contemporary journalists and intellectuals apart from Brooks and Gray have detected a resonance between his explorations of the metaphysics of violence and the events of 9/11. It is because of the unparalleled psychological depth and realism he brings to portraying the complex mindsets necessary to commit acts of homocidal violence for ideological reasons, or for what can to an outsider seem utterly gratuitous motives. It is well-trodden ground in Dostoevsky studies to show how his novel *The Devils* (also translated as *The Possessed*) published in 1872 reconstructs the cultural and philosophical milieu that had led to a *cause célèbre* in Moscow three years earlier, the murder of the left-wing radical Ivan Ivanovich at the hands of the leader of his own anarchist cell, The People's Reprisal. The crime that led to Ivan's body being unceremoniously weighted with stones and dumped through a hole in the ice was seemingly to have questioned the tactics of his leader, none other than Sergey Nechayev, whom we met in the last chapter as the Godfather of political 'nihilism'. The murder was to precipitate his flight to Locarno in 1870 where he renewed his close friendship with Bakunin.

Nechayev's ruthless act has sometimes been explained, indeed by Dostoevsky himself, as cynically calculated to create a psychological 'blood-bond' between the cell members. Whatever the ulterior motive, the murder was consistent with the philosophy of the 'end justifies the means' that we saw in the pages of his *Catechism of a Revolutionary*: the priority of fulfilling the revolutionary mission took precedence over all other humanistic or moral considerations. The French moralist Albert Camus was to explore a similar ethical dilemma faced by nihilists, but came down on the side of an anti-fanatical humanism, in his play *Les Justes* (1950). It dramatized the assassination of the Grand Duke Sergei Romanov, the uncle of Tsar Nicolas II, by a terrorist cell of Revolutionary Socialists in 1905, and contrasted Kaliayev, who retained humanist scruples, with Federov, whose dedication to the cause betrayed a commitment to the revolutionary programme of an unmistakable nihilist intensity, anticipating the later ruthlessness of Stalinists.

Dostoevsky's *The Devils* (which Camus dramatized in his 1959 play *Les Possédés*) is thus a novel on a highly contemporary theme. It offers finely nuanced psychological portraits of a group of would-be revolutionaries in a small town near St Petersburg who become implicated in the murder of one of their number, an act cynically instigated by their leader Verkhovensky – patently modeled on Nechayev – to forge a sense of conspiratorial solidarity between them. In depicting his discussions with Shigalyov, Stavrogin, Shatov, and Kirillov, each of whom embodies different facets of their search for a Gnosis of action, Dostoevsky explores the particular cultic milieu in St Petersburg that led so many of 'God's orphans' to formulate a mazeway resynthesis to lead their generation out of the labyrinth in what the author describes as 'a peculiar time' when 'something new

was in the air'. 'All kinds of rumours were circulating' along with a 'large number' of ideas which were 'perplexing' because 'in no way was it possible to orient
oneself or be certain what these ideas meant'.[3] They did not seek a totalizing solution to the crisis of modernity only for themselves or for their beloved Russia.
They longed to eject the disturbing and unwelcome guest of nihilism from the
door of an entire modern civilization which they saw as in profound, but *exorable*,
decline. The 'liquefying' effects of modernity were epitomized for them in the vulgar materialist 'might' of the British empire, the crassness of Prussian militarism,
and the spiritually hollow 'progress' of secular liberalism. Dostoevsky presents
their attempts to transcend the present as doomed to failure in their own terms,
yet also highly dangerous for the health of society.

The novel's passionate exposition of different utopian projects of a way out from
the historical cul-de-sac in which the nihilist generation felt trapped, is not just a
tribute to Dostoevsky's brilliance as a 'magic realist' of the soul. It also points to
a fascination, and even a deep kinship with Nechayev's extremist solution to the
country's moral and social malaise, a kinship explored with unrelieved intensity
in J.M. Coetzee's novel *The Master of Petersburg*.[4] This brings the novelist and the
terrorist face-to-face as if they incarnated two sides of an ethical and psychological
dichotomy, facing each other across the narrow divide separating a writer who
explores the moral abyss at the heart of modernity and a terrorist who declares
a purging war on it, between a contemplative Gnosticism and a Modernism of
the deed. At one point in their counterfactual confrontation Dostoevsky's bid to
mount a verbal defence of metaphysical humanism falls apart in the face of the
relentless logic of Nechayev's attack on his principles:

> And he does not believe himself because he has lost. Everything is collapsing:
> logic, reason. He stares at Nechayev and sees only a crystal winking in the light
> of the desert, self-enclosed, impregnable.[5]

Even without postulating that in a sense Verkhovensky is Dostoevsky's alter ego
in *The Devils*, the novelist certainly displays empathy with the delusory apocalyptic fantasies so characteristic of the nihilist generation and of all those desperate
to resolve a liminoid situation by precipitating a new era. Seeking to persuade
Stavrogin to let himself become the charismatic leader of a popular uprising,
Verkhovensky describes the Russian people as 'weeping for its old gods' and
'shrouded in mist', leading to 'an upheaval such as the world has never seen'.
Then they will need a 'new force' to emerge in society. Once the movement gathers
pace 'The earth will resound with the cry: "A new, just law [nomos!] is coming." '
At this point 'the oceans will seethe, the whole show will come crashing down,
and then we'll plan to set up a stone structure. For the first time! We shall build it,
we alone!'[6] God is no longer in the frame. The new stone edifice will be dedicated
to a secular utopia. Lyamshin, who finally betrays the group – unmistakably modelled on Nechayev's group The People's Reprisal – to the authorities, explains that
it aimed to promote 'the systematic destruction of society and all its principles'.
Then 'when society was on the point of collapse – sick, depressed, cynical, and

sceptical, but still with perpetual desire for some kind of guiding principle and for self-preservation – to gain control of it'.[7] This is the essence of creative destruction in a political key: first destroy the 'whole filthy system' and then build a new one, or even leave it to others to inaugurate that phase. First destroy. Dostoevsky has no doubt that attempts to bring about paradise on earth through terrorist violence are doomed to have effects which are 'diabolical', but he understands the metapolitical logic of waging a terrorist war against the Tsarist system and Western modernity all too well.

Building towers and destroying towers

Gray and Brooks are not the only political commentators to have suggested that Dostoevsky's study of nihilism in *The Devils* anticipated the events of 9/11. James Wood, writing in the *Guardian*, claims the novel exposes the 'murderous ravenousness that tears free of ideological accountability' which inhabits 'feeble physical specimens who plume themselves up with the thought of their private revenges'.[8] Similarly Adam Kirsch's review of the novel praises it for its unparalleled insights into the psychology of total commitment to a violent cause that led to 9/11.[9] Slavoj Žižek, by contrast, points out the fallacy of seeing Dostoevsky as anticipating the violence of Islamist terrorism, a thesis that became the subject of an entire book in Daniel Glucksmann's *Dostoievski à Manhattan* (2004). The Russian novelist, he claims, was exploring the extremism engendered by intellectuals for whom the universe had become Godless, whereas 'the lesson of today's terrorism is that if there IS God, then everything, up to blowing up hundreds of innocent bystanders, is permitted – to those who claim to act directly on behalf of God, as the instruments of His will'.[10]

However, neither Kirsch nor Žižek seem to grasp the significance of one of the points Gluckmann makes, admittedly fleetingly and in impenetrably florid prose. In his soliloquy on the singular moral force unleashed by the 9/11 terrorists that limpidly blue September morning on the banks of the Hudson river, he muses:

> Stopping at nothing, he goes the whole hog in ('total') revolution, in (absolute) war. *He undertakes the terroristic abolition of the (theological) difference between the earthly and the heavenly. Whether he sacralises the profane or profanes the sacred,* he leaps beyond his own shadow and transgresses the principle of the equality of all mortals before death. Believing he can rise above Death, and, in the role of its Exterminating Angel, installs himself as Death's destructive clone.[11]

What Gluckmann alludes to, but – frustratingly, at least for an Anglo-Saxon mindset – disdains to *analyse*, is the way lethal terrorist violence can result from two *different* types of fanaticism. It would have been illuminating if he had distinguished the different nature of the 'leap' and the 'shadow' for someone defending a beleaguered tradition, and someone condemned to be one of 'God's orphans', who thus desperately seeks out a new nomic home and cosmic principle for which to act as exterminating angel. For Zealotic terrorists the shadow is a futural one, a deepening darkness cast on reality by the destruction of their nomos which can only be banished through heroic action to restore the light that emanates from their religion or nation. The leap is thus into an apocalyptic mindset in which the fight is for a preordained divine or primordial national order which will appear *after* the *eschatos* or the Final Battle to reinstate and renew the old nomos.

For Modernist terrorists the leap is out of the shadow of the liminoid, out of anomy and into the light of a higher state of cultural being which will be accessible to all (or to 'their' particular elite segment of humanity), once they have fulfilled their mission to implant a new nomos in (their) history. In doing this, they are rising above the horror induced by 'the abyss of the future' which, according to Carl Jung, must be faced by all truly 'modern' human beings in 'their search for a soul' once they have been cut off from the traditional nomos. The inhabitant of the West, he declares:

> has become 'unhistorical' in the deepest sense and has estranged himself from the mass of men who live entirely within the bounds of tradition. Indeed, he is completely modern only when he has come to the very edge of the world, leaving behind him all that has been discarded and outgrown, and acknowledging that he stands before a void *out of which all things may grow*.[12]

In such works as *Notes from the Underground*, *Crime and Punishment*, *The Devils*, and *The Brothers Karamazov*, Dostoevsky places readers empathetically in the intimate circle of some utterly 'modern men' of the sort Jung talks about, thus leading them vicariously through the power of fiction to the very brink of the moral void of absolute anomy, absurdity, and nihilism 'out of which all things may grow'. Nechayev was one such man who built his house on the slopes of Vesuvius.

It is the hallmark of the 'great' postwar modernist novelists – André Malraux, Albert Camus, Jean-Paul Sartre, André Gide, Samuel Beckett, Friedrich Dürrenmatt, Günter Grass, Martin Walser, Norman Mailer, Joseph Heller, Don Passos, Jack Kerouac, Don Delillo, Luke Reinhardt, to name a very few – that their creative, 'narrative' selves stand vertiginously on the edge of a dark crater far below, swathes of sulphurous nihilism swirling around them in the rarified atmosphere. In this extreme, primordial, *cosmogonic* state of liminoidality, the peculiar strategy they find for resolving, or at least assuaging, their personal experience of the nomic crisis of modernity is to merge aestheticism (which has its own intrinsic renomizing and sacralizing function) with psychodrama, whether in comic or tragic key. If their works have a lasting effect, even across different ages, languages and cultures, it is largely due to the therapeutic release they provide in conjuring up through the illusionist magic of literature (however 'thick' the layers of realistic description and plotting applied), specimens of human being living *in extremis* whose responses to being alive express themselves *de profundis*. Each 'character' may reflect fragments of the author's own 'real' personality, or act as catalysts to the formation of entirely new imaginary personae which relate to each other, like the traces of sub-atomic particles in a laboratory cloud chamber, all fragments of the same original molecule.

It was in the experimental, fictional, but oneirically mimetic world of modernist fiction that Dostoevsky populated his 'realist' novels with personifications of elemental psychic energies – utopian and dystopian, constructive and destructive, life-asserting and despairing, loving and psychotic – which issue forth from the nomic abyss of modernity. A leitmotiv of his major works is a central character committed to or searching for an entire, 'totalizing' world-view and who may carry out extreme acts of violence as gestures towards a higher morality and a new life principle. But it is also a feature of Dostoevsky's later works that they leave open the possibility of a radical *restoration* of Christianity's nomos, a reaffirmation of Christ's original soteriological plan for humankind, now reformulated in terms of the salvation of Russia and its people from the encroachment of secularism and nihilism. Quintessentially 'modern' personalities condensed out of the Zeitgeist of urban Russia are the unnamed narrator in *Notes from the Underground* and Raskalnikov in *Crime and Punishment*.

Fittingly, his last major novel *The Brothers Karamazov* is thronged with different temperamental and psychological reactions to the liminoidality of the partially, and highly unevenly, Westernized Russia of the late nineteenth century. In a plot of considerable complexity many different narrative arcs and metaphysical journeys of individual characters intersect, each exhibiting a different variant of a 'Zealotic' retrenchment within traditional faith, 'Herodian' accommodation with Westernization, or a 'Modernist' bid to realize an alternative future for Russia. In the process scientism, liberalism, feminism, anarchism, nihilism, socialism, communism, aestheticism, and narcissism are all shown by Dostoevsky to be found wanting as the basis of a new nomos. By the time he wrote this novel in the late 1870s he had grown away (retreated?) from his own experimentation with variants of post-Enlightenment utopianism. He had also healed himself of his compulsive gambling, which could be seen as another psychological release from the pain of anomy. He had now come to embrace a blend of Orthodox Christianity with a Slavophile belief in Russia's destiny to save the world from perdition, a moderate form of Zealotry containing Modernist palingenetic currents.

Integral to his renewed faith was the acceptance of the objective existence of God and the immortality of the soul, seeing the fact of Christ, as opposed to the myth of Christianity, as dooming to failure *a priori* all attempts of human beings to find earthly solutions to the suffering and injustice of existence by the imposition of subjective human utopias. Everything hinged on this facticity of the metaphysical, for if the divine realm were (as Nietzsche later claimed) but a mere myth, then the suffering in the world would become instantly intolerable, and it would be morally imperative for society to be transformed through revolution. However, if there was *objectively* (and not just mythically) an invisible, divinely ordained cosmic harmony, then all the world's irrationality was only apparent, and suffering had to be accepted as part of a larger scheme of things, God's inscrutable plan for humanity.

Even so, there is more than a touch of the 'old' Dostoevsky in Ivan's insistence in his famous confrontation with Alyosha in the chapter 'Pro and Contra' of Book Four of the novel that not a single child should have to suffer in order to pay for 'the eternal harmony'. In this scene, Alyosha Karamazov embodies the restored sacred canopy of Christianity, Ivan, his brother, the modern rebellion against a traditional order based on the authority of a *deus absconditus*, a God who has removed Himself from the historical process and has unilaterally suspended communication with His Creation. The crucial point to emerge from the novel for our purposes is the deep affinity, portrayed as a blood relationship, between radical atheism and radical religious belief, indeed between all concerted efforts to create a solid narrative arc and moral order in the face of the liquefaction of nomic realities. In a crucial passage the narrator pinpoints the symmetrical relationship between an individual's commitment to a religious or to a secular fanaticism. The narrator comments on Alyosha that:

> As soon as he reflected seriously he was convinced of the existence of God and immortality, and at once he instinctively said to himself: 'I want to live for immortality, and I will accept no compromise.' In the same way, if he had decided that God and immortality did not exist, he would at once have become an atheist and a socialist. For socialism is not merely the labour question, it is before all things the atheistic question, the question of the form taken by atheism to-day, *the question of the tower of Babel built without God, not to mount to heaven from earth but to set up heaven on earth.*[13]

In a sense both brothers incarnate Janus-like facets of the same absolutist drive towards establishing a suprapersonal nomos that will stem the tide of anomy and decadence. Both men are psychological twins in their quest, and are equidistant from human beings indifferent to the metaphysical absurdity of the cosmos and seemingly blessed or cursed with minimal existential needs for any sort of self-transcendent purpose: Nietzsche's 'Last Men'. However, while Alyosha is still defending the traditional Russian–Christian nomos, Ivan is bent on creating a new one, on erecting a Tower of Babel under a Godless sky. As modern terrorists they would be pitted against each other in a cosmological civil war, the rearguard Zealot fundamentalist versus the avant-garde Modernist utopian, the Saint against the 'Devil'. Till the end Dostoevsky, the convert to Slavophile Christianity, was wrestling with his 'inner' nihilist, perhaps his true 'double'.[14]

Meanwhile others, capitalists, communists, and fascists, all filled with the modernist ecstasy of Gnostic certainty, would before long be constructing towers for humanity of stone, cement, iron, glass, and barbed wire which soared into empty skies. And in a little over century, a new caste of Zealots would have arisen to defend a beleaguered Islam, which would create its own cellular network of nomos-defending terrorists. A group of these would eventually take down two of the most iconic towers of the Babel of modernity to purge, in their eyes, the polluted heavens of the ungodly, and make a symbolic *tabula rasa* of Western values on the river-front of Lower Manhattan, now known by their 'enemies' as 'Ground Zero'.

Joseph Conrad: The terrorist as 'propagandist of the deed'

Over the next decades Russia's history was to be transformed not by any Slavophile vision of the regenerated nation under a reborn Church, but by 'Nietzschean' forces of creative destruction and positive nihilism. These were increasingly channelled into a coordinated Bolshevik revolutionary movement rather than individualistic acts of 'propaganda of the deed' which in practice, however spectacular, only reinforced the stranglehold of Tsarist reaction. If the allusion to Nietzsche smacks of the imposition of an abstract conceptual template on the far more down-to-earth factors that culminated in the Russian Revolution, then the testimony of Sergey Stepniak lends it some analytical weight. Having assassinated the chief of the Tsarist secret police in 1878 in the streets of St Petersburg, Stepniak escaped to the United States where he became a major campaigner for the overthrow of the Tsar. More importantly, *Underground Russia* (1882), widely read in Marxist and anarchist circles in Britain and the US, established him as a major theorist not just of nihilist anarchism, but of the basic principles of Modernist terrorism itself.

None other than the ardent socialist Eleanor Marx, daughter of Karl Marx, glowingly endorsed Stepniak's account of the revolutionary subculture which flowered under the Tsar:

> That a book on the Russian revolutionary movement, written by Stepniak, with a preface from the pen of Lawroff [Pyotr Lavrov was one of the first Russian activists to identify himself as a Marxist] would be of the utmost interest was to be expected. The little volume which Stepniak modestly calls a series of 'Sketches and Profiles', is in reality a work of the utmost historical value, for though written by an active Nihilist, it is full of just appreciation and critical insight. *It is to be hoped that all the romancing historians and would-be historical romancers; all the emotional and tender-hearted old statesmen, and tract-distributing prison-visiting divines will read it before again expressing their views on Russia and the condition of the Russian people.* In his excellent 'Introduction' Stepniak has, in masterly fashion, traced the history of the Socialist – or, as it is improperly called – Nihilist movement from its beginning in 1861 to its latest phase, the 'terrorist' phase of to-day.[15]

Stepniak presents the generic terrorist in explicitly Nietzschean terms as an important new historical actor, who 'combines in himself the two sublimities of human grandeur: the martyr and the hero', emphasizing not a communality of aim or tactic but a communality of creed which alludes directly to his or her sense of transcendent mission. 'Proud as Satan rebelling against God', the terrorist is 'immortal', endowed by his mission with 'that cool and calculating enthusiasm, that almost superhuman energy, which astounds the world'.[16] It is a theme elaborated in Stepniak's work of terrorist fiction *The Career of a Novelist* (1889) which portrays the female terrorist Tania experiencing a powerful epiphanic 'moment of moments' when she commits herself to the anarchist cause, outgrowing 'in an instant her girlhood and womanhood'.[17] The implication is that the terrorist, through his or her readiness to act for the sake of a future society, thus conquers the decadent, anomic time of 'normal' modernity and achieves fulfilment in a suprapersonal, though no longer suprahistorical, sphere.

The allusions to Nietzsche in Stepniak's presentations of the metapolitics of terrorism are significant. In *Ecce Homo* Nietzsche claimed he was dedicated to bringing to a head the profound 'collision of conscience' between the dying otherworldly view of the world and the rising tide of purely this-worldly values with no supernatural sanction. That is why he cast himself in the heroic role of being the first philosopher to use the power of thought to 'uncover' or 'take the lid off' Christian morality and expose it as a human-made fiction. His philosophy of demystification thus represents an 'unparalleled catastrophe' that has turned him into 'a *force majeur*' who 'breaks the history of humanity into two parts', before and after Nietzsche.[18] It is the pivotal role that he ascribes to his philosophy in bringing about the moment when the tectonic plates of Christian Europe and the new world of secular science finally moved apart that leads Nietzsche to see himself as 'dynamite'.[19]

In contrast, anarchist nihilists such as Stepniak saw themselves as changing the *objective* history of humanity through the power of violent deeds, sometimes using literal dynamite to do so. By being an articulate theorist, novelist, and militant of terrorism in a Nietzschean key that was given the seal of approval by committed revolutionary socialists such as Eleanor Marx, Stepniak built a narrow causeway between the two Gnostic rebellions referred to by Pellicani, contemplative and activist, against a world experienced as in desperate need of a transvaluation of values, of transformation, of rebirth. In doing this he demonstrated their common historical roots in the great nomic crisis of Western modernity, and simultaneously underlined their underlying kinship as two forms of modernist revolution against anomy.

The milieu that produced Stepniak became the subject of a major novel by Joseph Conrad. He was the son of a highly cultured Polish patriot exiled in 1861 to the far north of Moscow as punishment for being part of a communist revolutionary group ('The Reds') dedicated to fighting the Russian occupation of Poland, another example of modern Zealotry. Disaffected with politics, he devoted himself instead to an extraordinarily intense physical and emotional life as a seafaring adventurer, before embarking on a series of 18 novels, two of which, *The Secret Agent* (1907) and *Under Western Eyes* (1911), centre on the theme of terrorism. By the time he wrote *Under Western Eyes*, partly as a response to his reading of *Crime and Punishment*, the political climate of Russia was saturated with revolutionary energies. The Party of Socialist Revolutionaries (SR), which was founded 1901 and by 1907 boasted some 45,000 members, had a terrorist wing modelled on the Nechayev-inspired People's Will that had succeeded in assassinating the Tsar Alexander II in 1881. In the same period acts of 'pure' violence were being carried out by some anarcho-communist groups, most famously the Black Banner, advocates of 'motiveless terror'.

The novel fictionalizes the terroristic subculture responsible for the assassination in 1904 of the head of the Russian secret police, Vyacheslav von Plehve, blown up in his carriage by a member of the SR Combat Group (also in St Petersburg, then the world centre of terrorism). Clearly, *Under Western Eyes* has its own intrinsic literary importance as a Conrad novel. However, three points stand out in the present context. First, Viktor Haldin, the assassin, justifies the murder as an act not of destruction but liberation, freeing the world of the 'true destroyers', namely those who crush 'the spirit of progress and truth'.[20] Acts like his, he claims, will eventually sweep all falsehood from the world and allow a 'new revelation' to issue forth from the nation, thanks to the power of the Russian soul.[21] The assassination was thus not murder, but, from the terrorist's own point of view, an act of creative destruction, of *positive* nihilism.

Second, Conrad emphasizes how SR militants consider their terrorism a sacralized form of political activity. Thus Haldin sees his spirit living on to inspire the revolutionary cause even after his martyrdom, thus turning him into a sort of secular saint.[22] It is a belief consistent with the claim of the real life assassin of von Plehve, Egor Sazonov, that his 'Social-Revolutionary beliefs merged with religion': the party wanted to realize the demands of Christ within history by making His kingdom 'come to earth',[23] an image which evokes the temporal, this-worldly aspirations of the modern Babel described by Dostoevsky in *The Brothers Karamazov*. Finally, Conrad portrays the attempts by terrorists to liberate Russians from their spiritual slavery not just as a political struggle, but also as a metaphysical rebellion against a society which had degenerated, in his own words, into 'le néant', nothingness. In terms of our analysis, the Russian Underground was thus a bid to put an end to the spectral, liminoid, nihilistic state into which the nation had drifted under the Tsars. The Party of Social Revolutionaries is portrayed as driven as much by a metapolitical creed as a political ideology.

Against this historical backcloth several features of Conrad's earlier novel on terrorism, *The Secret Agent*, assume particular significance. As in *Under Western Eyes*, the novel supplies the fictitious back-story to a real episode in the history of nineteenth-century terrorism, the abortive attack on Greenwich Observatory in 1894 carried out (for historically unknown reasons) by the French anarchist Martial Bourdin, who was killed by his own bomb before he could reach the building. Conrad's fictional reconstruction highlights the uncompromising, arrogant, *totalizing* nature of the terrorist mindset, replete with an activistic Gnostic knowledge impervious to rational debate or empirical refutation. Thus Mr Vladimir, the *éminence grise* behind the forthcoming attack, explains that to have an impact on public opinion the ideal bomb outrage must be of a 'destructive ferocity so absurd as to be incomprehensible, inexplicable, almost unthinkable; *in fact*, mad'. In this way it is experienced as an attack on 'the whole social creation', and hence has the effect of what Alex Houen in *Terrorism in Modern Literature* calls 'an epiphanous devastation'.[24] That is why Vladimir explains that the outrage must be conceived in such a way that the public does not react in the way it does to other calamities familiar from newspapers and 'current affairs'. A successful terrorist attack is one that strikes at the heart of the public's sense of normality. It is thus an act of violence which is not primarily military and tactical, or even murderous, but is conceived to have the maximum symbolic and metapolitical impact. By breaking the normative frame of 'news' or 'information' it can be experienced *gnostically* as an event disrupting the established temporality of modernity itself. It is this subjectively 'world-shattering' effect that was achieved to an unprecedented degree on a global scale by the 9/11 attacks.

Vladimir's reflections explain the significance of the anarchist's choice of target. In 1884, ten years before Bourdin's attack, an international conference had decided that the Prime Meridian of the newly created International Date Line should pass precisely through the Greenwich Observatory, making it one of the first potent symbols of global rationality, of the myth of science-based progress, and of globalization itself. Its physical destruction had no conceivable pragmatic purpose, but was an anarchic gesture of the sort that Dostoevsky's anonymous and anomic narrator of *Notes from the Underground* (1864) would have liked to commit, merely to assert the primacy of an alternative universe of irrational human freedom in which, in his own words, two plus two makes not four but *five*. The symbolism may even go deeper still. Walter Benjamin records that 'on the first evening of fighting' in the July Revolution of 1830 'it turned out that the clocks in the towers were being fired on simultaneously and independently from several places in Paris'.[25] In the same way, Bourdin may have been setting out to 'make the continuum of history explode' at least symbolically.[26] At that point the original attack on the building was not merely synecdochic. It was an apocalyptic act of sympathetic, or even homeopathic, black magic aiming to 'blow up' Enlightenment time so to let in a new time, a time of revelation, of Gnosis, or what Walter Benjamin calls 'Messianic time'.[27]

Whatever the truth about the historical event (or non-event), *The Secret Agent* is a powerful exposition of the fact that alongside the numerous assassinations of heads of state and embodiments of state power committed in the 1880s and 1890s as acts of 'propaganda of the deed', the political imagination of the Modernist terrorist could also operate in an almost entirely self-contained symbolic universe. In this mythopoeic fantasy-world the 'enemy' or the 'hated society' was reduced to (for the attackers) a potent synecdoche of its alleged domination. The novel also reveals the fallacy of all synecdochic terrorism. What looms so large in the mind of the terrorist is inevitably of minimal impact on the 'real world' of external reality, and even 'taking out' a tsar, a president, or an iconic major building, cannot bring down the entire system they epitomize in external reality. The terrorist tendency to confuse the inner symbolic realm with the outer world means that, with few exceptions, even if 'subjectively' 'evil' is destroyed and Time transformed, objectively, in 'the real world', with a few exceptions nothing changes as the result of a terror campaign against the status quo. Life continues. History is not derailed or jolted from its course, let alone forced onto new tracks towards utopia, despite the deaths and terrible suffering caused, the panic, the fear, and the imposition of security measures which suck the vitality from social coexistence.

In a curious reversal of the mystical perspective insisted on by William Blake, instead of seeing the world in a grain of sand, in the most symbolically-charged and metapolitically-oriented episodes of terrorism, the world in all its complexity is reduced to a single person, object or space. Only by viewing reality through this ideological tunnel vision can the annihilation of the 'target' be envisaged as inaugurating a new beginning. Conrad mocks this delusional consciousness in both of his novels on terrorism. The fact that the Unabomber, Ted Kaczynski (whom we shall encounter again in due course) kept a copy of *The Secret Agent* in his hut in Montana as a source of inspiration for his own synecdochic bombings against technological civilization, does not say much for his understanding of irony. The acute distortion of the reality principle which stems from the terrorist's 'activist Gnosticism' is a subject we will return to in the next chapter.

André Malraux: The terrorist as existentialist

A different aspect of the non-instrumental, metapolitical, *existential* dimension of some forms of terrorism, which so fascinated Dostoevsky and Conrad, is illuminated in considerable depth in Malraux's *La Condition Humaine* [*Man's Fate*] (1933), a novel particularly important for understanding the process of renomization and resacralization of reality that takes place in the microcosm of the terrorist's inner world. This is once again a fictionalized version of an actual historical episode, the abortive uprising against Chiang Kai-shek's Nationalist government carried out by communists in Shanghai in 1927. The uprising was just one episode in an intensely real and bloody ideological and military conflict between rival visions of the new society to emerge from the collapse of Imperial China. Two conflicting regenerative nomoi were pitted against each other till the bitter end, marked by the establishment of a Maoist China. Once again the author has exploited the historically undocumented subjectivities of the protagonists to investigate moral and metaphysical dilemmas close to his heart. In this case the subject under the forensic examination of heightened prose is the ability of human beings to endow their brief lives with absolute meaning through idealistically motivated, and ideologically targeted, acts of violence committed under the empty skies of an intrinsically absurd universe. Each main character in the novel exemplifies a different permutation of the ethical problems posed by commitment to political murder carried out with the aim of changing history. It is a decision portrayed by Malraux as one which imbues life with a transitory significance both dramatically heightened and deeply threatened by the prospect of a horrific death if the mission fails (in the case of the Russian communist Katow, the price of such failure is to be thrown alive into the furnace of a railway locomotive).

As a distillation of the novel's insights into the metapolitics of a terrorist's creed, Derek Allan's penetrating analysis of the psychological process of individuation undergone by Ch'en-Ta-Eul, one of the principal terrorists, assumes particular importance. It stresses the need for readers to suspend rationalist assumptions about morality as a function of ideation alone, and to grasp the particular philosophy of *action* (what Pellicani calls an 'activist Gnosis') each character embodies when confronted with the reality of murder and death. To illuminate this point, Allan cites the reference in Camus's essay *The Myth of Sisyphus* to the particular response to the absolute absurdity of existence incarnated in 'The Conqueror', the warrior for whom action 'becomes the means through which the world is understood', for whom action 'defines reality'. In the same way that *The Just* and *The Possessed* reject fanatical violence for humanism, so Camus himself never endorsed the Conquerors' amoral cult of pure action. He thus condemned both the state terror of the French government and the counter-terror of the Front de Liberational Nationale (FLN) in the Algerian War of Independence.[28]

Camus's major existentialist works, *The Myth of Sisyphus*, *The Outsider*, and *The Plague*, can be seen as a series of reflections on the innate, *species-defining* impulse of humans to revolt against the anomic condition of modernity (sometimes confused with the 'human condition' itself) which endows it for the first time in history with the quality of bottomless absurdity. Parts of *The Rebel* [in French the ambiguous *L'homme révolté*, 'Revolted Man'] depict the experiments of totalitarian regimes to *renomize* the world through social engineering and ruthless purges of the enemy, thus dotting the map of twentieth-century Europe and Asia with gulags, concentration camps, and killing fields. The characters in Malraux's existentialist *roman noir*, *La Condition Humaine*, do not have the luxury of indulging in prolonged theorizing, however. Allan argues that it is made clear in the portrait of the communist cell's leader, Kyo, that 'the irreducible, primary Chaos of human experience – the confused and confusing kaleidoscope of men, things and events – assumes order and significance solely in terms of the practical demands of the action (the revolution in Shanghai) that he has chosen to espouse'.

Thus Kyo is interested 'not in theoretical abstractions but in tangible issues discernible *now*', an 'intensely pragmatic perspective' which at the same time 'provides a basis for *meaning* in experience'. It is Ch'en's longing to fulfil, through a premeditated assassination, his personal need for a nomos, to reach out through terrorist action 'for a universe constructed of fixed and immutable principles', and to find in murder 'the deeper solace of universal and eternal truth'[29] that is to shape his terrible fate. The first time he stabs to death a political opponent in his sleep he realizes, as he stands there, dagger in hand, that he has acted 'not as a fighter, but as a sacrificial priest'.[30] Malraux describes how 'Ch'en felt the stars in their eternal motion invade his being like the relief from the cooler outside air', and for the first time becomes one with 'Life'.[31] In the Gnostic act of murder, the victim thus becomes a ritual sacrifice to the higher cause, even a secular one.

In subsequently planning Chiang Kai-Shek's assassination, Ch'en seeks to repeat this epiphanic experience, renew his encounter with 'the eternal' and re-enter 'that world of permanent and universal truth that he discovered on the occasion of his first murder'.'(On this point Allan draws parallels between Ch'en and Alexei Kirillov in *The Devils*, who believes that by committing suicide serenely he can become the true God.) When Ch'en announces that his plan to kill the Nationalist leader will result in his own death, Souen responds 'You want to make a kind of religion out of terrorism', to which Ch'en replies significantly 'Not a religion. The meaning of life. . . . *Complete self-possession*'.[32] He dreams of inspiring through his martyr's fate a 'race of avenging judges, themselves condemned to death', all achieving a secular form of mystic fulfilment by performing their ritual killing in an ecstatic, epiphanic moment of self-transcendence. *La Condition Humaine* dramatizes the inner process by which, as a terrorist nears the 'fanatical' state (literally 'sacralized' state) needed to carry out a martyr assassination, he experiences a 'kind of apotheosis, a privileged moment of total communion with ultimate truth – a terrorist's grim equivalent of an entry into paradise'.[33]

Tom Robbins: The terrorist as anarchic individualist

Tom Robbins' *Still Life with Woodpecker* (1980) unceremoniously airlifts us by passenger jet from the lethal ideological turf-wars being lived out in the fog-bound alleys of 1930s Shanghai to an altogether more upbeat space and time: sun-drenched Honolulu at the height of the summer congress season. It examines terrorism through the kaleidoscopic narrative lens of postwar, post-existentialist, postmodern, post-structuralist, post-Vietnam, and ambivalently post-Hippy 'acid anarchism' close to the author's own vitalistic outlook. Robbins offers a mordant counter-cultural satire on the coreless core at the decentred centre of US life in the 1970s. While surreally and sometimes outrageously comic on the surface, the novel operates on another level as a sustained examination of collective human behaviour in an 'advanced' but increasingly anomic Western society.

It reveals how the vast majority of Americans who can afford to travel, though materially privileged and physically secure beyond the fantasies of earlier generations, are spiritually impoverished and isolated. They are thus condemned to join what has become a roaming herd of God's orphans in order to find a temporary existential foster-home or spiritual motel room by joining a mass-produced and extensively commodified idealistic or trendy 'cause' to devote themselves to. The temptation to succumb to what Nietzsche called *Herdenmoral* or 'herd morality' is the main target of satire in a book that entreats the reader in scurrilous fashion – one of the many subplots is a love–hate relationship with a state-of-the-art Remington SL3 electric typewriter – to break out of the emotional strait-jackets of 'group mind' into the freedom of authentic consciousness.

The opening paragraph locates the narrative – a blend of modern fairy-tale with postmodern morality play – in the acutely liminoid conditions of 'the last quarter of the twentieth century', a time when Western civilization was 'declining too rapidly for comfort and yet too slowly to be very exciting'. This left millions experiencing 'various combinations of dread, hope and ennui' as they waited 'for something momentous to occur'. True to Zygmunt Bauman's exposure of the inextricable relationship between modernity and ambivalence referred to earlier, the 'collective unconscious' cannot decide whether the coming event will be 'apocalyptic or rejuvenating? A cure for cancer or a nuclear bang? A change in the weather or a change in the sea? . . . Would Mona Lisa sprout a moustache? Would the dollar fail?'[34] It is a situation that has stimulated the millennarian fantasies of Christians, New Ageists, radical Greens, and romantics alike to fever pitch. What Robbins has captured in a single page of exposition is the way an intensification of the liminoid in society can stimulate the primordial human apocalyptic faculty which promptly conjures up scenarios for the imminent course of history that offer the prospect of imminent closure, whether in an earthly Hell or a New Eden. The result is a proliferation of 'revitalization movements': 'Despite the boredom and anxiety of the period, or because of it... tens of thousands seemed willing to lend their bodies, their money, and their skills to various planetary rescue missions.'[35]

As we have observed, it is the alchemical power of the palingenetic *imaginaire* to turn the deepening night of anomy into the dawning of a new age, and so transform the sense of an ending into the presentiment of a new beginning. However, under the dispensation of secular modernity most new nomoi available – at least to those who resist the powerful lure of addictions to anaesthetize the existential pain – will be temporalized utopias. The one which forms the setting for the novel's opening is the radical ecology movement, complete with a vast New Age entourage, which is about to hold an ecumenical 'Geotherapy Carefest' in Hawaii. The mega-jamboree's star billing is an address by a new *propheta* of eco-consciousness, the US's most famous political Green, Ralph Nader – the novel was written over 15 years before in real life he ran as Vice President on a democratic ecological ticket. However, the conference has also attracted the attention of someone whose self-appointed mission is to liberate the masses from the inauthentic superego of fashions and fads, however high-minded their ostensible cause. It is to this end that this man arrives in Honolulu to carry out a carefully premeditated terrorist attack.

With Bernard Wrangle, known to the world's media as 'The Woodpecker', Dostoevsky's Underground Man has come out of his solipsistic lair and wants to party. A self-styled 'outlaw', he started out his bombing campaign as a protest against the Vietnamese War by targeting military draft-boards as well as a chemistry faculty building in the University of Wisconsin campus suspected of working for the war effort (an allusion to the project to produce Agent Orange?). Now the war is over he has switched targets to focus on organizations that encourage a literally soul-destroying group-mind. He has come to Hawaii to *make* something momentous happen, namely by exploding a bomb in the Carefest (though first he explodes one at a UFO conference by mistake). As he tells the beautiful foreign princess (this is a fairy-tale) who is going to the Carefest as a 'believer' (and has a crush on Ralph Nader), his dynamite does not aim to teach but to 'awaken'. The explosion is intended to shake the participants out of their collective somnambulism and foster a climate of radical, anarchic individualism, a goal which clearly has its roots in the mentality of the 1960s counter-culture.[36] In a remarkable passage of authorial commentary on his own story, Robbins candidly reveals one of basic reasons he wrote the novel. It is to address the existential crisis of modernity, and the resulting loss of any stable access to the metaphysical, to the sacral, or to metaphysically *full* silences:

> In a society that is essentially designed to organize, direct, and gratify mass impulses, what is there to minister to the silent zones of man as an individual? Religion? Art? Nature? No, the church has turned religion into standardized public spectacle, and the museum has done the same for art. The Grand Canyon

and Niagara Falls have been looked at so much that they've become effete, sucked empty by too many stupid eyes. What is there to minister to the silent zones of man as an individual?[37]

With the loss of traditional nomoi, any Gnostic knowledge of the sacral has for most denizens of modernity become fragmented, randomized, commercialized. The epiphanic now leaps capriciously out at an undifferentiated, denomized consciousness from trivial moments of surreal incongruity to produce unexpected and inconsequential portals to the numinous in a way which evokes Lautréamont's celebration of the beauty of 'the chance meeting on a dissecting-table of a sewing-machine and an umbrella!'.[38]

How about a cold chicken bone on a paper plate at midnight, how about a lurid lipstick lengthening or shortening at your command, how about a Styrofoam nest abandoned by a 'bird' you've never known, how about a pair of windshield wipers pursuing one another futilely while you drive home alone through a downpour, how about something beneath a seat touched by your shoe at the movies, how about worn pencils, cute forks, fat little radios, boxes of bow ties, and bubbles on the side of a bathtub? Yes, these are the things, these kite strings and olive oil cans and Valentine hearts stuffed with nougat, that form the bond between the autistic vision and the experiential world, it is to show these things in their true mysterious light that is the purpose of the moon.[39]

The aim of the 'Woodpecker' in *Still Life with Woodpecker* is thus to use terrorism to transform the 'herd morality' bred by the mass-consumption of an *ersatz*, commodity-fetishized, and hence *unreal* reality into the authentic vitalism of a Nietzschean Superman, a Surrealist poet, or a Sartrean existentialist. The tone is deliberately ludic. One chapter provides four bomb-making recipes, while another offers an ecstatic eulogy of the 'magic of TNT', and of the role of the 'outlaw', who finds himself 'outside the law' (the prevailing nomos) and hence can have access to 'outlaw maps' (mazeways?) that lead to 'outlaw treasures': 'Unwilling to wait for mankind to improve, the outlaw lives as if that day were here, and I love that most of all'. As a result the Woodpecker can celebrate the unique sense of fulfilment he derives from being a liberator from the shackles of hegemonic consciousness, a 'Law' as perverse in its own way as the one wrestled with in Kafka's prose.

I am the happiest man in America. In my bartender's pockets I still carry, out of habit, wooden matches. As long as there are matches, there will be fuses. As long as there are fuses, no walls are safe. As long as every wall is threatened, the world can happen. Outlaws are can openers in the supermarket of life.[40]

It follows from this extreme form of anarchism, closer to the solipsism of Max Stirner than the communitarianism of Mikhail Bakunin, that Robbins' fictional terrorism has the primarily metapolitical and epiphanic function. This is to make accessible, even to modern human beings who keep a safe distance from the edge of Jung's abyss of modernity, what he calls 'the power of higher consciousness which, while universal, cosmic even, is manifest in the intimate'. This goal can only be fulfilled properly if the terrorist continues (narcissistically) to assert his idiosyncrasy and never forgets that:

> the movement, the organization, the institution, the revolution ... is only the backdrop for his or her own personal drama, and that to pretend otherwise is to surrender freedom and will to the totalitarian impulse, is to replace psychological reality with sociological illusion.[41]

In fact Robbins delivers a sobering health warning about 'exposure to politics':

> When a good idea is run through the filters and compressors of ordinary tunnel vision, it not only comes out reduced in scale and value, but in its new dogmatic configuration produces effects the opposite of those for which it originally intended.[42]

It is a principle that explains the failures of the World Health Organization, Christianity, and 'virtually every revolution in history'. In fact the Woodpecker has experienced the principle at work in his own crusade against society: the attack on the chemical faculty in Wisconsin accidentally killed a graduate student working for his doctorate.

True to his creed of idiosyncrasy, Bernard Wrangel finally abandons his outlaw persona and his one-man revitalization movement to find fulfilment within a tumultuous love affair. The thematic axis of the novel duly shifts to focus on another core existential issue: how can the intensity of love be maintained? But not before it has delivered a vivid exposition of how materially secure but existentially anguished, hyperconscious 'modern man' and 'modern woman' searched for a soul in 1970s America before the final dissipation of the American Dream.

Sunjeev Sahota: The terrorist as Zealotic orphan

The last fictional treatment of terrorism reverses the flow of Robbins' stream of hyperconsciousness. In Sunjeev Sahota's *Ours are the Streets* (2011), Imtiaz Raina, a second-generation Pakistani Muslim living in Sheffield, abandons a reasonably happy family life to take on a martyr bombing mission instead. It is a novel that stands out from the others we have considered in two respects. First, its theme is not the account of how one of God's orphans or runaways attempts to revitalize and renomize a decadent civilization through an act of Modernist terrorism. Instead it shows how a modern form of Zealotry, an act of fanatical violence against civic society, can be undertaken by the most unassuming citizen in defence of a largely virtual nomic community perceived as being degraded and destroyed. Second it is written exclusively from the perspective of the (would-be) terrorist. It takes the form of an extended letter to be discovered and read by Imtiaz's wife only after he has carried out a martyr bombing against the Meadowhall shopping centre in Sheffield, so that she can explain to their young daughter why she lost her father.

What she (and the police) will find is a highly impressionistic, stubbornly unanalytical and unliterary autobiographical account of his process of radicalization. There is no ideological ranting of the sort mercilessly parodied in the film *Four Lions* (2010) (which plays out in a similar social milieu), and no diatribes against the 'New Crusaders'' oppression of Islam. There is also minimal explicit motivation provided for Imtiaz to deprive his family of his existence. The novel could even be read as if he has sleepwalked his way to martyrdom because he is impressionable in the company of fanatics, and thus gives his life to the Islamist cause without any real conviction or commitment. Yet Malraux's study of Ch'en's path to 'complete self-possession' allows us to join up the dots of motivation that are there and supply some of the missing ones, to reveal a far more complex and profound psychological process of radicalization at work.

First, it is clear from Imtiaz's own account of his life that his experience of growing up in Sheffield as part of the Muslim/Pakistani diaspora has been one of brooding anomy and rootlessness. He drifts into marriage with a white non-Muslim, Becka, with whom he has had casual sex, and on into fatherhood, and has no clear sense of professional or religious vocation. His appetite for life fades. Urban anomy grows. At one point he watches TV like he used to in the early days with his wife, 'trying my hardest to get interested in what were on, but all seemed so bright and dead and pointless'.[43] Later, in Pakistan, where he has gone to bury his father, he finds himself telling his relatives how 'hard it is for kids growing up in England', referring not to material needs but emotional ones. In a semi-articulate expression of confused ethnic identity and liminoidality he complains 'I mean we are the ones stuck in the middle of everything. Like, we're not sure whose side we're meant to be on, you know', a situation that leaves him rooting for Liverpool Football Club (discreetly) but not for England, and 'defending Muslims against whites and whites against Muslims'.[44]

It is the death of his father, a taxi-driver, due to a heart-attack provoked by chasing a fare-dodger, that triggers an existential crisis of meaning in Imtiaz which is crystallized when he gets to Pakistan and lives with his cousins. He starts off thinking he will just be a sort of tourist, learning a bit about history but free to do what he wanted.[45] Yet there are soon signs that he is about to discover (invent?) his 'true' identity in Pakistan. He feels stung by the comment that he has been 'brought up in foreign lands, learning foreign ways'.[46] Then, when he tells one of the Islamists he meets, Ustaadji, he could not sleep well, he is told that it cannot be easy to sleep when his 'bed is made of bricks'.[47] Although Imtiaz does not understand, the reader knows that this is a reference to his intolerable crisis of cultural identity. We realize soon that it is the gradual resolution of this crisis in his commitment first to a fundamentalist Muslim identity, and then to a suicide bombing in Sheffield, that is unfolding on the pages before us with a minimum of introspection or self-analysis.

The man who had until recently been an existentially lost diaspora Muslim, soon comes to appreciate the fact that 'everyone treated me as if this were my real home, as if England were just some place where I happened to be born' and that when people fell out with him it was a sign they cared about him.[48] He finds himself irrationally drawn to an Islamic myth told in the tradition of oral history, which tells of the story of the Shadow of God. He is particularly impressed by the moment in the story when the hero takes out his weapon and declares: 'With this sword of justice I vow to return glory upon my religion and death upon the infidels'.[49] By the time the leading Islamist, Aaqil, speaks passionately about the international community of Muslim blood,[50] Imtiaz feels 'he were speaking directly to me'.[51] When they debate whether he should join the struggle (jihad), he is asked whether it is because he is 'called by Allah' or because he feels he owes his 'brothers and sisters something', and answers confidently that 'me feeling this way is just Allah's way of calling me'.[52] He has found his mission. Or rather the mission has found him. The prelude to this sense of *metaphysical* certainty is the remarkable epiphany he experiences when praying on a mountain top at sunrise. As dawn breaks he finds for the first time his timid prayer grow strong. Soon:

> we were all as one great boiling voice washing over the valley. Magic were spilling over me. The whole world was on fire, trembling with the force of us all on the crest of that hill. . . . no one could beat us: Mountain air a dreamy green, as if Allah Himself had chosen to lean down from on high and breathe upon this day. Ameen.[53]

By the end of his trip to a remote corner of Afghanistan where he lives for a few days with committed Islamists, he realizes that although where he has been is the most isolated place he has ever encountered, 'I don't think I have ever felt more connected to the world'.[54] He has discovered in Pakistan and within himself a lost nomos, like a private Atlantis submerged by tides of modernity. When he returns to his life in Sheffield it now feels more mundane and unreal than ever. He is determined to cling onto his new-found sense of cultural and sibling belonging, to his personal epiphanic moment of self-transcendence. He submits willingly to the grooming to become the next in line for a mission after another martyr attack is carried out on behalf of what is now 'his' community. At no point does he question the moral or tactical justification for attacking innocent weekend shoppers. His somnambulistic state is explained, however, not by apathy, but because he has found a transcendent purpose, a higher reality to which to sacrifice himself: a 'true' sacred canopy under which to briefly live and die in glory. When he alludes to the phrase from the Qu'ran, 'He who sleeps contentedly while his neighbours sleep hungry did not believe in my message',[55] it is clear that the conversion is less about theology than identity. He has found who his true spiritual neighbours are. His discovery of a sense of belonging means that instinctively he resolves to remain true to his (mythic) memory of his ancestors, to what they have suffered, and to their present humiliations and sacrifices. He must be 'loyal to the old wounds'.[56] He observes that when he pushed the boat into the water from the bank of a river in Pakistan 'I felt my stomach dip as we were freed from the green muddy lime'.[57] This can be read as a lived metaphor of his own liberation and self-purification.

It is the discovery of something worth dying for that resonates in one of the early messages he leaves for his daughter Noor. He tells her she must not live her life like her grandfather, who would return from a nightshift driving the taxi physically exhausted and emotionally drained, full of humiliation and shame. Nor must she live her life for 'trivial things like possessions'. She must live her life 'like you are proud enough to die'.[58] Unlike what he has been forced to feel for his own dad, he believes his daughter can celebrate his achievement of self-realization and his legacy to his family that was denied his parents. Before the trip to Pakistan 'I were always so and so's grandson or such and such's nephew or whatever. I were never just me, on my own'. But since, 'It were like for the first time I had an actual real past, with real people who'd lived real lives. Now I think that maybe when Noor takes her kids back home ... they'll sit in the shade of a banyan tree and listen open-mouthed to stories of the struggle that I, their baba, were part of.' [59] So powerful is the sense of emancipation and self-discovery Imtiaz has achieved through his terrorist mission that he dances joyfully on the eve of the attack. When he puts his hand on the bomb-jacket he can feel his 'desperate and thirsty' alter ego, his heroic avatar, longing to pull the cord to detonate the explosion.

The novel has been criticized for its failure to demonstrate Imitiaz's inner radicalization process explicitly and his indifference to fundamentalist ideology. Whatever the flaws of style, plot, and characterization which *Ours are the Streets* may exhibit as a first novel, however unaware the author Sunjeev Sahota may be of the deep structure of the journey to fanaticism he has traced in his protagonist, and how utterly ephemeral his book may prove to be in comparison to the novels of Dostoevsky, Conrad and Malraux, it has particular resonance within the present analysis. It can be read as the impressionistic fictional inner autobiography of an anomic, only partially educated and self-aware member of a liminoid generation growing up within Britain's sprawling diaspora Muslim community who submits to the deep-seated *subliminal* drive to renomize and resacralize his life through a terrorist act of mass murder. This holds true even if he exhibits only the most rudimentary awareness of the deeper rationale behind his commitment, as well as displaying considerable theological illiteracy, historical ignorance and tactical naivety about the Islamist cause for which he is about to martyr himself. His motivation is more existential than ideological.

Like one of 'God's orphans' described by Pellicani, Imtiaz can neither fully assimilate to the 'trivial' materialism and secularism of the West's post-Christian individualism, nor embrace the traditional, apolitical, mechanical Islamic faith of his parents' generation. A fatal logic thus dictates that his psyche seize the chance which presents itself to him in Pakistan to become a 'Zealot', and thus adopt, with a minimum of introspection, the Gnostic revelation of life's ultimate purpose in a martyr act of violence committed against the demonized 'enemy' that this demands, even if he personally feels no passionate hatred for his host country.[60] It is his chance to achieve 'complete self-possession'.

The fiction of the authors we have considered highlights different aspects of the metapolitics of the terrorist's creed. It can result from highly intellectual Nietzschean urges to overcome the death of God by building a secular Tower of Babel, a project which first demands the assassination of public figures to clear the construction site. It can express itself in symbolic attacks designed to undermine the rational assumptions of European civilization at the height of the Victorian age. It can lead to the murder of incarnations of an enemy ideology which is experienced as the ecstasy of self-realization. It can serve to waken a world of somnambulists from the inauthenticity of their group-minded and hence mindless lives. It can be a self-sacrificial gesture towards preserving a belatedly adopted ('discovered') cultural nomos from obliteration by modern multiculturalism and consumerism. Terrorism is clearly an irreducibly plural phenomenon.

However, taken together with the earlier chapters, our consideration of terrorism's treatment in fiction has put us in the position to extrapolate a core pattern in the process of radicalization which a terrorist undergoes on his or her inner journey to the defining act of purging violence, no matter how varied the motivation or the cause. It is a pattern thrown into relief once terrorist radicalization is considered on a metapolitical level, whether in Zealotic or Modernist forms, as a search for a transcendent act of self-possession through activist, not contemplative, Gnosis. The metapolitical dimension of terrorism emerges when it is viewed from an angle diametrically opposed to the one which focuses exclusively on its instrumental aspect. Like the second image in a child's lenticular lens which makes a tame lion roar when tilted, the metapolitical dimension in terrorism, the creed, is always present, however invisible it may be to those who reduce it, with the eyes of what William Blake called 'single vision', to criminality, madness, paramilitary operations, or political extremism. The novels we have considered highlight this second perspective, and allow us to see the fanatical violence it leads to *on one level* as a pre-emptive strike against the hostile, soul-destroying forces of nomocide or anomy to ward off existential dread, as an extreme act of resistance and rebellion against the entropy of higher meaning and purpose under the corrosive impact of modernity. In the next chapter we shall consider the syndrome of terrorist radicalization in more detail.

5
The Metapolitics of Terrorist Radicalization

Terrorist radicalization Stage One: Nomic crisis

So far we have encountered two artificially polarized 'ideal types' of terrorism, Zealotic and Modernist, and sampled some of the ways the mindsets of terrorists involved in planning or executing acts of violence have been presented in European and US fiction. This has put us in a position to suggest that a fundamental psycho-social syndrome is at work in the process that transforms a non-violent, non-militant, 'normal' individual, perhaps with feelings and values which are too inchoate, confused and contradictory to be dignified with the term 'worldview', into a fanatical devotee of a creed which demands the execution of an act of destruction that sends a message wrapped in terror to a target audience. Any syndrome postulated as being common to each process of terrorist radicalization is, of course, another ideal type. It thus involves reducing infinitely complex sequences of behaviour to a single pattern or dynamic model for the heuristic purpose of increasing their intelligibility and accessibility to researchers and policy-makers.

There is no suggestion here of applying a reductive 'one size fits all' approach to the individual trajectory that produces each terrorism, since the constellations of historical, socio-political, and personal factors involved in the genesis of terrorism have been extremely variegated, and are unique to each one of its manifestations, so that the act of violence commited can only be fully understood in terms of that uniqueness. Nevertheless, building on the first four chapters, a sustained exercise in 'idealizing abstraction' will be attempted here to identify the key steps in the radicalization process formulated as a generic 'syndrome', one which will hopefully illuminate and be illuminated by the individual examples of terror encountered in the subsequent chapters.

The first premise for this model was established at some length in Chapter 2, the innate need of human beings to feel their lives have a self-transcendent dimension and suprapersonal purpose. This dimension or purpose is variously described in the Human Sciences in terms of religion, culture, totalizing value system, narrative arc, transcendence, sacred canopy, nomos, or in some other formula which indicates they experience a meaning beyond, and hence of greater significance and duration than, their own brief, and, within a cosmic perspective, infinitesimally small and insignificant personal timeline. The corollary of this need is an instinctive, visceral fear of anything that threatens the coherence, vitality, or self-evidence of the nomos if it is already integrated within an individual's experience of the world, or the drive to generate a new nomos as the basis of such meaning if it has been destroyed or has always been missing. A second corollary is that growing up in the absence of a fully-fledged, 'solid' nomos – as so many modern individuals do – can make them, especially in the presence of objective forces of emotional, social, economic, or political deprivation or oppression, susceptible to the powerful negative emotions (affects) evoked by terms such as distress, dread, *angst*, terror, and ontological exile, loneliness, and homelessness. These may be experienced only fleetingly when the protective force-field provided by such factors as religious belief, ideological convictions, socialization, distractions, work, routine, obsession, or addiction breaks down. Yet even the occasional 'negative epiphany' that life is being lived out in a meaningless biosphere in an indifferent cosmos where everything passes may be sufficient to infiltrate liquid fear into an outwardly secure existence.

To the more empirically minded it may seem excessively speculative or bizarre to take a bleak existentialist premise about the black hole of absurdity that lies at the heart of the human condition as a premise to understanding the process of radicalization. It should thus reassure those of hale and hearty ontological disposition to find that several contributors to terrorism studies endorse this approach by attributing the origins of terrorist commitment at least in part to profound, even desperate, longings for ontological security. Thus the three authors of *In the Wake of 9/11. The Psychology of Terror* locate the ultimate roots of the Islamist attack in the threat posed by American foreign policy and by Westernization to Muslim religion, culture, and national identities. The book analyses the events of 9/11 and the response of the US government and citizens to it through the unusual lens of Terror Management Theory which we encountered in Chapter 2. As we saw, TMT's premise for understanding fanaticism is that it arises from a profound disturbance in the sense of belonging to a meaningful, purposeful cosmos guaranteed by a 'culturally derived worldview' that endows the world with 'order, stability, meaning and permanence'. Culture imparts to individual lives a sense of purpose deriving from the certainty that they are 'capable of transcending the natural boundaries of time and space, and in doing so, eluding death'.[1] Threats to cultural integrity, whether endogenous or exogenous, can thus create the conditions for extreme violence. Assaults on the integrity or self-evidence of the nomos, for example, the challenge of radically conflicting conceptions of reality or insidious cultural colonization by another society or other ethnicities, 'threaten to release the anxiety from which our conceptions shield us, thus undermining the promise of literal or symbolic immortality afforded by them'.[2] This, the authors add, can lead to the response of 'trying to annihilate' those who embody divergent beliefs, an impulse fully enacted in ethnic cleansing (which frequently involves terrorism) and genocide (which cannot, since there is no third party to be terrorized by the killings).

A similar conclusion is arrived at by Jessica Stern in *Holy Terror* as the result of numerous in-depth interviews with 'religious' terrorists to establish patterns in their motivation:

> Because the true faith is purportedly in jeopardy, emergency conditions prevail, and the killing of innocents becomes, in their view, religiously and morally permissible. The point of religious terrorism is to purify the world of these corrupting influences. But what lies beneath these views? Over time, I began to see that these grievances often mask a deeper kind of angst and a deeper kind of fear. Fear of a godless universe, of chaos, of loose rules and loneliness.[3]

Modernity, she realizes, 'introduces a world where the potential future paths are so varied, so unknown, and the lack of authority so great that individuals seek assurance and comfort in the elimination of unsettling possibilities'.[4] 'One-worlders, humanists, and promoters of human rights have created an engine of modernity that is stealing the identity of the oppressed'. Extremism is a response to 'the vacuity in human consciousness' brought about by modernity.[5] Chapter one of *Holy Terror* thus concentrates on the key role played by social and psychological alienation in fuelling terrorism.

In *The Blood that Cries out from the Earth*, James Jones reinforces these points. He stresses how modernization and globalization have failed to create a satisfying culture for millions in developing countries, such as Indonesia and the wider Islamic world generally, and has thus created a 'spiritual vacuum' which is the source of the appeal exerted by religious extremism.[6]

> In the anomie of our postmodern, global society with its smorgasbord of options and lifestyles, a religious conversion provides clear norms, a preordained answer to the postmodern dilemma 'who am I?' and a sense of rootedness in a timeless tradition that transcends and feels more substantial than the ever-shifting kaleidoscope of contemporary communities of reference.[7]

It is significant that none of these authors distinguishes between the nomic crises emanating from the breakdown of an existing nomos and inspiring what we have termed *Zealotic* forms of defensive aggression, and the type of nomic crisis into which the denizens of modernity are born and which they sometimes go to extreme lengths to resolve by converting to violent forms of programmatic *Modernism*. Nevertheless, there is a significant degree of convergence between our approaches. The fruitfulness of this line of inquiry into the roots of fanaticism is further reinforced by Eric Hoffer's slim but 'classic' treatise on political and religious fanaticism, *The True Believer*, written in the immediate aftermath of the Second World War when the memories of the mass rallies of Hitler and Stalin were still vivid. This offers a number of insights into the intimate relationship between anomy and blind faith in mass movements and in their leaders that apply just as well to the commitment of disaffected individuals to terrorist causes also. For example, he writes that when 'people who see their lives as irremediably spoiled' convert to a movement 'they are reborn to a new life in its close-knit collective body'.[8] The drive to belong to a community of faith, secular or religious, which provides a sense of ultimate purpose missing from an atomized, anomic individual existence leads to the 'selfish altruism' described by Dipak Gupta as intrinsic to the terrorist persona, and epitomized in the members of the jihadi movement whose 'acts of self-sacrifice transform them into god-like creatures, much beloved by God himself'.[9] Hoffer goes so far as to relegate the importance of ideology to a secondary factor, stating 'a rising mass movement attracts and holds a following not by its doctrine and promises, but by the refuge it offers from the anxieties, barrenness and meaninglessness of an individual existence'.[10] He sees all forms of self-surrender to a political cause as 'in essence a desperate clinging to something which might give worth and meaning to our futile, spoilt lives.'[11]

In the more clinical discourse of the post-9/11 social sciences, Arie Kruglanski endorses Hoffer's assumption by arguing that extremist ideologies exert a particular fascination on individuals suffering from inner confusion and a troubled identity because they are formulated 'in clear-cut definitive terms' and offer a sense of 'cognitive closure'.[12] They thus provide an antidote to what we have called the liquid, liminoid quality of modernity. In an era where all certainties are in meltdown, extremism offers a protective shelter from what Walter Benjamin called 'the storm of progress'. Kruglanski also contributed to an important multi-author paper which views 'diverse instances of suicidal terrorism as attempts at significance restoration, significance gain, and prevention of significance loss',[13] a phrase that contains the embryonic distinction between Zealotic ('significance restoration' and 'prevention of significance loss') and Modernist ('significance gain') terrorism.

Janja Lalich's study of the dynamics of the fanaticism generated by cults is also relevant here, since it highlights the role played in the process of radicalization by the need for 'cognitive closure' and 'personal significance' in an age of reality's permanent tendency to liquefaction. She carried out in-depth case-studies of two modern US cults, the New Religious 'Heaven's Gate' and the New Left 'Democratic Workers' Party' – of which she was a dedicated member before her voluntary de-radicalization and metamorphosis into a professional sociologist. On the basis of this field work she provides a sophisticated reconstruction of 'the intense reorganization of the person's inner identity, or sense of self' this process demands to transform a 'normal' person into a fervent adept, even (as in the case of the Heaven's Gate members) to the point of death.[14] She shows little interest in the initial state of anomy or personal life-crisis that may serve as a necessary but insufficient condition for what she sees as the twin process of conversion and commitment to a cult. However, she is highly lucid (perhaps because of her own experience) about what identification with a cult offers the convert.

At the heart of the new-found sense of belonging lies a discernible 'world-view shift' which endows life with 'meaning and purpose' combined with an 'activist stance' on everyday life underpinned by a 'transcendent belief system'. This is a world-view which offers a 'total explanation of past, present, and future, including a path to salvation' (a 'mazeway resynthesis', a *creed*) based on 'an exact methodology, or recipe, for the personal transformation necessary to qualify one on that path', or what we have called a 'totalizing nomos'.[15] Echoing the observations of Luciano Pellicani concerning the total certainty hungered for by God's orphans,[16] she calls the 'inner knowing' and 'true consciousness' which are 'necessary for salvation' a 'Gnostic' form of knowledge deeply bound up with dualistic ideas of good and evil.[17] The correspondence of her phraseology and Pellicani's concept of 'activist Gnosticism' is striking.

Lalich finds that what sustains the increasingly intense psychological commitment to the cult is its ability to satisfy the adepts' craving for 'personal transformation' which is subjectively fulfilled the more they feel they are being initiated into a new world of transcendence. It is an experience accompanied by a powerful sense of metamorphosis, of living on a new level of consciousness. This experiential 'opening up' is of necessity the concomitant of the *closing down* of the 'old world' of ambivalence, ambiguity, complexity and plurality. The liquid turns solid. This insight leads Lalich to talk of achieving 'personal closure'[18] within a 'self-sealing' system. It is a system made up of charismatic authority emanating from a 'guru-like' leader figure,[19] ritualized procedures of control imposed by the group or cult, and an overarching belief-system, producing a transformation in world-view which may eventually come to take over the inner and outer lives of initiates to the point of fanaticism and violent action. The freedom with which the 'gurus' in Lalich's analysis cannibalize various ideologies and beliefs to create the unique syncretic vision and ritual adopted by the cult has obvious resonance with Wallace's theory of 'mazeway resynthesis' as the basis for cultural revitalization. In short, conversion to a cult puts an end to what has been for the convert a distressing experience of anomy and the liminoid.

It is clear from Lalich's approach that the shift from a modern world of cognitive ambivalence to febrile, fanatical certainty is not brought about as the result of 'brainwashing'. It is due to a symbiosis between an inner drive towards transcendence and forms of external reinforcement or cognitive coercion which can be experienced as a sensation of 'freedom'.[20] Hence the paradox of 'bounded choice' which is so central to her analysis.[21] Though few cults are terroristic, or even violent, Lalich herself refers to the cultic dimension in the Ku Klux Klan, Timothy McVeigh's attack on the Oklahoma Murrah Building, the Aum Shinrikyo attack on the Tokyo subway, the Symbionese Liberation Army, the Weathermen, and the eco-terrorists of Earth Liberation. I would go further and argue that there is a cultic dimension to all radicalization, even if the charismatic authority and cultic community to which terrorists belong remain virtual and no violence ensues, and even if there is no other member of the cult than a single fanatic.

Stage Two: Splitting and the Manichaean world-view

If the initial situation of terrorist radicalization is one of nomic crisis or exile, then the path to total commitment can be seen as one of increasing psychological investment in defending, restoring, or regaining a nomic home (the Zealotic path), or finding a new one to adopt or establish through the realization of a (frequently utopian) project (the Modernist path). It is an impulse that may be experienced in far less metaphysical terms by the actors themselves as a process of overcoming a deep experience of humiliation,[22] of exacting revenge through retributive violence, or of transcending a sense of worthlessness and emptiness by finding a specific cause which seems self-evidently important and 'real'.[23] Except in the rare cases of someone creating a terrorist movement *ex nihilo*, the Modernist variant of the process is usually initiated when a disaffected individual predisposed to search for total solutions comes into contact with extremists (or their ideology) with whom (or with which) there is some sort of cultural affinity. The cell of God's orphans which formed around Verkhovensky in *The Devils* is an example. The Zealotic process can be triggered when something awakens a latent or weakened sense of belonging to a lost or beleaguered nomos, the central event in *Ours are the Streets*.

However, in the age of the Internet, radicalization may occur in the absence of a movement or cell of actual people. Certainly a guru or charismatic leader may be involved in the initiation. Lalich has shown this to be an important component in the most intense processes of cultic initiation that lead to total commitment to a cause to the point of death, but again, this may not be a living presence.[24] Especially within a Western context it may equally well be a virtual community made up of websites, pamphlets, and video-clips on YouTube, whose impact is perhaps augmented by sporadic 'human' contacts in real time, conversations, or radicalizing harangues by priests or leaders of extremist parties. However, all that is needed as a catalyst to conversion in some cases may be a revelatory text or group of texts (such as the Nechayev's *Catechism of a Revolutionary*, Mao's *Red Book*, Julius Evola's *The Revolt against the Modern World*, or William Pierce's *Turner Diaries*), or alighting upon a website which provides a voice and a narrative for long-held frustrations and hatreds.

We should not expect there to be a regular behavioural pattern in the early stages of radicalization. There must be some 'Road to the Damascus' epiphanies of the rightness of a terrorist cause, but many more gradual initiations into the closed universe of a fanatical vision. Nevertheless, whether initial contacts with the cultic milieu of radicalization are serendipitous or integral to the person's entire cultural background, the prospect of a nomic crisis or spiritual exile being about to end must sooner or later precipitate a powerful, almost alchemical transformation in his or her personality. Anomy is suddenly and dramatically, or gradually and piecemeal, transmuted to a sense of total nomos. Frustration, impotent rage, humiliation give way to a sense of empowerment. A sense of futility is replaced by a sense of destiny. Rays of light from a higher dimension penetrate the gloom to show a way out of the sense of isolation, alienation, or despair. The individual starts to feel that he or she is the agent of a higher cause or will.

It is at this point that an originally amorphous existence lacking any sort of coherent narrative arc starts to 'take shape', a shape that endows a previously anomic existence with distinctive mythic, dramatic, and aesthetic qualities. The feeling of having been born to serve a higher will or destiny, of being 'sent' to fulfil a suprapersonal historical, or even supranatural divine purpose crystallizes in the 'mission'. This locates the individual life within a powerful living drama in which the 'enemy', the source of decadence and evil, is unmasked and identified, enabling the solution to be visualized in a heroic struggle to establish, or to re-establish, purity and good. Jessica Stern alludes to the aesthetic, narrative aspect of radicalization when she comments that the mission 'must be so compellingly described that recruits are willing to violate normal moral rules in its name'.[25] Its psychological function is clear: to lift the previously anomized individual into a renomized or nomized temporal sphere of transcendence which is experienced as religious or secular salvation.

It is this redemptive, soteriological aspect of the terrorist's creed, the dramatic dimension of commitment that Hafez alludes to when he speaks of 'the discursive practices that inspire individuals to engage in self-sacrificial terror', and of the 'logic of liberation and personal redemption' that inspire people 'to make the ultimate leap toward a "heroic" end'.[26] His observations are echoed in Robert Robins and Jerrold Post's study of 'political paranoia' and 'the psychopolitics of hatred':

> The individual whose world is falling apart is experiencing his own psychological apocalypse. From this state of ultimate powerlessness and meaninglessness, *some create a world of meaning in their mind, a new world in which they have power and significance.* Through this vision they have found personal redemption.[27]

The intensification of the sense of mission can lead to the point where it becomes a fixation, a primary reality relegating to secondary importance all other aspects, including family and personal relationships and even survival itself, just as Nechayev demanded in his *Catechism of a Revolutionary*. For this to occur, a well-established process has taken place known in psychology as 'splitting'. Splitting, a concept first developed in the discipline of child psychology, involves the projection of 'bad feelings' and 'feelings of badness' experienced by the future terrorist onto out-groups to a point where the contemporary world eventually comes to be seen as a theatre of cosmic war.[28] He or she can then become enlisted in a Manichaean[29] fight to the death between opposing metaphysical, cultural or (for racists) biological principles on which the survival or death of humanity (or a chosen segment of it) depends.[30] From that point on all psychic and physical resources are devoted to achieving the 'symbolic objective'[31] of not just changing the status quo, but triggering the advent of a new era.

James Jones, a clinical psychologist, puts particular emphasis on this factor in his account of religious terrorism, emphasizing how the dichotomized, bipolar metaphysical world portrayed by organized religions predisposes ontologically insecure individuals who show 'impatience with ambiguity and an inability to tolerate ambivalence' to 'a splitting of the world into polarized all-good and all-evil camps and the demonizing of the other'.[32] In similar vein in his contribution to *The Fundamentalist Mindset* he states that the 'psychological preconditions for religiously sponsored terrorism and violence' is a preoccupation with 'purification'. As a result 'the search for reunion with the source of life can become subsumed into unconscious dynamics such as splitting and a Manichaean dichotomizing of the world'.[33] Mazarr makes a similar point when he locates the roots of the need for a culturally created, totalizing identity that dehumanizes others who do not share your world-view in the experience of existential dread, commenting that ethnic and religious strife are 'ultimately the result of a psychological inability to tolerate those who do not share one's death-denying illusions'.[34]

This line of analysis is further corroborated by Daniel Hill in his study of the psychological processes that engender religious fundamentalism. He argues that the 'mentalization' which enables a properly individuated person to tolerate ambivalence, embrace otherness, and experience empathy can become blocked in an existentially insecure person, leading to 'the projection, splitting and Manichaeanism' which are hallmarks of the fundamentalist mindset and the precondition for religious violence.'[35] But it is another terrorism analyst, Jerrold Post, whom we encountered earlier as an expert on political paranoia, who alludes to an equally important but neglected aspect of the radicalization syndrome when he adapts the term 'splitting' to refer not just to the dichotomization of the world, but to a phenomenon within the personality of the future terrorist. Once embarked on his mission he 'idealizes his grandiose self and splits out and projects onto others all the hatred and devalued weakness within'.[36] In other words, splitting is accompanied by the birth of a new personality, an enhanced, aggrandized self, one elevated beyond the impotence, inadequacy, and humiliation of the anomic self. The grandiosity[37] of the new self empowers him to act out the role of hero in the narrative drama of the mission with which he is charged. This new self is thus licensed to commit violence for the sake of the 'sacred' cause which they would never have felt morally permitted to perform in their 'private' lives and selves.

Heroic doubling

The phenomenon of self-aggrandizement that is the concomitant of splitting has been illuminated by a major writer on the social psychology of extremism and terrorism, Robert Lifton. In language that echoes Zygmunt Bauman's sociology of modernity's 'liquefaction', *The Protean Self* warns us in the opening sentence that 'we are becoming fluid and many-sided. Without quite realizing it, we have been evolving a sense of self appropriate to the restlessness and flux of our time ... The Protean self emerges from confusion, from the widespread feeling that we are losing our psychological moorings.'[38] One of the solutions to the dilemma which the psyche finds to cope with physically or morally painful situations is a strategy he calls 'doubling', a phenomenon he witnessed in Hiroshima victims, Nazi doctors and nuclear scientists. Lifton portrays it as a form of functional dissociative state maintained by *psychic numbing*.[39] In another chapter he explains that 'the self can respond to historical pressures not only by opening out but also by closing down'. In doing so it is taking refuge from the torments of identity and the liquid fears which proteanism bring by constricting itself to the point where it becomes a totalizing, simplistic 'fundamentalist self' (in the *non*-religious sense of the term).

Lifton sees 'doubling' at work not just in religious fanatics but in other 'true believers' such as Nazis, Maoists, and the proponents of ethnic cleansing, all of which tend to conjure up Manichaean fantasies of a world divided into good and bad. The 'fundamentalist self' they develop to carry out extreme violence is convinced of precipitating an 'end time' which will inaugurate a new era.

His characterization of the Christian conversion experience which leads to 'the fundamentalist self' is particularly relevant:

> We found that conversion usually followed upon a sense of severe life crisis, often involving a subjective experience or threat of falling apart, of disintegration or fragmentation of the self. That sequence – from the collapse or death of the self to illumination and rebirth – then takes its place at the centre of one's life narrative and one's identity as a Christian.[40]

It seems clear that Christian conversion is one permutation of the reconstitution of the anomic self in a new, fundamentalist self, fuelled by a religious or secular totalizing ideology (often, as we have seen, the product of an intense process of syncretism, of mazeway resynthesis).[41] This new self, though 'psychically numbed' in terms of conventional morality, can achieve a high level of psychic vitality and intensity within the framework of a terrorist mission. Experientially the fragmented, anomic, conventional self has often been left as a facade or shell of normality, while behind the mask the psyche has undergone a process of *heroic doubling*, resolving the existential problems that crippled the earlier persona's ability to feel alive and purposeful, born again as a 'new man' or 'new woman'.[42] In this context it is significant that Gregory Lande and David Armitage, who stress the centrality of the role 'splitting and doubling' to the terrorist radicalization process,[43] draw attention to the process of heroization and of psychological palingenesis which is integral to it:

> How does a person take on the role of terrorist? The psychological transformation of a person who is acutely aware of his frailty, into a person who is a heroic and potentially destructive bearer of an ideological or religious message is a dramatic one. The terrorist group provides the structure for this transformation. It provides a new belief system [creed]; ... it defines the terrorist act as morally acceptable; and, it presents a plausible way of achieving the outcome – all of which defines the terrorist act as serving the greater good.[44]

Seen in this way terrorist radicalization is no more than a special example or species of a much more general phenomenon that occurs whenever someone takes up a cause which implies a radical change in the status quo, even in a pacifist spirit. Thus the activists of the anti-capitalism movement of the new millennium 'see themselves as soldiers in an existential battle for redemption of the world from the evils of globalization'.[45] It is the same psychological process of 'cosmizing the self' through the terrorist *persona* that is explored in fictional detail through the character of Verkhovensky in Dostoevsky's *The Devils* and Imtiaz in Sahota's *Ours are the Streets*. Mazarr suggests that the need to find an existential home in the world can produce 'a desperate and sometimes violent search for the zealous embrace of a tightly bound community in service of a heroic cause' which can drive individuals into a terrorist network.[46] However, it is important to note that, in line with Lifton's theory of the protean self, the original, unfanaticized self is rarely totally replaced or destroyed by the process of doubling: it lurks unredeemed and unconverted in the background, needing constant reinforcement by the 'self-sealing system' and ready to leak out in special circumstances and allow a return to 'normality' or 'pre-existing self' which is, crucially, the key to the possibility of *de-radicalization*, a theme we shall return to in the last chapter.[47]

The recurrent magazine and media fantasies of heroic doubles (e.g. in the films *Superman, Spiderman, Wonderwoman, Batman, Iron Man, Heroes*, and so wonderfully parodied in the cartoon *The Invincibles*), suggest that through enacting in his life a process of self-heroization within a Manichaean scenario, the terrorist is living out an archetypal compensatory fantasy in which he is *at war* with an enemy identified by the totalizing myth that frames their lives. Ruth Stein argues in her Freudian reading of terrorist motivation (which places considerable emphasis on the Oedipal father complex), that the purpose of the letter which the 9/11 bombers read on the eve of the attacks 'was to transform a young Muslim into a warrior, instilling spiritual motives that create inner peace, fearlessness, obeisance, and lack of feeling during the killing', a clear case of heroic doubling.[48]

This transformation from civilian to warrior is considered by Stein a decisive moment in the radicalization process. Once someone suffering from a nomic crisis feels 'enlisted' by a higher cause this way it imbues him or her with a 'warrior ethos', thanks to a special psychological process discussed in Christopher Coker's book on the 'transformative' impact of war.

> [War] allows a warrior to tap into the vein of his own heroism. It allows him to lead an *authentic* life. In that sense, his life is never quite the same again. Battle can be akin to an epiphany or a religious experience. When we talk of the warrior soul, we do so because many of us must find a place for the sacred in our lives, and it is more than symbolic that the two words 'sacred' and 'sacrifice' etymologically share the same root. Sacrifice is the key to the warrior ethos.[49]

It is by living out and *realizing* through violence the metaphor of the 'warrior' that 'ordinary' persons with no prior military training can achieve the mental strength required to fulfil a deadly mission with no thought for their own lives or the suffering they cause. An archetypal account of this process is offered in nineteenth-century tract on the Japanese ethic of Bushido, *Hagakure*, translated as *The Way of the Samurai*, which celebrates the fact that 'it was a requisite for samurais of old to cut off heads before they reached fourteen or fifteen years of age'.[50] The manual can be seen as a psychological treatise on how to 'grow' a warrior self through a life of sustained stoicism and unpitying military self-discipline. This allows the individual to cultivate an intimate relationship with death so as to transcend the fear of death and death itself and so achieve that state of complete separation from the realm of compassionate humanity advocated by Nechayev in his *Catechism of a Revolutionary*.

Hagakure teaches the novice that he must 'die anew every morning and every night': 'If you continually preserve the state of death in everyday life, you will understand the essence of Bushido, and you will gain freedom in Bushido'.[51] Bushido is thus a total nomos in which the prospect of nothingness is not just glimpsed but stared into with defiant resolution until passive nihilism gives way to a form of vitalism fuelled by the readiness both to commit acts of extreme violence, and to die or commit ritual suicide (*seppuku*). The result is a state of 'postive nihilism' maintainable in everyday life within the elite community of the samurais. The text makes it clear that the warrior (as opposed to the professional 'soldier') can be thought of as existing in a 'heterotopia',[52] a special ethical and existential time and space which can be imagined – especially in the case of 'suicide terrorism' – as an intense microclimate of absolute nomic energy beyond self-doubt and fear. Within it he or she peers into the abyss of mortality and experiences the anguish resulting from the death of the 'small' self as transcended by the certainty of living according to a higher set of values accessible only to a small, courageous elite, and the possibility of living on in the collective memory as a hero and martyr.

The heroic double empowered by a warrior ethos is an archetypal fantasy encountered in the many epic cycles of the world's myriad religions and oral story-telling traditions, of which the Greek legends, Norse myths, and the Hindu Mahabharata are just those better known in the West. But the heroic double also has affinities with the universal religious topos of the believer perfected through faith, devotion, and self-sacrifice, the Nietzschean 'superman', and the 'new man' who has been the subject of totalitarian utopias of the left and right in modern times.

The self-heroization undergone during the process of terrorist radicalization has a number of important correlatives. One is that as the personality becomes 'Titanized', it enters a transformed experience of time-and-space, namely that of an end-time. For the Zealot the final showdown between a beleaguered tradition and its enemies is approaching. For the Modernist the decadence and anomy of contemporary history are seen as the death-throes of an old order which are, simultaneously, the birth-pangs of new one. The manic mood inspired by feeling part of a movement that is bringing about the transition to a new era is captured in Goebbels' autobiographical novel *Michael: A German Destiny* where his fictional alter ego writes, 'I am no longer human. I am a Titan, a god!... If we are strong enough to form the life of our era, it is our own lives that must first be mastered. A new law is approaching'. A new nomos. This passage expresses the profound link between heroic doubling and apocalypticism in terrorist radicalization. As Charles Strozier and Katherine Boyd observe:

> The apocalyptic indulges in dualistic thinking, violent images, and desire for the end of the world. A discourse wherein one's paranoia and rage are explained, justified and given direction. The apocalyptic provides fertile soil for the violent potentials in the fundamentalist mindset.[53]

The terrorist mindset can be energized by the fantasy that the dying culture can be protected from its enemies through violence or that the continuum of history can be exploded or broken in two, that the present can be made into a *tabula rasa* so that a utopia can be realized, but only through heroic acts of purging violence and blood-sacrifice. Jones finds the work of René Girard particularly illuminating for understanding the importance of the archetype of blood-sacrifice to the terrorist mindset. In *Violence and Sacrifice* he argued that in tribal societies the ritual slaughter of the scapegoat enabled the community to be reconciled and healed.[54] He went on to suggest that instinctively even modern, purportedly rational revolutionaries have followed the mythic logic according to which a holy war must be fought, blood must be shed, and evil in its human incarnations must be purged for a new social order to be established.[55]

A second correlative of the self-heroization involved in generating extreme violence has been illuminated by Klaus Theweleit in his classic study of the psycho-dynamics of Nazi radicalization, *Male Fantasies*. The ecstatic Titanization which can accompany heroic doubling is the subjective experience of becoming 'a new and self-born man within an apparatus which strips [the individual] of his ego boundaries'.[56] Such 'self-birthing' is undergone by those who are, in terms of mature individuation, 'not-yet-born' when they join a redemptive cause. But their new warrior personae can only be a travesty of genuine individuation. In psychoanalytical terms the terrorist has developed a false 'true self'.[57] Such an interpretation is consistent with the observation of Jerrold Post about the motivation to become a terrorist – though he clearly does not have in mind cases of radicalization which occur within concrete situations of enemy or state oppression, and which often involve physical threat and life-shattering psychological scars that have nothing to do with intrinsically unstable or split personalities:

> The act of joining the terrorist group represents an attempt to consolidate a fragmented psychological identity, to resolve a split and be at one with oneself and with society, and, most important, to belong.[58]

The Alice Syndrome

It is symptomatic of the perversion of healthy individuation that radicalization within a terrorist narrative arc is generally accompanied by an acute distortion of the relationship between inner and outer reality, in which the psychic inner world of the 'new self' assumes far greater significance than external reality. This can be seen as a special manifestation of condition which is known to psychiatrists as the 'Alice (in Wonderland) Syndrome', named after the scene in which Alice first shrinks and then grows after ingesting different sides of a (hallucinogenic?) mushroom. As the subjective self splits and doubles in the radicalization process, and the internal fissures are cosmized into an epic Manichaean worldview, the previously threatening, oceanic, amorphous external world is reduced to a miniaturized simulacrum divided between good and evil. By destroying symbols of 'evil' some particularly delusional Titanized minds believe they will be able, through the equivalent of sympathetic magic, to bring about the collapse or destruction of the whole 'bad' world they represent.[59] This fantasy was common among dynamite-wielding anarchists in the nineteenth century.

In his analysis of the absolute lack of concrete, realistic, achievable goals, which he sees as a characteristic of Italian terrorists in the 1970s, Franco Ferracuti cites approvingly Francesco Bruno's description of their conflict as a 'fantasy war', namely 'a process in which the terrorists believe themselves to be soldiers in a war against society, and in which the struggle to achieve a utopian world fulfils needs the terrorists cannot satisfy through the usual channels of socialization'.[60] (However it should be stressed that such an analysis obviously should not be applied to situations where terrorists pit themselves against objective, highly concrete forms of enemy or state oppression, as in the case of the Sicarii, Chechens, and Tamil Tigers, whose war was anything but 'fantasy'.) As Robins and Post have pointed out, the demonization of the Other in a Manichaeanized world involves dysfunctional cognitive processes akin to paranoia, no matter how 'functional' and technically proficient the cult member or terrorist remains in serving their cause and fulfilling their mission.[61]

In the paragraph headed 'On the Spur of Madness' *Hagakure* provides the personal testimony of a major samurai concerning the extreme mental state that the terrorist warrior must enter in order to kill efficiently without being paralysed by the compassion or guilt felt by 'normal' people in committing extreme acts of violence. He (or she) feels cut off from the concerns of 'the world' but not as a murderer filled with hatred, but as the proud member of a privileged, ascetic elite dedicated to ethical purity and the service of others in spirit of self-sacrifice, effectively anaesthetizing or numbing the conventional human conscience:

> Being that you are samurais, be proud of your valor and prowess and prepare yourselves *to die with frenzy*. Keep in mind to purify your everyday diction, thinking, development, and the like. And try hard to do it. The way to serve is to consult with people you can confide in.... And also realize that you are to devote your lifelong services to the interests of others. It is better for you not to know general information.[62]

Such a passage leads us directly into the peculiar kind of 'madness', or 'frenzy' which may often be concealed by a sustained façade of calm, icily-controlled 'normality' that often characterizes the fanaticism of the terrorist. It is inseparable from the terrorist's creed, the private nomic universe that makes it possible to transcend the dread of the abyss and dissolution, and instead act on behalf of a higher moral order, one which has its own internal logic and authenticity, no matter how 'mad' and contrived it may appear to outsiders. As Mazarr says, 'The fanatic grabs feverishly for reality by creating unreal, mythologized versions of it, and hopes to become authentic by playing a fabricated role in the myth they have thus authored.'[63]

It is the distortion of the reality principle by the false process of self-individuation into the hero of an apocalyptic narrative that helps account for what Hoffer calls 'the monstrous incongruity between the hopes, however noble and tender, and the actions which follow them. It is as if ivied maidens and garlanded youths were to herald the four horsemen of the apocalypse.'[64] As Hoffer implies, the recurrent *topos* of the heroized and fundamentalized mindset, whether in Zealotic or Modernist extremism, is the role of retributive violence and purging destruction as the magic catalysts to revolution. Pedahzur and Perliger observe that 'in both Jewish and non-Jewish religious terrorism' – and in non-religious terrorism as well – 'many perpetrators are driven by some sort of grand vision of a new order, believing their violent act will be the catalyst for this epic transformation'.[65]

Such a serious misreading of events is yet another symptom of the dysfunctional reality principle and the sustained confusion within the terroist psyche between the 'magic time' being played out in the interiority of the terrorist's psyche and what Walter Benjamin calls in *Theses on the Philosophy of History* the 'homogeneous, empty [anomic] time' of external reality. It leads to the fanatical, hermetic imposition of a palingenetic, apocalyptic narrative born of the revolutionary's longing for Gnosis onto the myriad brute, meaningless facts of a human world under the permanent dispensation of chronos, symbolized in Francisco Goya's famous painting of the Roman God Saturn feasting upon one of his sons. It is a time which of itself knows no grand narrative, end times, no *eschatos*, no apocalypse, thus parts of 'the external world' come to be ruthlessly butchered by an overexcited metapolitical imagination so as to force it to fit the Procrustean bed of the activist's utopia.

Dr Günter Rohrmoser, contributor to a government-sponsored investigation of West German terrorists in the early 1980s in the wake of the mayhem caused by the Red Army Faction, stressed this discrepancy between utopianism and mundane reality in their vision of the world, while also referring perceptively to the dualistic, apocalyptic mindset that underpins it:

> What do the terrorists want? They want The Revolution, a total transformation of all existing conditions, a new form of human existence ... the total and radical breach with all that is, and with all historical continuity. ... There is no voice that could call them back to reason. For them there is no connection between the vision that drives them and the existing reality. ... They are fascinated by the magic of extremes, the hard, uncompromising either/or, life or death, salvation or perdition. ... They are driven by a pitiless hatred for what they regard as their enemies, a hatred fed by disgust with what they regard as a morbid, decadent society.[66]

It is as a result of the processes of splitting and heroic doubling undergone in the course of their radicalization, that formerly anomic, disempowered, and spiritually exiled human beings find their suprapersonal home. They are thus able to derive ontological meaning and security from the prospect of committing acts of sacrifice of 'others' (what the Germans call *Fremdopfer*), even at the cost of sacrificing themselves (*Selbstopfer*).

Stage Three: The bliss of completion

The third stage in this ideal type of the radicalization process is the mindset in which the sanctity of the mission has been so internalized that acts of violence against society can be carried out not just guiltlessly, but with a sense of pride, and even of cosmic self-fulfilment. Rohrmoser's reference to 'salvation or perdition' in the context of Germany's highly secular terrorism in the 1970s is telling, once it is understood that the psyche experiences the nomos as holy even if it is an entirely secular, anti-clerical utopia. If the inner conversion process is complete, fanaticism is a state of grace, again underlining the significance of the etymology from *fanum*, meaning a sacred temple. In this final state of extremist consciousness, geared not to mystic contemplation but to violent action – and even martyrdom – on behalf of the cause, ordinary norms and parameters of existence fall away. Subjectively these modern 'warrior priests' are living in an apocalyptic, kairotic time outside linear, chronic history.[67] However, time is short.[68] It is *now* that the sacred tradition must be defended, the primordial holy nation created or recreated, the murder of innocents halted, the True Faith restored, the race purged of decadence, the Millennium imposed, the end of History 'forced' to its conclusion, the desecration of the planet prevented, the ideal society established.[69] History has reached its crisis point, the iron gates of Time are molten enough to be forged into a new shape through violent intervention. For the protagonist of the assault on the 'enemy' or the status quo, conviction has taken the place of confusion, partial knowledge has been replaced by redeeming Gnosis, the feeling of being mired in society's 'filth' has given way to being the chosen agent of its purification, the liminoid has been resolved into a definitive narrative, society's outcast has become the avenging angel of its nemesis, impotence has metamorphosed into complete self-possession, despair into bliss.

To use bliss in the context of terrorists may sound a discordant note, but here is the testimony of Jessica Stern on the basis of her extensive interviews with terrorists:

> Although we see them as evil, religious terrorists know themselves to be perfectly good. To be crystal clear about one's identity, to know that one's group is superior to all others, to make purity one's motto and purification of the world one's life's work – this is a kind of bliss.[70]

She also concedes that she has come to see 'that apocalyptic violence intended to "cleanse" the world of "impurities" can create a transcendent state' and can understand 'why the killers [she] met seemed spiritually intoxicated'. She goes on to state that 'all of them describe themselves as responding to a spiritual calling, and many report a kind of spiritual high or addiction related to its fulfilment'. People join religious terrorist groups 'partly to transform themselves and to simplify life',[71] in other words, to change anomy into nomos, thereby simplifying and sacralizing their lives.

Ruth Stein is able to use her psychoanalytical lens to dissect this blissful state further:

> The promise of fulfilment is not that of happy beatitude, of sated envelopment and plenitude, but of ascetic overcoming of oneself, transcendence of time and the body, and an assenting sacrifice of one's will in the service of a higher will. The regressive process of becoming mentally subjugated is both intensely relational and has affinity with the process whereby hate and fear are transformed into a perverted, enthralled 'love'.[72]

Nor are Stern and Stein alone in recognizing that the path to terrorism is the path to some form of fulfilment, to transfiguration. In a remarkable aside Mazarr alludes to the phenomenon we have called 'heroic doubling' which allows terrorists in the run-up to an act of murderous destruction committed by their warrior avatar to endure the utter banality of ordinary, anomic reality till their kairotic moment of special time finally comes. They thus resemble spies or secret agents working for a higher power, using their 'anomic' self as a cover story for the actual drama unfolding, like a real-life Clark Kent/Superman:

> But one is hard pressed not to think of the stolid, brutal authors of September 11, going about their placid lives and smoothly traversing their petty cares – going to the bank, filling their cars, greeting their piloting instructor with a smile and a handshake, brushing their teeth, watching a television sitcom – sustained by the conviction that they had taken their death inside, bought and owned it, and therefore achieved wholeness, achieved greatness, achieved authenticity.[73]

From his Swiss mountain top Nietzsche announced that 'The secret of reaping the greatest fruitfulness and the greatest enjoyment from life is to *live dangerously!*'[74] The most extreme Modernists of the deed wrench this principle out of the safety of the philosopher's snug mountain refuge, put on their boots, and set out along impossible ridges and slopes to create an avalanche, which in their distorted vision, will deluge the world. Meanwhile the Supermen and Superwomen of modern Zealotry carry out their heroic martyr missions to wreak death and destruction so as to save their threatened nomos or prevent the whole world sinking for ever into an ocean of degeneration. Naturally, the precondition for the mission's completion is that the nebulous Manichaean world-view has undergone a process of *focusing* which enables the most abstruse, utopian vision to externalize itself as a lethally practical form of terrorism. The totalizing vision has been channelled into producing a practical *plan* in which a specific material or human target is selected as a synecdoche of the forces of 'evil', 'the enemy', or 'the system' for attack, a target whose destruction will have a particular symbolic or emotional resonance for the intended audience which augments its terror effect on it. At this point we leave the sphere of terrorism's metapolitical creeds and make way for the many experts in terrorist tactics, campaigns, technologies, and actions to take up the story of specific attacks and campaigns.[75]

Two Hollywood takes on the metapolitics of radicalization

This three-stage model of radicalization may become considerably less abstract for readers if we consider how it applies to the plot of two major American films which will be familiar to at least some of them. Paul Schrader's *Taxi Driver* (1976) explores the intuitive, unreflecting struggle for a meaningful existence of Travis Bickle, an ex-Marine and Vietnam veteran whose life when we first encounter him is one of totally non-intellectualized disorientation, anomy, and moral squalor. Yet the disgust and anger grow to the point where he decides to take a personal stand against the physical and moral decadence he witnesses nightly in his job as a New York cabbie. He tells Charles Palatine, the presidential candidate who sits in his taxi, that the next president:

> should clean up this city here ... because this city is like an open sewer, it's full of filth and scum. Sometimes I can hardly take it.... Sometimes I go out and I smell it. I get headaches, it's so bad. It's like ... They never go away. It's like the president should clean up this whole mess here. He should flush it down the fucking toilet.[76]

Bickle certainly lacks the intellectuality, asceticism, and cold reflexivity of a Nechayevan Nihilist. Nevertheless, traumatized by his experiences of combat, denied any sort of recognition or gratitude for his sacrifices by the US society he had purportedly fought for, his hopes in an intimate personal relationship shattered, and the faith he placed in Palatine dashed, he, like his Russian counterpart, set about taking a personal stand against what *The Catechism of a Revolutionary* called 'the whole filthy order'. He equips himself with the fearsome armoury of a vigilante and transforms himself physically with a Mohawk haircut (the metamorphosis provides one of the most famous scenes in the history of the cinema). Bickle has created an alter ego, an avenging avatar. He has entered the liminal phase of the triadic *rite de passage* from citizen to terrorist, becoming a lone warrior in his own Manichaean drama of eradicating degeneration from New York. Spontaneously, with minimal politicization, he has carried out a process of heroic doubling to pursue the cause of a morally cleaned up city: half Zealotic, defending the homeland of a 'true' America, half Modernist, forging a new social reality where scumbags have been finally driven out.

After the unpremeditated shooting of a man attempting to rob a grocery store, he makes an abortive assassination attempt on Palatine, and then vents his rage against society's depravity in a raid on the brothel where an underage girl (Iris), whom he has decided to 'save', receives her customers, shooting dead the pimp, the bouncer and a client. They are the synecdoche in his Titanized world of the 'filth' to be flushed out. He only fails to take his own life because his gun is empty. He was prepared to die for his cause. As he repeatedly pulls the trigger he is serene. By taking on a suprapersonal mission he has overcome anomy and achieved redemption and self-possession. He is complete.

At one point the woman he tries to have a relationship with (who works for Palatine's campaign) says he reminds her of the character in the Kris Kristofferson song *Pilgrim Chapter 33*. The lyrics conjure up the image of a social misfit or drifter who had elements of 'poet', 'prophet', 'pusher', and 'pilgrim', making him a 'walkin' contradiction, partly truth and partly fiction'. The song also describes him as 'runnin' from the devils, Lord, and reachin' for the stars', and 'searchin' for a shrine he's never found', while 'losin' all he loved along the way'. On one level, then, Travis Bickle resorts to the identity of an urban terrorist to overcome a cosmic sense of abandonment, of being one of 'God's orphans'. As Travis gazes longingly at the signs of intimacy shown by a couple in the streets of New York he says in voice-over 'Loneliness has followed me my whole life, everywhere. In bars, in cars, sidewalks, stores, everywhere. There's no escape. I'm God's lonely man'. This is a direct allusion to Thomas Wolfe's poem *God's Lonely Man* that serves as the epigraph to Paul Shrader's film script. Metaphysical longings for purity, transcendence, sacrifice, and transfiguration, the hunger for a nomic home, lurk under Travis's inarticulate but highly eloquent actions.

Chuck Palahniuk's novel, *Fight Club*, published in 1995, opens with the unnamed narrator (called here for convenience 'Jack' as he was in the original film script) on the top floor of 'the world's tallest building' in New York which is about to be blown up, its foundation columns destroyed by home-made blasting gelatine. Meanwhile the 'space monkeys' working for an anarchist terrorist group called the Mischief Committee of Project Mayhem 'run wild' in the 191 floors below, 'destroying every scrap of history'.[77] Tyler Durden is holding a gun in Jack's mouth for reasons that gradually become apparent as the novel unfolds. Jack muses 'It's weird to think the place where we're standing will only be a point in the sky.... The photo series of the Parker-Morris building will go into all the history books', the last shot showing how it 'will slam on the national museum which is Tyler's real target'. Tyler comments 'This is our world, now, our world ... and those ancient people are dead.[78]

Both the novel and the film (1999) seemed to catch the Zeitgeist of post-Cold War America, the dark underbelly of Fukuyama's triumphalist 'end of history'. It quickly enjoyed a cult status, briefly turned 'fight club' imagery into a fashion statement, and launched a splattering of real fight clubs all over the world. Given the events of September 2001, the central terrorist event of the novel now exudes an oneiric premonitory quality: the attack on the financial district of Manhattan, chosen as a symbol of a society based on credit cards, consumerism, and conformism, the wilful destruction of a sky-scraper in New York to smash an icon of national culture and historical memory, the onslaught against Western culture and modernity. However, it is a novel that also provides a fascinating fictional case-study in the syndrome of radicalization we have been examining. In the extended flashback of the events that led to that moment of imminent death and urban catastrophe on the top-floor of the Parker-Morris building, we find that the narrator 'met' Tyler in an intense period of anomy. He is stressed out and alienated by his job as a cost–benefit analyst responsible for deciding whether defective cars should be recalled or not on the basis of the number of likely victims of accidents they cause and the resulting compensation claims.[79] He is apparently without friends or family, permanently jet-lagged, insomniac, increasingly convinced that he has lost control of his life. He attends several different support groups for people with serious life-issues (which means faking their symptoms) to try to get in touch with real feelings, but his life just gets weirder.

His understanding of the extent of his nomic crisis is revealed epiphanically to him only after he meets Tyler Durden, his anarchic, reckless, wild alter ego, who it is gradually revealed is as much an intimate part of his own persona as Hyde is of Dr Jekyll or the Steppenwolf is of Harry Haller.[80] Mediated through the agency of this Dionysian, nihilistic doppelgänger, Jack blows up his own flat, an artificial paradise of immaculate order and tidiness constructed from IKEA furnishing units, achieves a sustained awareness of his alienation, and takes drastic action to change his life. 'They' found a fight club where people let out all the pent-up hurt, humiliation, anger, disappointment, grief, bitterness, sense of failure and futility, angst, and fear by taking part in extremely violent bare-fist, no-holds-barred, bruising, bleeding punch-ups, a closed cultic community of cathartic violence, which eventually transmutes into Project Mayhem. Jack comments that 'Most guys are at a fight club because of something they are too scared to fight. After a few nights, you're afraid a lot less'.[81] After a few weeks the fight club is ready to act out its hatred of the society that made them so afraid, frustrated, and impotent. Its members focus and fine-tune their apocalyptic vision and select for ritual destruction the Parker-Morris bulding as a synecdoche of everything they hate.

The portrait that emerges of Jack before his 'conversion' to the life of a terroristic Steppenwolf is a case-study in the anomy experienced by millions trapped in the illusory existential security of a routinized modern, 'comfortable' life-style. It shows educated, 'successful' people painstakingly constructing 'iron cages' of rationalization out of flat-pack pine for themselves to live in an intrinsically absurd universe, and then spending the rest of the time anaesthetizing the pain of confinement and repressing the rebellious irrationality their situation incites. It also presents an intense psychodrama of what can happen if one day the psyche can bear the repression of authenticity and vital energies no longer, and makes a desperate escape attempt, violently breaking out of the trap created for it by tamely conforming to society's norms. Jack feels acutely the lack of a fixed point, a centre in modern life: 'Nothing is static. Everything is falling apart'.[82] He feels insignificant compared to Tyler, his vitalistic, psychotic alter ego, who makes nitro-glycerine out of human fat removed in liposuction operations (shades of Tom Robbins here), and whose obsession with authenticity makes him threaten to shoot a petrol-pump attendant if he does not give up his bum job and work to realize the dreams of a career he once nurtured in his adolescence. Jack feels so worthless that he deliberately drives into traffic to kill himself, his would-be last thoughts being: 'I am helpless. I am stupid, and all I do is want and need things. My tiny life. My little shit job. My Swedish furniture ... kill me'.[83] At another point during a particularly violent fight at the club Jack punches out his stabs of inner pain to the rhythm of 'everything you ever love will reject you or die. Everything you ever create will be thrown away. Everything you're proud of will end up as trash. I am Ozymandias, king of kings'.[84]

With the entry of Tyler into Jack's life, or rather with the emergence out of his protean self of an 'evil twin'[85] (Tyler is referred to at one point as Jack's 'identical twin')[86] who acts as mentor or 'psychopomp',[87] Jack's anomy is transformed by stages into an increasingly manic sense of mission which leads Jack/Tyler to invent Project Mayhem, whose aim is to disrupt the city's life with wanton acts of anarchy and vandalism, culminating with the plan to blow up the skyscraper. It is important for an understanding of terrorism in general that several motives are given for this campaign in the course of the book, reflecting the mixed motivation of terrorism in general. Consistent with Cozzens' analysis, they blend instrumental, utopian, and personal existential factors. One is

'negative nihilism', destructiveness without any ulterior end-purpose, a metaphysical Spartacus rebellion of *ressentiment* against a system in which the militants of
the Fight Club feel they have no place, no roots, no community. It is in this context that Tyler talks about the club's members as being 'the crap and the slaves of
history', and it is Jack's recognition of the truth in this description of himself that
makes him want 'to destroy everything beautiful I'd ever seen', to make 'the whole
world hit bottom'.[88] 'I wanted to burn the Louvre. I'd do the Elgin Marbles with
a sledge-hammer and wipe my ass with the *Mona Lisa*'. The purpose of Project
Mayhem is to 'blast the world free of history'.[89] Tyler claims that 'with enough
soap ... you could blow up the world',[90] and takes an infantile culinary delight in
cooking up explosives, in what he calls 'the nouvelle cuisine of anarchy'.[91]

However, in other moments the nihilism assumes a positive, *creative* aspect.
Tyler reflects that they have been born in an in-between age without 'a great war'
or a 'great depression', so, with nothing to shape their lives, they have to create
a 'great war of the spirit', and carry out a 'great revolution against the culture'.[92]
In this mood Project Mayhem is an act of positive nihilism 'that's going to save
the world' bring about 'a cultural ice age':

> Project Mayhem will force humanity to go dormant or into remission long
> enough for the Earth to recover. ... Like fight club does with clerks and box
> boys, Project Mayhem will break up civilization so we can make something
> better out of the world.[93]

It will also have the effect of empowering the participants, of allowing them to
overcome their sense of impotence and irrelevance. Its goal 'was to teach each
man in the project that he had the power to control history. We, each of us, can
take control of the world'.[94] Other passages make explicit Jack's underlying quest
for a nomos, something that transcends a cosmic void, even if it is experienced
as the wrath of a patriarchal God. The passage expressing this thought is directly
reminiscent of Pellicani's description of 'God's orphans'. Jack explains that, just
as some children behave badly to get the parents' or teacher's attention, so metaphysically exiled, abandoned, 'modern ' human beings may commit outrages to
grab cosmic attention:

> You spend your life searching for a father and a God. ... Could be, God hates
> us. ... God's hate is better than his indifference. ... We are God's middle chil-
> dren with no special place in history and no special attention: unless we get
> God's attention we have no hope of damnation or redemption. ... Only if we
> are caught and punished can we be saved. ... The farther you run the more God
> wants you back.[95]

Žižek has referred to this aspect of public violence as 'phatic',[96] a semiotic strategy
designed to draw attention to the presence of someone who feels ignored rather
than to communicate a definite message or pursue a clear strategy. But the phatic
violence of Project Mayhem here assumes the existential, religious dimension of
asking 'is there any higher force out there to punish me?' There is even an allusion

to a far less manic, more intimate aspect to the Project, that echoes the theme of bliss encountered in Ch'en's epiphany of 'complete self-possession' through political violence explored in Malraux's *La Condition Humaine*. Tyler muses 'Maybe we didn't need a father to complete ourselves'.[97] Such a thought implies that radicalization is a journey of self-discovery, of peeling off the false selves to come to the essential core, of completing a botched process of individuation that had become confused with socialization. It is echoed in a remarkable passage where, as their car hurtles through the streets at break-neck speed, the driver, referred to simply as 'the mechanic', shouts that as long as you are in the fight club you are not your job, your money, your family, your name, your problems, your age, or who you tell yourself'.[98] On one level the fight club thus provides the raw sensation of being alive, of living dangerously, of a vitalism uncluttered by any of the inauthentic roles ascribed to use by society: 'You aren't alive anywhere like you're alive at fight club'.[99] Its members have thus become existential heroes. The mechanic reassures Jack after his hair-raising drive he has just had a 'near-life experience'.[100]

Terrorism's pyrrhic victory

But what Palahniuk also brands in the mind is the psychological cost of this victory over anomy. Tyler Manichaeanizes the world into the 'good' fight club pitted against not just the whole of present society, but its whole past, all of which must be destroyed with only the faintest hope of anything positive emerging eventually, 'when the earth has recovered', to take its place. This radical splitting is accompanied by the most dramatic depiction of doubling. His process goes far beyond Bickle's make-over to become a Mohawk Indian. Jack literally creates a fully embodied double from his psyche who fights him, beats him up, blows up his flat, takes over his life while remaining invisible on security cameras. In fact the fight club and Project Mayhem may even themselves be mere figments of Jack's psychotic mind.

Indeed, one of the most powerful features of Palahniuk's novel, and of the subsequent film, is its sustained POV exploration of the confusion of subjective and external reality (in which all events are seen from the 'point of view' of the protagonist) which is the hallmark of what I have termed the psychological Alice Syndrome which is so often a feature of the terrorist mindset. By focusing on the existentialist crisis that precipitates the psychological rebellion against his fetishistically conformist life, the desperate quest that can motivate acts of apparently wanton violence is made accessible and intelligible even to those who have never had the conscious urge to 'break free'. This is no 'cry for help' in the conventional sense, though it does resemble the metaphysical cry that opens the first of Rainer Maria Rilke's *Duino's Elegies* and is immortalized in Edvard Munch's iconic painting, *The Scream*. It is the search for a more vital, more fulfilling, more real life, for community, for higher meaning, for the sacred, for nomos. *Fight Club* lays bare the inner mechanisms of a sociopathic psychosis, and externalizes the apocalyptic fantasies born of the fundamentalist self in conditions of extreme dissociation and alienation. It explores the process of Titanization that can condemn individuals *in extremis* to be engulfed in their inner symbolic world to the point where their role in the cosmic drama being enacted inside them dissolves the reality principle that inhibits fantasies of cathartic, sacralizing violence being enacted on fellow human beings.

When he believes the Parker-Morris building is about to explode, Jack states 'This is like a total epiphany moment for me'.[101] But the bomb does not explode. The recipe was wrong (or was there a bomb at all?). Recovering in hospital from the bullet he fired through his cheek, he is questioned by 'God' who sits behind a walnut desk taking notes on a pad and who tries to convince him that 'each of us is a sacred, unique snowflake of special unique specialness'. To which Jack's response is 'We are not special. We are not crap or trash either. We just are, and what happens just happens'. There is no epiphany, no release from contingency, no redemption, no completion. The third stage of the terrorist's triadic rite of passage is withheld. But nor he is completely cured from his addiction to the fantasy terrorist solution to anomy. The hospital cleaner reveals himself to be a member of Fight Club. 'We miss you Mr Durden.... We're going to break up civilization so we can make something better of the world'[102]

Fight Club, both as novel and mainstream film, had an extraordinary social resonance (as Palahniuk's Afterword of the 2005 edition documents). This was surely because it captured not just the post-Cold War and the post-everything mood of permanent liminoidality and nomic crisis in the citadels of modernity, but also the subliminal psychotic fantasies of 'smashing up civilization', of 'destroying the world to save it', of 'breaking history in two', of literally 'exploding the continuum of history', taking the stand against the nihilism of the 'last men' out of the impotent verbal histrionics of Nietzschean futurists, Dadaists, and constructivists, and turning them, at least fictionally, into what we have termed a 'Modernism of the deed'. Filippo Marinetti declared bombastically in point 10 of his Futurist Manifesto of 1909 that 'We want to demolish museums and libraries, fight morality, feminism and all opportunist and utilitarian cowardice'. But this was pure rhetorical melodrama, histrionic logorrhea. Tyler and his space monkeys set about actually demolishing the tallest building in New York, the epitome of modern civilization, so as to destroy the national museum, using nitro-glycerine made from home-made soap cooked from human body fat. *Fight Club* steals cultural modernism from the libraries and art galleries to which it is consigned, suitably catalogued and mummified, once its shock-value and novelty have died, and transports it into an arena of terrorist destruction which wants to wipe it out along with all history to make a *tabula rasa* of Western civilization, the ultimate minimalist installation, turning cityscapes into a Rothko canvas. Jack becomes a Modernist terrorist in the fullest sense. The book explores the pathological level of destructiveness that the terrorist creed can lead to, producing a state of mind where the external world has been totally subsumed within the solipsism of the 'warrior'. The terrorist's victory over anomy is thus a Pyrrhic one. Those who found the film simply 'cool', an inspiration for genuine fight clubs or fashion accessories, were sadly missing the point.

Yet Palahniuk is still a writer. *Fight Club* is still a novel – and a Hollywood movie starring Brad Pitt. Exquisite irony in the authorial perspective in both the novel and the film withholds certainty about whether Project Mayhem is any more than a paranoid fantasy even in the fiction of the narrative. The historical phenomenon of terrorism occurs when the real life equivalents of Verkhovensky, Mr Vlademir, Ch'en, the Woodpecker, Imtiaz, Bickle, and Tyler, and their counterparts in religious societies still not completely ravaged by modernity's anomy, burst out of the torments of their subjective inner world and cross the Rubicon to step onto the land of fanatical action transformed into cosmic warriors on a mission. This chapter has suggested that to take that decisive step their amorphous, chaotic world-view has, thanks to the combined processes of splitting and heroic doubling, taken on, whether gradually or suddenly, the distinctive narrative shape of a Manichaean drama in which they experience themselves as what Bob Dylan in the song 'Gates of Eden' calls the savage soldiers of good pitted against the forces of evil. Armed with the ideal types of Zealotic and Modernist terrorism and of the *rite de passage* from normality to fanaticism explored in the last four chapters we are finally in the position to sample actual episodes of terror that have occurred over the last 150 years to see what they have gained in intelligibility by losing some of their mind-numbing and reality-liquefying 'otherness'.

6
Modern Zealots of the Sacred Homeland

The modernization of Zealotry

The last four chapters have been devoted to establishing some basic heuristic tools for investigating the metapolitics of terrorism, the terrorist's creed. These, it should be stressed once again, constitute only *one* generic, but neglected, level of causation alongside the highly specific, 'concrete' social, economic, political, military, cultural, historical, and economic factors that condition each individual episode of fanatical violence. It would be a perverse reading of this book, one certainly *against* the intentions of the author, to form the impression that the defence of an existing nomos or establishment of a new one is somehow the 'real', or 'essential' subliminal motivation of the terrorist, all other factors being merely incidental epiphenomena. Equally, it should be borne in mind that the existence of a 'nomothetic' (i.e. nomos-creating)[1] level of terrorist motivation is relevant only to understanding the most ideologically motivated, genuine *fanatics*, who have made their religious or secular cause 'holy', not those who participate principally under duress, for reasons of personal vengeance, material gain, or criminal intent, or because of fear, emotional blackmail, a gang mentality, or the intrinsic, psychotic attraction of violence itself. 'Real' terrorists want their violence to communicate a symbolic message to a third party or target audience (which makes it in Žižek's vocabulary an act of '*phatic* communication'),[2] a message that cannot be ignored – like an 'offer that cannot be refused' – and hence to receivers who are *not* the immediate victims. The aim is to make the survivors, often placed at a safe distance from any personal threat, feel psychologically pressed into changing their behaviour or policies (or even their beliefs), or at least to feel deeply insecure in the world they call normality and which they hitherto took for granted as 'real'.[3]

After so much abstract modelling and a lengthy fictional excursus it is (high) time to put empirical flesh on the conceptual bones by considering some modern manifestations of what I have defined as the Zealotic species of terrorist acts of fanatical violence. Before this can be done, it is necessary to highlight the subtle impact that modernity has had on attempts to preserve a traditional nomos from destruction or re-establish its temporal security. In the modern age, the most fervent representatives of an intact religious-cultural tradition, though superficially the equivalent of the ancient Zealots or the medieval Alamut sect of Assassins defending Nizari Ismailism, turn out on closer inspection to have made significant concessions to secularization, the arch-enemy of all metaphysical cosmologies. This is because their nomos has been adapted to, and thus grown symbiotically connected with, the very modernity which they so forcefully resist through cathartic violence.

The intensifying forces of secularization and globalization of the last two centuries have over time accentuated the earthly foundations of sacred canopies which, before the advent of 'Western' modernity, always lay not in human institutions, temporal power, or expressly secular human utopias, but in one of myriad versions of an eternal metaphysical Law born contemporaneously with the primordial cosmogonic act which created the universe. As a result, the 'firmament' was in premodern cultures, however paradoxically to a modern sensibility, synonymous with the Heavens; it was the invisible, suprahistorical, *eternal* dimension of the spirit that supplied 'firmness' and solidity to the world, thus preventing its instant liquefaction and evaporation into chaos or nothingness. The intrinsically evanescent, illusory, *unreal* quality of human time before the age of secularism is powerfully dramatized in the cyclic conception of the universe recorded in the sacred Hindu text *Surya Siddhanta*. This posits a single *mahayuga* stretching from universal rebirth to final conflagration as lasting 4.32 million solar years. A single day of Brahma measures 994 *mahayugas*. A human life thus lasts less than the batting of an eyelid.

With the onset of modernity, the firmament comes to rest on an earthly, transient, and eventually entirely 'man-made' *terra firma*. The realm of the supratemporal and eternal are no longer substantial or self-evident enough to support the load-bearing pillars of ultimate reality, so this becomes secularized into a suprapersonal, but no longer supra-*human* or metaphysical entity grounded in secular time. Accordingly, the supernatural realm is increasingly borne aloft by events within historical time. The primary reality principle, once divine, starts to become 'temporalized', and achievements made within its orbit are judged in terms of a terrestrial, solar rather than an eternal, cosmic, or mythological timescale. At this point, the mythic Tower of Babel, originally built like a siege tower to scale Heaven, changes its nature. Already in the Book of Genesis the edifice is referred to as 'a city with a tower'. With the onset of secularization, Babel is gradually transformed into an inhabited, intrinsically meaningful structure in its own right: it becomes the world's first skyscraper, teeming with this-worldly life. The terrestrial sky sinks lower, the heavenly sky recedes. With the rise of secular reason and the gradual temporalization of utopia and the Beyond, totalizing human projects, despite their secularity and ephemerality, gain substance as purposeful undertakings with their own nomos-making, cosmogonic power and legitimacy.

This humanization and terrestrialization of sacred time is illustrated magnificently by Pieter Brueghel the Elder's *The Great Tower of Babel*. It was painted in 1563, when Europe's Christian cosmology had been thrown into turmoil by the combined effects of the recuperation of Classical knowledge in the High Renaissance, the proliferating geographical discoveries of 'new worlds', and the dizzyingly rapid strides of theoretical and empirical science. By the nineteenth century, the rise of Christian, then secular humanism, had led to what the German poet Friedrich Hölderlin called 'the flight of the Gods'. In their absence, towers of Babel had come increasingly to be built in the mind's eye, not to mount from earth to heaven, but to set up 'Heaven on Earth',[4] producing the entirely earth-bound Babel envisaged by socialists in Dostoevsky's *The Brothers Karamazov*. Within this cultural climate, even the most other-worldly traditional nomoi become ever more desacralized, politicized, and even militarized. Premodern battles for secular power were probably always conceived in religious terms or fought under a sacred pretext. However, with the onset of modernity, fundamentalist religion could take on the totalizing political aspirations of secular utopianism to be realized 'on earth'. Alternatively, the 'land and the people' could be sacralized to a point where they formed a nomos to be defended as zealously as any scriptural truth or sacred creed, with or without an admixture of traditional religion.

Zealotry in the modern age can thus still take the form of a belligerent religious fundamentalism (of course not all fundamentalisms are violent), but many of its most militant sects now pursue an agenda which involves changing human society or history itself through political violence which is no longer exclusively religious in character. Or else it is expressed in a form of ultranationalism, a modern phenomenon asserting the interests of an allegedly 'sacred' people bound together by such non-religious indices of ethnic homogeneity and distinctiveness as shared culture, language, historical continuity, customs, primordial homeland, 'race', or a blend of any of these components. For millions a suprahistorical heavenly or divine sphere has receded into the realm of myth rather than being a lived reality. However blatantly this-worldly the resulting nomos may be when analysed 'objectively', it displays magic prophylactic properties to protect human beings from the abyss of absurdity when it is experienced psychologically as 'sacred'. Maurice Barrès' famous lecture of 1899 on 'La Terre et les Morts' ('Land and Ancestors'), and the popularity of the name he gave to the road which carried hundreds of thousands of tons of supplies to the fortress town of Verdun when it was on the front line in 1916, 'La Voie Sacrée', are just two of countless examples of the modern Zealotic nomization and sacralization of a people constituted as an organic *ethnie*. In such cases the nomos is no longer imagined by a combination of culture, ritual, tradition, and metaphysical cosmology, but by a holy people or nation[5] threatened with degeneration and disintegration from within, the fear of which haunts Barrès's fiction, or an enemy from without. George Mosse's two groundbreaking studies of the 'sacralization' of the nation in nineteenth-century Germany, *The Nationalization of the Masses* and *The Crisis of German Ideology*,[6] chart this process which was to have such catastrophic results for Western 'civilization' between 1914 and 1945, resulting directly or indirectly in the deaths of scores of millions.

Religious fundamentalism again

A major source of insight in clarifying the process by which Zealotry assumes a partially or wholly secular dimension is Shmuel Eisenstadt's sociological analysis of the ideological dynamics of 'fundamentalism, sectarianism, and revolution'.

He offers a global survey of how modern history is shaped by the interplay of these three forces, and adduces wide-ranging evidence to show that they have all arisen in response to the growing dilemma induced by a modernization process. Consonant with the analysis of modernity suggested in Chapter 2, he sees the origins of the dilemma in the way this process undermines all the 'totalizing world-views' (i.e. 'nomoi') so vital to human culture and existential survival. He thus endorses the stress which Max Weber places on the 'contradiction...between an overarching vision through which the modern world becomes meaningful, and the fragmentation of such meaning generated by the growing autonomy of the different institutional arenas – of the economic, the political, and the cultural' under the process of rationalization.[7] On the basis of this approach, Eisenstadt locates a 'central dividing point' in modern political discourse, namely between pluralists and anti-pluralists. While the former defend the value of competition between multiple views of what constitutes the common good or ultimate value as necessary to promote liberal democracy, individual freedom, and rational progress, the latter viscerally reject the resulting pluralism, experiencing it as a source of life-threatening (i.e. nomos-threatening) anarchy and decadence. Clearly anti-pluralists tend to develop the 'fundamentalist mindset' discussed earlier.

When anti-pluralists commit themselves to eradicating any 'heterodoxy' or deviations from the norm they seek to impose in the name of a new social order freed of ambivalence and doubt, it produces what Eisenstadt calls ideal-typically 'Jacobinism' in a way which parallels Pellicani's use of the term 'activist Gnosticism' we encountered in Chapter 4. This he defines as:

> the strong predisposition to develop not only a totalistic world-view, but also overarching, totalitarian, all-encompassing ideologies, which emphasize a total reconstruction of the social and political order and which espouse a strong, even if not always universalistic, missionary zeal.[8]

Jacobin ideologies hold that 'totalistic political action' is necessary – as well as the violence, death, and destruction such action implies – in order to implement a 'transcendental vision' of the ideal society.[9] For Eisenstadt, the Jacobin interpretation of the French Revolution personified in Saint-Just and Robespierre is paradigmatic of such a totalizing ideology, leading to a 'reign of terror' to revitalize the project of destroying the *ancien régime* and creating a new social order inspired by the transcendental vision of a future world based on liberty, equality, and human solidarity. Between 16,000 and 40,000 citizens died in the name of the new order, victims of the totalizing force of modern utopianism. However anti-modern for those who naively equate modernity with democracy, Jacobinism 'developed fully in conjunction with the political programme of modernity' and is hence itself a form of political modernism. When manifested in a militant form of religious fundamentalism, it assumes the paradoxical form of a 'modern Jacobin anti-modern utopia',[10] a form of activist Gnosticism that seeks to destroy the present order in order to install, or make room for, an alternative modernity under a new sacred canopy.

In an important passage Eisenstadt highlights the fact that it is not just secular ideologies of total societal change – corresponding to what we have termed political modernism – that assume Jacobin qualities (though the liberalism of the French Revolution retained deistic notions in the concept of 'Supreme Being'). What distinguishes the 'proto-fundamentalism' of the Jewish Zealots from modern religious fundamentalisms is the way the most militant religious fanatics now pursue the modern *Jacobin* goals of bringing about a radical socio-political transformation within secular history. They dedicate themselves to a struggle not to usher in a divinely ordained 'End Days' like sixteenth-century Christian millennarians, but to bring about a permanent new order brought about through human agency inspired by God's purpose for humanity as laid down in scripture (according to their reading of it). For Eisenstadt it is 'the specific Jacobin tendencies or characteristics that constitute the most important common characteristics of these movements and which justify, in our mind, the term fundamentalism for all of them'.[11]

Elsewhere the Israeli sociologist draws a distinction between 'fundamentalist' movements (e.g. the radical form of Shi'ite Islam that established the Iranian theocracy after the 1979 Revolution) and 'communal-nationalist-religious' struggles. These seek to secure cultural hegemony and political independence for a particular territory mythically conceived as defined by a unique, geographically-delimited nomos often in a Jacobin, totalizing spirit, but without emphasizing the primacy of religion as the sole ethnic marker, let alone seeking to universalize a (highly politicized and militarized) fundamentalist form of it as the destiny of the whole globe.[12] Akin to 'communal-nationalist-religious' struggles are 'communal-national' ones where the religious element is a secondary factor in defining a unique nomos of cultural identity, or may have disappeared altogether from the way the ethnic community is imagined. However, in all three cases the living nomos to be defended or renewed still has its roots in an idealized religious or historical past and is not created *ex nihilo* in a utopian future. Thus all three, with their 'strong tendencies to the ritualization of violence',[13] thus correspond to what I have called 'Zealotic' forms of politics as an incubator of terrorism.

Eisenstadt contrasts these with radical anti-traditional, anti-religious, and anti-democratic movements which produce the *secular totalitarianisms* exemplified in communism and fascism.[14] These clearly correspond to what I have called 'Modernist' forms of politics, left and right,[15] which seek to resolve the nomic crisis of modernity by realizing a totalizing project for an alternative modernity which does not attempt to restore or defend an existing nomic order. In other words, while Eisenstadt uses Jacobinism as a blanket term for totalizing schemes for revolution, this book proposes the distinction between Zealotic (fundamentalist, communal-nationalist-religious, communal-national) movements and Modernist assaults on the status quo, left or right, all of which can assume violent, terroristic forms of expression.[16] It emerges from this analysis that contemporary Zealotic terrorism will tend to contain a modern, secular, Jacobin dimension, just as there is a 'religious' element in secular Modernist terrorism deriving from the sacralizing dynamic of fanatical revolutionary activity. It is a situation evoked by the taijitu, the dynamic Taoist yin/yang circle, and underlines the fact that both 'Zealotic' and 'Modernist' are are ideal types which have a purity that cannot be matched in reality. Chapter 8 will show how in certain circumstances the two types can actually form hybrids in which they become inextricable.

Chechen rebels and Tamil Tigers revisited

The value of Eisenstadt's analysis for understanding the metapolitical basis of contemporary terrorisms lies in the emphasis it places on the 'Jacobin' elements of secular, futural, and hence *Modernist*, utopianism which has insidiously infiltrated, or been proactively appropriated by, militant religious fundamentalism. This approach is particularly revealing in the evaluation of Islamist terrorism as a blend of Zealotic with Modernist elements in Chapter 9. Yet while 'Jacobinism' may be the appropriate generic term to refer to the totalizing 'transcendental visions' which Modernist terrorist movements seek to impose on the historical process, it would be misleading to use it to cover the fanatical defenders of a traditional nomos. These have no totalizing or revolutionary agenda to start historical time anew in an unprecedented new order, but rather seek to get it back on track after a deviation into decadence. Also the slippage detectable in Eisenstadt's highly schematic and abstract categorization of terrorism between (religious) 'fundamentalist' and 'communal-national' movements demands empirical clarification. In practice, the 'modern anti-modernism' of contemporary Zealotic terrorism is a highly complex, dynamically changing product of historical and contemporary forces, each case displaying a unique constellation of factors which can make the distinction between the two movements difficult to draw.

To illustrate this we will briefly revisit the extremism of the Chechens and Tamil Tigers encountered in Chapter 2, before considering Sikh and Jewish struggles to secure, create, or complete the sacred homeland. We have already seen that in the first phase of their protracted struggle with Tsarist Russia an idiosyncratic form of Islam blending Sufism with pagan traditions served as an ethnic marker for the Chechens in their Caucasian homeland in a way which would suggest that their struggle was 'communal-national'. Yet after centuries of perfunctory Islamization, Sufi missionaries finally succeeded in transforming Chechens into practising Muslims in the eighteenth and early nineteenth centuries, so that Jeffrey Bale, who has studied modern Chechen terrorism in depth, warns against assuming that 'in the 1990s the Chechen resistance movement was essentially a secular, nationalist movement with irredentist aims' concealed behind an Islamic façade.[17] In reality, Islam had become integral to the nomos that Chechens were seeking to defend. From the mid-1990s, Chechnya underwent a process of Islamic radicalization as Saudi-backed Wahhabism swept aside Sufism. Chechnya was declared an Islamic Republic and, under the influence of the Global Salafi Jihad, plans were developed within the new Chechen fundamentalist communities to conquer neighbouring Dagestan and create a larger Islamic state.[18]

Thus the metapolitics of Chechen anti-Russian guerrilla warfare and terrorism has shifted over the last 200 years from communal-national, to communal-nationalist-religious, to internationalist fundamentalist. This has produced tensions between secular and traditional Sufist Muslim Chechens, both concerned principally with securing freedom for their homeland, and a new generation of religious fundamentalists who insist that Chechnya is one of the many battle fronts in the apocalyptic world war being fought against the *kuffar*, or infidels, and world of *jahiliyyah* (apostasy and moral decay) by the warriors of an Islam now seen as the global solution to all humanity's ills (thus introducing a non-fundamentalist, Modernist, hybrid element into their ideology).

As a result of the ensuing radicalization in the demonization of 'the enemy', Islamist rebels executed a number of non-Islamist Chechen leaders, civil servants and clerics in 2001 in circumstances recalling the Zealotic assassinations of Herodians as an 'enemy within' 2000 years ago. To categorize the creed of any one episode of Chechen terrorism thus demands a forensic investigation of the worldview and motivation of the individuals responsible, and of the purpose of the attack almost on a case-by-case basis to establish whether Chechen paramilitary units are 'simply' trying to restore a (heavily idealized and mythicized) pristine Chechen ethno-cultural-linguistic 'submerged' nation, or are working beyond that, or even instead of that, to restore the lost Islamic Caliphate on a new global scale as the basis of a new world order. In the terminological shorthand we have just established, is their cause a communal-nationalist-religious, fundamentalist, or a hybrid of both? This in turn is a classification that has to integrate the recognition that Islamism itself is not a 'pure' example of fundamentalism. Instead, it contains elements of hybridization with theologically extraneous, temporal ideological causes and goals typical of what Eisenstadt calls the 'Jacobinization' of modern fundamentalism (a point which will be developed more fully when we return to Islamism in Chapter 9).

The metapolitics of the Tamil Tigers' fight for their homeland were constituted very differently. Michael Roberts' close study of the LTTE[19] quickly dispels any notion that they represent a form of Hindu fundamentalism, or that they had 'Jacobin' aspirations to impose a totalitarian nationalist state in northern Sri Lanka,[20] let alone Marxist ones, as some international socialists vainly hoped. Nor is it correct to allege that the militia movement used coercion and intense propaganda to brainwash the civilian population. The Tamil sense of nationhood, popular sovereignty, and cultural identity which became such a powerful political, paramilitary, and terroristic force in the second half of the twentieth century, had deep roots in the unique ethnic-cultural and historical self-awareness forged by the Tamil settlement of Sri Lanka from the tenth century BC onwards. This has its own intricate ethnic, military, and religious history which refutes essentialist claims concerning a 'pure' Tamil nation (of course, all claims of ethnic, racial, or religious purity reveal themselves on closer inspection as being based on mythic thinking).

Between 1949 and 1970, Tamil identity was expressed in a 'sectional nationalism' nested within the powerful surge of Sri Lankan national identity unleashed by the granting of independence from the British colonial rule. Although overwhelmingly Hindu in religion and tradition, Tamil nationalism, as we saw in Chapter 2, accommodated a sizeable Muslim minority (with whom ethnic tensions have sometimes flared up) as well as a small Christian one. Initially Tamils sought peaceful coexistence with the vastly more populous and territorially extended ethnic Sinhalese population. The centre-ground of early Tamil politics was a moderate federalism, pursuing not separatism, but legally guaranteed social, economic and linguistic inclusion in the new nation with a degree of regional autonomy. The nomos was not yet experienced as being beleaguered or threatened to the point where it could breed the paramilitary attacks, fanaticism, terroristic violence, and the relentless succession of atrocities and martyr bombings which became the order of the day in the 1980s. It was the draconian programme of Sinhalization and the increasingly violent regime of military repression imposed by the majority Buddhist government that inevitably led to the emergence of Tamil secessionist and irredentist ultranationalisms – especially after the destruction of the Jaffna library in 1981. It fell to the most ruthless and fanatical of these groups, the LTTE, to assert its hegemony over its most radical currents. It is worth noting that 'irredentism' comes from the Italian *terre irredente*, 'unredeemed lands', and already contains religious connotations about the 'sacrality' of the homeland.

From the start, the LTTE was thus a 'communal-national' rather than a 'communal-nationalist-religious' movement, though it was dominated by Hindu cultural consciousness. In the 1970s the group even adopted the vocabulary of radical socialism, but, apart from a genuine hostility to the caste system and administrative corruption, this was largely cosmetic, reflecting the way anti-colonial and secessionist struggles the world over used Marxist discourse at the time. This became clear when the movement dedicated ever more energy to perfecting an elaborate political religion whose purpose was to encourage identification of all Sri Lankan Tamils with the 'sacred' cause of Tamil Eelam now in mortal danger (a predominantly *secular* goal which did not involve the fundamentalization of Tamil religions). Once threatened, this nomos, in the spirit of all beleaguered organic nationalisms, assumed for those who based their existential creed on it an increasingly intense transcendental and 'eternal' significance, one that dwarfed the importance of any individual life, and held out the promise to those who died heroically for its sake at least a temporal immortality in the collective consciousness of the Tamil people.

Significantly, Roberts refers to the way the concept of Tamilttay ('Mother Tamil') provided the 'overarching "parasol"' for LTTE ultranationalism. Once the Tamil motherland rather than religion was idealized as a 'sacred canopy', hyperpatriotic Tamils could experience total identification with the Tamil 'people-nation-state' to the point where the 'gift' of their own lives as a 'weapon' in the fight for this cause was seen as 'a form of fulfilment, rather like an arduous pilgrimage or rolling on the ground for miles in the course of a meaningful religious festival invoking a deity's beneficial power'. This is no simple metaphor. Roberts claims that an important factor in developing the fanatical mindset which made so many Tamils prepared to die for Eelam was the secularization of the Hindu tradition of Kavadi. This obliges the devout to make propitiatory offerings to deities, a penitence which has always led a small minority in all the world's Tamil communities to endure a rite of 'ascetic mortification'. This sometimes involves extreme *self-inflicted* suffering to complete the process of purging all desire and attachment to the world. The deeply personal and private sense of existential self-possession experienced by Ch'en in Malraux's *Human Condition* had become under the LTTE a collective, almost mass-produced experience of public, *spectacular*[21] self-sacrifice.

Maintaining the Tamils' new 'sacred canopy', or 'sacred parasol', to meet the nomic needs of a people literally threatened with extinction required the rapid deployment of cultural resources to create a new political religion. This was successfully carried out through an intensive process of mazeway resynthesis which integrated suicide terrorism within a cult of 'Tamilttay'. Roberts documents the emergence of elaborate ceremonies commemorating past battles, heroism, and communal suffering, lushly painted backdrops replete with the traditional imagery associated with dance and folk theatre, as well as ancient martial, lyric, and lament music disseminated in DVDs, cassettes and videos, all produced 'to glorify the achievements of the Tigers'. Integral to this total mobilization of culture in the fight to preserve the Tamil nomos – a blend of traditionalism and media-savviness characteristic of modernity – was the cult of the leader Prabhakaran, finally killed in the massacres of May 2009. The new political religion appropriated an ancient Hindu tradition, originally entirely metaphysical in content, of 'adoration (bhakti, pattu) offered to many human beings perceived as harbouring something divine, whether it is great musical talent, rhetorical power or the strength to keep a family together'. Far from being cynical propaganda, Roberts is convinced by the evidence he has seen that LTTE 'personnel of all ranks and ages' maintained 'a devotional regard for Prabhakaran as a brother (annai) with god-like qualities'. Everything about the movement's creed at the height of the war with the Sinhalese government suggests a deep process of temporalization of originally metaphysical categories of ritual and belief had taken place to supply the Tigers' creed.

What also emerges clearly from Roberts' account is the impossibility of understanding LTTE terrorism without taking seriously the elaborate metapolitical cosmology that rationalized its Nibelungen-like 'last stand'[22] in May 2009 to defend the vision of Tamil Eelam to the last man and woman. He reveals the unique way the Tamils forged, out of indigenous religious and cultural resources, their own version of the 'religion of nationalism' which has always shrouded 'the political in the symbolism of a "higher purpose"', thereby turning the nation into 'the object of devotion'. In other words, the LTTE successfully transformed 'Tamil Eelam' for many, if not all, Sri Lankan Tamils into their sacred nomos, using cultural and religious traditions to sanctify their cause and turn a significant section of the Tamil population into Zealotic terrorists. Typical of this process was the way their increasingly fierce warriors' ethos sanctioned the most ruthless murders, and the way accounts of bloody self-sacrifices were infused with motifs from ancient Cankam poetry, the 'devotional elements of the bhakti religious movements of Southern India' and the 'practices of surrogate sacrifice that are commonplace in Tamil Saivite worship'. The result was a death cult reminiscent of the Japanese kamikaze pilots and the terrorists of the Romanian Iron Guard. The underlying

affinity between Tamil communal nationalism and Hindu religious fundamentalism is thus stronger than might first appear, even if it was not formally based on a
fanatical reading of Hindu scripture.

It is worth noting that the porosity between fundamentalism and ultranationalism is illustrated differently, but no less clearly, in the state Buddhism
whose modern warriors eventually crushed the LTTE. Since the earliest Buddhist
occupation of the island, Sinhalese Buddhism has been distinct from its mainland parent, much as Tibetan and Japanese Buddhism have their own marked
idiosyncrasies. Over the centuries it has developed rituals and myths to tolerate
the presence of non-Buddhists in an island that some considered the cosmic centre
of the Dharma, and the mythical origins of the Sinhalese Buddhist nation were
held to lie in a mingling of immigrant Hindus, Indian Buddhists and indigenous
peoples.

Navarila Dhammaratana, an Indian Buddhist monk who has made a special
study of Sinhalese Buddhism, has traced how in the late nineteenth century the
Buddhist counter-reformation in Sri Lanka was spearheaded, bizarrely enough, by
the Theosophist and close associate of Madam Blavatsky, Colonel Olcott. His missionary zeal led to the rapid 'theosophication' and Europeanization of Buddhism
in the 460 Buddhist schools he established on the island.[23] This remarkable development in turn set the scene for Anagarika Dharmapala, who, after a bourgeois
and Methodist upbringing, converted to Buddhism, and undertook the task of
transforming the pluralist indigenous tradition of his new-found faith into an
ethnocentric myth which proclaimed Sinhalese racial superiority over the other
ethnic minorities on the island. Now imbued with the Aryan mythologies of
superior and inferior races so prevalent at the turn of the century and latent in
Theosophy, Sri Lankan Buddhism was now equated in school text books with
civilization and 'the racial individuality' of the Sri Lankan people, while the Judeo-
Christians and Tamil Hindus on the island were portrayed as carriers of a decadent
barbarianism. The lethal legacy of Dharmapala was to create an exclusive, modernized Buddhist nationalism on a par with other nationalist perversions of religion
which have sullied the history of Christianity, Judaism, Islam, Hinduism, Sikhism,
and Shinto.

After 1948 state Buddhism quickly lost its commitment to universal compassion and hardened into what one expert has described as 'Sinhalatva'a creed 'just
as rigid and uncompromising as Hindutva (Hinduness) in neighbouring India',
which has also been responsible for the rise of 'Saffron terrorism'.[24] This surreal term refers to numerous episodes of fanatical violence committed by Hindu
militants whose ideology was a blend of fundamentalism with a Modernist cultural nationalism reminiscent of the European New Right. It was enriched with
strands of extreme ethnocentrism and racism which, in the formative period of
the 1930s, was conditioned by the Nazis' myth of racial purity and organic nationhood (*Volkstum*). Thus one of Hindutva's most influential ideologues, Vinayak
Damodar Savarkar (1883–1966), wrote chillingly in 1938, 'If we Hindus in India
grow stronger in time, these Moslem friends of the league type will have to play
the part of German-Jews. . . . India must be a Hindu land, reserved for the Hindus'.[25]
In terms of the conceptual framework developed in these pages, Hindutva is thus

another example of a Zealotic-Modernist hybrid. It emerged from a convoluted process of 'mazeway resynthesis' necessary to adapt Hinduism to the realities of a rapidly modernizing post-independence India awash with acute socio-economic pressures and sectarian tensions. These posed a major threat to traditional Hindu communal life in Northern India. Thus Hinduism's successful translation into particularly robust forms of ethnic separatism in party-political, military, and terroristic forms since the creation of an India as a multi-faith secular state in 1947 is not an endogenous phenomenon. It is to be seen in symbiotic relation to the increased political radicalization, Islamization, and recourse to sectarian terrorism of Indian Muslims as a way of solving their own social marginalization, demonization, and identity crisis.[26]

The first ominous sign that Sinhalatva had poisoned Sri Lankan Buddhism to a degree that made the federal solutions sought by ethnic and religious minorities unrealizable was the attempt by Tamils in 1958 to stage a *Satyagraha*, a collective act of pacifistic civil disobedience pioneered by Gandhi to demonstrate the superiority of 'soul force' over violent confrontation. In the event, 10,000 peaceful demonstrators were fired on by the Sinhalese police, causing over 100 casualties. This policy of repression, rationalized by a fundamentalist corruption of Buddhism with strong Modernist components derived from ultranationalism and European racism, inaugurated the systematic use of state terror and deliberate nomocide carried out by the ostensibly democratic state of Sri Lanka. It was a policy that culminated in the systematic, some would say genocidal, extermination of the LTTE fighters and many thousands of innocent civilians in May 2009, not before Tamil fanatics had themselves committed large-scale terrorist atrocities on the enemy.

The Sikhs' quest for Khalistan

Sikh separatism provides another rich case study in the way 'Jacobin' and Modernist elements can infiltrate Zealotic terrorism, as well as the fuzzy boundaries that can separate its different varieties. Contemporary Sikh terrorism has grown out of a combination of a beleaguered religious tradition and a powerful current of 'submerged' secessionist nationalism, and hence displays elements of both 'fundamentalist' and 'communal-nationalist-religious' Zealotry. Though overshadowed by Islamism since 9/11, it has in the past been able momentarily to grab the attention of the world's media with spectacular attacks on civilian life. To mention airplanes and terrorism in the same breath now conjures up such images as German special forces storming the Boeing 737 of Lufthansa Flight 181, hijacked by Palestinian terrorists to Mogadishu to secure the freedom of the Baader–Meinhof Gang leaders in 1977, or the Lockerbie Disaster of 1988, when an explosion on board Pan Am Flight 103 cost all 259 lives. Most of all it brings back fleeting memories or ghostly imaginings of the passengers being flown to their deaths by the four planes used in the 9/11 attacks. What has been largely erased from collective memory, at least outside Canada, is the terrorist attack of June 1985 on a Boeing 747 of Air India Flight 182 travelling from Montreal to Delhi via London.

It was one of two mid-air explosions planned to occur that day when bombs hidden within radios loaded inside unaccompanied suitcases were detonated. By a twist of fate, the other device exploded before being put onto Air India Flight 301's cargo hold at Tokyo's Narita Airport. The Boeing that was struck crashed into the Atlantic, killing 329 people, including 280 Canadians, 27 British citizens, and 22 Indians. The simultaneous mid-air explosions had been almost certainly planned by a group of Sikh separatist nationalists, the Baabar Khalsa International (BKI), working in close collaboration with members of the International Sikh Youth Federation (ISYF), one of whom was eventually found guilty of making the bombs. They targeted the planes of India's international airline as a potent international symbol of an Indian state which they held responsible for the violation of their culture and the systematic oppression of their people by a state that in their eyes was effectively run for and by Hindus. Based in the diaspora Sikh community in Canada, the plotters realized their attack would attract far more media exposure than any outrage committed in India, and they were right.

Through this spectacular act of 'phatic communication' which touched the nerves of the whole 'civilized' world (i.e. the travelling public), the increasingly international Sikh separatist movement aimed to force the Indian government (the receiver of the message) to allow it to realize their dream of an autonomous Sikh homeland in the Punjab to be called Khalistan, 'Land of the Pure'. The attack illustrates once again how the Alice Syndrome can convince fanatics to substitute their mythic imaginings of the world for external reality to the point where they ruthlessly destroy what have for them become mere ciphers of the demonized 'enemy', thereby causing devastation to living human beings utterly unconnected with the sacred cause they pursue.

Such Sikh militancy has deep historical roots. It dates back to the early seventeenth century when the sixth Guru, Har Gobind, organized Sikhs into a militia to resist the threat of foreign occupation by the Moghul Emperor Jehangir. According to tradition, the religious identity they were defending, Sikhism, the last of the world's 'Great Religions', originated in the revelations which God made to Guru Nanak (1469–1539). Although raised in humble circumstances in the Punjab, the prophet then undertook a series of five epic journeys to discover Higher Truth, an undertaking that brought him into contact with the several locally-competing religious cultures (nomoi) in the Indian subcontinent and the Middle East, as well as Christianity and Judaism. The Punjab had always been an area of migratory settlement, invasion and cultural intermingling. However, in the late fifteenth century it found itself caught up in the imperial ambitions of the Mongols (known by their Persian name, Mughals) and the struggle for hegemony between Muslims and Hindus. It was thus a period of profound anxiety and liminoidality.

The revitalization movement led by Guru Nakuk exemplifies the highly creative syncretism that weaves a new nomos apparently from nothing, a process of mazeway resynthesis involved in the genesis of all new religions, but whose mythopoeic mechanism can only become apparent to non-believers. By hybridizing Hinduism – particularly elements of Vaishnavism with its stress on active devotion ('bhakti') – with Islam – especially its monotheism and Sufi mystic tradition – a new monotheistic religion was born rejecting the polytheism or idol worship found in Indian popular culture, and emphasizing the need to break free from *maya* or illusion, a basic principle in both Hinduism and Buddhism. In principle, Sikhism cultivates a powerful sense of divinely ordained cosmic order by sanctifying the numeral one as the signifier of an omnipresent and infinite God (*ik onkar*), visible only to the inward heart and eye of the enlightened. These are not confined to any one race or gender (God is ungendered in Punjabi), because through meditation all human beings, whatever their culture, can learn to experience God directly as the creator of life, not just on earth, but on other worlds within the universe. One of Guru Nakuk's pronouncements was that 'There is no Hindu, there is no Muslim, so whose path shall I follow? I will follow God's path. God is neither Hindu nor Muslim'.

A strong sense of primordial cosmic order thus pervades Sikh theology, since God's will (*hukam*) existed before creation and brought the material universe into being in a way reminiscent of the primordial *logos* of Biblical cosmogony. *Prima facie*, Sikhism thus would seem to contain from the beginning an ideal doctrinal basis for various forms of nature mysticism, transcultural humanism, and inter-ethnic harmony. The stability and growth of this remarkable New Religious Movement which put down roots and flowered in a region of intense cultural and political wars, was guaranteed by the principle of 'Guru Succession'. This principle (reminiscent of the Christian Apostolic Succession) lasted until 1708 when it was abolished by the Tenth Guru, but by then it had ensured the constant refinement of Guru Nakuk's original teachings, and the adaptation of the scriptural and ritual traditions in which they were enshrined to a constantly changing historical situation. This innovation allowed Sikhism to become the core of an expanding, self-confident religious community.

The transformation of Sikhism into a political religion celebrating the warrior ethos was – again, according to tradition – the work of Hargobind, the Sixth Guru of the Sikhs. Legend has it that he carried two swords symbolizing spiritual and temporal power, the *mīrī* and *pīrī*. This abrupt militarization and 'ethnicizing' of the Sikh cosmology can be attributed to the growing success of the Sikhs in establishing their own independent state and unique political identity in the Punjab, which had brought them into direct conflict with the Moghuls. In 1699 the tenth Guru, Gobind Singh, founded the Khalsa as a warrior caste combining strict religious observance with political obligations and military discipline to defend the infant Sikh community from attack. From this time on, the global humanism and pacifism latent in original Sikhism was eclipsed by a powerful tradition of militancy and patriotism reminiscent of the Judaic Zealots and the Ismaili Assassins. The effectiveness of the new Sikh Confederacy made up of warrior bands known as *misls*, put the temporal leaders of the Sikh community in the position to take advantage of the subsequent decline of the Moghul Empire in the region. By the death of Maharaja Ranjit Singh in 1839 the Sikh empire stretched from Peshawar in Afghanistan to the borders of China.

The nemesis of the Sikh empire was not the Moghuls but the British, who under the East India Company fought the two bitter Anglo-Sikh wars (1845–46, 1848–49) to secure their economic and thus political and military domination of the Punjab. Inevitably groups arose to agitate for Sikh independence from the British empire, notably from within the Namdhari religious sect, and there were notable conspiracies and acts of defiance by militants, but it was the gathering momentum of the Indian independence movement after the First World War that provided the context for Sikh separatism to become an organized paramilitary force in the Punjab. The Babbar Akali was established as an underground terrorist movement in 1921, and was only crushed after pitched battles with British police. Sporadic murders of British soldiers and police officers followed, but the most famous incident was the assassination in 1940 of Michael O'Dwyer in London's Caxton Hall. He had been Lieutenant Governor of the Punjab at the time of the Jallianwala Bagh massacre of 1919 when some thousand Sikhs were killed on the occasion of one of the major Sikh religious festivals being held in Amritsar.

The Indian Independence Act of 1947 created autonomous ethnic states for Muslims, but the legal assurances that Sikhs would enjoy a semi-autonomous status in the new India came to nought. Having survived the threats posed to their nomos by the Moghuls and the British, many Sikhs now felt that their culture was about to be marginalized or engulfed by an independent but overwhelmingly Hindu India. It was a situation that inevitably fostered secular 'communal-national' separatism, but also militant forms of fundamentalism (invoking Sikh scripture) that supported the Khalistan Movement,[27] such as the Akhand Kirtani Jatha (AJK) group that arose in the 1980s. However, until the late 1970s the separatist aspirations of the Sikh community were, like those of their Tamil counterparts, still largely channelled into peaceful protests and democratic lobbying for language rights, equal representations, and an end to discrimination. Yet despite some concessions, many Sikhs continued to suffer from the relegation of their unique culture to the pariah status of a religious and ethnic minority, and the psychological pressures imposed by social exclusion and anomy were growing.

The tipping point for the radicalization of Sikh separatism into a major international terrorist force was Operation Blue Star carried out by the Indian Army in June 1984 on the orders of Prime Minister Indira Gandhi. Its ostensible aim was to show respect for the Golden Temple (*Harmandir Sahib*) in Amritsa, the most sacred space in Sikh culture, by putting an end to its occupation by hundreds of armed political activists who had taken refuge there. They were members of Damdami Taksal (DT), a fundamentalist religious group supporting Sikh secession from India. Its real motive was much more likely the tactical one of attacking Sikh terrorists. The bitter fighting led to 83 military deaths and some 500 civilian casualties. But aside from the sheer scale of the bloodshed, it was the material destruction of the temple and of over 1,500 rare manuscripts held by the Sikh Reference Library it housed which marked out the operation as a deliberate act of nomocide by the Hindu state. There are striking parallels between this state-sanctioned act of desecration and biblioclasm in Amritsar and the burning of the Jaffna library by the Sinhalese three years earlier.

222222

The fanatical defence of the Sikh nomos now entered its most violent phase. On 31 October 1984 Indira Gandhi was assassinated by two Sikh bodyguards. It was an act of calculated vengeance against the person who had ordered Operation Blue Star, but also the synecdochic destruction of the ultimate personification of Hindu state power. A year later Air India Flight 102 was brought down in the Atlantic by Babbar Khalsa International, whose name deliberately evoked the original warrior caste formed by the Sixth Guru. It originated in 1978, not as a result of clashes of Sikh separatists with Hindus, but with members of the Sant Nirankari Mission, a Sikh 'New Religion' which invokes the transcultural humanism of early Sikhism to establish Universal Brotherhood throughout the world. More spectacular kidnappings, assassinations, and attacks on the Indian state followed, culminating in August 1995 with the suicide bomb detonated outside the government complex in the capital of the Punjab, Chandigarh, killing the chief minister of the Punjab state along with 15 aides and security guards. It also sent shock waves through one of Le Corbusier's most iconic modernist buildings.

Modern Sikh terrorism is a highly complex phenomenon, organizationally and ideologically, which has been responsible in four decades for many hundreds of lethal attacks on the Indian state and many thousands of deaths. It is symptomatic of the general rise in parts of Asia with a deeply embedded tradition of sectarianism tensions, of fundamentalized, politicized, militant, and terroristic forms of Hinduism, Buddhism, and Islam. This phenomenon is the natural expression of growing ethnic tensions and struggle for economic and social resources in areas of dramatically expanding populations, mass poverty, and economic development where modernization and globalization are occurring in major cities at a vertiginous pace compared with nineteenth century Europe. It is a nexus of factors that is creating a profound nomic crisis for all traditional communities, not least for the seven million of the Sikh diaspora.

What is significant for understanding the modernization of Zealotry is the emergence of over 16 groups prepared to fight for the creation of the Khalistan homeland and thus preserve the sacred Sikh canopy from destruction, not by fighting for the restoration of religious purity, but by establishing the temporal state necessary to safeguard the nomos from destruction: a temporalized utopia. The Heavenly City of the first Guru accessed through meditation has now become for Sikh fundamentalists an Earthly City located in the Punjab where an exclusive faith can be practised, or, for Sikh communal-nationalists, an end in its own right. The notable fundamentalist separatists are the AKJ, DT, and the Bhindranwala Tigers Force of Khalistan, a name which invokes both the DT's religious leader killed in Operation Blue Star and the Tamil Tigers.[28] The communal-nationalists are such groups as the BKI, ISYF, and the Khalistan Commando Force. The large number of diaspora Sikhs sufficiently fanatical about the Khalistan cause to join organizations such as the International Sikh Youth Federation (banned as a terrorist organization under Indian, British, Canadian, and US anti-terrorist legislation) are overwhelmingly communal-national rather than fundamentalist in orientation.[29]

Thus, while the early history of Sikh militancy illustrates the tendency of all beleaguered traditions, in this case a fledgling one, to resort to Zealotic violence to defend the nomos, the later history shows how modern Zealotry tends to channel its nomos-preserving energies differently. Religious sects arise not only concerned with restoring the purity of the original religion from corruption or defending the faith from attacks by the militants of rival religions, but also with creating a territorial homeland and sovereign political state within which this purity can be institutionalized and defended from external aggression, thereby subtly secularizing and Jacobinizing the religion. Or else communal-national groups appear whose pursuit of an independent homeland takes precedence over metaphysical issues of doctrine and orthodoxy, even to the point of operating as a secular paramilitary formation and committing mass atrocities. In the Sikh case the quest for a homeland has resulted in acts of indiscriminate violence against civilians, their futility recalling the bombings carried out as 'propaganda of the deed' by nineteenth century nihilists. Meanwhile the sovereign Khalistan remains as much a mirage as it ever was. Undeterred, its terrorist devotees persist in rejecting one of the original tenets of their faith which asserted that divine truth is not invested in any one faith. As far as they are concerned, Guru Nanak was wrong: God is not Muslim, nor Hindu, but *Sikh.*

Recovering the Promised Land of the Israelites

Extremist violence born of Zionism, both before and after the creation of Israel, is no less revealing for an appreciation of the complex metapolitical dynamics of modern Zealotic terrorism for several reasons. First, as we saw in Chapter 1, it was the Zealots under Roman occupation who created the context for the emergence of the Sicarii, the first well-documented terrorist group dedicated to the defence of their territorial and religious nomos. Their memory has been invoked by Jewish militants in the twentieth century to inspire the struggle for Israel, underlying the continuity of what Eisenstadt calls 'proto-fundamentalist' (premodern) with (modern) 'fundamentalist' religious violence characterized by its Jacobin dimension. Second, the ensuing Jewish Disapora, which lasted some 2000 years, demonstrates the extraordinary ability of what became, in time, a geographically scattered and ethnically and linguistically heterogeneous people, one generating many internal sectarian differences and heterodoxies, to retain an overwhelming sense of collective identity and destiny. It was enabled to perform this feat through the power of religious and cultural traditions to preserve intact the memory of a primordial nomos identified with a sacred territory despite the advent of modernity.

Central to this feat was the fact that, in the times of the Torah (the Old Testament of the Christians) the Israelites were granted through their religion[30] a powerful sense of their own ethnic superiority, their elect status within God's plan for the earth, and exclusive possession of metaphysical Truth with respect to all other peoples and cultures, thanks to their unique relation to the single, omnipotent creator deity. Moreover, part of this privileged status, which was transmitted largely through bloodline rather than conversion, was exhibited by the divine promises enshrined in the Holy scriptures. These revealed that the Jewish people's ordained destiny and sacred duty within historical time is to inhabit a Holy Land or Promised Land and repossess it if lost. The concept of Palestine as the 'Holy Land' (in Hebrew *Eretz HaQodesh*), and the notion of Jerusalem as its holiest city, is common to Christianity and Islam, but only in Judaism has the obligation to return and resettle the Land of Israel (*Eretz Yisrael*) been an integral part of religious observance, with commandments (*mitzvoth*) that can only be observed on Jewish soil. In the words of one commentator, the Jewish territory thus becomes a portal to the divine, metaphysical realm that is the only true reality:

> The uniqueness of the Land of Israel is thus 'geo-theological' and not merely climatic. This is the land which faces the entrance of the spiritual world, that sphere of existence that lies beyond the physical world known to us through our senses. This is the key to the land's unique status with regard to prophecy and prayer, and also with regard to the commandments.[31]

The Holy Land within Jewish thought thus represents an outstanding example of the ideal type of the premodern sacred canopy, amalgamating myth, ritual, ethnicity, cosmology, secular and sacred history, culture, tradition, and Hebrew conceived as the 'true', divine language of worship, whatever other language was spoken. As a result of this unique combination of factors moulding Jewish national consciousness and identifying it with a particular sacred territory, metapolitical myths were to play a vital role in modern times in sustaining the successful political and paramilitary irredentist campaign of Zionists to create the secular State of Israel. However, as with Sikhism and Islam, 'fundamentalism' in Eisenstadt's specialized sense is a problematic term to apply to political Judaism since there are so many discrete Jewish theological traditions. Long before the tribulations and persecutions of modernity culminating in the Shoah, particularly embattled Diaspora communities in Spain and Eastern Europe were developing ultra-orthodox variants of Judaism with no irredentist aims. This was in marked contrast to the rise of ultra-assimilationist variants in other Jewish communities in which Jewish culture increasingly replaced Jewish religion as a source of identity with the result that Jewishness became extensively hybridized with the culture of the host society.

The more secularized elements within the Ashkenazi communities of Europe thus provided a social habitat receptive to the rise of European ultranationalism, and hence communal-nationalist notions of the Jewish nomos, in the mid-nineteenth century. In the wake of the tide of anti-Semitism unleashed by the Dreyfus affair in France and the rise of political anti-Semitism in Vienna – a development also reflected in pogroms in Russia and Eastern Europe – the idea of a heroic movement of irredentist nationalism to reclaim Palestine as its historic homeland had a powerful resonance in the more integrated and assimilated Jewish communities. The most powerful expression of this project was provided by Theodor Herzl, the founder of Zionism, in the political manifesto *Der Judenstaat* (The Jewish State) of 1896, and the utopian novel *Das Altneuland* (The Old New Land) of 1902. These envisaged a secular state retaining the best of European liberalism and culture, including religious tolerance, where Jews and Arabs could live in harmony. Under Max Nordau's influence, early Zionism also embraced eugenic principles and set about changing the perception and self-image of Jews by promoting a cult of the 'warrior Jews', close to the land, physically strong and courageous, and embodying 'muscular Judaism'.[32]

Herzl's legacy was a strong wave of 'ethnic nationalism' focused on the creation of the sovereign secular state of Israel in line with liberal European principles of self-determination and nationhood. It took ideological form in the continuation of Herzl's Political Zionism, the Labour Zionism that became dominant in the 1930s, and the Revisionist Zionism of Ze'ev Jabotinsky's New Zionist Organization founded in 1935, dedicated to the principle that the 'Jewish homeland' could only be liberated by force. (Note the assumption that the primordial Holy Land was under foreign occupation.) All pursued a 'communal-national' solution to the increasing threat posed by unfolding events in Europe to the Jews. However, it should be noted that the Judaic religious tradition had instilled into all three groups the vision of a national territory broadly coterminous with the Biblical Holy Land, however liberal or egalitarian the system of government envisioned, so even the most secular Zionism had a latent religious component. This component was naturally far more pronounced in Religious Zionism, a strand of 'religious politics' that initially spread among a section of Orthodox Jews under the influence of Rabbi Kook in the first years of the twentieth century.

Even before Herzl's utopian novel was published, the Rabbi had published the first of three articles which anticipated the later orthodoxy of Religious Zionism. He claimed, not only that the creation of the State of Israel in Palestine was the fulfilment of certain prophecies in the Torah, but that the irredentism of Political Zionists contained, unbeknown to them, a divine Jewish spark which Religious Zionists would one day turn 'into a great light', a subtle appropriation of secular Jewish irredentism. This is a supreme example of the modern temporalization of what was originally an exclusively religious vision. Another source of religious inspiration for Zionism was provided in 1902 when orthodox Jews at a conference in Vilna founded Merkaz Ruchani, devoted to the principle 'The Land of Israel for the People of Israel according to the Torah of Israel'. Reflecting Eisenstadt's distinction between 'proto-fundamentalism' with its largely other-worldly orientation, and 'fundamentalism' as a 'modern anti-modern' ideology with Jacobin elements, the state-building project of Religious Zionism was rejected as excessively secular and heterodox by spokesmen of the older ultra-orthodox (still 'proto-fundamentalist') traditions, such as the Sephardhi, Haredi, and Hasidic Jews.

In contrast, Religious Zionists conceived the reconstitution of Israel as a precondition of the fulfilment of Biblical prophecy. Whereas Political, Labour and Revisionist Zionism displayed purely metaphorical elements of Messianic thinking in their evocation of the imminent new beginning for the Jewish people, the Messianism of Religious Zionism was literal. (The fact that one of the factions of Revisionist Zionism was called 'the Messianists' points to the religious currents bubbling up from underneath Revisionism as well.) In the heaven-directed cosmology of Religious Zionists, any political or eventual military campaign to repossess Palestine was considered justified by ancient passages in the Torah, as in this one, taken from Numbers 33.50–55 in the Hebrew Bible:

And ye shall drive out the inhabitants of the land, and dwell therein; for unto you have I given the land to possess it ... But if ye will not drive out the inhabitants of the land from before you, then shall those that ye let remain of them be as thorns in your eyes, and as pricks in your sides, and they shall harass you in the land wherein ye dwell.

Such words led Religious Zionists to believe that by reclaiming and reoccupying the Promised Land, they would hasten the arrival of the Messiah and the salvation of God's chosen people.

What can be gleaned from this complex tangle of overlapping sacred canopies, stretching from 'cultural', secular, and pluralistic to ultra-orthodox religious, all successfully resisting the nomocidal forces of modernity endangering the Judaic nomos? In the context of Zealotic terrorism, what stands out is the emergence of two basic strands of Zionism by the early twentieth century. One was overtly secular and nationalist (communal-national) in the modern sense, the other more 'communal-nationalist-religious' and fundamentalist (Messianic), but both bore a Judaic imprint in the way they imagined the homeland. This dichotomy helps explains the emergence of two separate terrorist campaigns. The first was waged by Revisionist Zionists to recreate the nomos and reoccupy Eretz Yisrael. It was fought with genuine religious zeal directed towards carrying out retaliations against Arabs, putting pressure on Labour Zionist 'moderates', and murdering British soldiers defending the Palestine Mandate and keeping the peace between the conflicting Arab and Jewish communities. It is no coincidence that the context for the first outbreak of Jewish Zealotic violence was the Great Arab Revolt in Palestine (1936–39) and the imposition of the British Mandate in Palestine, both perceived by Jewish nationalists as a deep threat to the restoration of their people's nomos. The second, far more sporadic terrorist violence would occur after the creation of the State of Israel in May 1948, and was the work of Religious Zionists directed at Palestinians and 'Herodian' fellow Jews perceived as betraying the divine mission to complete the settlement of the Biblical homeland and hence allowing the nomos to come under threat.

Irgun, also known as Etzel, was active from 1931, and in 1937 became the paramilitary wing of the New Zionist Organization under Jabotinsky who led it from 1937 to 1940. Now the militant arm of Revisionist Zionism, it assassinated Ralph Carne, head of the Jewish unit interrogating terrorists captured by the police, and carried out scores of less infamous but no less brutal outrages against Arabs and British soldiers. Its most notorious attacks were the bombing of the King David Hotel in Jerusalem on 22 July 1946, and the Deir Yassin Massacre of April 1948, a month before the creation of the State of Israel, in which over 100 Palestinian villagers were killed, complete with summary executions in the streets and hand-grenades thrown into family homes. After independence, Irgun formed the basis of the Herut or Freedom Party, which eventually mutated into Likud, the dominant force in Israeli politics since 1977. The party was founded by Menachem Begin, Irgun's leader from 1943 to 1948, in its most violent phase, and Israel's Prime Minister from 1977 to 1983. The campaign against the Mandate for

Palestine is a rare instance of the politically successful use of sustained irredentist terrorist violence.

The Deir Yassin atrocity was committed together with militants of the Lehi organization, which originated as a radical faction that had broken away from Irgun in 1948. Also known as the Stern Gang after its leader Avraham Stern, Lehi was virulently anti-British, and identified consciously with the ancient Zealots in their fight against the Roman occupation and its fighters were proud to be called 'terrorists'. The organization was responsible for the assassination of Lord Moyne, the British Minister Resident in the Middle East, and the United Nations mediator, Folke Bernadotte. In the case of Lehi the boundary between communal and communal-nationalist-religious (and even fundamentalist violence) becomes very difficult to draw. In his article 'The Logic of Ethnic Terrorism', Daniel Byman makes a sharp distinction between ethnic terrorism and 'violence committed for religious purposes', and has no hesitation to classify Irgun and the Stern Gang as prime examples of the ethnic variety.[33] However, another scholar, Nachman Ben-Yahuda, points out that, even if Lehi members were not practising Orthodox Jews, the founding documents of Lehi are 'saturated with mystic statements regarding the divine nation of the people of Israel, their divine right to the land, based totally on Biblical sources, even to the point of reconstructing the Third Temple'.[34] Stern himself changed his name to Elazar Ben-Yair, the last commander of the Sicarii in their doomed battle with the Romans on top of the fortress of Masada, and was generally known as 'Yair', a classic example of heroic doubling.

The curious blend of the secular and religious in the Lehi mindset is obvious once again when Yitzhak Shamir, one of the three leaders of Lehi after 'Yair' Stern's assassination, cites as its heroes not just the figures Gideon and Samson of the Torah, but also Giuseppe Garibaldi and Tito, and the militants of the Russian and Irish revolutions. Shamir was later to become Israel's seventh prime minister. On the basis of such considerations it seems safe to suggest that Lehi represents an extreme form of communal-nationalist-religious terrorism strongly imbued with Jewish fundamentalism. Just how intermingled the secular political and cultural nationalism is with the orthodox religious in its thinking is illustrated by the last three of Stern's *18 Principles of Rebirth*:

> **Power:** The Hebrew nation shall become a first-rate military, political, cultural and economical entity in the Middle East and around the Mediterranean Sea;
>
> **Revival:** The revival of the Hebrew language as a spoken language by the entire nation, the renewal of the historical and spiritual might of Israel. The purification of the national character in the fire of revival.
>
> **The temple:** The building of the Third Temple as a symbol of the new era of total redemption.[35]

The fanatical mindset which Lehi inculcated into its followers in their mission to reconquer the Holy Land is reflected in the following article published in its underground newspaper *He Khazit* (*The Front*):

Neither Jewish ethics nor Jewish tradition can disqualify terrorism as a means of combat. We are very far from having any moral qualms as far as our national war goes. We have before us the command of the Torah, whose morality surpasses that of any other body of laws in the world: 'Ye shall blot them out to the last man'.[36]

The Jewish paramilitary irredentism of Irgun and Lehi made a vital contribution to the creation of the State of Israel and can be seen as one of the most successful terrorist campaigns in the world. By 1947 many hundreds of activists were involved, responsible for countless episodes of violence, but even the most violent groups were integrated into the new state under a general amnesty and many leaders went on to have brilliant political careers.

The restored Jewish Holy Land, in the form of the new State of Israel, found itself under immediate threat from a military alliance of hostile Arab states, and from Palestinian and Lebanese terrorist groups, but the first two decades of the new State were largely free of Jewish terrorist incident. Things changed with the Six Day War of 1967. Religious Zionists saw the sweeping victory as sign of divine intervention and were particularly incensed by the progress towards the two-state solution for the Middle East sought by secular liberal or left-wing politicians. Their determination to forestall peace with the Palestinians led to the formation in 1974 of Gush Emunim, which agitated for intensive settlement of West Bank and Gaza Agudat, provoking the hostility of non-religious Zionists.[37] The alarm which coursed through the new organization at the signing of the 1978 Camp David Accords between Egyptian President Anwar El Sadat and Israeli Prime Minister Menachem Begin (a former Irgun leader) provoked its most fanatical elements into forming the Jewish Underground. This cellular terrorist organization was responsible for a number of bomb outrages against Palestinian officials and students. Its main goal, however, was to blow up the Dome of the Rock in Jerusalem, the Muslim Holy of Holies. The plan was foiled, but it provides a perfect example of synecdochic and nomocidal terrorism at work: deliberately destroying not people, but a material target which is the sacred symbol of a people's nomos in order to disseminate fear and inflict psychological damage on third parties. The Jewish Underground was a long way from the amateur world of Joseph Conrad's *The Secret Agent*, but the impeccable logic articulated there about the need to create 'epiphanous violence' by the attack on the Greenwich Observatory is the same.

The foiling of a simultaneous attack on six Arab buses led to the destruction of the Gush Emunim's terrorist network in 1984 before it could destroy the shrine, but since then there have been a number of notable terrorist attacks by ultra-orthodox 'lone-wolves'. Several of them were directly or indirectly radicalized by Rabbi Meir Kahane's aggressively anti-Palestinian Kach Party, which called in the Knesset for the expulsion of Arabs from Israel and Palestine, and eventually was banned as a terrorist movement. These attacks include the pipe bomb attack against leftist intellectual Zeev Sternhell, and the murders of a Palestinian taxi driver and a West Bank shepherd committed in 1997 by Yaakov Teitel, an American

Orthodox Jew, who came to Israeli specifically to play a heroic role in the struggle for Eretz Yisrael; and the gun attack on a bus by Natan-Zada in 2005, a 'born again' religious Jew who fell under the influence of Kahanism and his demonized depiction of Arabs as stealing sacred land from its rightful owners.

The most spectacular attacks were committed after Israel had signed the Oslo Peace Accord in 1993, granting a degree of PLO autonomy in Gaza and Jericho. Baruch Goldstein, an American-born Israeli physician, radicalized by the Kach movement, carried out the 1994 Cave of the Patriarchs massacre in the city of Hebron, in which he shot and killed 29 Muslim worshippers and wounded another 125 before being killed by the survivors. A year later Yigal Amir assassinated Yitzhak Rabin for sanctioning the Oslo Peace Process. He claimed to have been following orders from God, and that the murder was legitimate under the Talmudic principle of *din rodef* ('pursuer's decree'), permitting extrajudicial execution of a person if it saves Jewish life. He had been radicalized by the Eyal movement, which had in turn been greatly influenced by Kahanism. In all such cases a narrative template adapted from Jewish religious orthodoxy prompted a radical process of 'heroic doubling', encouraging an 'ordinary' individual to experience himself as playing a leading role in the climax of a divinely ordained cosmic drama being lived out in historical time and now reaching its Messianic conclusion.

Inferences about Zealotic terrorism

A number of significant points stand out from our 'thick' description of the modern Zealotry generated by separatist or irredentist nationalism. First, even the most 'modern', 'normal' individuals, male and female, may *in extremis* prove susceptible to experiencing as the ultimate 'sacred cause' worth dying and killing for the defence and preservation of an endangered homeland (as in the Chechen and Tamil liberation struggles), or its *re*creation in the case of a lost homeland (as in Sikh secessionism and Jewish irredentism). As a result, the mission to defend or establish the territorial basis for an ethnic national, or a religious nomos has become a major source of fanatical violence in the modern age.

Second, it should be emphasized that it is not out of self-aggrandizement or megalomania that there are those for whom the land and culture (communal nationalism) and the religious cosmology identified with it (communal-nationalist religion), or the religious cosmology itself and the territorial home to ground it in secular time (fundamentalism), represent a 'Holy Land'. They believe it is the basis of existence for the present, past, and future generations of all their 'people' to whom, in their most ecstatic moments, they feel linked organically and eternally, so that their role in defending it becomes *infinitely* more important than their private existence. Indeed, the most militant patriotic fundamentalists or secular ultranationalists fighting to protect, conquer or reconquer their endangered nomos can imagine themselves fighting not just for their own lives and their descendants, but for their ancestors.[38] These are metaphysically preserved and 'present' in the collective memory, in tradition, and in the 'sacred texts' of their culture of the sort destroyed in Jaffna and Amritsar, and would be obliterated by allowing the nomocidal forces to win out. Every struggle for the homeland thus automatically metamorphosizes the freedom fighter into a holy warrior in a cosmic battle against a demonized enemy, providing for some an indescribable sense of nomic purpose and transcendence. It is only when that metamorphosis fails to take place or the official heroic myth offered fighters fails to convince them of the sacredness of their cause that a tormented, sardonic, but sublimely elegiac war poem such Wilfred Owen's *Dulce et Decorum Est* (1918), or a visionary novel of transcultural humanism such as Erich Remarque's *All Quiet on the Western Front* (1929), the film banned by Goebbels four years later, can be written.

Third, within the Zealotic mindset the Holy Land does not occupy the same time–space continuum as other stretches of land, sea or sky, so that its special-ness is destined to remain invisible to Google Earth. This is because its 'sacrality' is the result of a unique, laser-like projection of culturally and experientially conditioned mythopoeia filtered through upbringing, custom, language onto a historical situation, a territory, and a struggle. The examples of the most ded-icated Chechen, Tamil, Sikh, and Jewish nomic warriors show that when the homeland serves as the sacred canopy, it provides an eternal firmament. It embod-ies the metaphysical community, historical continuity, and collective memory which provides each existence lived under their protective shield with transcen-dence, whether it is lived within the physical borders of the homeland or in a diaspora.

There is, of course, nothing new or particular to terrorism about this. The readi-ness to defend a Holy Land through violence has probably been a permanent feature of human nature since the dawn of language and communal conscious-ness, and with the rise of ultranationalism in the modern age has shaped – and sometimes punched frenetically into shape – the contours of modern history. Every war monument and cemetery in the world bears testimony to the sacraliza-tion of the people, its territory, and its heroic dead epitomized in the oxymoron 'God and Country'. The film *Dances with Wolves* (1990) fictionalizes the desperate attempt of Native American Indians to defend the sacred canopy of their existence from the 'White Man'. The Aztecs' desperate fight to protect Tenochtitlan (now Mexico City) from the nomocidal Conquistadors is one that has yet to be told from the vantage point of the defeated. But these are just two of the innumerable episodes of nomocide that litter human history, the vast majority of which will never be told. Down through the ages peoples and cultures have destroyed other peoples and cultures, leaving the anguish of many millions at the loss of their physical and metaphysical homelands unrecorded. A recent episode which is well documented is the extreme, and often suicidal violence with which the Japanese fought to defend the island of Iwo Jima in 1945, a fanaticism largely explained by the fact that it was not an occupied island, but the first territory within the sacred Japanese homeland (*furusato*) to be invaded by the US forces.[39] This passage from the SS newspaper, *Schwarzes Front*, when Germans were ordered by the Third Reich to defend their own nomos from invasion (and stave off the discovery of the atrocities committed in its name) expresses sentiments that can be empathized with by all soldiers and terrorists prepared to kill and die for their sacred country, whether a 'Holy Land', a 'Mother Country', or a *Heimat*:

> The soldier hurling himself against the charging hordes of the enemy knows there lies behind him a home which embraces *everything which gives his life meaning*: first and foremost father and mother, wife and child, bride and lover, but also the city, the village, the farm, the meadow, the forest, ... the old fairy-tales ... everything which has grown and has taken shape, *the fruit of centuries and the seed of the future*.[40]

The appeal in this passage to the SS soldier to identify entirely with the sacred (and utterly un-Christian) nomos and so become a self-sacrificial 'holy warrior' in the fight against the 'enemy' (thoroughly demonized and dehumanized in the rest of the passage) is palpable. It is a passage that might also speak to the most militant and disaffected of the many millions forced in recent decades into migration and their own inner diaspora all over the world who feel their 'Holy Land' is being lost forever, predisposing them to one day be enlisted into a 'sacred cause' to preserve it from oblivion.

Fourth, it has hopefully become clear how insidiously the modern age secularizes the sacred nomos so that the struggle to defend it to the death, like the Sicarii at Masada, now involves secular projects of state building, creating a new society, achieving political sovereignty, and forging an original variant of modernity, a process that can reduce religion to a mere marker of ethnic difference and cultural continuity, or even dispense with it altogether. Categorizing national struggles and the terrorism they produce into religious and ethnic, fundamentalist, communal-nationalist-religious, and the more secular (but still sacralized) communal-national causes is clearly very tricky. However, some such typology is needed if the deeper layers of motivation of terrorists are to be understood. Doubtless, the conceptual schema we have suggested here could be further tested for its heuristic value by considering in detail other defensive, irredentist, or separatist national struggles against national cultures threatening to overwhelm them, such as those of the Irish, the Basques, the Palestinians, the Iraqis, the Afghans, the Kashmiri Muslims, the Tibetans, the Lebanese, and the Kurds. My own preliminary reconnaissance of these cases suggests, however, that the causal patterns generating Zealotry which have been identified in this chapter, and the taxonomy used to classify them, would be refined rather than invalidated by such an investigation. Hopefully, further research into this topic would illuminate an important topic not even touched on here, namely why some national struggles for independence or sovereignty generate terroristic violence and some do not. A comparison of Basque with Catalan, or Irish with Scottish separatism might be instructive on this matter, but it is an issue that goes beyond the scope of the present work.

Finally, readers might have noted the absence of any sustained reference to the 'radicalization syndrome' so elaborately constructed in the last chapter. Yet it has been implicit throughout this chapter that the premise to the rise of Zealotic terrorism, ancient or modern, is a crisis within the nomos which precipitates in some a process of splitting and heroic doubling in which the external threat to a culture (the 'enemy') is demonized and its defenders become cosmic warriors in a life or death struggle. In this context it is worth citing the most authoritative book on Jewish religious terrorism available in English, Ami Pedhazur and Ari Perliger's *Jewish Terrorism in Israel* (2009). In the preface the authors question the heuristic value of explaining religious violence in terms of theological radicalism or strategic calculation. Instead they offer an 'alternative framework' which 'focuses on the analysis of the sociological and cultural traditions that contribute to the radicalization of communities and the socialization processes among peers that eventually lead to the formation of terrorist cells'. They start with an observation about what has been termed here 'splitting' and 'Manichaeanism': 'Totalistic ideologies are based on a division of humanity into dual categories such as the saved versus damned, godly versus demonic, and dark versus light forces.' Such totalism reinforces 'the impulse to validate an absolute worldview by confronting demonized exemplars of evil as contrasting symbols'. They then suggest that pluralistic societies everywhere tend to host religious countercultures committed to a totalizing world-view. This sets up the scenario that when 'an external event' occurs that 'poses a potential threat to the community or its most cherished values' (nomos), the 'community leaders' within the counterculture begin 'framing the event as catastrophic', calling for a war 'between the forces of light and the forces of darkness'. In other words the nomic crisis generates an apocalyptic mood of imminent catastrophe and palingenetic expectations of salvation mediated by religious authorities.

At this point 'the slide into violence by some community members will be unavoidable'. Those who take the path to terrorism are those who have 'extremely high levels of identification with the community and commitment to its values',[41] precisely the sort of total and totalizing identification liable to generate a *second* identity, an avatar engaged in a cosmic drama through the process of what I have called 'heroic doubling'. With or without religious convictions, the disoriented, politically impotent, atomized individual who psychologically and mythopoeically becomes one with his or her 'nomized' and 'cosmized' ethnic community is transformed into a sacred warrior for a higher cause. Pedhazur and Perliger imply that theological motivation for 'religious terrorism' is somehow subordinate to the role of sociological and cultural factors, the drive to defend the community's 'most cherished values'. As will become clear, the position adopted in this book instead is that when established religion is still integral to social and cultural cohesion and hence to the community's 'most cherished values', then religious fundamentalism can still play a defining role in shaping the radicalization process and determining the ideological rationalization of the acts of violence committed in order to preserve or restore the nomos. Indeed, in these circumstances the religious is inextricably linked to sociological and cultural factors. In the case of religious Zionism, which in the past has frequently 'slid into violence', the terrorist creed is surely to be seen as a blend of fundamentalist and communal-nationalist-religious terrorism rather than being 'simply' communal-national, even if it has become so involved with founding and preserving the State of Israel state building that it has inevitably acquired Modernist Jacobin and not just Zealotic Jacobin elements.

Before we consider the phenomenon of the hybridization of the Zealotic with the Modernist in more detail, the next chapter will investigate further the situation of those who, even with no traditional nomos to defend, are able to find a suprapersonal cause to fight for in order to solve the nomic crisis they are experiencing. Once they have created their heroic avatar, they play the starring role in a cosmic fantasy which has replaced reality and demands a ruthless commitment to 'Modernism of the deed', extreme acts of violence inflicted on the bodies and lives of real human beings which are calculated to induce, sooner or later, the birth of a new reality out of the prevailing decadence and anomy. It is a commitment ultimately driven by the fear of falling through the holes being torn in the sacred canopy and falling into the icy wastes of the infinite void.

7
Modernist Terrorism Red, Black, and White

The vitality of terrorism before 9/11

'Great events cast their shadow before them', the German poet Wolfgang Goethe stated cryptically. However, the constant foreshortening of historical perspectives in an increasingly present-centric 'media age' has been aggravated by selective memories induced by the current 'War on Terror' (i.e. on Global Salafi Jihad) in the decade following 9/11. The combined effect tends to blank out from our reading of contemporary history the long, menacing shadows of terrorism, both religious and secular, that had already fallen over many parts of the world in the two decades preceding that limpid, innocent, early autumn morning in New York. It is easy to forget, for example, that in 1984 the Reagan Administration had already declared a 'War against Terrorism' as a reaction to the truck bombings of the US Embassy in April 1983 and then the barracks of the French and US Multinational Force of peacekeeping troops six months later, an attack causing the most serious casualties inflicted on the US and French military in a single day for decades. The assaults were carried out by the Shi'ite Muslim terrorist organization operating under the name Islamic Jihad (AKA Hezbollah) during the Lebanese Civil War. It led to the withdrawal of the Multinational Force from the Lebanon, another rare example of terrorism actually succeeding in its immediate aims. Although Islamic Jihad was commonly referred to as 'fundamentalist', in Eisenstadt's terms it should perhaps be more precisely considered communal-nationalist-religious because of the importance of its territorial ambitions.

The Civil War in the Lebanon was an extraordinarily tangled and bloody sectarian conflict in which kidnappings, murders, bombings, and terrorist atrocities became normal occurrences as competing religious and secular factions – Syrians, Shi'ites, Sunnis, Druze, Christians, communists, socialists, Pan-Arabs – fought piranha-like at the cost of ordinary citizens over control of 'their' country to decide who had the right to impose their political ideal, their religion, and their nomos, on the war-torn nation and its mutilated body politic. But the Lebanon and Palestine were not the only hot spots of fanatical violence in the years before Bush declared his own war on terror. The launching of *Terrorism: An International Journal* in 1977 (now *Studies in Conflict and Terrorism*) heralded the birth of a new discipline. It was followed by *Terrorism and Political Violence* in 1989, and the creation of the Centre for the Study of Terrorism and Political Violence (CSTPV) at the University of St Andrews in 1994. For a snapshot of the world-wide problem political violence had become by the end of the Cold War, it is worth consulting the overview of terrorist movements offered by Yonah Alexander in 1992 as the background for a study of communist militancy in Europe.[1] Many of the scores of movements listed are dedicated to ethnic separatism, irredentism, or resistance to enemy occupation (e.g., the IRA, LTTE, PLO, Hezbollah) and thus are clearly Zealotic in nature, whether communal-nationalist-religious or communal-national. However, two recurrent types of violent militancy listed by Alexander as occurring in the US, Europe and parts of Latin America and Asia pursued the vision of socio-political revolution to bring about an alternative modernity: 'Red Terrorism' (variants of revolutionary anarchist or communist movement) and 'Black Terrorism' (neo-fascist, neo-Nazi, or White Supremacist violence). These correspond to the secular left-wing and right-wing groups in Bale's categorization and the species of Modernist terrorism established in Chapter 3 of this book, since instead of defending or recovering a nomos, they aim to create a new one.

We will first sample these two categories before looking at one other example of fanatical violence prompted by the need to create a new totalizing nomos for society to live, kill and even die for. Our case study in Red Terrorism will be the *Rote Armee Fraktion* (RAF), better known as the Baader–Meinhof Gang – responsible, along with *Revolutionäre Zellen* (whose creed was a heady cocktail of Marxism–Leninism, anarchism, anti-imperialism, anti-racism with feminist, anti-Zionist and anti-Semitic elements typical of modern ideological 'mazeway resyntheses') and *Bewegung 2. Juni* (a branch of an anarcho-leftist urban guerrilla movement)[2] – for a sporadic series of terrorist actions directed at the capitalist and political system in West Germany between the early 1970s and the late 1990s. Black terrorism will be represented by Franco Freda, one of the many ideologues and activists of extreme right-wing terrorists in Italy between the late 1960s and mid-1980s, whose shadowy cellular organizations for a time spread a pandemic of public anxiety and sense of national crisis through a series of murderous attacks on Italian society whose authorship and purpose were never determined. In both countries there were times, particularly during 'The German Autumn' of 1977,[3] and the 'Years of Lead' in Italy between the late 1960s and the early 1980s,[4] when the German and Italian state seemed under a permanent state of siege by the threat of terrorist violence. In all, well over 2000 civilian lives were lost, and thousands more injured, not to mention the blighted lives and incalculable anxiety of those most affected, while millions of pounds worth of material damage was caused, all without any specific demands or ultimatums to be met beyond the release of prisoners. It should be added that according to some analysts, especially on the left, the Black terrorism of the years 1969–74 was part of a 'strategy of tension' to destabilize the government to a point where a right-wing coup could be carried out by anti-democratic elements within and outside the state. The ostensive aim, some have claimed, was to stop in its tracks the rise of socialism and the far left that peaked in 1969's 'Hot Autumn' of massive strikes in Northern Italy.[5] Yet the tangled threads of this convoluted story will probably never be fully unravelled and the world-views of some of the authors of the violence are so outlandish that looking for rational tactical goals may be a false premise. The meaning of 'White terrorism' will become clear in due course.

The radicalization of an 'in-between generation'

It is consistent with our model of modernity as a disenchanting, denomizing force, that the background to the US and European episodes of both Red and Black terrorism in the period 1960–85 was, in contrast to the rise of extremism in inter-war Europe and to terrorism outside Europe, not characterized by objective conditions of economic and political crisis. Instead, there spread through the first postwar generation, growing up in the superficially prosperous and stable Western societies, a deep subjective malaise, a disaffection with the current state of society experienced by a large cohort within the younger generation that had not experienced the war and could not identify with 'actually existing' postwar democracy. They were products of what Tyler in *Fight Club* calls an 'in-between age'.

In the case of the US, the nomic crisis that struck so many of the younger generation within two decades of the death of Hitler, as well as the powerful youth rebellion *against* anomy, was amply documented at the time, for example, by Paul Goodman's *Growing Up Absurd* (1960). It was even accorded official recognition when in July 1979 President Carter made a major speech to warn that America faced a 'crisis of confidence' which 'strikes at the very soul and spirit of our national will' visible in the 'growing doubt about the meaning and purpose of our lives and in the loss of unity of purpose for our Nation'.[6] When an interviewer with a plummy English voice asked Bob Dylan in the early 1960s why he did not wear, or even own, a tie, it was clear that a rift valley had opened up between the war and postwar generations, and that the times really were 'a-changin'. A vociferous minority of students, at least in countries where they enjoyed freedom of speech, showed signs of wanting to go beyond song lyrics in their attempts to bring about a new beginning in the civilization that was in their eyes vitalistically, creatively, and sexually challenged and had also waged so many horrific wars within three generations.

As a result, the profound nomic crisis experienced by the 1960s youth (trivialized by references to 'Hippies') generated myriad bids to find a new 'sacred canopy' at an individual or collective level, leading to a plethora of heterogeneous 'modernist' experiments in achieving transcendence. Some of these were purely epiphanic – such as the use of psychotropic drugs and the quest for mystic, often oriental sources of enlightenment. Others were programmatic, forming through revolutionary social and political movements which aimed to overthrow the core values of the 'system' and realize alternative ways of living more in harmony with society, other peoples, the planet, and the cosmos. The 'New Age' palingenetic climate generated by the mounting despair in the rationality, morality and sustainability of actually-existing democracy was articulated in all its rich creativity in a series of books by Theodor Roszak with such suggestive titles as *The Making of a Counter Culture* (1968), *Where the Wasteland Ends* (1972), *Unfinished Animal: The Aquarian Frontier and the Evolution of Consciousness* (1975), and *Person/Planet: The Creative Disintegration of Industrial Society* (1979). In 1978 William McCloughlin also offered penetrating testimony to the widespread feeling that America was undergoing a sea-change in values, or 'a Fourth Awakening'. He dates the perceptible breakdown of the old order to 1960 after which 'norms no longer matched experience' and a critical loss of faith spread among the young in science, technology, state, and the official concept of progress. These led to radical experiments with new life-styles, a new openness to oriental mystic traditions, and a widespread longing for 'ecstatic rebirth' which embraced sex, drugs and music.[7]

In the US, the prevalent form taken by 'programmatic modernism' among the young was the rejection of 'straight' society in mass student protests against the Vietnam War and the 'system' that was waging it, but there were also radical and violent groupuscular expressions, such as the bid to renomize society through extra-parliamentary political agitation. A fascinating case study in one individual's conversion to a cultic, fanatical, but non-violent, communist faction, the Democratic Workers Party, is offered by Janja Lalich in *Bounded Choice* which, as we saw earlier, explores the dynamics of initiation to cults.[8] Some particularly disaffected idealists could be lured into even more extreme positions and take up a cause that demanded the readiness to commit terrorist violence to precipitate change.

McCloughlin cites Paul Goodman's prescient observation that 'Alienation is a powerful motivation of unrest, fantasy, and reckless action. It leads ... to religious innovation, new sacraments to give life meaning. But it is a poor basis for politics, including revolutionary politics'.[9] This is borne out by Alston Chase's investigation into the cultural background to the 'lone-wolf' terrorism of the Unabomber Ted Kaczynksi. Chase sees the confluence of the pessimistic climate created by the threat of nuclear catastrophe, the Cold War, and the Vietnam War with a loss of confidence in a future based on technocratic reason, democracy, and capitalism as 'tearing a hole' in the fabric of US society by the early 1970s. At that point 'terrorism began to fill the hole',[10] spawning on the extreme right such groups as a revived Ku Klux Klan, the Minutemen, the American Nazi Party, the Order, and the Aryan Nations, and on the left the Black Panthers, the Weather Underground, and the Symbionese Liberation Army.

Unlike the extreme racist right, still licking its wounds after the defeat of Hitler, the apocalyptic mindset of the radical Left could at least rationalize its messianic vision. To the believer, unmistakable portents of the imminent end of capitalism could be read into the remarkable constellation of events which together betokened a global revolutionary change: the 1968 student revolts in France, Mexico City, Berlin, Rome, and London; the abortive Prague Spring; the Northern Ireland Civil Rights movement; the impact of Uruguay's Tupamaros organization as well as Marxist-led independence movements throughout Africa; Mao's Cultural Revolution; and in the US the rise of the Black Panther Party and growing unrest in black neighbourhoods in the most deprived inner cities.

Meanwhile in Europe, the youth of individual nations on both sides of the Iron Curtain were undergoing their own crisis of confidence in the 'system', capitalist or Soviet. The formulation of radical left-wing alternatives could draw on currents of neo-Marxism, the New Left, neo-Anarchism, feminism, radical ecologism, Zen economics ('Small is Beautiful'), Third World solidarity, 'Hippie' critiques of consumerism, the Puritan Work Ethic, and straight society, as well as counter-cultural attacks on the technocracy (all this when global warming was still only a twinkling in the eye of some climatologists). The subversive political underground they created remained profoundly energized by the anti-Vietnam protest, especially by campus student protests in the US. Meanwhile, on the right the White Supremacist mindset was fuelled by the rapid growth of mass immigration and multiculturalism, accompanied by the very real sense outside the US of being increasingly dominated by American, Anglo-Saxon, or in the US by 'One World' values which were threatening an indigenous and superior ethnic identity. It was a situation where all those who tolerated or conformed to the status quo could be seen as reactionary defenders of a doomed old order, actively delaying the emergence of a just society or accelerating the destruction of cultural and ethnic homogeneity. This perception encouraged the most profoundly alienated and inwardly desperate to adopt utopian alternative value systems, some of which led to 'Modernism of the deed' in the form of left- or right-wing violence.

Since both the genuine communist or ethnically pure societies they postulated were apocalyptic utopias – unlike in most separatist struggles there was no coherent plan to achieve them – they went hand in hand with the process of splitting and demonization. This in turn triggered the Alice Syndrome: a delusional overestimation of the possibility of changing the world through targeted violent action accompanied by a fatally weakened reality principle. It was a situation that condemned to futility all acts of terrorist violence against the 'system' or 'capitalism', no matter how fervently the protagonists believed in the scenario which demanded them. They caused physical pain and psychological devastation to innocent human beings to no objective purpose, the passion for creation often degenerating into not 'positive' but cynical, nihilistic acts of destruction for its own sake, without any visible purpose other than making obscene phatic gestures against the status quo and the *ennui* of everyday life. The situation recalls the famous lines in W.B. Yeats' *The Second Coming*: 'the best lack all conviction, while the worst are filled with passionate intensity'. This trait was accompanied in the case of Red and Black terrorism and the more idiosyncratic forms of it encountered in this chapter by a number of additional psychological defects. These include an adolescent sense of self-importance, a confusion of abstraction and rhetoric with reality, and an utter breakdown of empathy and humanity, and a deficiency in common sense, humour and self-irony, all products of the radicalization syndrome we have described. 'And in their promises of paradise you will not hear a laugh'.[11]

The post-nihilism of the Baader–Meinhof Gang

It was from within a peculiarly West German variant of the nomic maelstrom of the late 1960s that Andreas Baader, Ulrike Meinhof, and Gudrun Esslin conceived their utterly unwinnable war on society. To be part of the 'in-between' generation in the Federal Republic of Germany (FRG) added a number of special ingredients to the counter-cultural leftist mode of alienation from the state witnessed in other countries at the time. There was the contempt of youth for the 'Auschwitz generation', the physical proximity of the GDR and the Soviet Bloc (especially in Berlin), (rhetorical) solidarity with the Palestinians and Vietnamese in their struggle against 'imperialism', a highly vociferous and superficially politicized student generation bent on emulating their French and Czech comrades, the emergence of new gurus of rebellion such as Herbert Marcuse and Rudi Dutschke, the brutal repression of anti-Shah protests of 1967 in which Benno Ohnesorg was shot dead by a policeman (who, ironically in the light of the RAF's claimed GDR sympathies, turned out to be a STASI undercover agent). It was a nexus of factors that conspired to convince many caught up in the youth protest movement that the Federal Republic was a 'police state'. The external history of the Baader–Meinhof Gang, AKA the Red Army Faction or RAF, has been reconstructed in great detail.[12] The highly disparate paths that led the leaders Baader and Ensslin to become leaders of a red terrorist cell, shortly to be joined by Meinhof, are well established, underlining that it is as futile to search for a 'terrorist personality type' as it is a proto-fascist 'authoritarian' one.[13]

Baader was a former car-thief addicted to sex and drugs, who was drawn into the terrorist underground largely through his relationship with Gudrun Ensslin, and revelled in the opportunities life in the underground gave for him to indulge his compulsion for eroticism, hedonism, vitalism, narcissism, violence, and crime behind a smokescreen of virulently vulgar Marxist anti-system rhetoric. An utterly different trajectory led the highly idealistic and literate Ulrike Meinhof from Lutheranism to Communism, and from being one of the country's leading left-wing journalists to a PLO-trained urban guerrilla operating in West Germany. Closer scrutiny reveals the profound personal and existential crisis that she experienced in her private life that was never fully resolved.[14] The ideological driver of the gang was not Meinhof, but Gudrun Ensslin, rebellious daughter of a Lutheran pastor who had colluded with, but never actively supported, Nazism. She was interviewed by a psychiatrist when she was in prison awaiting trial for one of the first of the Gang's strikes against the 'capitalist West', an arson attack which was meant to bring home to Germans the horrors of the American troops' use of napalm against the Vietnamese. He detected in her 'a heroic impatience', an urge to break out of 'the inadequacy of our existence', and 'put into action what she had only learned about in the parsonage'.

Her father's comment on her motivation for the crime, made at the time of the trial, is even more striking. His daughter wanted to prevent the restoration of the society that had committed genocide and could not stand idly by and allow 'the hopes for a new beginning, reformation, rebirth, to be destroyed'.[15] He also expressed astonishment that Gudrun:

> who had always thought things out very prudently and intelligently, essentially experienced a state of euphoric self-realization, a holy self-realization, in the sense that one speaks of sacred humanity. For me, that is a greater

signal than the arson itself, that a child of Man commits such deeds *to achieve self-realization.*[16]

It is surely disturbing that Pastor Ensslin was prepared to compromise his Christian faith to sanction his daughter's commitment to a cause which would soon lead from firebombing a clothes shop to murder, maiming, kidnapping, hijacking, and terrorizing the nation. But in this comment he shows rare insight into the way Gudrun might have found in her terrorist action the epiphanic sense of existential completion and nomic certainty expressed by Malraux through the persona of Ch'en.

More insight is given into the metapolitical aspect of the Gang's activities by Stefan Aust, then the editor of *Der Spiegel*, in the lecture he delivered to the German Historical Institute in Washington in 2008. It offers a lucid account of how the RAF's self-appointed mission to trigger a general uprising against the crypto-fascist state they believed they lived in, took shape within a climate of profound alienation from a Federal Germany. In their eyes their native land had not purged itself of Nazism, tacitly approved of the sufferings being inflicted on Vietnamese peasants by the US army and the regimes of Israel and the Shah, and crushed legitimate peaceful civic protests with SA-like brutality. He highlights the significance of evidence that the RAF's leaders identified with Captain Ahab, alone in a small boat on a vast, hostile ocean seeking to kill the Leviathan, the Great White Whale of the State. Aust comments that Ensslin's choice of names from *Moby Dick* as the Gang's code-names in prison enabled him to understand:

the degree to which the prisoners had romantically imbued their struggle against reality. *They transformed themselves into icons, and they became icons* [avatars], with all the consequences that entailed, with all the severity and brutality against alleged opponents, innocent bystanders, against their comrades and, in the end, against themselves.[17]

In terms of our conceptual framework, such an observation confirms that sustaining the frenzied terroristic activity of the first generation RAF involved a radical (but, in the case of Ulrike Meinhof, incomplete) act of splitting and heroic doubling. Whether the deaths of Meinhof, Baader, and Jan-Carl Raspe – Irmgard Möller survived four stab wounds near her heart – in the Stammheim Prison on the evening of the hi-jacking failure on 18 October 1977 was collective suicide or extrajudicial execution has never been resolved. Möller herself claims she was stabbed by prison guards, and the repeated blows with the knife seem *prima facie* inconsistent with self-harm. But there is no doubting Holger Meins' determination to starve himself to death, nor the extreme lengths all the leaders were prepared to go to expose the 'true' nature of the Federal Republic. By the time of their deaths they had acquired a glamorous, guru-like status within broad swathes of disaffected young Germans who felt orphaned not just by 'God', in Pellicani's sense, but by the imperfectly de-Nazified Germany of the 'economic miracle', and an 'imperialist' West still locked in a potentially lethal boxing clinch with the Communist world.

As a result, even while the original leaders were in jail, a new RAF was formed by a small cadre of their more sociopathically inclined admirers to continue the struggle. At first their goal was to free them. Then, when the plane hijacking carried out by the Popular Front for the Liberation of Palestine to force the government to release them went so disastrously wrong in Mogadishu in October 1977, they dedicated themselves to avenging their deaths. This commitment demanded an intense radicalization that turned a number of educated Germans of apparently normal intelligence and psychology into ruthless urban Sicarii, prepared to kidnap and execute symbols of Germany's unpurged Nazi past in pursuit of their fantasy jihad against 'the system'. Various aspects of the RAF campaign suggest that all three of its generations were in the powerful grip of the 'Alice Syndrome': its counterfactual, if not paranoid, assumption that it could trigger a revolution by provoking the state to reveal its true identity as a 'fascist state' in its draconian response to terroristic violence; the dark pit that separated their goals and their achievements; the grotesque mismatch between their squalidly hedonistic, criminally violent, egomaniacal, cruel lives and their self-image as warriors waging a holy war against persecution and oppression on behalf of the deceived 'people'.

Even when it announced on its website in 1998 that it had disbanded officially and recognized the inadequacy of its revolutionary tactics, the communiqué, a detailed essay about the history, aims, and eventual failure of the RAF, expressed no regrets for the deaths, suffering, fear, and chaos its members had caused. Instead, it restated the legitimacy of its assault on the state's authoritarianism and capitalism.[18] While the RAF are regularly referred to as 'Marxists' on the basis of such self-characterization, there are grounds for thinking that their Marxism was neither orthodox nor fundamentalist, but rather as superficial as the 'Christianity' of Timothy McVeigh or Anders Breivik, or the Islam of Black Power, more a gesture towards a lost identity than the basis of a creed. They had not studied Marxism, had not worked their way up through Marxist organizations, and had no real sympathy for the East Germany which gave them refuge and support when necessary. Marxism was a semiotic marker that indicated they were anti-liberal, anti-capitalist, anti-fascist, anti-police, anti-Nazi, anti-US, anti-imperialist, and anti-Israel, while being pro-Vietnamese, pro-PLO, pro-'liberation' and pro some ill-defined 'revolution' against an equally nebulous 'system', undertaking acts of violence which would create a 'new society' in which 'people' would be 'free'.

Given its divorce from reality and the lack of any sort of ideologically coherent revolutionary tactics or goal, the RAF's violence thus has far more in common with that of Russian nihilists and French anarchists than it did with Lenin's Bolsheviks or the KPD under Hitler. They were as inept as urban guerillas as they were as ideologues, and the PLO trainers were appalled by their lack of discipline and blatant hedonism which was an offence to Islam. Nechayev would probably have had no time for them either, especially the infantilism and self-indulgence of Baader, whose attitude to revolution, in particular, is far better illuminated by the portrait of Tyler Durden in *Fight Club* and his account of Project Mayhem than by any treatise on Marxist revolutionary theory. The RAF's violence might thus be called post-Marxist or even 'post-nihilist', devoid of substantive ideological creativity or reality as a response to the postwar German malaise, more phatic than strategic.

The holy warriors of the Kali Yuga

At the time when the FRG felt most under siege from the RAF, namely in the 'German Autumn' of 1977, Italy had been experiencing 'the Years of Lead' for nearly a decade, a period when the Italian public was constantly exposed to the possibility of terrorist attacks from the extreme right or the extreme left, whose unknown authorship and purpose only intensified the sense of insecurity and crisis.[19] Among the most notable of these outrages were the Piazza Fontana (1969)[20] and Piazza della Loggia (1974) bombings (by the right), the kidnapping and assassination of Aldo Moro in 1978 (by the Red Brigades with possible state collusion),[21] the bombing of Bologna station in 1980 (by the right), and two aborted neo-fascist coups reliant on the collaboration of elements within the state (1970, 1974). The corruption and structural inefficiencies of fascist sympathizers within the Italian judicial system of the day mean that the authorship of many attacks is still shrouded in doubt (a situation effectively dramatized in Marco Giordana's 2012 film *Romanzo di una Strage*).[22]

Whatever the many unresolved issues arising from the period of Black terrorism in Italy, there is no doubting the major impact on its core vision of the world achieved by the writings of Julius Evola (1898–1974). Evola entirely supplanted Mussolini as the main ideologue of the groupuscular neo-fascism that flourished, largely undetected, outside the parliamentary fascist Movimento Sociale Italiano (MSI) between the 1960s and the 1980s. This underlines how important it is to take into account the creed, the metapolitical dimension of ideology when attempting to address, not just the effects of terrorism, but its underlying causes.[23] Though largely unknown outside Italy except in the extreme right-wing intellectual circles of the European New Right, Evola is by far the most important advocate of the need for a total 'Conservative Revolution' in postwar Italy and Europe to create the basis of a new, healthy, organic society. Dadaist painter, dilettante, voracious autodidact, occultist, creator of an esoteric total history of civilization, prolific cultural pundit, political essayist, 'spiritual racist', anti-Semite, anti-feminist, anti-Hippie, apologist for the International Brigades of the Waffen-SS as the precursors of a spiritual reborn, heroic, chivalric, Aryan Europe, his life spanned the Fascist regime, the war, and the emergence of postwar fascism. It uniquely allows the evolution of fascist thought to be tracked from ethnic and biological ultra-nationalism and militarism to pan-Europeanism and culturalism.

Combining traits of René Guénon, Oswald Spengler, Ernst Jünger (whom he admired), Mircea Eliade (who admired him), and Alain de Benoist (whom he influenced), Evola produced from the mid-1930s a series of books offering a radical diagnosis of modernity's decadence. According to his alternative world history, 2500 years of perverted ideas of rationality, humanism, and progress have produced a fatally flawed and spiritually bankrupt civilization. The only hope lies in a metapolitical process of rebirth brought about by a spiritual elite, a palingenesis he saw announced in the rise of Fascism and Nazism, but which in the post-fascist period has been indefinitely postponed. In the 1970s, his total explanation it provided for the nomic crisis of the West could exert a deep fascination on a new generation of men (his was a deeply patriarchal world-view) alienated by materialism, disgusted by consumerism, and rabidly opposed to communism.

Armed with the magic key Evola provided to making sense of the anarchy and spiritual catastrophe of the West, some responded inwardly to his call for a new elite charged with a sacred mission to restore the lost Tradition by creating a society once more ruled by the caste of warrior-priests epitomized in the Indian *Kshatriya*. It is important to note the element of Zealotry involved in protecting and eventually restoring in a new society the Traditional nomos. Just as Zealotic ideologies now contain an element of Modernism, so Modernist ones contain a Zealotic component, albeit reduced to the fantasy of reviving the essence of some lost sacred canopy, whether as primitive communism, the Aryan world, the Roman Empire, or Christian Europe. Evola's works, written as a prophet rather than an academic – he regarded academics as 'mummifiers' of truth – offered voluminous Gnostic revelations to God's orphans. By convincing them they were invisible heroes living in spiritual exile in a decadent age, like undercover agents for the lost Tradition, he precipitated a process of heroic doubling in the more metaphysically demanding milieus of the extreme right for whom the fascism of Mussolini and the MSI was vulgar demagogy. Once converts to his esoteric vision felt driven to break out of the spell cast by fantasies of epic struggles between good and evil metaphysical forces[24] and into the world of violent action which he implicitly celebrated (but refrained from himself), he stepped onto a path that could all too easily lead his faithful to commit to terrorist violence.

The context for Evola's profound impact on Black terrorism in Italy[25] was the generational malaise of the second postwar generation we have already described, which in Italy was compounded by such unique factors as the defeat of Fascism, the collusion of both the Communist Party and the neo-Fascist party, the MSI, with parliamentary politics, Europe's domination by the US and NATO, the apparently impregnable power of the Soviet Empire and the threat of the New Left in Europe, economic stagnation, and a deeply sclerotic parliamentary system dominated by a profoundly undemocratic Christian Democracy and a state synonymous with corruption. With his seminal *Revolt against the Modern World* (1936) (a book admired by the Nazi Expressionist, Gottfried Benn) Evola had explained the roots of the West's democratic and communist decadence in terms of a millennial decline from the Golden Age of Traditional society known in the Hindu philosophy of history as the Black Age, Kali Yuga. His postwar books, *Man among the Ruins* (1953) and *Ride the Tiger* (1961) provided a spiritual survival manual for those who experienced deepening anomy under an increasingly Americanized, consumerist and 'plebeian' democratic world, and were viscerally repelled by the communist alternative. Evola explained that such was the state of degeneration that not just party political, but all revolutionary projects were doomed in the short term. The only solution was inner emigration into a state of *apoliteia*, 'apoliticalness'. However, this did not preclude acts of violence carried out against the vacuous 'normality' of a doomed society, as long as they were aimed less at changing things than sending a phatic message of solidarity to fellow spiritual warriors equally condemned to 'ride the tiger' of modernity until it collapsed in exhaustion at some point in the future.

Evola had a profound effect on some of Italy's most uncompromising theorists and orchestrators of Black terrorism – Adriano Romualdi, Pinto Rauti, Stefano della Chiaie, Franco Freda – and hence on such key neo-fascist terrorist groups as *Ordine Nuovo*, *Costruiamo l'Azione*, *Avanguardia Nazionale*, and *Nuclei Armati Rivoluzionari*, providing an abstruse rationale for a succession of murderous assaults, which was often mixed in syncretically with more conventional neo-fascist rationales for a war on democracy. While some groups remained faithful to the spirit of the Republic of Salò, the more Evolian, genuinely *neo*-fascist terrorists poured their energy into the gratuitous violence of radical *apolitieia* designed simply to destroy the illusion of democratic consensus. Others implemented a theory of 'spontaneismo armato' in a spirit closer to Evola's intention and reminiscent of some less instrumentally-minded, nihilistically inclined Russian anarchists, such as Nechayev's own *Narodnaya Rasprava* (The People's Reprisal).[26] Either way, they selectively drew on Evola's bizarre metapolitical vision to rationalize gratuitous acts of violence against the civilian population in the name of a nebulous 'higher' vision of the world.

In a fascinating passage, Franco Ferraresi, the leading Italian expert on the very real 'threats to democracy' in these years, contrasts the axioms behind Red and Black terrorism in the Years of Lead. For the Extreme Left, the future revolution justified all violence committed against capitalist society in order to bring it about. The world was now split into those who promoted and those who obstructed the transformation, relegating those who stood in its way to a subhuman status where their deaths had no moral significance. As an Italian expert on left-wing terrorism put it: 'The enemies are a category, which means ciphers: they are symbols not human beings'.[27] At this point murder and death become abstract, insubstantial when set alongside the sacred cause of humanity's emancipation from capitalism. By contrast, the Right regards death as transfiguring, and integral to purification. What characterizes modern societies is that the bulk of their citizens have 'learnt to live with heterogeneity, indeterminateness, ambiguity which are not perceived as threats'. These are what Zygmunt Bauman calls the 'ambivalent' and 'liquid' qualities of modernity. However, it is precisely this ambivalence and liquidity that threatens to plunge members of the extreme Right into a nomic crisis, triggering their retreat into the security of a totalizing vision and a 'fundamentalist mindset' (which in the context of modernist politics refers to the 'apocalyptic' perception of reality discussed in Chapter 5 without theological connotations of ultra-orthodoxy). It then only needs a breakdown of state law and order for them to feel their time has come and they are called upon to *act*.

Within the mythically structured, Manichaeanized cosmology of extreme right Italian militants of the 1970s, the process of heroic doubling, of substituting the ordinary self with the political or apolitical *Kshatriya* or sacred warrior, progressed to a point where they believed history had charged them with a mission which is the key to the survival of humanity in any meaningful sense of the world. Ferraresi sees in this fantasy battle for survival the roots of their obsession with restoring traditional rootedness and identity, regenerating the purity of the nation or race, and promoting the vision of a new order to be brought about *whatever the human cost*. Such a mindset, insulated from the real world by the Alice Syndrome, is prone not just to devise lethal forms of terrorist attack against innocent citizens to enact their palingenetic fantasy, but to cross the Rubicon from fantasy to physical violence in banks, squares and train stations.[28]

Franco Freda was for over a decade one of the leading ideologues and intellectuals of terroristic neo-fascism and was implicated in the Piazza Fontana bombing. His manifesto, *The Disintegration of the System* (1969), a seminal text for the Evolian, metapolitical brand of neo-fascist terrorism, calls for a campaign of 'eversione' (a form of subversion practically synonymous in Italian with terrorist violence) to 'precipitate and accelerate the process of the destruction [of the system] and add momentum to the work of breaking up the present political equilibrium'. He appeals to elements within Italy's radical left who would within a few years organize themselves into their own rival terrorist movement, the Brigate Rosse (the Red Brigades) to collaborate in the common cause of 'putting an end to the bourgeois infection', even if the struggle is for the Left 'exclusively human, historical, social', while for the Right it is 'superhuman, metapolitical, metahistorical.'[29] He calls upon his followers to develop the (Nechayevian) virtue of the fanatic, namely 'to take up an idea of the world, and once it has been acknowledged, to live it out, to strive towards its realization – subordinating everything to this objective and considering whatever means valid as long as it proves effective for achieving it'. The Right must abandon the constraints of legality, give up reformist illusions, and, inspired by the 'magnificence' of the revolutionary task before them, realize that 'in a political soldier purity justifies every form of hardness [i.e., ruthless violence], disinterest [i.e., a callous lack of compassion], and every tactic [i.e., bombing soft targets], while the impersonal character of the struggle absolves him of any moral preoccupations'.[30] Freda's text is based on the speech he gave to the steering committee of the *Fronte Europeo Rivoluzionario* held in Regensburg on 17 August 1969. The Piazza Fontana Bombing, in which he was widely thought to have been directly implicated, took place five months later, killing 17 people and wounding 88. The same afternoon, three more bombs exploded in Rome and Milan. The utterly futile metapolitical campaign of violence against against 'the system' (i.e., innocent citizens) had begun.

The terrorist acts of postwar anarchists, communists, and the racial or metapolitical Right are forms of fanaticism, as Freda proudly acknowledges. Yet, however shrouded in metaphysical mystification or a sacralizing discourse, this is clearly a *secular* fanaticism with a mission but no concrete plan. Indeed, such a fanaticism is bordering on the psychotic in its cult of creative destruction without any blueprint for the ensuing creative phase: an apocalypse without a millennium. For example, although *The Turner Diaries* are often called the neo-Nazi *Mein Kampf*, what stands out in contrast to Hitler's 'reckoning' with the present phase of history is the absolute absence of any forward planning. The construction of a new order lies permanently beyond the horizon of the present, over the rainbow, producing a strategy of burning everything to the ground (which in practice means sporadic acts of terrorist violence) in the vain hope that a new nomos will somehow arise phoenix-like from the ashes of the old (unfortunately the ashes of real people not CGI enemy hordes). Even when inspired by the Tradition, this is *Modernist*, revolutionary, anti-traditional terrorism that has occurred only since the middle of the nineteenth century. But Italy's Black terrorism was in the tradition of Nechayev, not of Marx or Hitler, let alone Mussolini. Proudhon's motto had been brutally truncated to read simply *Destruam*, 'I will destroy'.

It was a perverse utopian logic that could lead to a modern *Kshatriya* to leave a bomb set to explode at the central train station of Bologna on a Saturday morning in the middle of the holiday season when it would be packed with families. Bologna had been reduced, by the iconaclastic imagination of a fanatic in the grip of the Alice Syndrome, to a 'red' city, standing in the way of the rebirth of the Tradition. The explosion killed 85 and injured over 200, achieving nothing but yet more pointless death and suffering. While at the opposite extremes of the political spectrum on paper, the true ideological paternity of RAF, Revolutionary Cells and Italy's Black terror organizations in practice was not Marx or Evola but Nechayev, whose *Catechism* had declared that the true revolutionary 'must ally himself with the savage world of the violent criminal, the only true revolutionary in Russia'. They thus had more in common with the self-styled 'Nihilist Anarchists' who bombed the IBM's offices in Athens in May 1996 than any idealistic Bolsheviks or Nazis.

Timothy McVeigh strikes back against ZOG

It would be understandable if, after sampling the paranoid world of savage attacks on civil society inhabited by Red and Black terrorists each bent in their own way on the 'disintegration of the system', the inclusion of a section on the Oklahoma Bomber seemed anomalous. After all, McVeigh is regularly presented as a representative of religious terrorism, which is the subject of the next chapter. For example, Mark Juergensmeyer's *Terror in the Mind of God*, claims that 'Christian Identity ideas were most likely part of the thinking of Timothy McVeigh', going on to make the self-contradictory claim that he 'imbibed Identity ideas, or concepts similar to them...perhaps most of all from the book *The Turner Diaries*' which some referred to as 'his bible'.[31] For Charles Strozier, in his chapter on 'Apocalyptic Violence and the Politics of Waco', McVeigh epitomizes a 'baffling overlap of right-wing violence and apocalyptic Christianity'.[32] Meanwhile Jessica Stern in her *Terror in the Name of God* asserts that 'like more mainstream Protestant fundamentalists, adherents of the Christian Identity Movement (CIM) take the scriptures literally and focus a great deal on the Endtime'. She goes on to state that 'Identity Christianity has become the dominant religion of the racist right in America', and includes McVeigh among its converts.[33] In apparent corroboration of this thesis, the Sullivan County CIM website proudly claims him as one of their own, 'a product of Christian Identity and their holy war against ZOG'.[34]

If *The Turner Diaries*, *Hunter* (William Pierce's second terrorist novel), and Christian Identity were indeed expressions of Christian ultra-orthodoxy or fundamentalism, or if apocalypticism were a uniquely Christian or theological phenomenon, then the bombing of the Alfred P. Murrah Federal State Building in Oklahoma on 19th April 1995 would have been one of the most devastating episodes of religious terrorism in the modern history of the West, not just for its death toll, and the scale of the material damage caused, but especially for the deep scars which the first major terrorist attack on American soil left on the national psyche. Tragically, it was not to be the last. The clue to dispelling the widespread fallacy of seeing McVeigh as a Christian terrorist lies in CIM's reference to ZOG, the 'Zionist Occupation Government'. The Christian Identity which now forms an integral part of the American contemporary far Right is not to be confused with the extreme heretical sect of British Israelism which emerged in the nineteenth century claiming the British were the 'lost tribe' of the Israelites. The organization based on an aberrant but pro-Jewish reading of scripture was transformed into a racist sect – one which regards traditional Christians as heretics – by the American, Howard Rand in the 1920s. In a period which saw the rise of postwar xenophobia in the US and the revival of the Ku Klux Klan as a virulently White Supremacist, anti-Semitic, and anti-African-American organization, Rand elaborated and embroidered the theory of 'seedlines' to the point where by the later 1930s (by then under the influence of Nazism), the CIM was attacking Jews as the offspring of Satan.

Since the war, in tandem with the rise of neo-Nazism and a new incarnation of the Ku Klux Klan, Christian Identity has provided the metaphysical adhesive and cosmological script for the fundamentalist mindset and narratives of a bewilderingly wide range of racist groups in the US. But when CIM is integrated into extremist White Supremacism, it ceases to be a form of *Christian* fundamentalism in any meaningful sense, though it certainly retains an extreme form of fundamentalist *mindset* in the wider sense explained in Chapter 3. As James Jones explains clearly in his section 'The Divine Terrorist. Religion and Violence in American Apocalyptic Christianity',[35] those curious to see the terroristic imagination of genuinely *Christian* fundamentalism (in Eisenstadt's sense of the term) in all its gory, apocalyptic sadomasochism, then the place to look is not on Christian Identity websites. Rather it is in the Bible-thumping rantings of Christian Dispensationalists and Christian Reconstructionists, and especially in the 16 books of the *Left Behind* series by Tim LaHaye and Jerry Jenkins. The authors stated candidly on the talk show *Listen America*: 'We're in a religious war and we need to aggressively oppose secular humanism; these people are as religiously motivated as we are and they are filled with the devil'.[36] Such bandwagon riders of the Apocalypse could be seen as driven by their holy war against secular modernity as representing a form of 'Christianism', sometimes as ferocious in its rhetoric as Islamism, though generally a far more marginalized factor than Islamism in the threat it poses to civil society.

Total sales of the book series had, by 2007, surpassed 65 million, and it has been also adapted into a highly successful three-part film series and a video game. *Left Behind* depicts in obscenely graphic detail what for Dispensationalists is *literally* the end of the world. The *eschatos* of the Book of Revelation is being lived out in our time. Soon the Antichrist will rule the earth and only those with the sign of the Beast are safe. Eventually Christ shall return as the conquering Messiah, the good shall be saved and the wicked punished with eternal suffering, but only after the seas have been turned to blood in a Boschian nightmare of Armageddon. The novels are set specifically in the imminent time of the Rapture in the US where those 'left behind' have to fight for their lives against Satanic hordes in human form as the entire infrastructure of modern civilization is destroyed and the cities are filled with gruesomely evoked scenes of violence, death, pain, despair, grief, as planes crash, trains and cars collide, and chaos (or rather the Beast) rules.

In marked contrast, the racist activists who associate themselves with Christian Identity have no more fundamentalist theology in them than the third incarnation of the Ku Klux Klan which, after the war, became so indistinguishable from the utterly *pagan* neo-Nazis that they now hold their Aryan Fests together, along with Christian Identity racists.[37] The Christianity of such groups is directly comparable to that of the German Christians (*Deutsche Christen*) whose emergence from neo-paganism to supply an important ideological strand of Nazism has been studied in an investigation by Karla Poewe[38] which refutes any lingering delusion of Nazism being compatible with the theology of redemption through Christ's unique sacrifice so central to 'genuine' Christianity. The Christianity of White Supremacists is a bogus Christianity, the widespread category error of portraying McVeigh as a 'Christian terrorist' because of his links with the pagan racist strand of Christian Identity suggests that secular-minded academia should pay more attention to the core features defining religious creeds.

An indication of the essentially secular nature of Christianized White Supremacy in the US are the ideological acts that headlined the 2001 Nordic-Fest organized by the Imperial Klans of America. A CIM leader (Richard Butler) shared a platform with Matthew Hale, the leader of the World Church of the Creator – now known as Creativity – which, true to its slogan RaHoWa, 'Racial Holy War', is an openly *atheistic* celebration of race. The CIM component of White Supremacy in the US can thus do no more than give his cause a Christian, pseudo-religious veneer, providing racists with a home-grown metaphysical rationale and cosmic narrative that avoids the need to import them from neo-Nazism, which originated in Germany and whose public image is tarnished by associations with Hitler and the Holocaust. CIM's infiltration of white racism has been vastly facilitated by a peculiarly American tradition of religious freedom and non-conformism, allowing myriad evangelistic and fundamentalist Churches to exist alongside idiosyncratic derivatives of Christianity, such as the Mormons, and overtly un-Christian forms of religiosity, such as the Church of Elvis Presley, Heaven's Gate or the Reformed Church of Druids (which started out as a joke religion).

'New' Christian Identity thus has a closer affinity to Evolian metaphysics or the occultist Ariosophy, which cultivated its own theory of seedlines that helped radicalize Hitler's anti-Semitism in pre-war Vienna,[39] than with the religious zeal of Christian Dispensationalists and Bible Belt evangelists. Thus it should not surprise us to find that, Gary Yarborough, one of the leaders of The Order, a terrorist group inspired by *The Turner Diaries* but also identified with CIM, could write in 1993 an impassioned call to use violence in opposing the enemies of the White Race (not of Jesus Christ!), since peaceful protest was 'no longer profitable' and the time had come 'to fight terror with a greater terror'. He went on to declare a form of ecumenicalism which is far removed from the teachings of Jesus:

> Whether you are National Socialist, Klan, Odinist, Christian Identity, Skin Head, Creator, or any other cult, creed, faith or persuasion of our cause does not matter. For the essence of our cause, regardless of our diversity, is race, our common genetic heritage.... Our faith is our race, and our race is our faith![40]

The need to take the claimed religious convictions of racists with a pinch of salt is also illustrated by the tortuous ideological itinerary of David Myatt, whose *Practical Guide to Aryan Revolution* on a Canadian website probably influenced the London nailbomber, David Copeland.[41] Myatt studied Christianity and Buddhism, in what Kaplan calls a 'Siddhartha-like search for truth'[42] before becoming a neo-Nazi, and then converting to Islam in 1998, whereupon he embraced its most militant, anti-Zionist, Islamist forms. A writer of science fiction, he abandoned Islam in 2010 to dedicate himself to the elaboration of his own mystic philosophy of 'The Numinous Way'. Clearly Myatt, like so many racists, needs a metaphysical system to 'cosmize' and 'nomize' his hatred, paranoia, and split universe and provide his existence with meaning, but he is a dilettante of religious cosmologies, not a genuine convert who displays the quest for nomic certainty that drives the generation of New Religious Movements.

It thus makes sense if *The Turner Diaries*, McVeigh's 'bible', is also described by Jones as 'the bible' of CIM,[43] for there is absolutely nothing Christian about William Pierce's novel, as one would expect from a work by the leader of the largest neo-Nazi organization in America, the National Alliance. It describes the coming secular apocalypse from the perspective of Earl Turner, who becomes a member of an anti-government terrorist cell, The Order, and who eventually becomes a martyr to the cause of the White Race in the throes of its heroic self-liberation from degeneracy. Although written in 1978, it is set in the future, and takes the form of a diary recording events that climaxed in 1999 on the eve of a new millennium. However, this is not the Armageddon of *Left Behind,* but one spawned by a sustained neo-Nazi fantasy dramatizing the longed-for final reckoning with a multicultural, dysgenic world. (Hitler called his *Mein Kampf* 'a reckoning'.) Pierce's heroic avatar, Turner, predicts a 'cleansing hurricane' to purge the remaining healthy elements within the white race of *all* other human beings (who for Nazis are, of course, *sub*-human). The millennarian longings are directed, not towards the ultimate theocracy of the Second Coming, but the creation of a global white *ethnocracy,* through the seizure of power of what is, to Pierce, the objectively real, this-worldly, US-centred 'Aryan race'. If more proof were needed to demonstrate the book's lack of Christian credentials, it closes with dedication not to Jesus but to Adolf Hitler.

Having established there is no 'baffling overlap of right-wing violence and apocalyptic Christianity' in McVeigh's attack, I propose to draw on the abundant knowledge now available about his path to violence to consider him in the light of the 'radicalization syndrome' we proposed in Chapter 5. He was born in 1968;

was deeply affected by his parents' divorce when he was 10; was raised after the divorce by an emotionally distant father in a run-down part of New York; was shy with girls; got bullied at school; and dreamed of retaliating against his tormentors. He also was a brilliant computer hacker at high school, but an academic underachiever. In short, there was nothing out of the ordinary to suggest he would become a mass murderer, except, perhaps, that under his grandfather's influence he developed in his teens a profound interest in firearms and was incensed at government's attempts to limit the Americans' constitutional right to own a gun.

With no particular goal in life he enlisted in the army at 20, and soon displayed a passion for fitness training and a great prowess in weapons training. He was given a chance to put his prowess with the 25mm cannon to good effect when Operation Desert Storm was launched two years later. He was assigned the task of standing atop a Bradley Fighting Vehicle picking off Iraqi soldiers desperately fleeing the fate of being buried alive by the sand being driven into their trenches by enormous US tanks equipped with snow-ploughs. He later commented that the army taught him to 'switch off his emotions', by which he presumably meant his innate compassion for fellow human beings. McVeigh returned to the US a misfit and an outsider. But Robert Lifton suggests that something important had happened in the desert: 'McVeigh's death immersion in the Gulf War undoubtedly was brutalizing and numbing, yet it also seems to have created a hunger for meaning and transcendence.'[44] For a new nomos.

Once demobbed, he resented his dead-end job as a security guard after the perverse exhilaration and the (hardly heroic) military action which had won him the Bronze Star and the invitation to apply to join the Green Berets. He suffered a deepening sense of depression at the state of the nation and anger at the government, which might be explained partly as subliminally displaced distress at having to carry out orders to cold-bloodedly shoot down the soldiers of an enemy who had been overwhelmed by vastly superior military technology. His resentment against the US army was also not helped by having to pay back an overpayment of wages during the war.

In a letter to a newspaper he found a potent image to express the American public's general indifference to what he and his fellow-soldiers had been through in Iraq ostensibly on behalf of 'the nation'. He compares it to the way supermarket consumers choose to remain blissfully ignorant about the mass-slaughter of animals being performed daily, so that they could buy cellophane supermarket meat with no blood on their hands.[45] It is a profound metaphor. The chapter on this period of his life in his biography, *American Terrorist*, is entitled 'Nothingness',[46] referring to McVeigh's growing sense of listlessness, his lack of intimate relationships, his feeling of being an 'outsider', his bottomless anomy. His brief flirtation with gambling was, as for Dostoevsky, a symptom of a deeper existential malaise. The first outward sign of a splitting process occurring came in a letter he sent to his local newspaper in February 1992, the *Lockport Union Sun and Journal*, in which he expressed his deep anger with the nation's industrial and moral decline, and alarm at the way the American Dream was dissipating. It ends with the ominous questions 'Is a civil war imminent? Do we have to shed blood to reform the current system? I hope it doesn't come to that but it might.'[47]

It was the siege of the Branch Davidian ranch near Waco, Texas by the FBI and ATF (the United States Bureau of Alcohol, Tobacco, Firearms and Explosives) that was the tipping point in his life from the psychological state known as 'dissociation' to potential terrorist fanaticism. The 50-day day siege ended on 19th April 1993 in a furious fire-fight with the members of the sect, who were well armed, and the compound catching fire, causing the deaths of 76 cult members, including more than 20 children, two pregnant women, and the sect's leader, David Koresh. Already McVeigh had been frequenting gun shows where he came into contact with a broad spectrum of far right cultic milieu, and mixed with hard-core members of the militia movement, survivalism, Christian Identity, neo-Nazism, the Patriot Movement, and the Ku Klux Klan. He used these contacts to sell copies of William Pierce's novels, several scenes in which, but particularly the conditions of cosmic racial war it depicts, would directly influence his mission. He drove to Waco to witness the end of the siege in person, and experienced it as an apocalyptic event in miniature which crystallized into the epiphany that the Federal State was indeed waging a war against its own people, and he had to act. In the paranoid mindset of all the groups and literature that impressed him, the Federal state was just the front for ZOG, the forces of evil which were destroying the essence of America. It was time to carry out an act of retribution against the demonized State and so send a wake-up call to the mass of somnambulists deluded into thinking everything was 'normal'. With his army background, love of weapons, and an apocalyptic imagination fed by *The Turner Diaries* and *Star Wars*, it was bound to be an act of 'phatic violence' on an awesome scale.

From Waco onwards McVeigh was no longer one of 'God's lonely men'[48] or 'God's orphans'.[49] The world was now stably split between the forces of ZOG and their puppets, and a small heroic elite of white warriors determined to act. The mazeway resynthesis he carried out to create this Manichaean cosmology drew on the broad spectrum of paranoid politics in which he had steeped himself. Anomy had given way to a fundamentalist mindset enabling him to undertake a spectacular act of 'Modernism of the deed', its unprecedented destructiveness on US soil causing a national trauma that would not heal, but instead be eclipsed on 9/11.

By September 1994 the process of heroic doubling was complete. Following a pattern strangely reminiscent of Travis Bickle in *Taxi Driver*, McVeigh now reverted to his soldier persona, which carried him through to the completion of the mission not with a Mohawk haircut, but an army crew-cut. He was helped in maintaining his secret urban guerrilla identity, possibly known only to his one convicted collaborator, Terry Nichols,[50] by his identification with the crew of the Starship Enterprise in *Star Trek*, and especially with the role of Luke Skywalker in *Star Wars* in his mission to destroy the Death Star. In *American Terrorist* the split between the older, anomic and new, heroic self is dramatized by McVeigh's thoughts being expressed in the discourse of a soldier carrying out a dangerous mission, following orders which he gave himself to complete. The army's brutal lessons in how to switch off compassion and obey had put him in good stead for carrying out a large-scale massacre. It had produced a military avatar that now controlled his life.

Having decided to act, the syndrome of terrorist radicalization entered its final phase: 'focusing'. The nebulous, generic hatred of the demonized enemy was reduced to a specific target – an iconic Federal State building – and date, two years to the day after the ending of the Waco siege. Thus, as Juergensmeyer explains, both the time and place of the attack were steeped in symbolic significance to maximize the phatic power of the communication,[51] pointing to a powerful synecdochic imagination at work. He was assisted by using as a blueprint an almost identical attack described in detail in *The Turner Diaries*. Once the target and date were decided, McVeigh set about the arduous, elaborate, and risky process of making the bomb and planning the logistics of the attack with the meticulous, professional efficiency typical of someone whose 'small-self' qualities of humanity, compassion, and moral conscience have been anaesthetized by the process of heroic doubling and by the sacred significance of the act itself.[52] It is symptomatic of his success in totally renomizing his life through the mission to carry out a single terrorist act, that McVeigh was ready to die for his cause. He was perfectly prepared to explode the bomb manually if the timer malfunctioned, and utterly stoic in confronting his eventual execution by lethal injection.

Clearly McVeigh's project was holy to him, in the sense that every nomos is experientially sacred for its zealots. It was a sacralization of the profane made easier by having immersed himself in a counter-culture which regularly announces the holiness of racial war. But it should by now be abundantly clear that in the absence of religious belief he had used a process of syncretism, of *bricolage*, in a deeply modernist sense, to create his own defensive trench against the desert of absurdity. The resulting compound of ideas was a militant racist's equivalent of T.S. Eliot's act of 'shoring up fragments' against his 'ruins' in *The Wasteland*, the iconic poem of interwar poetic modernism. He was so determined to complete a symbolic strike against the evil Galactic Empire of ZOG, stretching from the FBI right up to the United Nations, that, in the profound grip of the Alice Syndrome, the Murrah Federal State Building from which troops were sent to Waco could, as it were, morph into the Death Star. He could now play the heroic role of Luke Skywalker as a Jedi Knight pitted against the forces of evil. There was an element of Zealotry in defending the beleaguered nomos of a mythicized original America and pure White race from further degradation by symbolically attacking the 'enemy within': the Federal State. But his action was also a vague gesture towards a racially healthy new order. His response was not of a reactionary, but of a Conservative Revolutionary. As Charles Strozier puts it, the violence in Oklahoma was supposed to initiate a process leading to 'rebirth, redemption, hope, freedom, indeed a New Age', but of a secular kind.[53]

As Peter Osborne explains in his seminal *The Politics of Time*, the ideologues of Conservative Revolutionary extremism 'understand that what it would "conserve" is already lost (if indeed it ever existed, which is doubtful), and hence must be created anew'. Such an extremist 'recognizes that under such circumstances the chance presents itself to fully realize this "past" *for the first time*.'[54]

It is an analysis that leads him to conclude that 'from the standpoint of the temporal structure of its project, fascism is a particularly radical form of conservative revolution'. As such it is 'neither a relic nor an archaism', but a '*form of political modernism*'.[55] It is thus important for an understanding of the metapolitics of terrorism, that, except when it is pursuing the defence, restoration, or regeneration of a past or existing nomos, or seeking to fulfil the millennarian fantasies of a scriptural prophecy of the end days, apocalypticism is not Zealotic but Modernist. The Manichaeanism, the fantasies of death and total destruction, the notion of a hurricane of ethnic cleansing, of regenerating a nation through blood, whether through the sacrifice of others or through martyrdom, celebrated throughout the extreme Right, are not 'perversions of Christianity', let alone signs of Christianity. They are universal archetypes of the revolutionary imagination, which, as Pellicani has shown so clearly, is innately *apocalyptic*.

If McVeigh sought to win any sort of immortality, it was that of Earl Turner, the fictional martyr to the White race. As a 'White terrorist' such immortality was not of the heavenly sort, but of the temporal kind so lucidly expressed by Adolf Hitler:

> To the Christian doctrine of the infinite significance of the individual human soul ... I oppose with icy clarity the saving doctrine of the nothingness and insignificance of the individual human being, and of his continued existence in the visible immortality of the nation.[56]

The cleansing power of blood

When he left the hired truck in front of the Alfred P. Murrah Building, it was loaded with the same type of fertilizer-based explosive used in the 1993 Islamist attack on the World Trade Centre two years earlier, but which had also been described in *The Turner Diaries*. As he dispassionately carried out his plan, McVeigh wore a T-shirt bought at a gun-show. It carried on the front a picture of Abraham Lincoln with the phrase shouted by his Confederate assassin: *Sic Semper Tyrannis* ('Thus Ever to Tyrants'). On the back was a stylized tree, running through its branches the words of Thomas Jefferson: 'The Tree of Liberty Must be Refreshed From Time to Time with the Blood of Patriots'. Once again it would be fallacious to read Christian connotations into the myth of blood sacrifice McVeigh had concocted. It is a topos which is as central to the Aztecs as it was to Christianity or to the ritual slaughter on the altar of the nation in the First World War, producing such chilling declarations as the one made by the Irish nationalist leader Pádraic Pearse in 1913: 'Bloodshed is a cleansing and sanctifying thing, and the nation which regards it as the final horror has lost its manhood.'[57] These words would take on new connotations in the four-year hecatomb of the First World War, which was also hardly a 'Christian' slaughter, as Wilfred Owen's 'The Parable of the Old Man and the Young' recalls. In the poem Abram ignores the Angel's instruction to slaughter a ram caught in the bushes instead of his son, and the whole of Christian Europe has continued to ignore it day after bloody day for the duration of the 'Great War', sacrificing 'half the seed of Europe one by one'.

It was Eric Voegelin, one of the pioneers of the study of political religion in the 1930s, who reminded us that:

> In the imaginary reality of the ideologists, this killing of men in revolutionary action is supposed to produce the much desired transfigurative, or metastic [palingenetic] change of the nature of man as an event in 'history'. Marx has been quite explicit on this point: Revolutionary killing will induce *Blutrausch*, a 'blood-intoxication' [blood-frenzy]: and from this *Blutrausch* 'man' will emerge as 'superman' into the realm of 'freedom'. The magic of the *Blutrausch* is the ideological equivalent to the promise of the Pauline vision of the Resurrected.[58]

Lest sceptics still insist this is Marx's adoption of a Christian topos, note these words from the Islamist ideologue Abdullah Azzam: 'History does not write its lines except with blood. Glory does not build its lofty edifice except with skulls'.[59]

Meanwhile, in the external world of non-fantasy, of a flesh-and-blood reality far removed from the perverted, perverse perspectives of the Alice Syndrome, the explosion that was meant to help refresh with blood America's tradition of freedom from excessive government – an anarchist dream as well as a White Supremacist one – went off underneath the day-care centre of the Murrah Building, killing 19 children. It also killed 149 adults and injured another 800 people. The bomb had 'worked', like the bombs of the Piazza Fontana bank and Bologna train station had worked. But like the Red and Black terrorists, and the nihilist and anarchist terrorists before them, McVeigh's act of White terrorism was part of no real plan or blueprint for how precisely the nation's rebirth would come about after the explosion. No real plan other than some vague, infantile daydream that the massacre of the innocents and the spectacular material destruction would wake up 'real' Americans to the crushing power of ZOG, thus sparking the war to end wars with the government as prophesied in *The Turner Diaries*.

McVeigh was a psychologically damaged White racist terrorist with 'active nihilist', and hence sociopathic, tendencies, who escaped the collapse of his inner world or his own slide into passive nihilism by taking refuge inside an alternative world shaped by the fantasies of the US's sprawling counter-culture of paranoid racist politics and apocalyptic projections.[60] Perhaps his T-shirt should just have carried the single word *Destruam*. It could have been spelt out in letters of blood running through the charred, leafless branches of a burnt out oak, the remains of a scorched children's tree house still visible.

8
The Hybrid Metapolitics of Religious Terrorism

The intricacies of 'religious terrorism'

In the decade between 11th September 2001 and 22nd July 2011, the day when Anders Breivik carried out a car-bombing and mass-shooting against material and living symbols of Norway's pro-immigration political establishment, publications of academic and airport books and articles on 'religious terrorism' soared. Presented visually as bar charts, the statistics assume a sinister seismographic quality.[1] They register in palpable form the irresistible, tsunami-like wave of concern that swept in slow-motion from New York and Washington over the psychological defences of 'the West'. The barriers separating a vast subjective (and essentially mythic) homeland of normality, predictability, civil peace, and security from a threatening 'other world' in various states of anarchy, poverty, violence, and civil strife had been breached. Like giant graffiti written in the language of destruction, stark phatic messages obsessively transmitted that day by the world's media on behalf of Global Salafi Jihad could just be made out or guessed at through the clouds of dust and smoke: 'We will avenge Muslims for what "you" have been doing to us for centuries'; 'You have enemies pledged to rid the world of your evil civilization', or simply 'We are here too'. Thanks to global live TV coverage, a previously unimaginable act of 'triadic' violence had reached a target audience of unprecedented vastness that had been deliberately terrified *ontologically*.[2] Academics (myself included) hastily retrained to be able to contribute to the updating and reprogramming of the SatNav systems provided by the human sciences to monitor, map, and make intelligible the unfolding world process.

The disproportionate role played in the history of terrorist metapolitics by its religious manifestations can be gleaned from earlier chapters highlighting the ferocity with which Sicarii, Assassins, Sikh separatists, religious Zionists, militant Hindus, and the militias of a Buddhism tailored to justify an implacable *raison d'état*, have been prepared to use their religion to legitimize their cause or kill in the name of their faith. But these chapters have also made it clear that significantly different levels of religious commitment lurk within different terrorist episodes or campaigns. Hinduism, however important culturally, played a minor role *theologically* within the Tamil struggle for Eelam, while the role of Islam for Chechen rebels ranged from being just one of several ethnic markers, to the basis for locating anti-Russian resistance firmly within Islamism's global war against the West. We have also encountered the specious role played by religion in any meaningful theological, soteriological, or mystical sense, both within the most actively racist branches of Christian Identity, and as a factor in McVeigh's savage attack on ZOG. 'Religious terrorism' is clearly a fuzzy concept that demands considerable care if it is not to reinforce stereotypes, simplifications, and prejudices. However, there are several factors militating against conceptual lucidity or taxonomic clarity.

First, there is the extremely thorny problem of defining religion itself, which continues to have repercussions not just for religious studies, but in such specialist fields as philosophy, anthropology, and international law,[3] while posing particular issues for an exclusively (secular) scientific mindset.[4] It is a problem compounded by the innate human capacity to endow anything which assumes vital significance (the homeland, football, cars, fashion) with a sacral or numinous aura enshrined in ritualistic behaviour. When 'religion' is qualified by terms such as 'traditional' or 'revealed' to limit confusion, this then makes it more difficult to decide what qualifies as a 'new religion', while dualistic talk of a heavenly realm precludes monistic metaphysical systems such as Buddhism and Taoism. Then there is the question of religion's relationship to cultural myth and traditional ethics. Was the elaborate mythology of ancient Greece its 'religion', or was it the sign instead (along with import of mystery religions from the East) of the *decline* of an earlier 'genuinely' religious cosmology, and hence the erosion of its culture's metaphysical core? Does state-sponsored Confucianism, set to become an official source of ethical values for millions of Chinese in the new millennium, qualify as a 'religion' because of its concern with cosmically ordained patterns in human and social affairs and the official cult of veneration for its founder?

Finally there is the profound ambivalence of many religions as the source of moral conduct and a barrier against hatred, conflict, and violence. It would be very convenient for the secular human sciences when attempting to analyse religion's role in promoting or justifying nationalistic, military, and terroristic violence if the ethical core of the world's major faiths could be identified with pacifism, respect and compassion for all human beings irrespective of ethnicity or creed, and love of the created universe. This would allow all acts of hatred or violence committed in the name of religion to be treated as the product of heterodox, perverted interpretations of the original creed carried out in the name of a secular entity (nation, empire, wealth), and hence a form of heresy, idolatry, or decadence. Unfortunately this would be to ignore the profound ambivalence of not just the scriptural and exegetic traditions, but also the social, political, and military histories of the major faiths, Judaism, Christianity, Islam, Hinduism, and Sikhism. All supply texts or precedents in abundance that admit a 'fundamentalist' reading of religious truth justifying the demonization of the enemy (cast as infidel or impious) and acts of savage violence against the human incarnations of evil. Moreover, a study of the Aztec culture shows how ritual violence can be hardwired into some cosmologies with no room for compassion being extended beyond the core 'people'.[5] Moreover we have already seen in our account of Tamil separatism in Sri Lanka how even a religion as intrinsically pacifistic as Buddhism can be retooled into an instrument of ethnic cleansing on the basis of an idiosyncratic sectarian reinterpretation of its racial basis. In the absence of a higher clerical authority within the faith that can pronounce on the theological authenticity or legitimacy of such an idiosyncratic reading, it is impossible to condemn Sri Lanka's state Buddhism as a heresy with any objectivity.

Defining religious terrorism

For the purpose of discussing 'religious terrorism' in the present context, the working definition of 'religion' proposed here is:

A totalizing cosmology, generally formulated within an extended, and constantly evolving, scriptural and ritual tradition and admitting many variant sectarian interpretations, postulating a suprahuman, metahistorical order which is manifest in atemporal laws or metaphysical patterns, and which endows human life with a narrative shape, ethical values, and ultimate meaning conceived as independent of human agency or will.

This approach retains a basic secular/religious distinction (which some experts in the field of religious studies would doubtless contest), but fully accepts that the religion does not exercise an exclusive monopoly over the human experience of the sacred or the process of sacralization, which, especially since the advent of globalizing modernity, can endow terrestrial pursuits and objects with a numinous aura. It is this possibility which predisposes religion to hybridization with secular phenomena and ideologies, as routinely happens in the case of 'political religions'[6] – in the sense both of the sacralization of politics and the politicization of the sacred, often with an admixture of established religion, a process that occurred on all sides in the First World War to such devastating effect.

Such hybrids require particular scrutiny within terrorist studies when associated with ethnic or paramilitary violence to establish their religious content. It is also worth bearing in mind Eisenstadt's claim that a defining feature of fundamentalist religion under modernity is that – in contrast to 'proto-fundamentalism – when attempting to erect a barrier to the nomocidal forces of modernity it tends to assume certain 'Jacobin' aspects of modernity itself. In particular, theological cosmologies become infused with secular concepts of totalizing state power and illiberal modes of sovereignty, which are implemented through the application of advanced technologies of communications, administration, finance, and destruction. Nor should the 'liquefaction' of reality under modernity be ignored. Its permanently liminoid state fosters mutations in established religions, and the emergence of new heterodoxies and 'mazeway resyntheses', or even new religions, though the supratemporal, genuinely metaphysical credentials of such new nomoi merit careful scrutiny. Meanwhile, at the personal level, religion may become a 'floating signifier' of questionable authentic theological content, allowing individuals to undergo paradoxical trajectories in the search for the truth. This we saw with David Myatt – allegedly the ideological 'groomer' of the English terrorist David Copeland – who converted from Nazism to militant Islam, before becoming the creator ('designer'?) of his own New Age religion. The conversion of the Swiss neo-Nazi Ahmed Huber to Islam is also a revealing case study in this context.[7]

Once we accept the importance of suprahuman metaphysics in approaching religious terrorism, Eisenstadt's crucial but unelaborated distinction between 'fundamentalist' and 'communal-nationalist-religious' projects to counter modernity assumes a fresh significance. All religions are affected by the temporalization of the metaphysical under modernity. Where a religion's function is reduced to supplying an ethnic or sectarian marker which rationalizes mythic projections of a homogeneous, organic community of the 'good' pitted against political or ethnic 'enemies' in a Manichaeanized universe, then it becomes an integral part of a secular 'ethnicity' and a territorialized identity. Any terrorist violence it helps inspire is thus 'communal-nationalist-religious' rather than simply 'religious', and certainly not 'fundamentalist'. Such a distinction is particularly salient when analysing Zealotic politico-religious struggles which may develop both 'fundamentalist' and 'communal-nationalist-religious' expressions, as we saw in the case of the fight of both the Chechens and Sikhs for an independent territorial nomos. Communal-nationalist-religious terrorism is at bottom a secular, *non-religious* form of violence, no matter how many clerics may abuse their vocation by endorsing it. It is distinguished from communal-nationalist violence only by the fact that here religion was unable to provide an extra affective ingredient to the myth of ethnic distinctiveness.

The secular dimension of some 'religious conflicts'

Just how entangled (communal) religious and secular factors can become within ethnic disputes is highlighted by the analysis of identity politics in the collection of essays entitled *Religion and Conflict in South East Asia*. What stands out is the minimal role played, in the various case studies, by fundamentalist beliefs in the clerical sense when religiously self-defined ethnic groups clash in the defence of their threatened communities or nomoi. In fact 'religious terrorism' in the pure sense of elaborating fundamentalist readings of scripture as a legitimation of paramilitary violence against an entire 'system' is conspicuous by its absence from the volume. Indeed, Kumar Ramakrishna suggests in his essay on the psychological roots of conflict in the area that:

> Religious violence is less about religion per se than about the underlying social psychological and, in particular, mimetic dynamics driving it. As noted, the religious cause merely provides a *legitimation* for the violence the warring parties *already* feel compelled to commit.

In particular, the invocation of religion allows the protagonists of secular (communal-national) conflicts to view each other in '*absolutized, sacralized, and transnationalized cosmic war terms*' (original emphasis). This corroborates strikingly both the cosmizing and renomizing model of fanaticism we have proposed in our own model of terrorist radicalization, since Ramakrishna sees fundamentalism (used somewhat loosely to apply to communal-nationalist-religious movements as well as Islamism's globalizing religious war on the West) as a way of countering 'the perceived ideologically and spiritually debilitating effects of globalization', approving of the verdict of one psychologist that it is 'the mark of a those who have a very limited ability to live with the ambiguity inherent to healthy human life'.[8] Such a verdict echoes the stress which Mark Juergensmeyer, widely considered the world's foremost expert on religious terrorism, places on the way Sikh, Christian, and Islamist militants all see 'globalization and the new world order' as their main enemy, leading him to conclude that 'acts of religious violence' are 'religious responses to a political problem. They are responses to the perception that the world has gone awry'.[9] Under the intense pressures of modernity, liquid fears become the hydraulic power of religious fundamentalism and paramilitarized sectarian conflicts.

As a result the communal violence in East Asia proves to have a closer affinity with the sometimes terroristic secessionist campaigns of the Kurdish separatist *Partiya Karkerên Kurdistan* (PKK) and the Basque *Euskadi Ta Askatasuna* (ETA), which have no official religious aspect. As in the case of all secessionist or irredentist struggles, 'Kurdistan' and 'Euskal Herria' remain largely imaginary homelands for largely imagined communities. The only reason why these groups did not invoke an ultimately specious religious rationale is that the majority Islam of Kurds and the majority Roman Catholicism of Basques are shared with the very territories from which they want so desperately to secede. When scriptural religion does play a prominent generative role in a territorial cause, as we saw in the case of the Zionist quest to re-enter the 'Promised Land', it is precisely because it does provide a significant inclusive and exclusive ethnic marker. It hence can supply potent metapolitical legitimation for the justice of the mission, and is not necessarily an indicator of fervent personal religious beliefs as such. In each case the result is a modernized Zealotic defence of mythicized primordial nomoi.

This is demonstrated by one of the most lethal and protracted episodes of terrorism of the last century, the campaigns of 'ethnic cleansing' carried out between Orthodox Serbs and Catholic Croats, and perpetrated on Muslims (Kosovans and Bosniaks) by both ethnicities during the Yugoslav wars of 1991–95, but also inflicted by Bosnian and Kosovar Albanian Muslims on Christians when circumstances permitted. Precisely because religion provided the most powerful cultural, nationalist, and historical marker of ethnic difference,[10] overriding extensive communalities of language, genetic heritage, and the recent experience of common statehood under the Communists, it helped rationalize acts of war crime, nomocide, sadism, torture, systematic rape, and mass murder on a mind-numbing scale.[11] They were mostly carried out by trained soldiers and 'normal' citizens with a calculated hatred and cynicism that challenges naive assumptions about progress and civilization, and underlining once more the way nebulous world-views can be translated into devastatingly effective 'rational' tactics. Ethnic cleansing in the Balkans can be seen as a hybrid of genocidal violence, whose pragmatic rationale is to exterminate as many of an 'enemy race' as possible, with strategic terroristic violence (in this case both state and anti-state), calculated to send a powerful semiotic signal to other members of the ethnic community to flee or be massacred. But as a generic phenomenon it also has a profound cathartic, expressive, sacral (but only superficial religious) dimension for the protagonists irreducible to pragmatism. Though rarely included in surveys of the history of terrorism, ethnic cleansing is arguably one of the most potent and effective forms of state and anti-state terror, its legacy discernible in the permanent scars now branded in the collective memories and psyches of the post-Yugoslav states, jeopardizing the prospects of inter-community harmony within a multicultural Balkans for generations. This blend of apocalyptic utopianism with the capacity to pursue devastatingly effective short-term political and military strategies is called by the Arabist Michael Doran 'pragmatic fanaticism'.[12]

The temporal immortality of 'the inner thing'

Another familiar example of the specious role played by religious faith in terrorism is the conflict in Northern Ireland where, for historical reasons, the ethnic divide between indigenous Irish and 'British Irish' correlate to Catholicism and Protestantism. This is because most Loyalist Irish now concentrated in Northern Ireland are descended from the Protestants who (were) settled in Ireland in one of the waves of 'Plantations' forced on the island under mainland rule from the time of the Tudor conquests onward. Despite the importance of religious sectarianism in the way the most militant members of the two communities define themselves, the essentially cultural, non-theological nature of the 'religious divide' is shown not only by the utter disregard of Christian ethics of forgiveness, neighbourly love, and Samaritan compassion in every act of recrimination and reprisal, but also by the general lack of interest shown by militant Loyalists and Republicans alike in providing theological or scriptural rationales for the killings. It is consistent with the ultimately secular basis of the conflict, that factions within the IRA espoused Marxist theories of 'popular front' anti-colonialism in the 1960s, a development paralleled by some 'Muslim' terrorist groups in Algeria, Palestine and the Lebanon in the same period. Long before this shift to the left, the Welsh and English Catholic Church had officially condemned the IRA, though the Irish Catholic establishment kept its counsel.[13]

A rare insight into the psychological and metapolitical dynamics of personal commitment to the IRA cause is provided in Denis O'Hearn's semi-hagiographic biography of Bobby Sands, MP,[14] the Provisional IRA's most famous terrorist and 'martyr'. It traces the way the resentment of the British troops and Loyalist persecution of the Catholic community in Belfast which Sands had inherited as part of his birthright came to be transformed by stages into a principled political stand, paramilitary violence, imprisonment, and a leading role in the campaign for IRA detainees in the Maze Prison to be granted the status of political prisoners, culminating in his death by hunger-strike. There is no suggestion at any point that Catholicism for him was a religious faith in the theological or mystic sense. He wore it as a badge of Irishness. Unusually for a terrorist, Sands was a consummate protest poet and protest singer. He bequeathed in his verses a number of unique flashes of insight into the extraordinary motivation and resolve it demanded of him to die for his cause in the squalor of a British jail. Exposed to mental torture, privations of every sort, and then self-inflicted starvation, he was psychologically stripped down to his essential being in a way reminiscent of Ivan Denisovich in Solzhenitsyn's novel about life in the Gulags and the testimony of dehumanization in Auschwitz conserved in Primo Levi's *If This is a Man*.

In the process, Sands seems to have found in his existential isolation and terror a cluster of ontological principles to maintain his resolve until the excruciating end. He clung tenaciously onto his inner sanity, or what he called his 'window of the mind'. He maintained an unshakeable belief in the justice of the IRA cause *unto death*. He identified with the Irish men and women, famous and unknown, who had suffered under the British for the cause of independence down through the centuries. The poem *The Rhythm of Time* shows he also felt part of a vaster, even older invisible, *metaphysical* community of brothers formed of all those who had fought for justice throughout the ages against the overwhelming odds of tyranny in its various guises. These included not just Christ and the first Christian martyrs, but the Roman slaves who took part in the Spartacus rebellion, the English peasants who followed Wat Tyler, the Parisian poor who stormed the Bastille (marching 'upon the serpent's head'), and the Native Americans who defied the charges of the White Man's cavalry till none were left standing.

Irrespective of the objective moral justification for the IRA's struggle or for Sands' contribution to it (if such a thing exists), the flashbacks to epic heroic stands against tyranny in the past convey powerfully his belief in a suprapersonal, cosmically heroic dimension to his struggle which inspires his resolve to resist the British. Though conveyed within a sacralizing narrative, his stoicism stems not from God, but from a primordial instinct in human nature beyond the confines of creed or race to rebel against oppression and injustice and to kill or be killed, armed with an unshakable, fanatical faith in the rightness of the cause, namely to be recognized not as a criminal but as a political prisoner, a prisoner of war, a holy warrior. The song expresses, like no academic analysis ever could, the psychic power unleashed by the process of splitting and heroic doubling which can allow a terrorist not just to feel unrepentant to the end, but to find the courage needed to conquer extreme pain and the fear of annihilation. Had Albert Camus, the author of *The Rebel*, and Bobby Sands read each other, they may well have sensed an elective affinity between them. The first two verses and two of the last three, which frame the poem's evocations of an eternal rebellion against the foe, read:

> There's an inner thing in every man,
> Do you know this thing, my friend?
> It has withstood the blows of a million years,
> And will do so to the end.
>
> It was born when time did not exist,
> And it grew up out of life.
> It cut down evil's strangling vine,
> Like a slashing searing knife

. . .
It is found in every light of hope,
It knows no bounds, nor space
It has risen in red and black and white.
It is there in every race

. . .
It lights the dark of this prison cell.
It thunders forth its might.
It is 'the undauntable thought', my friend,
The thought that says 'I'm right'.[15]

Sands' biography demonstrates in graphic, sometimes gruelling detail, how an essentially secular communal-national terrorist cause only partially legitimized by a religious ethnic marker can, under extreme duress, be cosmized, nomized and *sacralized* into a suprapersonal mission demanding absolute faith to the point of the 'ultimate sacrifice'. It also shows that this process can take place without introducing the *suprahistorical* metaphysical and theological dimension that would mark it out as a form of fundamentalist, as opposed to merely semiotically religious, terrorism. Such a realization lends weight to the argument that it is not religion that produces violence any more than secularity, but the radical act of mythopoeia that produces monomania and fanaticism, an act that certainly may draw on a religion to endow a struggle with a heroic metapolitical dimension, but can equally turn to profane sources if the cultural context is more propitious.[16] The IRA struggle was (and still is for the Continuity IRA which continues it today) essentially Zealotic in its defence of a (mythicized) national homeland from alien occupation, but also Modernist in the powerful futural thrust of the mythic longing for a different Ireland, even for some activists a Marxist Ireland, returned to a homogeneous people freed from oppression and social injustice, the revolutionary dream which inspires so many anti-colonial struggles. If Sands wrote *The Rhythm of Time* now it would probably contain an allusion to Nelson Mandela and the cause he suffered for in his 27 years of imprisonment as a leader of the African National Congress, and even to its terrorist wing, the MK, the Spear of the Nation, which he co-founded.[17]

Sands' testimony also calls into question some assertions made by Mark Juergensmeyer. He claims that the postmodern era has given rise to a 'post-verbal, image-driven kind of political message . . . conveyed by a kind of terrorism that is *wholly different from traditional terrorism*' (my emphasis). Shaped by religion, the acts it inspires are 'less tactical than symbolic'. The terrorists 'are less engaged in a real struggle, one that has immediate goals and gains, than one that is transcendent', conceived as a 'cosmic war', 'an almost Manichaean battle' between good and evil. The result is acts of terror intended as 'a kind of performance, a kind of demonstration'. Mohammed Hafez makes a similar point in his essay on the 'making of suicide bombers': 'Religious reframing can enable moral disengagement by imbuing acts of extreme violence with meaning, purpose, and morality.

It transforms cruel terror into sacred missions in the minds of terrorists.'[18] Yet Sands reminds us that all terrorism, even separatist or irredentist struggles with a precise political goal, has a transcendent metapolitical dimension, and that, however secular the mission is, it can be sacralized to the point of fanaticism and the suppression of empathy with victims in the name of 'freedom' or 'justice'. We also saw earlier that all terrorist violence is both tactical *and* symbolic in its choice of target, since the destruction it carries out is *by definition* a message or 'demonstration' to a target audience, and that the psycho-dynamic process that enabled it to be carried out always involves an inner process of splitting the world into a Manichaean struggle between good and evil.

As for the alleged lack of a precise goal in religious terrorism, this may apply to the more utopian aspects of the Islamist struggle (though the lack of concrete strategic goals is not to be exaggerated),[19] but not to the Sikh or Jewish fundamentalists pursuing an independent homeland, a goal as precise as that found in many secular causes. Indeed, it is the violence of much nihilist, Black, Red, and White terrorism (which are surely with respect to Islamism 'traditional') that has lacked any sort of tangible strategic goal, certainly when compared with the Madrid attacks by 'religious fundamentalists'. Although these were part of a campaign to reconquer for Islam the Andalusian territory 'stolen' from them in the Reconquista, presumably as one stage of global Islamization, the timing of the attacks soon led to Spain's withdrawal of troops from Afghanistan which was probably one of the main goals of the attack, the result of a blend of utopian fanaticism with what Michael Doran called the 'pragmatic' variety. In each of these cases the terrorism was fully 'religious' in the sense that political and social conflicts were perceived by the protagonists themselves as earthy manifestations of supernatural clashes between metaphysical forces of good and evil. This gulf that divides 'secular' from genuinely 'religious' terrorism at the level of *creed* is better understood by considering a well-documented case of terrorism of an exclusively metapolitical nature that derived its rationale, not from a traditional but from a New Religion, in a process that allows the dynamics of nomos formation and terrorist radicalization to be examined in some detail.

'Cosmic truth' in an ocean of anomy

On 20th March 1995 five different subway trains converged on Kasumigaseki Station in the heart of Tokyo carrying bags leaking sarin gas into the crowded compartments. The members of a high profile New Religious Movement (NRM) who had left them there aimed to kill hundreds of thousands, instead of the twelve fatalities and over 5000 injuries actually caused, some of them permanent. Ironically for an NRM obsessed with purity, it was the impurity of the sarin that prevented the intended national catastrophe from occurring, but even so the psychological effect on Japan's sense of security was more profound than that of the Great Hansin earthquake of the previous January which had devastated Kobe. The incident acquired an even more chilling aspect when investigations established that the organization behind it, Aum Shinrikyo (Om Supreme Truth), was bent on building up a vast stockpile of biological weapons, and planned to build or buy nuclear devices in order to wage a war against 'society' on the global scale envisaged at the end of *The Turner Diaries*, though this time to wipe out not racial but spiritual enemies. Within a month of the Tokyo disaster McVeigh's bomb, designed to trigger the type of apocalyptic race war William Pierce had hoped for, would explode in Oklahoma having a profound impact on the US national psyche.

Experts on religious, millennarian, and terroristic violence have painstakingly pieced together the utterly outlandish motivation for this potential terrorist catastrophe in Japan's capital, which would have eclipsed 9/11 in its death toll, if not its global iconoclastic potency. It is a motivation which only becomes intelligible in terms of the arcane religious vision of society and history with which the sect's members were (mostly voluntarily) force-fed. Within the strictly controlled ideological micro-environment of the Aum cult, imposed by its guru Asahara Shoko, the logic of its apocalyptic strategy was impeccable. It was to 'force the end' of the present decadent era of history,[20] which meant hastening the process of society's disintegration and the onset of a Third World War. This in turn was only the prelude to a 'Buddhized' Armageddon ushering in the transformation of Japan into Shambala, the Tibetan paradise, as the spiritual base-camp for the world's final transfiguration through the agency of the Aum movement.

The secondary sources available even in English, which include a particularly sophisticated investigation by Robert Lifton, reveal a textbook case of the metapolitical syndrome underlying terrorist radicalization. It is one which, as the attempted realization of an exclusively metaphysical religious vision, is uncluttered by the pursuit of discernible strategic goals in any material, political, military, or territorial sense. The data collected allow the fatal progression to be traced from Asahara's deeply personal and multi-factorial nomic crisis, to his stage of splitting and Manichaeanization, where these combined with a paradigmatic case of ever intensifying heroic doubling. The concomitant Alice Syndrome took hold to the point where a leader and his followers – here a guru and his adepts – were imbued with a sense of higher mission to carry out acts of violence with a symbolic, metaphysical significance within the Aum narrative, but of unimaginable and utterly pointless destructiveness in the 'real world'. It was during the final phase, when the cosmic war was 'focused' tactically into a series of planned terrorist attacks, that things started going wrong within the parallel metapolitical universe that Asahara had created for his adepts. The botched sarin attack and the discovery of the cult's secret arms factories by the state police precluded the final phase of completion and fulfilment.

The acute nomic crisis which forms the precondition for all NRMs and terrorist radicalization, including Aum Shinrikyo, stems from the permanently liminoid conditions or 'liquid' conditions created by modernity, often combined with other local destabilizing factors. These conditions have fostered the generation of countless new religious nomoi of various permanence and public support since the late nineteenth century. They emerge particularly strongly in 'post-religious' societies where modernity has largely sapped the vitality of traditional religious cultures, but left a widespread dissatisfaction with the spiritual vacuity of the globalized materialism of 'the West'. Although they surface sporadically in all Westernized societies, they thus are a particular feature of parts of the US, Brazil, and South East and Eastern Asia.[21] Some new religions have hit the headlines because they produce group, or even mass, suicides, such as 'Heaven's Gate' in the US, 'The Order of the Solar Temple' based in Switzerland, and 'Peoples Temple', which ran the colony in Jonestown, Guyana where in 1978, 918 sect members and their children 'voluntarily' died, either stabbed or poisoned. New Religions have sometimes been associated with self-defensive violence, most famously at the shootout of the Branch Davidians with the FBI at their ranch near Waco. However, until the Aum cult none were associated with terrorism.

If a terrorist NRM was going to emerge anywhere it was likely to be in Japan. Already in the early part of the century, the country's feat in achieving its rapid transformation into a leading industrial and military power, without dismantling its feudal system, had produced religious convulsions, and given rise to a number of significant New Age cults. The much more fundamental postwar transformations carried out in the aftermath of defeat in the war, the dropping of atomic bombs on two major cities, and the destruction of the Emperor system, only intensified the liminoidality already endemic to its modernity. Soon the country was awash with symptoms of profound anomy: addictive mechanical and electronic games, a sprawling subculture of 'extreme' science-fiction, B-movies with apocalyptic scenarios involving giant monsters, comics portraying 'fantasy' military and erotic violence, powerful student protests and public displays of violent utopian politics left and right. These included the attempt to re-enact the officers' revolt of the 'February 26 Incident', which failed like its predecessor, leading to the ritual suicide of the famous writer Yukio Mishima in a protest against contemporary 'Western' decadence. From the 1970s onwards, bizarre cultic New Religions mushroomed, all symptomatic of the thick substratum of anomy lying just below the surface of the new prosperity, all offering existential shelter from the storm of materialism, the aching psychological loneliness, and turmoil of spiritual confusion. Peculiarly Japanese social traditions predisposed some young Japanese to surrender themselves blindly to a cult, especially if it demanded material and physical sacrifice. Among these was the readiness to endure extreme pain in macho initiation rites, and to undergo a process of psychic self-emptying or 'self-annihilation' so as to be filled with the will of the leader.[22]

Lifton stresses the role played by an 'unmoored state' in Asahara's path to guru status,[23] a state of anomy accentuated by poverty and near-blindness. Driven by a longing for the transcendence of materialism, he joined the new religion Agonshu in 1981. Within four years he had founded his own religion, which in 1987 had been renamed Aum Shinrikyo, – Aum representing the primordial sound of cosmic creation and Shinrikyo meaning 'Supreme Truth'. Having assumed the role of a *propheta* endowed with special powers to lead the disaffected away from a doomed society and into a spiritual paradise, Asahara embarked on a sustained act of 'mazeway resynthesis', typical of all NRMs,[24] to assemble the highly syncretic nomos which would be the basis for the 'ideological totalism' of Aum Shinrikyo. He fused elements of (Tibetan) Buddhism, yoga, the Shiva cult, the prophetic role of Jesus,

Christian millennarianism, the eschatological prophecies of Nostradamus, astrology, notions of 'sacred' science, and the apprehension of higher planes of reality cultivated by the drug underground and the Hippie counter-culture to produce an apocalyptic variant of Eastern mysticism, complete with an elaborate hermetic discourse, hierarchy, and ritual. The fulcrum of this Gnostic vision was the imminent 'Armageddon' which will only be survived by those with great karma or by membership of Aum.[25] On one level it was a project rooted in Zealotic fantasies of preserving and harnessing reservoirs of ancient wisdom buried by modernity – an exercise of recuperation and restoration of Perennial Wisdom undertaken by nineteenth-century Theosophy and many New Age cults since such as the Neo-Druids. But this nomos-conserving impulse was fused with the nomothetic drive to create a new sacred canopy to restore the spirituality of the world through revolutionary acts of 'Modernism of the deed', deeds of cataclysmic annihilation. As in all such cases of Nechayevian 'positive nihilism', precisely how lethal attacks on society would lead to the new era in practical terms was of no concern. The palingenesis would simply unfold as the corollary of Armageddon, following the dream logic of all apocalyptic fantasies based on 'creative destruction'.

In the process of concocting the Aum doctrine, Asahara had Manichaeanized the world in a way which split it into a handful of the saved fighting an invisible war against billions of damned – an elite even smaller numerically than the non-dysgenic Whites left after the 'cleansing hurricane' depicted at the end of *The Turner Diaries*, or those taken in the 'rapture' portrayed in the *Left Behind* series. But Aum's elite would not be 'taken'. Their job was to stay and survive the end of the world. Asahara knew this because he had himself written his own version of an apocalyptic narrative of the sort that dominated the popular imagination in postwar Japan, the most famous example in the West being the *Godzilla* film series.[26] The world was deep in the throes of the age of darkness, the Kali Yuga of the Hindus, the *mappa* of the Buddhist scheme of history, the *eschatos* of the Book of Revelation (even the end of the world was conceived syncretically in Aum doctrine!). The moral decadence, the earthquakes, the social unrest were all portents of the end and harbingers of palingenesis.[27] It was a script which naturally gave Asahara himself, or rather his cosmic avatar, the starring role of prophet, messiah, exterminating angel, cosmic guru, and elemental God, an act of heroic doubling on a truly megalomaniacal scale. From within his ideologically 'locked-in' state of mind, displaying the paranoia, conspiracy theory, and apocalypticism typical of the 'fundamentalist mindset' referred to in Chapter 5, Asahara planned and began executing his own global Project Mayhem on a scale far greater than anything Tyler Durden could have dreamt up even in his most manic moments.

He was able to deliver a pragmatic dimension to his fanaticism thanks to his success in attracting so many well-educated, technically expert, money-generating supporters only too anxious to join his private *communitas*, secede from a doomed society and achieve transcendence, even at the cost of intensive painful, humiliating rituals of self-mortification. The indoctrination process followed to the letter the one described so perceptively in Lalich's *Bounded Choice*. Helped by a long Japanese tradition of leader and hero worship, highly professional but spiritually unmoored young men willingly became 'clones' of the leader. This could involve taking the Nazi concept of 'working towards the *Führer*' one stage further by wearing a special headset to listen to Asahara's brainwaves – a hi-tech version of the Emperor's New Clothes principle.[28] Interviews carried out by Lifton[29] and Juergensmeyer[30] with former Aum cult members bring out how successfully the barrage of brainwashing techniques endured by cult members produced a permanently altered consciousness. It appears that many of them emulated the guru's heroic doubling to the point where they believed they had found the nomic certainty they craved.[31] At that point some internalized the Armageddon scenario as the only lens through which to experience contemporary events even beyond the sarin attacks. One of them explained that the cult's success was due to the fact that 'it spoke to the needs of people to find certainty and a framework for understanding the unseen forces in the world around them'.[32] Lifton goes further. The 'ecstatic merger of leader and follower' induced by the cult facilitated the experience of a highly addictive 'rapturous state', of 'bliss', of the 'joy of self-surrender', of 'ecstasy', of an 'experiential transcendence' so 'intense and all-encompassing that in it time and death disappear'.[33] For some within Asahara's thrall the Aum creed had replaced the lost nomos.

From fantasy war to act of religious terrorism

The degenerate time and death of the Buddhist *mappa* or Hindu Kali Yuga, or the Christian 'end days' would not be transcended until the old order had been destroyed in a cosmic conflagration. Though Asahara started off with a relatively benign, non-destructive interpretation of his sacred mission, the failure of Aum to win electoral support and the first hostile comments on his group's activities in the press seem to have intensified his paranoia and triggered ever more apocalyptic fantasies, which he naturally claimed to be prophetic visions. (There are striking parallels with the *propheta* role played by Jan Bockelson for the Anabaptists of Munster).[34] Aum's vast financial and human resources were channelled into creating facilities for building weapons of mass destruction (WMD) to launch a war on a fallen world so as to accelerate the advent of Shambala, and the Buddhist principle of *poa* (delivering a humane death to those already fated to die) was perverted (and even hard-boiled relativists would surely agree this was a perversion) to justify mass murder. When assassinations began occurring to cover up what was going on, the police started to investigate.

The radicalization of Aum and its guru now entered the final stage: focusing and the practical implementation of a plan. The campaign of unleashing WMD to trigger Armageddon was brought forward, the nuclear attack was to be preceded by a lower-key assault on the complacent citizens of the *mappa*, and the target was selected: the Tokyo subway system. Unlike the 7/7 bombers, whose choice of the London underground stations seemed arbitrary, Asahara displayed an exquisite iconoclastic imagination when planning the subway attacks, so as to maximize the intensity of the symbolic message it conveyed. The emissions of the chemical warfare agent, sarin gas, were planned to be at their most intense when the five trains converged at Kasumigaseki station, a nuclear bomb-proof space deep under the centre of Tokyo's government buildings and the Imperial Palace. Aum would strike right at the mythic heart of Japan's sense of security following the same symbolic logic that led Conrad's character in *The Secret Agent* to select for destruction the temporal centre of global modernity, Greenwich. As in the novel, Asahara's plan failed, and led to a massive security operation which uncovered his cult's vast complex of secret research and weapons facilities, including a giant microwave for incinerating the bodies of enemies and defectors. The guru and his adepts were denied the ecstasy of seeing Armageddon unfold before their eyes.

The Aum cult represents an extreme example of the Alice Syndrome in operation. The gigantization of Asahara's leader-hero persona – as guru he bestowed on others the warrior-hero persona of executing the actual murders – magnified to *manga* comic proportions by the success of his cult and adoration of his followers, eventually led to a total breakdown of the reality principle. This enabled him to give free rein to a Manichaeanized fantasy world dominated by paranoia, megalomania, conspiracy theories, apocalyptic visions, and psychotic fixations which equated destruction with purification, a terrorist world war with the purging of a degenerate humanity. With the right technical assistance his fully ideologized psychosis[35] might have led to the deaths of hundreds of thousands had the various WMD worked properly, producing an act of 'propaganda of the deed' against the modern world compared with which anything undertaken by Modernist terrorists working in the Nechayevian tradition of active nihilism, Red, Black, or White, would have paled into insignificance. Asahara's crusade was thus a prime example of what Franco Bruno called a 'fantasy war',[36] whose inner dynamics are captured in one of Robert Lifton's penetrating observations:

> In psychological terms, what we need to realize is that what happens within the personality of a man like Asahara is that 'self' and 'the world' become combined. But instead of the self becoming, so to speak, a part of the world, the world becomes an aspect of the self. The projection of Armageddon, buttressed by various forms of ideology, becomes, in a psychological sense, a reading of the self, a projection of the self and an assertion of the self that contains the world.[37]

In other words, Asahara was in the thrall of the Alice Syndrome, his 'real self' utterly overpowered and neutralized by his grotesque cosmic avatar, a plot all too familiar from children's science fiction.

Lifton points to parallels with the case of the paranoid schizophrenic, Daniel Schreber, meticulously recorded by Sigmund Freud, who also became haunted by a sense of the world's imminent annihilation at his hands, a destruction only he would survive so as to take up the mission to renew mankind. He was thus the 'human being on whom everything turns', 'the Saviour of the World and the Ruler of the World'.[38] The crucial difference is that Asahara's psychosis was the product of a protracted period of cosmization and nomization carried out within the protective shell of his own cult, and that he took the destructive phase of his palingenetic vision to the threshold of strategic and technological realization. True to the fatal logic of totalitarian 'creative destruction' that so terribly disfigured the twentieth century, a revitalization movement had become an annihilation movement. One of the 'underground men' described by Dostoevsky a hundred years earlier had now left his subterranean lair and turned his *ressentiment* into a totalizing eschatological cosmology as lethal as any bomb waiting to go off, and had formed his own terrorist underground movement of disciples to enact it. Some would have had the advanced scientific technological know-how and fanatical devotion to use their Master's resources to place not plastic bags of sarin, but a 'radiological dispersal device', a 'dirty bomb', in the heart of Tokyo instead, to realize Aum's version of Project Mayhem to carry out a single symbolic strike against the evil of modern urban civilization. It was the turn of God's orphans to be Gods themselves. History, WMD technology, science fiction, forgotten wisdom, ancient religions, millennarian prophesies, and psychotic fantasies would then all have come to fruition simultaneously in one blinding flash of purification, cartoon-like in its fantasy-time apocalypticism, but deadly serious in its consequences for living human beings in real time.

Bobby Sands and Aum teach us how in the liminoid conditions of modernity secular motives for terrorist violence can become hybridized with elements drawn from established religion or imbued with genuine sacrality through instinctive but idiosyncratic mystic impulses, or else an elaborate home-grown act of religious syncretism can be radically secularized by carrying out sociopathic acts of violence against existing society. We are hopefully now in the position to make more sense of the terrorist creed that for over a decade has dominated the attention of media, terrorologists, and counter-insurgency forces, even to the point of detracting attention from other potentially destructive causes: Islamism.

9
Islamism's Global War against Nomocide

The elusive nature of political Islam

So far in this volume there has been fleeting talk of Islamism only in the context of the call from 'terrorologists' Jeffrey Cozzens and Jeffrey Bale for more attention to be given to the cultural, non-instrumental, 'expressive' aspects of Global Salafi Jihad (GSJ) in Chapter 1, and the replacement of a more traditional Sufism-oriented commitment to Islam by Salafism among the dominant factions of Chechen rebels noted in Chapter 6. Yet this book, like so many of the analyses, conferences, and documentaries on terrorism that have proliferated in the last decade, is obviously written in the sinister non-shadows cast by the absent Twin Towers which still subliminally dominate the Manhattan skyline in such ghostly fashion. The thorny issue of Islamism must thus be addressed head-on in any sustained investigation of the 'terrorist's creed', even if the task is undertaken by a non-Muslim such as myself with no knowledge of Arabic and only a second-hand, mediated knowledge of Islam's extraordinarily diverse history, culture, religion, and politics.

I am not alone. After the Iranian Revolution of 1979, the joke circulated that Pentagon experts on the Middle East were 'speed-reading the Quran'[1] for clues to the unexpected success of the Ayatollah Khomeini's revolution in deposing the pro-US Shah. It would seem that, with the honourable exception of a handful of longstanding non-Muslim specialists in Middle Eastern historians, religion, and politics, most of the West's 'post-Christian' political scientists and historians of terrorism are still pretty clueless about what may well be, at least in devotional rather than simply nominal terms, the world's most demographically and culturally dynamic religion – estimated at 1.5 billion followers and rising. For the rest of us the 'methodological empathy' needed to understand the deeper motivations of Islamist violence is inevitably problematic at a cultural and theological, if not a human level, even though that does little to prevent a steady stream of simplistic or ill-informed opinion on the subject in the Western press and some would-be 'expert' publications. As Olivier Roy, author of *Globalized Islam*, points out, even before discussing Islamism's relationship to Islam there is the problem of establishing what constitutes a Muslim:

How do we begin to isolate and categorise the complex and multilevel practices of more than one billion Muslims living in many different social, cultural and geographical conditions? How are we to designate a specific attitude as 'Muslim' or 'Islamic'?[2]

One of the few qualified to act as an effective mediator between the intensely variegated Islamic world and Western academia, is the Damascus-born Bassam Tibi, who was steeped in Islam's religious and social culture before becoming a German citizen, and eventually found his vocation as a tireless protagonist of a moderate 'Euro-Islam'. Trained as a Western political scientist, he devoted considerable energy in the decades before and after 9/11 to attacking Islamist extremism on theological, historical, and humanistic grounds. It is thus wise to heed his warning not to pronounce dogmatically on political Islam without the prerequisite knowledge, since 'in order to talk about Islam, Islamism and Islamists you have to go, talk to them, live among them'. He is particularly disparaging about self-proclaimed experts on Islamism whose 'language capacities do not go beyond restaurant and hotel requirements'.[3] Another major expert in this area, the German academic Kai Hafez, whose name suggests a Turkish and Muslim family background, goes so far as to claim that serious studies of Islamic politics remain a 'marginal academic field' eclipsed by journalistic polemicists, 'while the real specialists at best make it into the media during periods of extreme crisis'.[4]

To take just one example of the problems encountered by the non-specialist, the question of Islamic orthodoxy and heterodoxy, which holds the key to judging whether a particular Islamic creed is a 'perversion' or 'hybrid' of 'genuine' orthodox faith, is no less fraught than in the case of Christianity, which has had its own intensely fissiparous history since the Reformation. The main Sunni and Shi'ite branches, both of which have national and regional dialects, and the many smaller off-shoots such as Sufism and Wahhabism, not to mention the proliferating variants of modern fundamentalism, all claim historical and scriptural legitimacy as the true version of the Islamic faith in a way reminiscent of zealous Protestant sects in Europe and the US since the sixteenth century, with the added problem that there is no equivalent of the Vatican or the Holy Synod to pronounce authoritatively on the theological issues raised. The topic of Islam as a source of 'religious terrorism' is further complicated by a plethora of terms used in its Anglophone analysis which can sometimes make it difficult to establish precisely what is under discussion.[5] For example, in reference to Al Qaeda and its associated organizations, Political Islam, Radical Islam, Global Salafi Jihad, Salafi-Jihadism, Jihadism, and Salafism are current as alternatives for 'Islamism', while one expert, Jonathan Githens-Mazer, uses 'radical violent *takfiri* jihadism (RVTJ)' for what appears to be substantially the same phenomenon.[6]

Nor does it help when the debate is framed by the deployment of such typical products of Neocon Newspeak as 'the Axis of Evil' and 'Islamofascism'. Such terms had gained currency even before 9/11, and in its immediate aftermath understandably resonated for a time with wide strata of the US public on a 'gut' level while revanchist nationalist passions were high. Even in Europe many more of those transfixed by the images of the towers crumbling to dust may have been seduced by a reductionist perspective which assumes that Islam's militancy in the West somehow represents its only face, thereby ignoring the existence both of a 'humanistic' strain in classical and historical Islam, and the emergence in the twentieth century of factors leading to its moderation, whether for idealistic or pragmatic reasons. This now makes the *de facto* acceptance of multiculturalism statistically far more representative of sentiments within the Muslim diaspora than jihadism, a point to which we will return.

Nevertheless, contrary to the wishful thinking of Islamophiles, which seems to include most academics, fantasies of a global *umma* have been integral to Islamic aspirations for the world ever since the days of the Prophet. With the rise of Islamism in the 1930s a strident minority of Muslims were already interpreting contemporary history as a 'clash of civilizations' long before Samuel Huntington's book appeared as a riposte to the Panglossian optimism of Fukuyama's *The End of History* in 1996. Despite the events of the last 20 years much 'liberal' opinion in the West adopts an 'apologist' stance towards Islam, keen to play down the centuries of its imperialistic struggle to colonize and convert large parts of Europe, and to minimize the risk posed to democracy not just by Islamist 'extremism', but by the globalizing aspirations and 'occident-phobia' of many non-violent Muslims. Although post-Christian Europeans are now supposed to feel remorse about the savagery of Christian knights exhibited during the Crusades, there is no equivalent call within the Islamic world for Muslims to recognize centuries of savagery displayed in the construction of its vast empires by nominally Muslim rulers. This leads some of the more rigorous scholars to dissociate themselves *both* from tendentially racist 'Islam-bashing' in the popular press, and from overcompensatory ultra-liberal 'Islamophilia' within academia.[7] Fortunately, a number of Western, often Anglophone, experts[8] have spent years acquiring the prerequisite skills to approach Islamic radicalism from 'inside' and arrive at more considered assessments, on which the following analysis can draw.

Clearly, few original revelations about Islamism can be expected here. The intentions of this section are more modest: to highlight those aspects of Islamism and Islamist terrorism already established by serious scholars which acquire a fresh significance in the light of our general thesis on the metapolitics of the terrorist's creed as a response to modernity. What stands out clearly whatever source is consulted is that traditional Islam is undergoing a deep and protracted nomic crisis under the increasing impact of a globalizing secularization, one that in the long term may genuinely threaten its very existence as a living faith and existentially effective nomos. According to our model of modernity, this is true of all religions exposed to its nomocidal forces, but Islam's increasingly liminoid situation, both within the Islamic world and among its growing diaspora community, is particularly intense and deeply resistant to generalization. An individual Muslim's sacred canopy is exposed to different pressures according to whether it is being maintained in a democratic, authoritarian, or theocratic Islamic state, one with or without deep sectarian divides, in an 'enemy-occupied' or submerged Islamic nation, or in a multicultural and multi-faith Western, Eastern, or African society containing significant communities of diaspora Muslims. Particularly in the secularized West, diaspora Muslims face a daily struggle with nomocidal forces, which makes them a vital source of recruitment to the most radical forms of political Islam.[9] Generation, education, and class also condition individual Muslim reactions to modernity.[10]

To complicate the situation for would-be commentators further, there are also deep-seated, seemingly atavistic factors feeding 'occident-phobia' among extremists, notably collective Muslim memories of the extraordinarily bloody Crusades[11] carried out by fanatical 'Christianists' nine centuries ago (which makes the term 'crusade' by a recent US president so laden with negative connotations to Muslim ears). *Ressentiment* is also exacerbated by a diffused sense, especially pronounced within the younger generation, that the once glorious Islamic Empire – which at its height included sizeable territories in Eastern Europe – has been humiliatingly eclipsed by a technologically and militarily more powerful but spiritually hollow, even 'infidel' West. In addition, there is also the important but widely neglected fact that Islam has a particularly tormented relationship with the world of secular democracies because it has largely retained its collective charge of religious faith at a premodern level of intensity reminiscent of the fervour which characterized Western Christianity in the sixteenth century, when Europe was awash with religious fanaticism and hosted violent reactions to the socio-economic and political upheavals of early modernity, not least the cosmological turmoil of the High Renaissance. Threatened by an acute multifactorial liminoidality, Europe generated 'fundamentalist' passions bent on preserving the Christian sacred canopy intact, unleashing outbursts of millennarianism, religious wars, the sporadic persecution and exquisitely barbaric torture of heretics and 'witches', as well as a systematic conquest of New World native American cultures regarded as 'pagan' which was carried out with at times an almost genocidal fury in the name of God.[12] In addition, there are numerous historical, geopolitical, ethnic, and theological factors peculiar to Islam which fuel its internal factionalization[13] and intensify its problematic relationship with modernity.[14]

However, it is Islamism as the basis of anti-state terrorism, not Islam's 'predicament with modernity' that must be our focus in this chapter. Rather than attempt to synthesize expert accounts of Islamism's genesis or recent history, I propose to identify six ideal-typical responses of Islam to the modern world within which to locate it. This will hopefully allow new aspects of the relationship of Islamist terrorism to mainstream Islam (or rather Islams) to be thrown into relief that can easily be lost sight of in a detailed 'diachronic' account of its emergence.

Six Islamic reactions to the threat of nomocide

One reaction of Muslims to modernity is a process deeply familiar to those conversant with the history of Christianity over the last 300 years, since it consists of the gradual 'privatization' of faith.[15] In pragmatic terms this has the effect of imparting Islam with an everyday, outward tolerance of the non-Muslim 'Other', whether religious or secular, but without it being articulated as a conscious ideal, let alone

expressed as a fully elaborated theory of 'liberal Islam' and the values of tolerance and pluralism at its core. The result is a *de facto* moderate Islam, which may
still exhibit considerable religious zeal and fundamentalist strictness both within
the religious community and within the domestic sphere, and hence behaviour
incompatible with secular concepts of individual human rights. It is made possible by the innate capacity in human beings for operating a functionally stable
and normalized psychological division between the collective social sphere (society at large) and the specific community or family to which they belong. It is
the default situation of the many millions of diaspora Muslims, as well as the
members of many other religious and ethnic communities, living in pluralistic
Western democracies from Amsterdam to Toronto. It allows them to maintain a
personal, familial, and communal sacred canopy, while avoiding stressful tensions
with other belief-systems within the shared social space, particularly conflicts over
the many norms of the 'host' nation which contradict Islamic mores.

If the Islamic experience were to follow that of Christianity, then this privatization of Islamic faith within Westernized societies would over time lead to a gradual
secularization and 'cooling off' of faith to a point where mass apostasy would
result at an experiential level, even if the external communal and ritual trappings
of Islam were retained with respect to annual religious festivals, birth, marriage,
and death. Naturally pockets and islands of sectarian and fundamentalist fervour
might remain, as it does in the scattered evangelical Christian communities of the
contemporary US. However, the continued intensity of Islamic faith in pluralistic
religious societies such as India and Indonesia would indicate that the privatization of faith as a basis for coexistence with other religions that have retained their
vitality need not necessarily lead to secularism.

Another category of Islamic reaction to modernization is represented by those
states formed under the impact of European nation-building, either after the collapse of the Ottoman Empire in 1923 or in the wave of decolonization following
the Second World War. These states, often authoritarian regimes if not out-and-
out dictatorships, became *de facto* secular political systems at the level of executive
power, attitude to economics, stance on technology, civil bureaucracy, and foreign
and social policy, with no attempt to make clerical theology or Shari'a law the basis
of society. Post-liberation Algeria, the Egypt of Nasser and Mubarak, Ba'athist Iraq
and Syria, Arabia under the Saud dynasty, and the Sudan before the fundamentalist regime installed by Colonel Hasan al-Bashir in 1989[16] provide examples of
this highly variegated phenomenon. It involves a process of partial modernization which encourages the division between personal, communal faith and the
civic life imposed by a political regime, a division comparable in some respects to
the evolution of Islam among diaspora Muslims. The political classes and media
in the West seem keen to convince themselves that the 'Arab Spring' represents
a groundswell of fervour for liberal change led by a logged-on youth embracing
Western values. Only time will tell whether each country where it has taken place
will in fact undergo a sustainable transition towards a democratic society based on
a 'modernized' Islam that genuinely embraces a cultural and religious pluralism
upheld through 'people power'.There may result instead an era of deep instability

in which reinvigorated and regrouped authoritarian forces struggle for hegemony with groups locked in sectarianism conflict with each other. One of the main opposition groupings is a speciously 'democratic' Islamism which will shed its parliamentary façade at the earliest opportunity, concreting over the green shoots of anything resembling religious humanism or secular individualism with slabs of Shari'a law. It should not be forgotten that Europe's liberal and socialist 'spring' of 1848 was followed by the authoritarian winter of 1849–50 where autocracy reasserted its hold over European societies in a number of guises.

The privatization of Islam inside or outside the direct Islamic sphere of influence, though rarely acknowledged by Muslim clerics as a viable or desirable strategy for the long-term survival of their religion, offers one potential route to the conservation, at least in the medium term, of a still existentially vital but tolerant and pacifistic Islamic faith within 'modern' multi-ethnic and multi-religious societies, one which would place it on a par with the many other privatized faiths whose peaceful coexistence is accommodated by liberal societies. The interiorization of faith envisaged here can build on the firmly established 'cultural schizophrenia' which already makes millions of Muslims happy to operate the fruits of the West's technological rationality while still rejecting on theological grounds the premises of secular science that created them.[17]

A third ideal-typical Islamic response to modernization is represented by (mostly educated, Westernized) Muslims who consciously embrace the separation of faith from State and reject on principle the use of violence and oppression by a theocratic regime to impose a conservative Islam as their society's total and exclusive sacred canopy, let alone its imposition over the whole world. Instead they proactively work towards the emergence of an ideologically elaborated, non-secular but liberal form of Muslim participation in democratic civil society both nationally and internationally. Its underlying premise is that humanism need not be based on an aggressively atheistic brand of Western secular humanism informed by the Darwinian premises about human history and nature represented in the Anglophone world by Richard Dawkins and the journal *New Humanist*. Moderate Muslims see the 'humanization' of Islam as pragmatically necessary for it to thrive within a globalized modernity, as well as being legitimized theologically by a neglected 'deep structure' of tolerance of the Other within Islam itself. Advocates of moderate Islam point to theological corroboration of their positive stance on civic values and human rights familiar within Western liberalism in certain passages in the Quran and their associated Hadiths which promote compassion and harmonious coexistence with non-Muslims. These date from the Meccan period of Islam's history when Muslims constituted a small community subject to persecution, and hence predating the supremacism of the Medinan period.[18] Optimists about the prospect that the 'Meccan' face of Islam will prevail over its deeply engrained 'Medinan' version should remember that in its infancy Islam had to confront the existence of *religious* pluralism and coexistence, and not the far more challenging task of surviving as a scattered continent of ardent faith in an ocean of secularism.

For its protagonists this 'submerged' moderate patrimony of 'true' Islam, inevitably highly contested by conservative traditionalists and jihadists, makes it compatible with religious pluralism, social justice, gender equality, progress in the natural sciences, the rationalization of state governance, globalized technology, and transcultural humanistic values,[19] even if major issues remain concerning the degree to which Islamic science can ever accommodate a non-Creationist view of the cosmos. Some liberal Muslims idealize the seven centuries of *La Convivencia* in Southern Spain (711–1492 AD) as a Golden Era of tolerant Islam, but it is important not to romanticize a period in which in Muslim Spain (Al-Andalus) non-Muslims were treated as second-class citizens (*dhimmi*) subject to social exclusion and occasional persecution despite the intense intellectual exchanges between Muslim, Jewish, and Christian scholars.

None of these three reactions to modernity are conducive to radicalization processes leading to acts of 'religious terrorism', even if nominally Islamic autocracies may well resort to (essentially secular) state terror to maintain their grip on power in the face of popular sectarian or democratic unrest, as was so dramatically illustrated in the Arab Spring. The fourth reaction to be considered is highly conducive to violence, however. It comprises what we have earlier called 'communal-nationalist-religious' movements whose primary concern is to ensure that state power is not yielded to foreign or non-Islamic interests, and to protect the hegemony of the Islamic nomos within a particular territory as the identity marker of a particular ethnic group or 'people', but without attempting to install a theocracy run by clerics or pursue a global Islamization. It thus fulfils the criteria of the Zealotic terrorist movement we already encountered in Chapter 6, one which arises in societies threatened by foreign occupation or divided by irredentist, separatist or sectarian conflicts generated by internal struggles over power, territory, resources, or identity. It recruits support from a minority of Muslims with a militant disposition able to imbue their lives with meaning and purpose by 'sacrificing' themselves to the temporalized cause of their beleaguered community and tradition under the banner of their faith.

Although the 'heroic doubling' they experience may convince them they are enlisted in a metaphysical battle against a demonized enemy, closer inspection reveals their struggle not to be a 'religious war' in any meaningful sense, and as such it tends to have more immediate political and social causes than a war against a disenchanting 'modernity'. The inhuman refugee situation in Gaza and on the West Bank created by the annexation of Palestinian territory to create the State of Israel in 1948 and the subsequent wars provided the ideal conditions to incubate the Palestinian Liberation Organization and foster the emergence of Fatah as its largest faction. Meanwhile, the extraordinarily factionalized Lebanese Civil War (1975–90), which cost over 200,000 lives, brought into being an Islamic movement such as Amal, pursuing secular goals thinly veiled in religious rationales in a way that parallels the ideology of the first generations of Chechen separatists.

In Iraq too, many of the devastating acts of sectarian violence between Sunnis and Shi'ites since the US occupation are expressions of communal-nationalist-religious tensions of a civil war intensity, rather than being part of a war against the West as such (although, as in the case of both the Taliban and the Chechen separatists, recruits to such movements may well prove highly susceptible to

Islamization and a concomitant globalization of long-term objectives). For the moment both factions attempt to ensure that the new Iraq will adopt their model of an alternative, specifically Islamic, socio-political modernity in their conflict-torn region. Their effort to preserve the traditional nomos have thus in practice made considerable concessions to secularization and *Realpolitik*.

All these four responses to modernity's nomocidal forces would be rejected as a betrayal of true Islam by our last two ideal-typical responses to modernity, which together constitute what has come to be known as 'Islamism'. Indeed, their differing concessions to pluralism and the temporal are seen by Islamists not just as symptomatic of the moral decay of Islam and its shameful subservience to 'the West', but of the slide of the vast majority of the world's Muslims and Islamic governments into a state of *jahiliyyah*. This is an Arabic term denoting apostasy, or more precisely the 'ignorance of divine guidance' that existed before the revelations of the Prophet Mohammed, the religious equivalent of what came to be called 'decadence' in nineteenth-century Europe. For Islamists urgent, violent action is essential before the sacred canopy of Islam is lost forever.

Maududi, Qutb, and the first wave of Islamism

As should have become clear by now, 'Islamism' is used in these pages to refer to the project of not just preserving the Islamic sacred canopy, but imposing it as the unique nomos for all humanity. This means gaining universal hegemony for a fundamentalist version of Islam which, as will become clear, has assumed several features of a modernized version of a totalitarian, globalizing, and violent religious creed. Its ultimate goal was summed up succinctly in November 2011 by Dr Muhammad Badi, the supreme leader of the Muslim Brotherhood in Egypt, as 'a rightly guided Caliphate and *mastership of the world*'.[20] Such mastership necessitates the universalization of Islam via the creation of the global *umma*, or community of Islamic faith, one which has achieved theological, moral, social, economic and political ascendancy over all other cultures and political systems. At this point the nomocidal threat of the West to Islam's nomos, along with that of any rival religion, will have been eliminated once and for all.

For Islamists this utopian goal is to be achieved through one of two strategies, both guided by what its proponents believe is the spirit of the Prophet Himself and the true will of Allah. The first – our fifth ideal type of Islamic responses to modernity – is to establish Islamic states based on Shari'a Law as bastions against Westernization as the precondition for reversing the process of Westernization in a gradual but inexorable movement towards Islamic world power. This 'Statist Islamism' is thus intrinsically hostile to liberal concepts of humanism, pluralism, and a civil society. Yet it does not preclude the purely tactical short-term involvement in democratic and electoral politics in a way reminiscent of the interwar Communist theory of 'entryism'[21] in order to gain power. This strategy has unfortunately deceived some Islamophiles into believing that Islamism has the potential to mutate into a moderate form of Islam, something which it could only do by ceasing to be Islamism.

The second form of activist Islamism, and our sixth ideal type, has adopted the tactic of fighting a de-territorialized holy war, or 'jihad' with the West which is not based on the state's deployment of armed forces or directed exclusively against conventional military targets. Instead it exploits the devastating modern potential to disrupt democracies through acts of terrorist violence carried out against carefully selected targets within civil society. It corresponds to what we have already encountered as Global Salafi Jihad (GSJ). State Islamism and GSJ Islamism correspond to what Peter Demant calls the second and third waves of Islamism, the first of which he identifies as a sustained phase of ideological elaboration and dissemination (1967–81). This was followed by the State phase of the 1980s dominated by the establishment of an Islamic theocracy in Iran, and then by the GSJ phase (1991–2001) dominated by the emergence of Al Qaeda and culminating in the 9/11 attacks on New York and Washington. The post-9/11 period Demant treats as a fourth but unnamed phase in which all three manifestations of Islamism, ideology, Statism and Jihadism, play a crucial role in asserting Islamism's bid for ascendancy.[22]

Before considering Statist and GSJ Islamism as strategies to protect the Islamic nomos from being ravaged by nomocidal modernity, it is worth considering the first wave of Islamism's elaboration as a globalizing project. It was the period of acute liminoidality for Islamic culture following the end of the Ottoman Empire in 1923 that saw the first explicit formulations of Islam in modern totalitarian terms. In other words, Islamism was a product of the same era of acute nomic crisis that gave birth to Bolshevism and fascism as totalizing forms of political modernism. Thus Jeffrey Bale describes Islamism as the 'third major totalitarian ideological movement to arise in the course of an immensely destructive twentieth century',[23] a position endorsed by Mehdi Mozaffari[24] and Bassam Tibi.[25] The two most influential ideologues of the pre-1939 period were the Indian Abu Al-Ala Maududi and the Egyptian Hassan al-Banna, founder of the Muslim Brotherhood, both of whom conceived the project of overthrowing the hegemony of the West by establishing Islam as the sole basis of a new world order which would resolve once and for all the deepening crisis of anarchy and spiritual decay that they saw engulfing the world. In a speech made in Lahore in 1939 under the title *Jihad in Islam*, Maududi spelt out the global nature of the Muslims' earthly mission to secure the (spiritual and certainly not material) wellbeing of all humanity:

> The sole interest of Islam is the welfare of mankind. Islam has its own particular ideological standpoint and practical programme to carry out reforms for the welfare of mankind. *Islam wishes to destroy all states and governments anywhere on the face of the earth which are opposed to the ideology and programme of Islam regardless of the country or the Nation which rules it.*[26]

It is deeply significant in the context of our analysis of the metapolitics of fanatical violence that in order to transform Islam from a metaphysical world-view into a creed of global this-worldly political transformation through destruction, Maududi created a hybrid of Zealotic with Modernist terrorism. His calls to arms are based on classical Islamic conceptions of the duty of Muslims to spread Islam until it dominates the whole world, and hence of coexistence between Muslims and 'infidels' as a temporary arrangement. Yet the discourse of Islamic imperialism has been modernized under the influence of 'communist ideas about the party as a vanguard of the revolution', and a concept of the 'state as an explicitly ideological institution meant to produce a utopian society'.[27] This new vision of the state's role as the key to the re-Islamization of the world had a major influence on other fundamentalist militants, notably the Ayatollah Khomeini himself, whom he met personally in 1963 and who translated his works into Farsi. In this way Maududi exerted direct influence on the foundation of the Iranian theocracy. However, perhaps his most enduring legacy was the hybrid connotations he imparted to '*jihad*' by infusing the traditional ideal of the 'striving on the path to God', which could under prescribed circumstances sanction the recourse to violence to defend Islam from its enemies, with the modern Marxist connotations of a revolutionary struggle to usher in an imminent new world order through human agency. In Maududi's own words:

> In reality Islam is a revolutionary ideology and programme which seeks to alter the social order of *the whole world* and rebuild it in conformity with its own tenets and ideals. 'Muslim' is the title of that International Revolutionary Party organized by Islam to carry into effect its revolutionary programme. And '*Jihād*' *refers to that revolutionary struggle* and utmost exertion which the Islamic Party brings into play to achieve this objective.[28]

It was after the Second World War, however, that Islamism found its most influential ideologue. When Gamal Nasser overthrew the Egyptian monarchy and attempted to introduce a form of authoritarian socialism to modernize the country, it unleashed profound internal religious and political conflicts. This created the ideal environment to incubate intensely politicized fundamentalist reactions among disaffected Egyptians who not only rejected any concessions to the modern world, but declared war on it. Such a response to the contemporary nomic crisis resonated with the teachings and programmes of the Muslim Brotherhood, and found their most influential expression in the writings of Sayyid Qutb, notably his *Milestones* (1964). A major turning point in Qutb's life was when he won a scholarship to study the US education system at first hand. His subsequent time in Colorado (1948–50) was one of acute isolation, anomy, and of social, psychological, and religious torment. Threatened to the core of his being by the way the US hedonistic and materialistic way of life so casually flouted Islamic mores, he seems to have undergone a spontaneous radicalization process. As a result of the 'splitting' that ensued, Qutb divided his world into two opposed forces. On the one hand, there was a statistically minute vanguard of spiritually enlightened Muslims who, by going back to what they saw as the basics of their faith, discovered, understood and embraced their revolutionary mission to renew

Islam. On the other, there was the whole of 'fallen' humankind in the throes of spiritual self-destruction.

Milestones, published in 1964, paints an apocalyptic portrait of the world in which nearly everyone is wittingly or unwittingly living in a doomed *jahili* society, one that 'does not dedicate itself to the submission to God [Allah] alone, in its beliefs and ideas, in its observances of worship, and in its legal regulation'.[29] Writing before the Iranian revolution this included every society on earth because 'all the so-called "Muslim" societies are also *jahili* societies'.[30] Indeed, 'the whole world is steeped in *jahiliyyah*', the 'rebellion against God's sovereignty on earth'.[31] As a result 'mankind today is on the brink of a precipice... devoid of those vital values which are necessary not only for its healthy development but also for its real progress'.[32] Materialism, democracy, humanism, communism, secular science, loose sexual mores, addictions of all sorts are patent symptoms of the decadence of the non-Islamic world which was steadily contaminating the Islamic world as well. Of course, true to the fatal logic of *palingenetic* nihilism, they also signalled for Qutb the fact that the world is ripe for rebirth through a sustained campaign of creative destruction which will restore the canopy and save humanity from annihilation.

A 'vanguard' charged with the mission to revive and purify Islam will 'march [sic] through the vast ocean of *jahiliyyah* which has encompassed the entire world',[33] and establish the Divine Law (*al-Shari'ah*) over all humanity.[34] Armed with the true interpretation of Islamic jihad, this warrior elite has the right to attack 'institutions and traditions to release human beings from their poisonous influences, which distort human nature and which curtail human freedom'.[35] *Milestones* is thus the declaration of a fight to the death against every form of existence that is not founded on the most reductionist, totalitarian, bellicose interpretation of Salafism, a form of Islam which claims to be based on the faith and experiences of the first three generations of Muslims following the Prophet Mohammed's revelations. It invites all 'true' believers to turn wherever they are into a battle front within the cosmic war being waged between Islam and *jahiliyyah*. Each page of *Milestones* is imbued with the certainty of someone who has been granted exclusive access to cosmic Truth, and been uniquely blessed with divine understanding of the revolution needed to save the world. As for Muslims who are blind to the justice of the Islamist cause, they are '*jahili* Muslims', *kafir* or *kuffar* (infidels, or 'concealers of the Truth') to be converted or destroyed. It is a vision reminiscent of Asahara's vision of the mission of his Aum to purge the world of a defiling humanity through cathartic destruction. Nor is Qutb's version of Islam free of external influences. John Larsen has documented the impact on Qutb of the French apologist for Nazi eugenics, Alexis Carrel.[36]

Clearly the alienated, socially disempowered Qutb trapped in Colorado when Elvis Presley was at the height of his career, had undergone a spectacular process of heroic doubling. The soft-spoken fanaticism he exudes in his writings as he calmly sets forth his project for the destruction of all the world's infidel civilizations is symptomatic of an extreme form of Alice Syndrome at work. Meanwhile, his obsession with the 'filth' of the non-Islamic world in the grip of decadence which must be expunged from the earth puts him in the company of Sergey Nechayev, Travis Bickle, William Pierce, Timothy McVeigh, Tyler Durden, and Saloth Sar – better known as Pol-Pot – and all the other 'political Gnostics', 'revolutionaries of the apocalypse', and 'positive nihilists' we have encountered in these pages dedicated to the purification of the world through blood and destruction.[37] The metapolitical syndrome of radicalization we presented in Chapter 5 is completed when Qutb cites the Quran's promise of the ecstasy promised to each martyr who fulfils his task: 'They are jubilant at the favour from God and his bounty (3:169–171)'. Qutb thus proposes a concept of martyrdom as the fate that a Muslim willingly takes on himself as member of a vanguard at war with *all* societies, their armies, their governments, and their civilians before the new era of global Islam has dawned. A suicide bombing thus becomes a sacred ritual joyfully performed for God and willed by God.

The 'second wave': Statist Islamism

The visions of Maududi, al Banna, and Qutb, and their many Sunni clerical and militant proselytes could only be realized through the establishment of a theocratic Islamic state, but the closest they have come to political implementation so far is in the Islamic Emirate of Afghanistan (1996–2001). It was Shi'ite Islamism, with its distinctive apocalyptic and messianic tradition of Mahdism, which in the event provided the radical variant of Islam that could provide the basis of a stable theocratic regime in the Middle East, the Islamic Republic of Iran established by the Ayatollah Khomeini in 1979. There has also been a sustained struggle for power between nominally Muslim government forces and Islamist factions in Sudan, Pakistan, and more recently Bangladesh, while Statist Islamists currently assuming a moderate guise also seem destined to play a key role in determining the constitutional and civic future of several Islamic states as the 'Arab Spring' moves into a new season.

The hallmark of Statist Islamism is the insistence that the key to the organization of society, politics, and every aspect of morality and law is supplied by clerical interpretations of the Quran and associated Hadiths. It is fully fundamentalist in Eisenstadt's sense[38] in that by applying this deeply conservative, ostensibly scripture-based vision of state-building within an extensively globalized, secularized, and technologized world, it is forced to become a 'modern anti-modern' force. It is based on particular clerical interpretations of sacred texts, combined with the uncompromising conservation of traditions regarding gender politics, social mores, and punishments, yet at the same time (unwittingly) acquires a totalizing Jacobin element: the desire to create a theocratic Islamic state forced to be selectively integrated into and have restricted dealings with the international community.

The original Taliban can be seen as a major example of Islam's fundamentalist response to modernity, its ideology, regime, and violent campaign against democratization in Afghanistan representing a sustained attempt to keep the forces of secular life and the globalization of materialism at bay in the wake of

Russian withdrawal, though primarily within an Afghanistan and Pakistani context. Like the Chechen Muslims, Talibanism itself became increasingly absorbed into GSJ Islamism after the US invasion scattered its clerics and militants. Its fanatical resistance to Western liberalism betrays a radically Zealotic reflex of nomos-conservation reminiscent of Cromwell's Puritan Commonwealth or the Jesuit counter-reformation led by Loyola. Indeed, its lack of an elaborated agenda for modern state-building before the NATO occupation (in marked contrast to the one formulated by the Iran of the Ayatollahs) led Eisenstadt to refer to it as 'proto-fundamentalist'.[39]

Yet this is to ignore the significance of the Taliban's readiness to host Al Qaeda training camps while it ruled Afghanistan from 1996 to 2001. In doing so they gave concrete backing to the de-territorialized, Islamist vision of Islam's revolutionary mission which first took practical shape in the 1980s when the Mujahideen became the US-backed supranational fighting force which proved so deadly at combating the Russian occupation. Their successful campaign provided the essential context for Al Qaeda to be founded by the Saudi Arabian Osama bin Laden under the influence of the Palestinian Islamist theologian Abdullah Azzam.[40] The transformation of idealistic Muslims into supranational terrorists in remote areas of Afghanistan gave substance to Azzam's bloody vision of a jihad being waged by an invisible army of guerrilla fighters and terrorists engaged in a global war fought on numerous fronts against the enemies of Islam, whether in Chechnya or New York, Iraq or Bali.

The Taliban may have been predisposed to encourage the Islamist terrorists in its midst because its own ideology blended traditional Pashtun tribalism with the radical Puritanical theology of the nineteenth-century Deobandi Islamic Movement. This originated within the walls of the same Indian *madrasas* where Maududi had studied Islam before the Second World War. In the course of the twentieth century Deobandism developed into the extreme form of puritanism and fanaticism which has promoted powerful forces of societal Islamization and radicalization in modern Pakistan, a legacy of the reign of President Zia-ul-Haq (1977–88). Yet it is not the Taliban's Afghanistan, but the transformation of Iran into a theocratic state in 1979 after the deposing of the Shah that Demant sees as the outstanding feature of the second wave of Islamism. Significantly, the totalitarian ideology on which this process was based blended traditional Shi'ism with Islamist ideology as well as with extraneous modern elements. Kai Hafez goes so far as to claim that 'Khomeini was as little rooted in the Shia tradition of government as was the late medieval monk Girolamo Savonarola in Catholic traditions when he established the "divine dictatorship" in the Florence of the late fifteenth century, creating an unprecedented form of theocracy'.[41]

Certainly Iran's combination of clerical government and the embrace of Shari'a law with a state constitutionalism based on authoritarian Western models coupled with a technologically advanced industrial-military complex underlines the impossibility of establishing a 'pure' Islamic state in the modern age. It also highlights the marked tendency for fundamentalism to assume Jacobin elements once it is translated into political institutions able to maintain a degree of state efficiency and autonomy in the modern world of secularization, globalization, and international politics based on states, international capitalism, nation-states, and superstate alliances rather than empires.

Renomizing the world through terror

Both the Taliban and Iranian regime have had recourse to state terrorism in order to crush ideological and social forces they regard as undermining their efforts to impose an Islamist nomos on the entire culture under their control. However, this book is concerned exclusively with anti-state terror. As such it is one of the thousands of publications and initiatives since 9/11 whose combined effect is to act as enzymes enabling the Western world to 'digest' the full implications of that traumatic day. This section thus attempts to complement the vast amount of information already gathered about GSJ Islamism and its most infamous organization, Al Qaeda, by reviewing them in terms of the way they have confronted the nomic crisis to which modernity subjects all the world's religions. In a sense, this is the litmus test of the cogency and heuristic value of our exploration of the terrorist's creed in the earlier chapters, since, despite its inconspicuous beginnings in the late 1980s, GSJ has gone on to establish itself, with or without Osama bin Laden, as the most powerful, resilient, and effective anti-state terrorist force the world has ever seen, not just in its Al Qaeda incarnation, but perhaps even more so in the many hundreds of shadowy groupuscules and cells[42] all over the world which strive to put into practice the ideology of Islamism. The ideas of Maududi, al-Banna, and Qutb are now perpetuated in a constant flow of speeches, sermons, articles, web-articles, and downloadable videos which circulate freely within the radical subcultures of Islam all over the world.

The first point to stand out is that GSJ Islamism is a totalizing project of 'renomizing' and 'recosmizing' the world. As such it is loyal to Qutb's original vision of the task to 'abolish all concepts, laws, customs and traditions' based on 'selfish desires' (individualism, materialism, hedonism) 'and to replace them with a new concept of human life, to create a new world on the basis of submission to the creator',[43] a *'libertas Islamica'*, that is, brought about by liberating the world from the grip of *jahiliyya*. This religious diagnosis of the world's ills translates into Islam's theological terminology what our own secular social scientific analysis has described as the permanent liminoidality into which the whole world is inexorably sliding as once powerful religious *nomoi* become progressively undermined and 'denomized' by modernity. The attempt to create a global community of Muslims (the global *umma* under a global Caliphate) in a historical scenario shot through with apocalyptic and millennarian *topoi* is absolutely consistent with the pattern followed by all revitalization movements at a time of acute nomic crisis, a primordial pattern which, as we saw in Chapter 2, can be studied in considerable detail by reconstructing the responses of Zealotic Judaism to a nexus of threats to its integrity from the first century BC onwards. It is a scenario which, as in the case of Hitler's palingenetic nationalist, racial, and imperialist vision of the new world order to be imposed by the Third Reich, dooms to failure any attempt at appeasement, rapprochement, or compromise between convinced Islamists and liberal democrats.

The broad thrust of this analysis is corroborated by the observations of several serious students of Islamism. In the introduction to his translation of original writings by major GSJ Islamists, Raymond Ibrahim argues that 'the source of such elemental loathing [of liberal Western civilization] in these texts proves to be lost honour, humiliation, attendant envy, and the ensuing fear that the Islamists' "authority will pass away" ',[44] in other words, the elemental fear of the loss of the Islamic nomos. Similarly, Roxanne Euben, writing before 9/11, has argued that the jihadic struggle arose as a response to the 'widespread conviction that contemporary life is plagued by a multifaceted alienation requiring redress'. Its emergence is thus to be seen as 'part of the larger attempt among various groups and theories to "re-enchant" a world characterized by the experience of disenchantment'.[45]

It is consistent with this approach that Marc Sageman stresses the way joining an Al Qaeda cell allowed new recruits, many of them highly educated but in scientific disciplines which do not inculcate freedom of thought, to find a solution to the existential problems experienced particularly by Muslims cut adrift in a sea of modernity: 'they sought a cause that would give them emotional relief, social community, spiritual comfort, and a cause for self-sacrifice'.[46] Similarly, Charles Lindholm and José Zúquete argue that 'for uprooted and alienated youth, ahistoric and universalistic revitalization movements such as al Qaeda offer structure, meaning, identity, and emotional release', and allow them to feel they have found 'a lost ideal', and recovered their 'spiritual moorings'.[47] Meanwhile John Gray, in his survey of the rise of 'apocalyptic religions'[48] in the modern age, recognizes that underlying Islamism's quest to renew society through violence is the eternal human need for myths which 'answer the human need for meaning'.[49] The 9/11 hijackers, each in his own way a victim of modern anomy, 'turned to terrorism more to secure a meaning in their lives than to advance any concrete objective'.[50]

The second feature of Islamism to be thrown into relief is that all the main phases of the radicalization syndrome recapitulated in Chapter 5 are clearly at work. Its cognitive world has become a Manichaean realm in which 'true' Islam is pitted against both non-Islam and 'bad Islam' (the equivalent of the Zealots' loathing of Herodian Judaism which we encountered in Chapter 2). It is particularly significant that in demonizing the West and the US as the 'far enemy', the emphasis is not on their aggressive imperialist and military policies, but on their moral decadence. As for Sergei Nechayev, Travis Bickle, and so many religious Puritans, millennarians and fundamentalists, this is experienced in terms of the primordial trope of demonization and psychological dehumanization: filth. Qutb declares:

> The society may be drowned in lusts, steeped in low passions, rolling in filth and dirt, thinking that it has enjoyment and freedom from chains and restrictions.... The Believer from his height looks at the people drowning in dirt and mud.... He remains the uppermost with the enjoyment of the taste of belief.[51]

In such passages the visceral dread of the sacred canopy's imminent annihilation by a nomocidal modernity, of the absolute devaluation of the individual believer's life, of plunging into the abyss of nothingness now the cosmic shield has been removed, is transmuted by the alchemy of the palingenetic mindset into a fanatical sense of the utter worthlessness and impotence of the fallen 'world' and the absolute indestructibility and power of the creed whose redemptive mission it is to re-impose itself on humanity so as to 'save' it. Hence the famous opening of Qutb's *Milestones*:

> Mankind is on the brink of destruction ... because humanity is devoid of those vital values which are necessary not only for its healthy development, but for its real progress. ... At this crucial and bewildering juncture, the turn of Islam and the Muslim community [*umma*] has arrived.[52]

As we saw earlier in the case of Qutb himself, and in the analysis we offered in Chapter 5 of the letter to be read by the 9/11 conspirators on the eve of the attacks, such a metamorphosis from impotence and anomy to the sense of being in the vanguard of a movement to redeem the world involves an intense process of heroic doubling, the transformation from isolated civilian into cosmic warrior. One of the key features of Islamism is that, just as the French Revolutionaries saw themselves as incarnating the heroes of Republican Rome, so Islamists believe they are reviving the zeal and courage of the days of the Prophet. Thus the Taliban saw itself as renewing the first Caliphate, while bin Laden and his followers identified themselves with the first disciples of the Prophet Mohammed. The globalization of the Islamist mission enables all militant supporters of GSJ, even if it is only when logged on to a jihadic website, to cast themselves in the role of one of Allah's soldiers engaged in the front line of a battle against the forces of evil.[53] In their mind's eye they are thus re-enacting – though surrounded by the trappings of twenty-first century modernity – the Medinan phase of Islam inaugurated in 622 AD when the Prophet engaged in a sustained military campaign against Islam's enemies.

Burke goes so far as to assert that:

> Helped by a powerful surge of anti-Americanism ... the language of bin Laden and his concept of the cosmic struggle has now spread among tens of millions of people, particularly the young and angry, around the world. It informs their views, and increasingly, their actions.[54]

It follows that GSJ is to be seen as the outstanding 'fantasy war' of modern times, activating in its followers a powerful Alice Syndrome which Titanizes the previously anomic, disoriented ego, and reduces the whole of external reality to the dualist category of 'for' or 'against' Islam in such a way that the capacity for feeling compassion or assessing the real human and socio-political consequences of acts of terrorist violence is disabled. The result is an extreme state of dissociation reminiscent of the Russian nihilists, Timothy McVeigh, or the adepts of the Aum cult, but which has now been successfully disseminated and reproduced (cloned

even) throughout many thousands (though surely not 'tens of millions') of converts to Islamism. It is vital to note, however, that the extreme utopianism of
the Islamist universe, rather than preclude, seems to have actually fostered 'pragmatic fanaticism' to an extraordinary degree. As a result, the lethal sophistication
of the crucial 'focusing' phase of the radicalization syndrome, in which targets
are selected and practical plans for their destruction are meticulously devised and
ruthlessly carried out, has become one of the outstanding features of Al Qaeda and
its emulators.

Islamic terrorism thus comprises all the stages of radicalization analysed in
Chapter 5: the passage from anomy and nomic crisis, via a process of splitting and
heroic doubling to becoming cosmic warriors fighting evil within a Manichaean
conflict between a totalized Truth and a demonized Other. It is a metaphysical
battle which allows material symbols of evil to be identified and destroyed with
ruthless efficiency using the technological fruits of decadent modernity in a way
calculated to spread terror among the target population of the enemies of Islam.
Nor is the final stage of the process, 'the bliss of completion', to be overlooked.
Apart from the ecstatic state displayed (or at last feigned) in some martyr videos,
the most eloquent testimony to the existential core of the terrorist creed, the
final transcendence of anomy by becoming one with the eternal nomos, is a passage in the last instructions to the 9/11 hijackers taken from the 'manual' we
used earlier to document the heroic doubling the terrorist attack demanded. Their
imminent deaths are portrayed as the portal to an ecstatic state of fulfilment and
everlasting joy:

> When the moment of truth comes near, and zero hour is upon you, open your
> chest welcoming death on the path of God. Always remember to conclude with
> the prayer, if possible, starting it seconds before the target, or let your last words
> be: 'There is none worthy of worship but God, Muhammad is the messenger of
> God.' After that, God willing, the meeting is in the Highest Paradise, in the
> company of God.[55]

Islamism as a 'mazeway resynthesis'

On a psychological level the purpose of the manual is to maintain intact the
fanaticism of the hijackers' 'heroic double', the integrity of their Islamist's avatar,
a sacred warrior fighting his way along the path to God, right up to the point
where the planes crashed into their target. But it also brings out the hybrid nature
of Islamism as a political ideology, interspersing practical instructions for carrying
out a terrorist attack with references to Islamic faith, rituals and scripture, super-
imposing a metaphysical grid of absolute significance over the contingent texture
of everyday reality in a way typical of the fundamentalist mindset we considered
in Chapter 5 locked into its metapolitical delusions.

This hybridity proves to be deeply engrained within the value-system of GSJ
once its ideology is scrutinized. A number of experts have sensed the intru-
sion into its variant of religious fundamentalism of an extraneous element, an
apocalypticism that owes much to Western schemes of an imminent temporal,

this-worldly utopia. It is thus important to realize that from its earliest beginnings Islamism generated its own apocalyptic and millennarian currents of thought which were to become became a vital component of Shi'ite Mahdism and on which modern Islamists can draw without 'borrowing' them from the West.[56]

Laurent Murawiec thus seems to underestimate the role played by classical Islamic millennarians when he detects in Islamism a 'Gnostic' belief structure which makes its fanatics behave not like Muslims, but more like European millennarians and Bolsheviks.[57] A similar unfamiliarity with Islam's own millennarian tradition may have led Jean Rosenfeld to argue that 'the religion of bin Ladin' has more in common with movements that arise out of a 'cultic milieu' than with genuine Islam, making 'the religion of jihad' a type of 'revolutionary millennialism'.[58] It is the political philosopher and cultural critic John Gray who has focused the greatest attention on this aspect of Islamism. In *Al Qaeda and What it is to be Modern* he presents Islamism as 'a typical modern hybrid', with Islamic fundamentalism interlaced with elements of Leninism and Nietzsche,[59] and actually resembling both fascism and revolutionary anarchism in being 'unequivocally modern' in its strategy to 'remake the world by spectacular acts of terror'.[60]

This assessment is anticipated in his *Black Mass. Apocalyptic Religion and the Death of Utopia*. Here Gray presents Al Qaeda's politics as having both 'strategic and apocalyptic dimensions',[61] but insists that Islamism's 'apocalypticism' is to be associated not with religion as such, but rather to the Jacobins' draconian use of state terror during the French Revolution which was rationalized by the utopian belief that 'a higher type of human being' was within reach, 'but only once humanity had been purified by violence'. He goes on to argue that this faith in the cathartic, palingenetic power of violence has flowed into many revolutionary currents in the modern age:

> Nineteenth-century anarchists such as Nechayev and Bakunin, the Bolsheviks Lenin and Trotsky, anti-colonial thinkers such as Frantz Fanon, the regimes of Mao and Pol Pot, the Baader–Meinhof Gang, the Italian Red Guards in the 1980s, radical Islamic movements, and neo-conservative groups mesmerized by fantasies of creative destruction ... are all disciples of the Jacobins.[62]

However, once again we must be wary of seeing Islamism as essentially 'modern' or 'Jacobin' to the extent that Gray maintains. In the light of our own analysis the hybridity of Islamism is not the result of the 'modernization' or 'Jacobinization' of Islam, but rather a particularly potent example of the 'mazeway resynthesis' which has played such a key role in the genesis of new sects, religions, creeds, and ideologies throughout history. As we saw in Chapter 3, acute nomocidal and liminoid conditions have repeatedly triggered a process of cultural self-preservation. This involves the syncretization of selected elements of the traditional nomos with new, incongruous or even contradictory elements, often welded into a new ideological compound by being integrated within apocalyptic fantasies of destruction and regeneration, and dreams of renewal through cathartic violence. The integration of a 'Jacobin' element of secular millennarianism into Islam's own fundamentalist millennarianism is thus not a symptom of Islamism's modernity, but of its essential and *primordial* nature as a revitalization movement.

It is symptomatic of this aspect of Islamism that since it first arose it has generated a steady stream of charismatic *prophetae* figures who endow its ideology with the authority of Scripture, such as Maududi, al Banna, Qutb, bin Laden, Ayman al Zawahiri, Abdullah Azzam, not to mention the ultimate spiritual avatar of all devout Muslims: the Prophet Mohammed himself. Thus when approaching Islamism as a political creed it is important to give weight not just to the extraneous, 'modern' elements that has turned it into an 'ism', an ideology of action to be completed in this age within historical time, but also to its traditional Islamic basis. Peter Demant corroborates this approach when he shows at length how Islamism, though certainly an 'antimodern product of modernity',[63] initially arose out of ultra-orthodox Islamic fundamentalism. Similarly, Jeffrey Bale emphasizes that 'many of Ibn Ladin's militant interpretations of traditional Islamic concepts and generic anti-"infidel" attitudes are based on texts from the most authoritative Islamic sources (including key Qur'anic passages and the relevant sections in various collections of *ahadith* that are considered to be reliable)'.[64] A chilling example of what this 'fundamentalist' component of Islamism means in practice is the long treatise prepared before 9/11 'for the council of the jihad organization under the supervision of Dr. Ayman Al-Zawahiri' to provide justification for the killing of women and children in the pursuit of jihad. The text is replete with references to Islamic scriptures and theological disputes, culminating in a key passage reminding those with doubts about the morality of such acts that the Prophet Himself attacked the besieged city of Ta'if with catapults 'knowing full well that women and children would be struck, for it was not possible to differentiate between them'.[65]

However, as a syncretic political ideology typical of the process of mazeway resynthesis, Islamism's orthodox credentials as a form of fundamentalism are inevitably bitterly disputed among Islamic theologians and clerics, rejected as heretical by some and embraced by others. A fascinating document in this context is the 400-page refutation of al-Zawahiri's defence of the use of terroristic violence issued from prison by the leadership of the Libyan Islamic Fighting Group (LIFG) in 2009. Written in Arabic and argued in the dense discourse of theological scholarship, it renounces on *religious grounds* the 'use of violence to change political situations'.[66] Obviously the Islamist invocation of scripture to justify their struggle is anathema to moderate Muslims. Bassam Tibi, for example, has pointed out a number of ways jihadists deviate from the very Salafi Islamic tradition they claim to uphold, especially with respect to the strict rules and conditions laid down in the Quran that restrict the declaration of jihad.[67] This point is endorsed by Robert Brym, who cites approvingly the opinion of another Islamicist, Adam Silverman, that 'much of the so-called Islamic behaviour that the West calls terrorism is outside the norms that Islam holds for political violence'.[68]

It is also consistent with Islamism's nature as a product of mazeway resynthesis that it bears the hallmarks – not to say the psychological scars – of the permanent existential crisis engendered by a nomocidal modernity which it sets out to resolve through draconian counter-measures. Faisal Devji, for example, brings out in his idiosyncratic analysis the importance of seeing Islamism, not as a response to the traditional sense of the nearness of God, but a painful and highly modern experience of his absence. He finds something deeply *un*traditional, almost existentialist or Kierkegaardian, for example, in the way the Ayatollah Khomeini's last testament praises the Iranian people for achieving freedom 'in the absence of any access to divine authority'. This, he declares, showed they were 'far more faithful to their religion than the great and saintly personages of Islam's past'.[69] Such a statement leads Devji to the somewhat startling claim that 'the jihad is modern in a Kantian sense because it is founded upon humanity's freedom from external or supernatural authority.... It is far more preoccupied with the death of God than that of man'.[70] On a less metaphysical note, Devji also stresses the way the 'mediatization' of Islamism represents another radical break with tradition, claiming that its spectacular attacks, communiqués by video and internet, and filmed beheadings brings the jihad's frame of reference closer to the dreams and nightmares of the media than to any traditional school of Islamic jurisprudence or political thought. Indeed, he suggests that there may well be more to the way some terrorists seem to have 'modelled their behaviour on James Bond' than simply adopting a deep cover for their terrorist *personae.*[71]

Another highly qualified expert in this field, Malise Ruthven, confirms this interpretation of Islamism as the child of modernity's nomic crisis in terms even more compatible with the core premise of this book, namely humankind's innate needs for a nomos in the face of nothingness. He suggests the roots of Islamism lie in fear of the void rather than in fanatical faith in God, and goes on to suggest that the basis of all such messianic movements lies, 'one suspects, in the promise of escape from the burden of individual selfhood framed by the inevitability of death, the ultimate condition of chaos and dissolution'.[72] In other words, what drives Islamist terrorism is the metapolitical need for a sacred canopy to escape the modern condition of anomy and imbue existence with transcendental meaning. This line of thought leads to a remarkable passage in which he draws parallels between the personalities of Mohamed Atta (the leader of the 9/11 attacks) and Ulrike Meinhof.[73] It chimes in with our analysis of the core similarities of mindset underlying different terrorist creeds when he points out that the Arabic phrase '*ghadba lil-allah*', literally 'fury for God', used by an Islamist terrorist for his attack, was translated into English by a Muslim expert on terrorism as 'propaganda by the deed'.[74] (Is it sheer coincidence that the Al Qaeda in Iraq's emblem which signifies the aim of its Quran-based militancy to achieve a global Caliphate resembles a smoking nineteenth-century anarchist's bomb?)[75]

As we have seen, it is not just the existential dimension of Islamism that is modern, so is the historicized framework in which it sets out to achieve its goals, the temporalization of utopia resulting from the erosion of the metaphysical realm. This point emerges, for example, from a passage in which Olivier Roy, echoing the theme of global jihad as 'a fantasy war', argues that its goal, however horrifically real the consequences of the violence employed to achieve it, is essentially an imaginary *ummah* 'beyond ethnicity race and culture', just as much as the global

Caliphate is 'a virtual world'. He sees them as reflections, or rather mirages, of the radical deterritorialization that Islam has undergone in the modern age, the failure of Islamic statehood and nationalism, and the fragmented, factious state of the real *ummah* which has bred so much *fitna* (internal strife), another symptom of the *jahiliyya* that deeply troubled Qutb. They are fruits of the totalizing, globalized human imagination which only became possible in the age of globalization.[76] Yet here again the modern, extraneous element in Islamist syncretism is probably being overstated, betraying perhaps a subliminal attempt by liberal concerns to present Islam as a faith that reveals its true nature only when peacefully confined to its traditional communities and not pursuing zealous schemes of world mastership. Many medieval Muslims also found it natural to see the triumph of Islam over the world of the infidel and the establishment the global *umma* as their ultimate mission, even if the imagined world was much smaller then.

In short, while extraneous elements certainly exist in Islamism, it is perhaps too tempting for Islamophiles to demonize it as a perversion of true Islam and dismiss as modern aberrations a number of beliefs that have their roots in the classical Islamic tradition, particularly of the Medinan Phase. A remarkable example of this is Faisal Devji's argument that the Islamist vision of a globalized Islam follows a 'humanitarian logic', and that Al Qaeda sets out to bring forth the world's 'latent humanity' by their acts of sacrifice, thereby fulfilling 'America's promise of freedom for all'.[77] Surely this is a far too benevolent gloss on Islamism's campaign of 'creative destruction' against the existing world order. It ignores the bottomless capacity for hatred and violence that is engendered by dread when human beings fight for a nomos under attack, or for a new nomos which will enable them to avoid falling into the abyss of nihilism. It euphemizes the radicalness of Islamist determination not just to destroy the Prophet's enemies, but settle scores with the West.

This determination could be glimpsed, for example, in the notorious message that Osama bin Laden delivered to the West a month after the 9/11 attacks in which he declared that the purpose of such acts of aggression was to eventually achieve a 'balance of terror' with the West based on the principle that 'every time they kill us, we kill them'.[78] In case this is dismissed as atypical of Islamism now that bin Laden is dead and the Arab Spring may (possibly) be bearing some democratic fruit, it is worth noting that Islamists worthy of the name still 'work towards the leader' with clerical backing. During a sermon made shortly after bin Laden's execution by US special forces, the Sudanese cleric Sheik Ali Al-Jazouli exhorted Muslims to maintain the 'guiding principle' of Osama bin Laden, namely 'the importance of tipping the global balance of terror in favour of the Muslims for a "balance of terror" between Islam and the West'. It is a policy that has more in common with the US strategy of Mutually Assured Destruction at the height of the Cold War, also based on what was called at the time 'a balance of terror', than anything advocated in the Quran.[79]

Islamism results from our analysis as a hybrid of a particularly bellicose variant of Islamic fundamentalism with various elements of modern ideology seen in the subtle temporalization of its eternal universalizing mission, its embrace of technological modernity and the trappings of the spectacular society, and above all the existential dread of permanent anomy intensified by the erosion of the Islamic sacred canopy which fuels its campaign of revenge, retribution, and redemption on a global stage. Within the framework of this book it is clearly an intricate blend of Zealotic with Modernist terrorism, one which underlines how the anti-pluralist, militant, destructive side of orthodox religion combined with the most apocalyptically palingenetic side of secular utopianism can breed a world-wide leaderless, cellular terrorist movement of unparalleled effectiveness in weaving anxiety into everyday normality. Had Francis Fukuyama not been inveigled by his own totalizing neo-Hegelian nomos he might have recognized the possibility that the end of the Cold War might signal not the triumph of liberal capitalism, but the rise of increasingly fanatical bids by traditional religious cultures to re-enchant the world and rescue it from the dominion of the Last Men, but at the cost of the very religious purity that they set out to conserve.

The Aum cult and Islamism can be seen as the confluence of modern technology both with the search for a more fundamental, primal, anomy-defeating religious experience, and with a post-secular, and even postmodern dimension of hyper-reality consumed in X-rated video games. Perhaps each terrorist has forged in the furnace of his or her most intimate self, in the darkest recesses of an existentially desperate psyche – still called by some a soul – a new God to worship, a primeval deity, even if it (He?) wears the face (which for Muslims can never be portrayed by mortals) of familiar religious iconography.

The God of the 'religious terrorist' is one that demands blood sacrifice, like the Canaanite Moloch who exacted the immolation of children, the Aztec Huitzilopochtli who was placated only by warriors' hearts so as to keep the fifth sun burning, or the Indian Shiva to whom the Thugees sacrificed their thousands of victims. It is the same God for whom Wilfred Owen's Abram was so determined to kill his own son, perversely ignoring the angel's entreaty to substitute his own flesh and blood with a ram.[80] It is the bloodthirsty God whom Sheikh Abdullah Azzam worshipped in his heart when he wrote that 'the manuscripts of history are not scribed except with the blood of [Islam's] martyrs'.[81] This was the God invoked in the manual found in Mohammed Atta's luggage, the God in whose name the hijackers were to calmly slit the throat of airline passengers with box-cutters, not as an act of murder but of sacrifice: 'If God grants you a ritual slaughter, you should perform it as an offering on behalf of your father and mother, for you have debts to them'.[82]

It is a Divinity that inhales longings for purification and transcendence, and exhales the stench of suffering and blood, thus perpetuating humankind's eternally tragic drama of cosmic systole and diastole. It is a false God in any of the world's major religions because in order to reaffirm the value of Life it celebrates Death. The penetrating analysis of the Atta manual in *The New York Review of Books* concludes: 'The idea that martyrdom [and murder] is a pure act of worship, pleasing to God, irrespective of God's specific command, is a terrifying new kind of nihilism'.[83]

10
Afterthoughts on the Nature of Terrorism

Rethinking the dynamics of terrorism

In one sense, every book on the causes of terrorism written since 9/11 is an afterthought, a theoretical bolting of stable doors long after the riders of a fantasy apocalypse have galloped down their path to God. What this book has set out to do is to provide another bolt to that door by applying to the phenomenon of terrorism the understanding of the dynamics of Fascism and Nazism as a response to modernity which I explored in an earlier book.[1] The result has been a causal model of the psychodynamic roots of fanaticism in the human need for a sacred canopy, a classification scheme of two distinct rationales for terrorism which are prone to forming hybrids in the modern world, and an intentionally schematic radicalization syndrome expounded in the earlier chapters. Taken together, these are intended to provide a conceptual framework for investigating terrorism, which, as the etymology of the term 'concept' implies,[2] hopefully allows those working within the most humanistic sectors of academia, journalism, and policy-making to get a firmer theoretical grip on its non-instrumental dimension. As this book is an overarching theory formulated in a heuristic spirit, I would welcome corrections to the empirical gaffes I may have made, constructive criticism of my theory, or a suggestion for fruitful areas for further research which may help to corroborate or refine it.

Rather than cram in as many specimens of terrorism as space allowed, I have concentrated on outlining an artificially simplified taxonomy and causal syndrome illuminated by a small sample of case studies. It should be stressed once more that this was never conceived as a panoramic history of terrorism, but rather a sustained attempt to probe into the deeper, and all too often neglected layers of motivation for acts of fanatical violence. These I have suggested, whatever their immediate goals of vengeance, fighting for the homeland or religion, or apparently nihilistic destruction, are rooted in the human need for a transcendental meaning to life and for a mythic shield against absurdity. In short, the book makes the case for the integration into working definitions of terrorism and into policies, or counter-measures relating to it, references to its creed. This, as should now be clear, is the symbolic, phatic, existentialist dimension which

I have argued plays such a crucial role for the perpetrators of terrorism, even though this dimension may be invisible or incomprehensible to those directly affected or who are impotent spectators of the destruction and atrocities committed, and who naturally tend to reduce it to madness, criminality, or sheer evil. This seductive but reductive response has often been reflected in state propaganda and the popular media, but those 'professionally' concerned with terrorism are unwise to neglect the 'nomic' aspects of motivation which exist alongside more tangible instrumental and tactical considerations, or lose sight of the fact that if madness, criminality and evil is involved, they are of a special, meaning-seeking category. This more humanistic, anthropologically informed approach is not only important for the sake of gaining a fuller understanding of the nature of terrorism as a historical and social phenomenon, but also for two pragmatic reasons that should impress the most hard-headed investigator.

First, it is a leitmotif of this book that metapolitics play a decisive role in the individual motivation behind each act of terrorism at a psychodynamic and motivational level, and are thus deeply relevant to understanding why it has taken place, a process which demands methodological empathy with the mindset and value-system of the perpetrators, and hence to countering further attacks. Second, terrorism, we have argued, is to be understood *by definition* as an act of triadic violence whose direct object is the people and buildings destroyed, but whose all-important *indirect object* and real target is the third party (which may be an entire community, nation, political class, or civilization). This often nebulous entity is supposed to receive the 'message' wrapped in an envelope of grief and alarm at what has happened, and the visceral fear of further outrages. As a result, the symbolism, iconoclastic force, and semiotic significance of the attack for the terrorists themselves may prove to be as important as any strategic goal they hope to achieve, and thus demand to be given due weight by all those concerned with 'stopping terrorism'.

These intangible motivations should thus be decoded with at least as much care as was needed to defuse one of the Unabomber Ted Kaczynski's exquisitely crafted miniature IEDs (Improvised Explosive Device). Had the FBI profiled more intelligently the potential author of acts against the scientific community with their peculiar 'expressive' dimension he may well have been captured more quickly, and without being dependent on the pure chance that his brother recognized the style of Kaczynski's rants against the technocratic society. To take another example of how important on practical grounds it is to decipher the 'message' of a particular form of terrorism correctly, there is overwhelming evidence to indicate that Islamism, or rather Global Salafi Jihad, is fighting a multi-front war against the West in the name of a distorted concept of a 'sacred mission', namely to impose Islam by force on the whole of the planet as its only true faith. It follows that even resolving the Palestinian issue or withdrawing Western troops from the Middle East and Afghanistan cannot hope to appease dedicated Islamists and convince them to give up the struggle against *jahiliyya*, and that UK government initiatives to finance Islamist groups so as to convert them to moderation under the first Home Office Prevent strategy were wrong-headed to say the least.[3]

However, to stay with our example, once the non-instrumental nature of Islamism is appreciated it *is* possible to pursue policies which aim to minimize the appeal of the Islamist mission for potential converts to violent jihad in the wider Muslim community. This certainly demands a major international commitment to the resolution of major issues of foreign policy in the Middle East, notably the Israeli-Palestinian conflict, as well as avoiding policies and actions that fulfil Islamist stereotypes of the crass arrogance and moral evil of the West – such as the abuse of the human rights of Muslims in detention, or the reluctance to condemn atrocities and disproportionate violence committed by West-friendly states. In the domestic context this approach means taking steps to demonstrate that the (moderate) Islamic nomos is understood and respected, taking advantage of school lessons in religious studies and citizenship, for example, to acknowledge that Islam is a major world religion with an extraordinarily rich history, culture, and a demonstrable capacity for peaceful *convivencia* with other faiths. It is a policy which should be adopted towards all moderate forms of religions hosted in a democracy. Though this should not be taken to the point of compromising liberal rights to freedom of thought, expression, and worship for all believers won at great human cost over centuries, tolerating the abuse of the freedom of speech to be used by sectarian fanatics to incite hatred or violence, or conniving with offences against human rights by religious communities in the name of upholding 'multiculturalism'.

In short, this book is an appeal not just to the small army of terrorologists recruited since 9/11, but to the many more actively engaged in combating terrorism, to consider, if they have not already done so, the deeper causes behind what they are dealing with. This means appreciating more fully the nomic dimension of modern terrorism – of which Islamist violence is, of course, only one species, even if for nearly a decade it monopolized collective attention right up to the Breivik killings of July 2011. This in turn means taking into account the condition of permanent liminoidality which is being continually generated by modernity, and which may express itself in a substratum of anomy and angst lying just below the surface of everyday existence even in apparently fully integrated, 'well-adjusted', 'normal' citizens.

Against this background a particular constellation of factors can precipitate in a small minority of individuals not adequately 'moored' culturally or ideologically, and who are not blessed with a high tolerance of ambivalence, the process of splitting and heroic doubling leading to fanatical commitment to a terrorist cause. Such a scenario becomes more probable if the anomic individual has previously been exposed to a cultic milieu either in the form of direct personal contacts, or perhaps accessed via the web as a virtual community, in which terrorism has become normalized as a way of fighting back. (The 'lone wolf' terrorist is largely a figment of the media imagination, which ignores the network of ideological influences in which apparent loners are embedded.[4]) Such a milieu supplies a radicalizing medium which may turn the violent, but impotent rage and outlandish conspiracy theories characteristic of a fundamentalist mindset into commitment to an ideologically elaborated cause which 'pragmatic fanaticism' enables to be focused to the point of assuming the form of a specific 'mission' to carry out an act of semiotically significant violence. The appeal of such a cause to some believers convinced their nomos is under attack, or to one of God's 'orphans' desperate to create a new nomos, is that they are provided with a stable, action-oriented utopian or apocalyptic interpretation of the contemporary world which provides a sense of rootedness and purpose to an otherwise liminoid existence.

Rethinking the role of the sacred in terrorism

To offset the natural tendency to see all terrorism through the lens of 9/11 and of the attacks in Bali and on European cities that followed, it is important to bear in mind that it is not just Islamists who dream of 'mastership of the world' or at least their part of it. Literally any social, political, or religious cause can in principle be sacralized to the point of legitimizing violence in the mind of the terrorist, thereby underscoring the etymological link between 'fanaticism' and 'the holy'. The modern age has made us sadly familiar with the zealotry unleashed by struggles for 'sacred' homelands, for (highly mythicized) ethnic nations conceived as an organism to be purified, redeemed, or regenerated, or by missions to impose a particular religious or secular creed as the foundation of a new society. However, campaigns against abortion, vivisection, and the destruction of the environment have also given rise to terroristic episodes.

In 2008 eco-terrorism, not Islamism, was declared by the FBI the main domestic terrorist threat to civil society in the US,[5] and a year later left-wing vegan Daniel San Diego joined the FBI's Most Wanted Terrorist list,[6] presumably because in the US Islamist terrorism is viewed primarily as a foreign threat rather than homegrown danger, even if it successfully radicalizes some US Muslims. In September 2010 eco-activist James Jay Lee entered the Discovery Channel studios in Silver Springs, Maryland, waving a handgun and with bombs strapped to his body. He threatened to kill his three hostages and blow himself up if the network did not make its programming more planet-friendly. Before this he had posted a vehemently Gaia-centric and misanthropic manifesto alerting the public to the dangers that human overpopulation pose to the planet, a cause for which he gave his life when he was shot down after a four-hour stand-off.[7] 2011 saw the first terrorist attacks to save planet Earth from nano-technology.[8]

The most famous case of 'ecoterrorism' has already been mentioned. Between 1978 and 1995 the Unabomber, Ted Kaczynski, – as close to being a 'lone wolf' as it is possible to get – dominated the attention of the media and counter-terrorist agencies in the US with a sporadic series of mail-bombings, several of them lethal. His intended victims were academics and technicians unlucky enough to be working at or near a set of research labs chosen as a synecdoche of the scientific mindset that he believed was destroying humanity and the planet. His manifesto 'Industrial Society and its Future',[9] published by the *New York Times* and *Washington Post* in 1995 on condition he gave up his terrorist campaign (which he did not), is a well-researched and generally coherent diatribe against the social and ecological dangers posed by technocracy. It gives a rare insight into the meticulous, methodical way a terrorist may construct through rampant syncretism an alternative – but in most cases far less thoroughly articulated and rationalized – world-view with which to make sense of existence. It is within this idiosyncratic, totally nomized reality, hermetically sealed off from 'normality', that he or she comes to believe that calculated acts of violence against symbolically important targets will change history. In Kaczynski's case it was a self-imposed exile from a 'decadent' society lived out physically day by day in his Montana hut. On this basis he or she assumes the persona of a heroic avenger, or member of a revolutionary vanguard, or of the catalyst to a new age in which anomy, decadence, moral evil, or in this case, ecological destruction is banished.

It is thus with a certain inner consistency that Kaczynski refused to enter a plea of insanity at his trial: there was a fully documented, lucidly thought through method in his madness as far as the identification of a global problem was concerned, if not in his identification of a solution, where the Alice Syndrome took over completely and made him utterly misjudge the effectiveness of sporadic bombings in bringing about a change in the West's commitment to technocratic 'progress'. His biographer, Alston Chase, reveals how his concern for the 'planet' was a defining feature of the 1960s and 1970s counterculture,[10] but it took a complex interplay of painful personal experiences and personality traits to drive him into creating a universe split between nature and industrial society, not least the humiliating psychological experiments carried out on him in the name of psychological 'science' when he was a student. In symbolically attacking the scientific establishment which was allegedly destroying the planet he found a cause that gave structure and numinous meaning to an otherwise anomic, desperate existence.[11]

Kaczynski's case demonstrates that any issue taken up passionately – the tyranny of 'the system', a particular government policy, pensioners' or fathers' rights, the anti-G8 movement, a campaign for more state support for breast-feeding, or to get rid of mobile phone transmitters – can potentially spark terrorism. There are a host of fanatical rationales possible for an attack on McDonalds. For a cause to produce terrorism, though, it has to be processed through the filter of a mindset often fanatically committed to renomizing the entire world by focusing on one particular issue, perhaps one the vast majority might find trivial. It is the consistency and predictability of the way this mindset reconfigures reality once this cause has been identified by the nomos-seeking mind that makes it possible to reduce all terrorism to what we have identified as the three basic types of solution to a radicalizing nomic crisis: defending a nomos (Zealotic); creating a nomos (Modernist); and, through a Zealotic–Modernist hybrid, defending an existing nomos by recreating it as a new one within which it is subsumed. Kaczynski, for example, wanted to defend the primordial sacred nomos of Nature from the defiling ravages of the technocracy, which makes his campaign Zealotic. However, at the end of his manifesto he momentarily contemplates a 'religion of nature' as filling the vacuum left by the death of the cult of technology, a utopian projection onto the future that has a strong Modernist component. The phrase clearly betokens the process of 're-enchantment' and 'resacralization' of reality at the heart of all terrorist fanaticism, and points to the delusory state of mind in which Kaczynski lived out his time in his Montana retreat like the modern-day equivalent of a hermetic Hindu Saddhu living alone in his cave in the Indian countryside.

The Unabomber's road to extremism thus illustrates how every act of terrorism has at its heart an ideal to realize, a cause to sacralize, a creed to live out in reality, but also underlines how it requires careful research combined with considerable methodological empathy to piece together what the violence represents within each terrorist's private cosmology, no matter how unintelligible the violence to an outsider. In this respect his stand on behalf of the planet exhibits a unique permutation of the same syndrome we encountered in Bobbie Sands' act of ultimate resistance in the Maze Prison. The courage to stick to his hunger strike stemmed from his fanatical commitment to the totalizing nomos he had created to make sense of his life. By locating his alienating experience of life as a Catholic in Belfast within the historical framework of Protestant England's repressive colonial treatment of Catholic Ireland since Cromwell's time, Sands was able to create his own Manichaean universe in which he was on the front line in what he perceived as a centuries-old war between the defenders of the primordial Irish homeland and the British invaders bent on destroying it and settling it with their own kind. He was seeking to repel not only their expropriation of the indigenous population's right to rule their own country, but the subervsion of their culture and religion with the illegitimate form of Christianity and alien view of history of their oppressors. His excruciating self-induced physical and mental suffering is a testimony to the sincerity of his belief that in the Maze Prison, whatever the legal niceties imposed by the occupying British, he was a prisoner of war suffering for his sacred country, his Catholicism relevant only insofar as it signified the indigenous community and severed nation he belonged to. He was a martyr to the eternal struggle to wrest freedom from the clutches of tyranny.

Yet Sands' story also underlines once again how deeply the terrorist's sacralizing mission distorts the reality principle. By giving primacy to the metaphysical character of the violence so brilliantly expressed in his songs, he was blinded to the suffering the IRA campaign was inflicting on the lives of human beings reduced to a single category, the British, and to the futility of trying to bring about British withdrawal by using violence against civilians who also regarded Northern Ireland as their home. The subterranean link between sanctification of a cause and the ruthlessness born of fanaticism is illustrated as much in the IRA's struggle for the lost Irish nomos as in the determination of Loyalist terrorists to defend their nomos of territory, history, and religion as an organic part of a sacralized British history. The full horror of the atrocities committed and the personal and communal tragedies inflicted as a result of the 'nomization' of the conflict by both sides can perhaps only be appreciated properly from the perspective of the new 'post-Troubles' generation, most of whom now instinctively react with horror to the sporadic episodes of violence still generated by those determined to perpetuate the conflict.

The terrorist imagination is haunted by notions of 'sacrifice', 'redemption', the purifying value of 'blood', the purging, transformative power of destruction, especially destruction brought about by fire, explosions, and bombs. The human body is made up of molecules once forged in the furnace of the sun. In an analogous way the most modern terrorist's outlook on reality is generated by the same faculty for mythopoeia and sacralization that enables an objectively meaningless reality to be sacralised, that came into being when human consciousness first emerged into reflexivity, and the resulting knowledge of death and intimation of absurdity demanded a sacred canopy of magic and faith to be collectively constructed to protect life from the chill winds of nihilism. To study terrorism is to study the extreme product of this instinct for self-preservation through narratives of creation and destruction, good and evil, the sacred and the profane. To combat it means taking account of this sacral dimension.

Rethinking 'religious' and 'secular' terrorism

We showed in Chapter 6 that the fanaticism apparently expressed in acts of 'religious terrorism' may prove on closer inspection to be zeal not for religion as such, but for the *nomos*, a fusion of culture, collective memory, and sacred territory in which religion in the theological sense plays if anything a subordinate role. It is a point deeply bound up with the realization that the human capacity for sacralization is by no means restricted to the sphere of metaphysical revelations about supernatural orders of reality and truth preserved in scripture and doctrine. Even the ancient Zealots and Assassins were fighting not just for their Judaic or Islamic faith, but also for their material homeland, traditions, and collective identity. However, it is important not to overstate this argument to the point of losing sight of the continued importance of religion in ultra-orthodox or New Age forms as a rationale for terroristic violence in contemporary history.

For example, when the Israeli Prime Minister Yitzhak Rabin was assassinated in November 1995 by Yigal Amir, his action was true to the religious interpretation of Zionism according to which 'the Jewish people have entered the climactic era in Jewish history', a claim 'predicated on the theological significance of the creation of the State of Israel and renewed Jewish sovereignty over the Land'.[12] Hence it was deeply important for him that he could justify his act by invoking a Talmudic principle which sanctions murder to save Jewish life. He was also putting into practice the highly nationalistic version of Jewish fundamentalism which had been given extensive clerical approval and scriptural legitimation by a number of rabbis since the 1920s, most recently Rabbi Meir Kahane.

To take another example, we saw in Chapter 8 with what deadly earnest adepts of one of Japan's many New Religious Movements, Aum Shinrikyo, took its millennarian mission to 'force the end' of this doomed phase of history through biological and nuclear attacks. No matter how patently obvious it may be to non-believers that Shoko Asahara's creed was a grotesque pot-pourri of beliefs culled together by plagiarizing the world's major faiths and adding some pseudo-Hippy gobbledegook for good measure, his pronouncements had the force of divine revelations and holy prophesies to his followers, and he may well have suffered from religious delusions[13] himself about his Messianic status for the Elect. This example underlines how important it is for secular human scientists not to underestimate the role that religion can still play in sacralizing the goal of a terrorist attack in a post-religious age.

This insight is particularly important in making sense of Islamism, which is sometimes presented as a secular, essentially Western phenomenon which presents itself as an aberrant travesty of a true Islam that is inherently moderate. Typical of this tendency is Jason Burke's declaration about the motives of Al Qaeda Islamists:

> The militants believe they are fighting a last-ditch battle for the survival of their society, culture, religion and way of life. They also believe, as we in the West believe too, that self-defence can justify tactics that might be frowned on in other circumstances.[14]

It is central to the argument of this book that Al Qaeda is indeed fighting to protect its nomos from destruction, but that its reliance on a particular fundamentalist interpretation of Islam, which is in most respects not an aberrant heresy, but a scripturally founded ultra-orthodoxy, is crucial to the creed by means of which its fighters conceive and rationalize their cause. Hence the danger posed to democratic society by the presence of clerics such as Abu Qatada who remain unrepentant in using his scriptural knowledge and authority as a religious leader to legitimize Al Qaeda's war on the West to the point where he became known as 'bin Laden's ambassador in Europe'. This distinguishes Global Salafi Jihad from the struggle for homeland, culture, and religion that played such a crucial role for some of the participants of the First World War and Balkan Wars in which nation or race became one with God. John Gray minimizes the role of religious fundamentalism in the motivation of Islamism even more radically when he states that Al Qaeda, far from an attempted return to the sources of Islam, is a by-product of globalization:

> Radical Islam is often interpreted as a backlash against modernity, but it is striking how closely the lives of the 9/11 hijackers matched a stereotype of modern anomie. Living a semi-nomadic existence, they were not members of any community, and it is difficult to resist the impression that they turned to terrorism more to secure a meaning in their lives than to advance any concrete objectives. By taking up terror they ceased to be drifters and became warriors.[15]

Gray may well be correct about the soul-ravaging anomy that is the premise of radicalization. However in such assertions the role of religious faith has somehow been entirely edited out of the explanation of Al Qaeda's motivation and goals. Such approaches would make the warriors of Global Salafi Jihad not significantly different in motivation from the Sioux Braves who (helped out by Kevin Costner) fought to preserve their vital space against marauding Pawnees and supposedly genocidal Whites in the film *Dances with Wolves* (1990), or the existential desperados of Tyler Durden's Project Mayhem in *Fight Club* (1999).

Instead, as we suggested in the last chapter, it is important that any account of the beliefs informing Islamist terrorists' strategies and choice of targets recognizes that they see their actions legitimized by the 'true' face of Islam as revealed in the Quranic passages and Hadiths associated with the Medinan period of their religion under the prophet Mohammed. This was when the fledgling Muslim *communitas*, led by its charismatic *propheta* and armed with a new, rigorously monotheistic mazeway resynthesis drawn from syncretizing elements from several Middle Eastern religions, was fighting to establish its regional hegemony, and even found ways of justifying theologically the collateral damage to innocents to achieve this end. To lose sight of the centrality to Islamism of Islam as a revealed religion is to transform it into a socio-political ideology that may be more familiar and intelligible to secularized Western minds, but results in core explanatory elements becoming lost in translation. This in turn can lead to serious misjudgement of Islamism's potential for moderation and democratization.

Rather than focusing on sometimes spurious parallels between fundamentalist forms of religious terrorism and secular totalitarian ideologies, it would be more fruitful for the new terrorology industry to devote more scholarly time to the way several of the world's major religions lend themselves to being exploited as rationales for fanatical violence. Religious believers subliminally driven to create their own mazeway resynthesis to forge a sense of urgent mission to which to dedicate their lives are often able to exploit the profound ambivalence of their faith with respect to the legitimacy of extreme violence, vengeance, punishment, and the conduct of 'just' defensive and offensive wars.[16] We have seen that in the case of the Sinhalese government's war against the Tamil Tigers even an intrinsically pacifistic religion can be modified to turn it into a spiritual weapon to be used in a campaign of ethnic persecution of extreme inhumanity, a process analogous to the transformation of Shinto, an animistic 'nature cult', into a state religion helping justify imperialism of the most inhuman kind in Showa Japan.[17]

Although it is important not to go so far as Émile Cioran,[18] Christopher Hitchens,[19] or Richard Dawkins[20] in throwing out the humanistic, life-asserting, compassionate, creative aspects of some religions with the bathwater of barbaric fanaticism, the example of the Aztecs should remind those with an exclusively benevolent view of religion as a cohesive moral force of the 'dark side' of the human instinct to worship. There is abundant anthropological evidence for the thesis that religion's capacity for conferring sacral meaning on existence has often been inseparable from ritualized bloodshed, sacrifice and self-sacrifice, and apocalyptic fantasies of a cataclysmic end to history to be followed by a new age. These are all mythopoeic topoi which seem to lie dormant within the human psyche to emerge in new guises whenever secular projects are deemed to demand life-or-death choices or the destruction of innocent human lives purportedly in the name of a 'higher' cause.

An intriguing example of the way subliminal benevolent assumptions about Islam's true nature can distort the judgement even of someone who knows both Islam and Islamism inside out is provided by Ed Husain, famous for his 'de-conversion experience' documented in *The Islamist* before he co-founded the anti-Islamist Quilliam Foundation. Commenting on his success in bringing new recruits to the Islamist fold he writes: 'In addition to the many Muslims who "returned to Islam", or become "born again", several non-Muslims converted to the supreme ideology we had been promoting', drawn to Islam 'as a force, a power. Today, I doubt very much if they were humble hearts who turned to God.' He concludes it was not Islam that attracted them but a Westernized 'power-Islam'.[21] However, the concept of Islam as a potentially violent and intolerant 'power' is amply documented in fundamentalist readings of scripture. It is central to the way the faith is seen not just by modern Islamists, but by generations of rulers who for centuries ruled over and expanded through military conquest the many Islamic empires that had risen and fallen before the end of the last Caliphate in 1923. To dissociate 'power' from Islam as if it operates solely as a force for moderation and democracy is thus a deeply ahistorical and un-theological piece of wishful thinking. It suggests a subliminal process of 'defundamentalization' and liberalization at work in Husain's private understanding of his own faith parallel to the one that has taken place, though at the cost of much internal strife, dissent, and setbacks, within Catholicism and Protestantism since the Renaissance, enabling Christianity to metamorphose gradually into a 'liberal' force compatible with democracy, tolerance, and multiculturalism, at least outside the Bible Belt of the US and some evangelical African communities. Even as late as 1943 Catholicism was in cahoots with Fascism and Nazism, both 'power ideologies'.

In short, the violent aspect of major religions is not to be seen as the travesty of their true face, but rather as their 'evil twin'. Or perhaps Islamism could be understood in Jungian terms as Islam's 'shadow' self, sublimating the dread of death not into humility and submission to the compassionate will of Allah and the creation of awe-inspiring beauty in His name, but into projections of metaphysical evil onto the world. The corollary of this is the extreme hatred and destruction stemming from the will to serve Allah by expunging evil through ritual violence so as to force universal submission to His will in a global Caliphate.

It is precisely the 'power' side of a fundamentalist but historically largely orthodox exegesis of Islam that would help explain the over-representation of 'born again' Muslims or new converts to the Islamist cause. They are drawn to radical Islam by the prospect of replacing the anguish of existential doubt and psychological impotence by the absolute certainty and power offered by the Islamists' millennarian scheme of history and the chance to devote their previously meaningless lives to its imminent realization. In the Aum cult, of course, all members were by definition recent converts to Asahara's do-it-yourself religion, all of them lured by the practically hallucinogenic sense of breaking out of the anomy endemic to postwar Japan. We also saw earlier that the deadly gun attack on Arabs on an Israeli bus in 2005 was the work of Natan-Zada, a 'born again' religious Jew recently converted from apostasy to Kahanism under whose influence he now demonized all Arabs.

In the case of Islamism, too, it seems many become radicalized following a personal crisis of faith and identity (a nomic crisis), living an anonymous anomic existence (especially true of diaspora Muslims), or after recently converting from another faith or complete apostasy. It is as if the drive to embrace and be embraced by a nomos, and by the new (micro-)community that goes with conversion, is invigorated and 'turbo-charged' by a prior loss or absence of faith, the sudden release of pent up psychic energies producing a 'catapult' effect. The previous non-believer is propelled from despair – or the licentiousness and hedonism which despair can fuel – to the ultimate extreme of Puritanical fanaticism, even to the point of martyrdom, despite and *because of* a lack of any grounding in the theology of the commitment, or any sustained *practice* of the new-found faith. Permutations of this syndrome are discernible in the path to violence of Mahmud Aboulima, who led out the 1993 attack on the World Trade Centre, Mohamed Atta (the ringleader of the 9/11 bombers), the 7/7 bombers Mohammad Khan and Germaine Lindsay (a convert to Islam), and Nick Reilly (the Exeter Bomber), also a recent convert to Islam.

Once again Pellicani's insights into the fervent thirst for Gnostic knowledge of 'God's orphans' are instructive. Stranded in a no-man's land between traditional certainties and the total relativism and anomy of modern existence, they thus crave a third, action-oriented way out of existential despair, even if it leads straight into death's cul-de-sac, for it will be a *meaningful* death for a *higher* cause. Such an interpretation gives heightened significance to Jason Burke's observation that the militants of Global Salafi Jihad 'fit a model of revolutionary cadres over several centuries', found in 'Egyptian Islamists of the 1970s, Russian anarchists, Bolshevik activists and French revolutionaries of an earlier age'. They are over-represented by 'elements from the newly educated lower-middle classes in societies in flux' [liminoid societies], people 'who are so often at the forefront of calling for change, even if change is justified by retrospective appeal to a nostalgically imagined "just" golden age'.[22] It is part of this pattern that the 'born again' Islamist rejects those not burning with revolutionary passion as luke-warm 'non believers', as *kuffar*, thereby duplicating the reason for the Zealots' war not just on Romans and Greeks, but 'Herodian' Jews prepared to find an accommodation with the enemy.

This intolerance of moderation is inscribed not just in Qutb's dismissal of all Islamic states as *jahili*, but also the frequent rejection of the conventional Islam of the parents. It is a phenomenon testified to by Ed Husain in his account of his time as an Islamist. It is also analysed sensitively in a remarkably prescient short story and film by Hanif Kureishi, *My Son the Fanatic* (1997). The process of rebellion is driven by a thirst for an intense experience of truth that surely played a key role in the radicalization that led the four 7/7 bombers to blow themselves up, blasting themselves out of the close family lives they externally seemed to belong to. But secular humanists and moderate believers should not comfort themselves with the delusion that the truth which terrorists find in their flight from anomy, and the revolutionary violence and murderous hatred which their new-found creed demands from them, must necessarily be somehow a travesty and hence incompatible with a 'genuine' faith. Indeed, in scriptural terms it may prove even *more* compatible with orthodoxy than a modern 'moderate' version celebrating pluralism and individual freedom with minimal basis in scripture.

Rethinking what we read in the newspapers about terrorism

The widespread misunderstandings of the metapolitical causes of terrorism, and the role that religion, particularly Islamism, may play in them has had important consequences for its coverage in the media. The *Washington Post* of 27 January 2012 reported the case of Yonathan Melaku, a US citizen of Ethiopian background raised by Coptic Christian parents. The former Marine was arrested while on his way to desecrate the graves of US soldiers by scrawling 'Arabic statements on them' and leaving 'handfuls of explosive material nearby as a message'.[23] Months earlier he had gone on:

> a mysterious shooting spree that targeted the Pentagon, the National Museum of the Marine Corps and two other military buildings in Northern Virginia. A video found after Melaku's arrest showed him wearing a black mask and shooting a 9mm handgun out of his Acura's passenger window as he drove along Interstate 95, shouting 'Allahu Akbar!'

The article indicates that Melaku was a recent convert to Islam and had decided to carry out a series of attacks on buildings and 'sacred sites' of the US military, the synecdoche of the nation that Islamists see as the imperialist arch-enemy of their faith. Despite these clues, the article's headline reads 'Motive of Shooter who Targeted Military Sites is Unclear'. The fact that over a decade after 9/11 a patently obvious Islamist message did not get through to the journalists of the *Washington Post* suggests continuing failure to appreciate the semiotic dimension of what took place that day in the capital of the US.

Even more revealing of how poorly the ideological dynamics of terrorism are appreciated in the media was the flurry of confusing reports on the motivation behind the horrific twin attack in Norway carried out by Anders Breivik on 22 July 2011: a car-bomb attack on the residence of Norwegian Prime Minister Jens Stoltenberg and government buildings in Oslo, quickly followed by a 90-minute shooting spree at the AUF (Labour Party Youth) camp on the island of Utøya, which left 69 dead. Initially they were widely reported to be the work of a terrorist inspired either by 'Christian fundamentalism' or 'neo-Nazism'. The full story of Anders Breivik's radicalization process had yet to emerge when this book was going to press, when the trial was still proceeding, and hopefully good investigative journalism will eventually reveal more than the initial psychiatric reports (which declared him unfit to stand trial on the grounds of insanity) about the deeper psychological factors at work. However, enough has already been established to show how misleading many of the reports were, even when it had become clear that the attacks were not the work of Al Qaeda, but of a well-educated native Norwegian.

Preliminary investigations indicated Breivik had at one point been a member of the populist Norwegian Progress Party, which maintains a democratic stand against immigration and multiculturalism, and that he had corresponded with Nordisk, a right-wing web forum concerned with preserving Scandinavia's

Germanic heritage, but inaccurately described as neo-Nazi. But the main source of insight into the creed that had motivated Breivik in his attacks was the 1518-page PDF *2083. Declaration of European Independence*, that he had emailed to 1003 addresses culled from Facebook (including the White Supremacist Stormfront and members of the racist Odinist network), about 90 minutes before the bomb blast in Oslo. This was no declaration, but, in his own words a 'compendium' of notes, thoughts, self-interviews, explanations, practical information, and suggestions for further reading produced in a fluent but somewhat idiosyncratic English (to ease dissemination in Europe) on a variety of topics which he categorized under the following headings: 'The rise of cultural Marxism/multiculturalism in Western Europe; Why the Islamic colonization and Islamisation of Western Europe began; The current state of the Western European Resistance Movements (anti-Marxist/anti-Jihad movements); Solutions for Western Europe and how we, the resistance, should move forward in the coming decades; Covering all, highly relevant topics including solutions and strategies for all of the 8 political fronts.'[24]

The document's premise is that the general public's perception of Islam's history and the threat it poses to Norwegian and European history has been deliberately falsified and covered up by political and cultural élites, primarily 'politicians, NGO leaders, university professors/lecturers, writers, journalists and editors' preaching the values of Cultural Marxism, Political Correctness, and multiculturalism. These are all 'category A and B traitors' of Europe since they 'know that they are contributing to a process of indirect cultural and demographical genocide and they need to be held accountable for their actions. The truth needs to come out. We are in the very beginning of a very bloody cultural war, a war between nationalism and internationalism and we intend to win it.'[25]

Hundreds of pages are devoted to disabusing the reader of the illusion that peaceful coexistence with Islam is possible through an extended chronicle of the brutal war of conquest and colonization it waged on Europe as an imperialist power. These are followed by a lengthy set of notes on the extent of Islamic infiltration into European society in modern times and the threat of Europe being absorbed within a new empire, Eurabia, extending into North Africa and the Middle East. Breivik then turns to expounding the radical solution to the imminent prospect of the loss of Europe's political independence and unique, millennial culture for which it has fought so hard in the past: the development of a European Resistance Movement which will gather sufficient paramilitary force to fight a new crusade. By the symbolic date of 2083 (the 400th anniversary of the Battle of Vienna) this movement will have repelled the Islamic foe from Europe and re-established a culturally Christian, ethnically European continent for its genuine citizens.

The values that inform and misinform Breivik's project betray a number of disparate influences. There is the cultural, differentialist racism of the European New Right exemplified in Alain de Benoit's *Nouvelle Droite* and Aleksandr Dugin's pan-Slavism, as well as elements of Armin Mohler's vision of a Conservative Revolution against liberal democracy which had a major impact on neo-fascism. But there is a hint of an older type of biological racism when Breivik evokes the myth of the Viking hero Holger who will awake to save the Danes from danger and comments:

> Now, if even a trace of the blood of the Men of the North runs in your veins, or if you have lived long enough among them to have acquired some of their spirit, the hair on the back of your neck will rise when you read these words, and you will say, 'Yes! This is the hero, the man who will defend us during the troubles that are surely coming'.[26]

Above all the declaration shows the impact of the rise in Europe since the 1980s of neo-populism whose democratic forms genuinely embrace social liberal values and capitalism, but reject an open-door policy on immigration on the grounds that government policies in this area should be devised primarily for the bene-fit of members of the indigenous national community rather than for the benefit of foreigners. However, several populist parties (e.g. in Belgium, France, Holland, Hungary, Greece and Germany) have developed an extremist wing whose stand against immigration is articulated in terms of xenophobia, racial stereotypes, and a tendency to demonize foreigners, thereby legitimizing discrimination and racial violence. It is no coincidence if the British neo-Nazi BNP has spent a decade attempting to shed its extremist image and cultivating the image of a pop-ulist party on the model of Le Pen's *Front National*. In the context of Breivik's Islamophobia two populist leaders stand out apart from Le Pen: Geert Wilders in Holland and Pia Kjærsgaard in Denmark. But Breivik has translated the most extreme, racist interpretations of populism of the sort openly expressed by the non-electoral English Defence League since 2009, into a revolutionary ideology of violent paramilitary resistance to Muslim immigration. Its logical outcome would be a war of ethnic cleansing throughout the whole continent to purge it of Islamic influence, not to create a Nazi New Order but to give European democracy back to the 'Europeans'.

Two points emerge from this overview. Firstly, Breivik specifically dissociates himself from Christianity as a redemptive theology, though he embraces it fully as a cultural indicator of Europeanness and of ethnic distinctiveness with respect to Islam, explaining that:

> If you have a personal relationship with Jesus Christ and God then you are a religious Christian. Myself and many more like me do not necessarily have a personal relationship with Jesus Christ and God. We do however believe in Christianity as a cultural, social, identity and moral platform. This makes us Christian.[27]

But what it does not make Breivik and his future army of European Resistance is Christian in any theological, fundamentalist sense: quite the reverse. It is a cultural Christianity that also embraces the reverence for the Vikings shown by neo-pagan Odinists.

Secondly, Breivik is vehemently hostile to Nazism, which he claims was not only narrowly nationalistic and anti-European in its vision of preserving ethnic identity only for Germans, but whose genocidal persecution of the Jews in the Holocaust made any form of racism after 1945 taboo, thereby creating the postwar climate in which multiculturalism became the norm. Indeed, Breivik is convinced that 'multiculturalism would have never been implemented in Europe if it hadn't been for NSDAPs reckless and unforgivable actions', so that 'If there is one historical figure and past Germanic leader I hate it is Adolf Hitler',[28] hardly the affirmation of a neo-Nazi. A corollary of this is that Breivik supports Israel in its stand against Islam, and also expresses admiration for the militant Hindutva struggle to preserve Hindu integrity. At one point he suggests that European fundamentalists should emulate the Islamist cult of martyrs who fall in their fight for Muslim identity.

Thus the warrior caste of Knights Templars that Breivik wants to found incarnate not Christian or Nazi values, but a new 'European Religion' in which the whole continent has been mythicized into a sacral entity for which to die. Clearly we are dealing with a typically modern example of Zealotic terrorism inspired by a profound sense of the threat to his personal sacred canopy (configured as 'Norwegianness' and 'Europeanness' posed by modernity). This struggle has been mythicized into a war to the death against a demonized Islam. Yet, however much the vision of a Knights Templar resistance movement draws on a Christian-centred narrative of the medieval Crusades, it has a deep vein of Modernism running through it in the way Europe is conceived as an organic community, a total nomos of territory, ethnicity, and world-view (European Religion) locked in combat with a mortal enemy, a hybrization summed up in his own phrase: Conservative Revolution.

Aspects of Breivik's project for the salvation of Europe, so widely misrepresented in the press, take on enhanced significance in the light of the conceptual framework proposed in this book. The 1500 pages of the 'Declaration' document a protracted act of mazeway resynthesis demanding hundreds of hours of research and 'nomization' to become (what for him is) a cohesive world-view. As a lone wolf in his *modus operandi* (despite shadowy links to fellow Knights Templar), Breivik undertook the extensive process of self-radicalization needed to become his own *propheta* and follower, and set himself the task of producing a blueprint of the new *communitas* to be built by his European Resistance Movement. Information pieced together about his personal life suggests that the premise for the terrorist radicalization process was there: psychological disturbance resulting from parental divorce while he was still a child, a series of business ventures which won and lost him small fortunes, a stage of hermit-like withdrawal from society. This was followed by a process of splitting along ideological fault lines familiar from populist attacks on immigration which produced a Manichaean universe polarized between Europeans with sound instincts to preserve their millennial 'Christian' cultural heritage, and the 'Islamist' Muslim migrant communities and the 'multiculturalist Globalist-Marxists', the Norwegian democrats who, with the full support of the European Union, have encouraged the Islamic 'genocide' of Europeans, (or what we would call nomocide).

During the splitting process Breivik developed his heroic avatar, the Justiciar Knights Templar, enabling the psychological transition from a confused, anomic, and ineffectual emotional adolescent to a cosmic warrior destined to achieve a this-worldly immortality like all his fellow knights.

> You will forever be celebrated by your people as a martyr for your country, protecting your culture and fighting for your kin and for Christendom. You will be remembered as a Conservative revolutionary pioneer, one of the brave European Crusader heroes who said; enough is enough, it is time to take back our countries before our multiculturalist traitor elites actually manages [sic] to finalize their agenda and sell us all into Muslim slavery. Your sacrifice will be a great source of inspiration for generations of Europeans to come.

After their victory:

> Revolutionary patriots like the Justiciar Knights will then be celebrated as destroyers of Marxism and the slayer of tyrants; the fearless and selfless protectors of Europe, The Perfect Knights. For there is no greater glory than dying selflessly while pro-actively protecting your people from persecution and gradual demographical annihilation.[29]

Breivik thus solved his personal nomic crisis by syncretizing a fundamentalist mindset locked onto a palingenetic, millennarian vision of the world process. This he convinced himself was capable of being transformed within two generations thanks to the sacrifice of the vanguard of modern Knights whom his attacks would call into being, revolutionary patriots destined to win because, 'We do not only have the people on our side, we have the truth on our side, we have time on our side, we have the will of our ancestors and the will of God on our side'.[30]

A particularly fascinating feature of the 'declaration' is that it offers a 231-page case study in 'pragmatic fanaticism' at work, focusing the abstract Manichaean diagnosis of Europe's crisis into a functional terrorist mission which he carried out with lethal efficiency. It offers readers a detailed assessment of possible targets and the destructive properties and availability of the weapons needed to attack them, the way the firearms can be procured and the IED (Improvised Explosive Device) made, delivered and detonated, as well as the counter-surveillance techniques required to evade detection.

Another feature of the Breivik attack that stands out is the explicit link he makes between the terror the attacks will unleash within Norway's pro-multiculturalist political classes as the 'third party' targets of his message, and the wider historical metamorphosis this is meant to precipitate, accelerating a process of European rebirth that he is convinced has already started: 'Change is in the air, all over Europe. Europeans now gradually start to awaken from the spell of multiculturalism, Political Correctness and Muslim immigration, but they still don't know how deep the rabbit hole goes.'[31]

Our model of Zealotic terrorism also explains the logic of selecting members of the Norwegian Labour Party youth group for execution rather than Muslim immigrants. After all, they were, for Breivik, the 'real' culprits, the ones who had betrayed their cultural heritage and race and encouraged Norway's Islamization, just as the Zealots attacked the Herodians who encouraged Judea's Hellenization two millennia ago.

Finally, Breivik's Declaration provides precious insights into the complexities of the Alice Syndrome. It displays advanced autodidactic research skills, an impressive English, and synthesizes a wealth of accurate information about the imperialist and warlike aspect of Islam in history which make uncomfortable reading for Islamophiles who dismiss all fears of 'Islamization' as the hysterical result of racist scaremongering. At the same time, taken as a whole, the document offers a totalizing and deeply delusional Manichaean diagnosis of the present condition of Europe, especially in the later sections in which the preparations for the coming mass murder carried out on 22 July are described in forensic detail. Everything suggests a psychotic misreading of reality, a sociopathic mindset replete with elements of conspiracy theory, megalomania, narcissism, apocalypticism, and the urge to commit violence. This nexus of traits led to a total incapacity to feel compassion for the intended victims, a dissociated state of mind needed for dispassionate mass murder that he had trained himself in during the many hundreds of hours he spent by his own account playing the video-game World of Warcraft.

This analysis also offers a position on the issue that has vexed the court proceedings throughout his trial, namely whether Breivik is 'insane'. Certainly 'he lives in his own delusional universe and his thoughts and acts are governed by this universe'.[32] However, his 'paranoid schizophrenia' is of the particular kind exhibited by all those whose mind has locked into a Manichaean universe, in this case created through a private act of syncretism, which justifies terrorist killing for the sake of defending an existing nomos or creating a new one, and enables the 'cosmic warrior' to plan and execute the mission with pragmatism, resourcefulness and calm efficiency. If it is a psychosis then it is a self-induced, ideologically-elaborated psychosis. Hence Seena Fazel, a lecturer in forensic psychiatry at the University of Oxford, was right to be 'surprised by the diagnosis', pointing out that there was a contradiction between this assessment and the fact that Breivik had 'planned this [attack] extremely carefully over a long period of time and was terribly well organised', since 'usually with people with severe mental illness, their lives are slightly more chaotic than that'.[33] It may represent a triumph of liberal pluralism and tolerance that within months of the attacks the Café Teatret in Oslo was planning to perform the Declaration. However, much of the media coverage of Breivik's attacks on the proponents of multiculturalism suggests a voyeuristic trivialization, a refusal to probe into their deeper causal factors and the issues they were so perversely attempting to bring to the public's attention. The handling of the Breivik case, though a triumph of liberal democracy, nevertheless suggests that even many 'experts' fail to understand the powerful well-springs of nomic despair, identity crisis, and fanatical hatred lying just below the surface of plural modernity.

Rethinking terrorism's impact on the social imaginary

Despite the many words devoted to the military, economic, and political impact of terrorism on the West, relatively little thought has been given to its impact on what, under the influence of the psychologist Jacques Lacan's work on the 'imaginary order' which is the basis of the human reality principle, has come to be known as the 'social imaginary'. This was defined by John Thompson as 'the creative and symbolic dimension of the social world, the dimension through which human beings create their ways of living together and their ways of representing their collective life'.[34] It is in this sphere of collective interpersonal subjectivity that the contours and demarcations of shared social space are configured, the agenda of pressing problems 'out there' to be addressed through social or political action is set, and the unfolding of history is perceived.

It is thus precisely the affective sphere of the 'social imaginary', and not the material world, that terrorists intend to transform through the deliberate diffusion of terror through symbolically aimed acts of violence. When religious or ethnic separatists and Islamists, or 'loners' such as McVeigh and Breivik, set out to change the 'minds' of political leaders or 'wake up' the public to an issue that they fanatically believe has been complacently ignored, it is the social imaginary of particular groups they are gunning for, not the immediate victims. This realization is implicit when in *The Secret Agent* Conrad describes the ideal terrorist attack as being of a 'destructive ferocity so absurd as to be incomprehensible, inexplicable, almost unthinkable; *in fact*, mad', so it would be experienced as an assault on '*the whole social creation*'. There was some earnest debate after the Second World War whether literary creativity was still possible after Auschwitz,[35] but even before 9/11 one the most important analysts of contemporary American life, the novelist Don DeLillo, was suggesting terrorism had succeeded in drowning out Western culture's ability to communicate original insights into the human condition. This would indeed be a devastating blow to the West's social imaginary. It would be as if an odourless, colourless gas had seeped into the room and extinguished everybody's capacity for critical thought or creative intelligence to the point where their attention can only be engaged by quizzes, soap operas, and texting banalities to an ever-growing, but invisible and ultimately illusory cohort of cyberfriends. It is thus a proposition worth taking seriously.

DeLillo's *Mao II*, published in 1991, has now assumed the eerie premonitory quality[36] of the film *Don't Look Now* with its references to hijackers smuggling knives through security at three US airports, evocation of the enigmatic dialogue being held by the Twin Towers on the Manhattan skyline which invites an interruption, and the image of terrorists and novelist locked in a struggle for hegemony which art cannot win. In a passage containing a flash of horror sent forward in time from a decade before, we read:

> For some time now I've had the feeling that novelists and terrorists are playing a zero-sum game.... What terrorists gain, novelists lose. The degree to which they influence mass consciousness is the extent of our decline as shapers of

sensibility and thought. The danger they represent equals our own failure to be dangerous. *And the more clearly we see terror the less impact we feel from art*. . . . Beckett is the last writer to shape the way we think and see. *After him the major work involves midair explosions and crumbled buildings*. This is the new tragic narrative.[37]

In such passages the novel captured one aspect of the emerging post-Cold War Zeitgeist with clairvoyant lucidity. History was certainly not ending, *pace* Fukuyama, but its social imaginary was about to change dramatically. By linking the growing inability of his central character, Bill Gray, to finish writing his novel with the domination of headlines by terrorist violence in Lebanon to which he is destined to fall victim himself, De Lillo suggests that art's 'Shock of the New' was being neutralized, effaced by the cumulative effect on the public's sensibilities inflicted by the acts of 'Propaganda of the Deed' or 'God's Fury' becoming the daily fare of world news. Underlying this startling proposition is a rare intuition of the deep structural affinity that exists between the aesthetic modernism of serious artists and the programmatic modernism of 'nomos-creating' terrorists, both of whom in their very different ways want to break the continuum of history, alter 'normality', and create a new sensibility. It is this intuition that prompted one of the founding fathers of modernism in classical music, Karlheinz Stockhausen, to see in the destruction of the Twin Towers a 'work of art':

> Well, what happened there is, is of course – now you all have to adjust your brains – the greatest work of art that has ever existed. That spirits achieve in one act something which in music we could never dream of, that people madly practice for ten years, totally fanatically, for one concert. And then die. And that is the greatest work of art that exists for the whole cosmos. Just imagine what happened there. These are people who are so concentrated on this single performance, and then 5000 people are driven into resurrection. In one moment.[38]

Mao II suggests that even before the first abortive Al Qaeda attack on the WTC in 1993, DeLillo was concerned by the numbing effect on creativity of the liquid fear sporadically welling out from the sites of terrorist attacks in the Middle East and Europe, seeing in them a cumulative threat to the primacy of the artist in shaping the social imaginary in a vitalistic, humanistic spirit of freedom and invention. This fear would gush out like a geyser from Ground Zero a few years later.

Yet some critics have argued instead that DeLillo has misread the state of affairs, and postulated an even more depressing scenario for the future of art as a realm of human emancipation. Rather than a zero-sum game, they suggest it is a no-win situation. The terrorist does not 'stand outside' culture, as DeLillo asserts.[39] On the contrary, in a heavily mediatized, commodified, and spectacularized world, both 'terrorists and novelists have both lost the ability to shape the consciousness of the culture'. Neither can carry out what DeLillo calls 'raids on human consciousness', and the way things are going 'there may no longer be a human consciousness left to raid'.[40] Aesthetic modernism has been archived or finds itself displayed in museums like so many formalined entymological specimens. Terrorism's dependence on the media to maximize terror has become dependency. It has become a media-junkie, its attempt to dominate the media that feeds off the human misery caused by its attacks on society distorting the terrorists' perception of the world (already falsified by the Alice Syndrome) to a point where they fail to realize that whatever short-term media attention they grab nothing actually changes. The 'system' has won. The society of the spectacle, the public consumption of the spectacle, has triumphed. Individualism and authenticity are dead. 'The future belongs to crowds'.[41] But crowds whose capacity for creativity and humanity have been anaesthetized by the manipulators of the image on screens large and small. The terrorist has not defeated the Modernist artist as DeLillo claims: they have both been rendered equally impotent to reshape the social imaginary.

But this dismal line of interpretation misses an important reading of the novel, one which seems encoded in a subtext with which DeLillo intended to 'raid our consciousness' after all. It relates to 'our' addiction to news:

> The novel used to feed our search for meaning.... It was the great secular transcendence. The Latin mass of language, character, occasional new truth. But our desperation has led towards something larger and darker. So we turn to the news, which provides an unremitting mood of catastrophe. This is where we find emotional experience not available elsewhere. We don't need the novel. We don't even need catastrophes. We only need the reports and predictions and warnings.[42]

In other words, the symbiosis between modern terrorism and a globalized media has become possible, not because the semiotic messages of its destructiveness convince anyone, but because of consumer demand for a steady flow of packaged events and images that feed the public's insatiable hunger for vicarious, virtual catastrophes, a product that terrorism is uniquely well equipped to supply. As long as the occasional bloody outrage keeps journalists' blood coursing feverishly in their veins, as long as the threat of an attack is officially high,[43] those living away from the epicentres of anarchy can paradoxically feel more existentially grounded and *safer* by the proximity of a nebulous, imagined but extreme danger. The sensation that everything could end NOW seems to release a mythopoeic enzyme that casts us as imminent victims of a global apocalypse, and the myth of collective catastrophe is more comforting than the threatening state of permanent liminoidality. Victims of a corrosive void at the core of our lives that sucks us ever closer to the vortex of absurdity and nothingness, we are captivated by news which allows us to live out by proxy a catastrophic or eschatological scenario, the ultimate narrative to explain the chaos and decadence of the world.

DeLillo implies that while privileged Westerners pursue centreless postmodern existences on the surface, their/our subconscious selves are drawn to news bulletins, films, and video-games which provide psychodramas in which we can live out scenarios of imminent annihilation and possible rebirth. The collective impact of the rise of terrorism, especially since 9/11, on the social imaginary – at least of those living outside situations of social instability where radical political change may indeed be brought about by violence – is thus to have fed modern apocalyptic mythopoeia. It is based on the same archaic, primal, ritualized projections of life's fragility, death's violence, and the prospect of eternity that gave rise to the first human sacred canopies. This is why the prologue to *Mao II* takes the form of an outsider's description of a mass Moonie wedding ceremony performed in the Yankee Stadium. DeLillo asks 'When the Old God leaves the world, what happens to all the unexpended faith?', and suggests that the currency of belief now circulating under modernity in enormous unregulated quantities can be reinvested in cults such as the Moonies, in writing novels, in joining a terrorist movement.

In fact, in some ways *Mao II* anticipates the violence of Aum Shinkryo and its bid to bring about Armageddon which took place four years after its publication, just as presciently as it does the Islamist strikes on New York and Washington. The novel's terrorists are ethnic-religious Maoists fighting vulture-like in Beirut over the corpse of the Lebanese nomos. But the Moonie leader, like Asahara, attracts fanatical devotion of a different kind from his followers. He 'answers their yearning, unburdens them of free will and independent thought. See how happy they look.' As they chant they sense that 'the future is pressing in, collapsing towards them, that they are everywhere surrounded by signs of the fated landscape and human struggle of the Last Days'. But they are untouched, 'rayed with well-being ... immunized against the language of the self'. The Master 'lifts them out of ordinary strips of space and time and then shows them the blessedness of lives devoted to the ordinary, to work, prayer and obedience'.[44] This ecstasy of total Gnosis is portrayed as a benign escape from anomy here, but the 'crowd mentality' of collective belief also has a latent dark and destructive side which DeLillo reveals in the fanaticism of the Maoist terrorists who will eventually kill the demoralized writer at the centre of the novel. It was the same fanaticism that was to lead to sarin seeping insidiously out of bags in the Tokyo subway and the smoking rubble of Ground Zero.

One passage eloquently captures the raw emotional material of all secular and religious Zealotry born of a nomocidal, meaning-sapping modernity. The (Moonie) Master:

> leads them out past religion and history, thousands weeping now. They are gripped by the force of a longing...a longing deep in time, running in the earthly blood. This is what people have wanted since consciousness became corrupt [self-reflexive]. The chant brings End Time closer....They chant for world-shattering rapture, for the truth of prophecies and astonishments. They chant for new life, peace eternal, the end of soul-lonely pain.... They chant for one language, one word, for the time when names are lost.[45]

The fascination exerted on media-addicts who long for their next fix of sensationalism, and watch compelled as genuine catastrophes unfold in contemporary reality, is a passive, consumerist, existentially *lazy* version of the same desire to access apocalyptic time depicted here. Thanks to DeLillo the deeper meaning of *Knowing*, with its graphic dramatization of a subway disaster, a plane crash, and the end of the world, can now be grasped. Such films do not exorcise or transmute liquid fear, but dramatize and commercialize it like plastic bottles of Lourdes Water, enabling people engulfed in the 'ordinary time' of *chronos* to spend a couple of hours 'rapt', lifted into a virtual version of a cosmically significant 'end time', *kairos*, a time of civilization's destruction and rebirth whether in a new planetary era (*2012*), or in a parallel universe (*Knowing*). But there is no tragic catharsis, no Gnosis, no spiritual revelation in such films. Apocalypse is trivialized into 'entertainment' by the secular miracles of CGI effects. Afterwards spectators are delivered back to their anomic, popcornless lives in chronic time. Modernity's liquefaction of reality and erosion of the sacred canopy proceeds unchecked. As Paul McCartney put it in *Eleanor Rigby*, 'No one was saved'.

The terrorist solution to the dilemma of anomy is at the heart of DeLillo's novel: to reach a point of white-hot fanaticism in which the individual self is vaporized. It is replaced by the heroic double who transcends the fear of death by fighting for a cause which gives nomic weight to life. One of DeLillo's terrorists tells the journalist interviewing him that 'Mao said death can be light as a feather or heavy as a mountain. You die for the people and the nation, your death is massive and intense. Die for the oppressors, ... die selfish and vain and you float away like the feather of the smallest bird'.[46] The terrorist's creed gives the death of anomic individuals a substance it would otherwise lack, and hence gives paradoxical meaning and existential weight to their lives.

Yet DeLillo also hints at a way to escape anomy without recourse to fanatical violence, not in the text of the novel, but in the reader's response to it. At one point Bill Gray asserts 'a writer creates character as a way to reveal consciousness, *increase the flow of meaning*'.[47] This opens up a third possibility, a humanistic one – invisible to dichotomous thinking – in which the social imaginary can respond to the presence of terrorism instead of giving into the lure of the liquid fear it generates, or being seduced by the images of apocalypse it mass-produces. This is to refuse to accept either the anomic liquefaction of reality or its false nomic solidification within rigid, soul-destroying fanatical belief systems pursuing deadly utopias. Acupuncture claims to allow the *qi* energy, the *élan vital*, the 'life force' to circulate through the meridians (invisible to Western science) unimpeded. Humanism, whether secular or religious, can be seen as a social life force, promoting a healthy, meandering stream of creativity, both imaginative and practical, that transcends ethnocentrism, sectarianism, demonization, and Manichaean thinking, and embraces instead plurality, ambivalence, pacifism, and compassion. It offers a Third Way, a Fifth Element.

Having stressed throughout this book the lethal potential of some forms of human quest for nomic certainty and transcendence, it is good to be able to end with the example of a 'searcher' whose journey did not end with the transformation into a fully-fledged terrorist, nor with plunging back into the *lethe* of somnolent anomy. Instead it continued through fanaticism and beyond, enabling him eventually to channel his spiritual energy away into a religious humanism promoting *life-asserting* ways to make an impact on the social imaginary.

Rethinking the de-radicalization of potential terrorists

Ed Husain's *The Islamist* is a precious record of the step-by-step process of radicalization undergone by one diaspora Muslim growing up in London. It is a reconstruction illuminated by the introspection of someone deeply concerned to understand what brought him to the threshold of becoming involved in terrorist activities and allows the first stages in the syndrome of radicalization to be followed in great detail. Husain clearly is endowed with a low threshold of tolerance for absurdity and ambivalence. He describes the conflicting pressures on identity experienced by a Muslim in East London, and how even when he had become a militant Islamist 'there was a vacuum in my soul where God should be'.[48] In fact, the driving force in his soul turns out to have been not power, but the search 'for spiritual solace, for meaning in my life'.[49] At first Islamism seemed to provide an answer to his nomic needs, both spiritual and social, and when a writer like Qutb appeared to offer a total solution to the world's problems he had already been drawn into familiar patterns of cultic consciousness.

The splitting of reality soon followed: 'We were believers, Muslims; all others were *kuffar*. And we were no ordinary Muslims, but superior to others.'[50] Soon he was treating non-Islamist Muslims, including his own parents, as *kuffar*, and believing ever more fervently in the God-made politics being preached at the East London mosque. Here he was called upon to do '*da'wah* work', to spread the Islamist word of God, and prepare for the future Islamic state in Britain which would supersede existing institutions and culture. By 1994 he was working enthusiastically to realize the Islamist mission to conquer the world for Muslims, convinced that 'we were on the verge of a new world order',[51] with Islamic states being created 'throughout the Middle East'.

In the grip of the Alice Syndrome Husain utterly misread the political impact of a conference he helped organize which was to trigger the Islamization of Britain: 'Nothing happened. There was no Islamic state, no military coup, and no caliph.'[52] Disillusionment started to set in as his 'real self' started growing again at the expense of his heroic double. He realized that his 'relationship with God had deteriorated', and that his group which was working so hard 'to establish God's rule on earth', 'reverse history' and 'allow a return to the glory days of Islam' was actually 'clueless' about the Quran or Muslim practice.[53] The murder of a Christian student of Nigerian ethnic background who had been 'offensive' about Muslims, the direct result of the violent anti-*kuffar* rhetoric of his group, served as a 'wake-up call'. However, his group, Hizb ut-Tahrir al-Islami (Islamic Liberation Party), blithely issued a condemnation of the murder, claiming to be opposed to violence. Husain comments:

This myth was swallowed by investigators who never really understood the seriousness of the Hizb's form of violence. Even today, a primary reason for Western failure in the War on Terror is the same cause: an innate inability to understand the Islamist psyche.[54]

Clearly, someone who has been a convert to Islamism understands the importance of the terrorist's creed.

But Ed Husain had seen enough. He now saw Islamism as 'an empty, bankrupt ideology'.[55] The power of his new heroic avatar waned, and with it his uncompromising commitment to terrorist violence. He ceased to be an Islamist. Yet he did not return from the solidarity and artificial solidity of Islamism's Zealotic-Modernist firmament to the bottomless black pool of anomy. The emotional warmth he experienced in his relationship with a Muslim woman enabled him 'to reconcile my mind to the modern world and come to terms with the reality that surrounded me, rather than trying to dominate it in the name of religion'.[56] Thus he did not become apostate. Instead he gave up a well-paid job to concentrate on Quranic studies bringing about a deepening of his faith in Allah, at last filling the spiritual void he had experienced as an Islamist.[57] As a result the 'flow of meaning' in Husain's life increased dramatically. A Third Way had opened up for him.

His time spent in Damascus, where he was able to experience how Islam is lived in Muslim countries, and become familiar with the rich historical, religious, and ethnic complexity of cultures in constant interaction and symbiosis, deepened and *redirected* Husain's spiritual quest. He became impressed by the fact that:

> Repeatedly the Koran called for reflection, meditation, and contemplation of the world.... The Koran desired *yusr*, or ease, and not hardship in adherence to faith. There was an elasticity, nuance, and plurality in the message of the Koran that Islamists had somehow overlooked, in the process reducing our noble faith to terrorism, anger and conflict.[58]

As his world became de-Manichaeanized and he ceased to be a cosmic warrior for good, Husain became conscious of the common ground between Muslims and Christians and their ability to co-exist without Zealotry, worshipping the 'same' God from within different faiths. His frequent visits to a Sufi mosque 'cleansed the soul'. Teaching English for the British Council in Syria, he found himself ardently defending liberal humanist values of tolerance and pluralism, and spontaneously contesting the demonized portraits of Britain as the enemy of Islam planted in the heads of students by Islamism. By the time he left Syria the tunnel vision imposed by his 'Islamist blinkers' had been cured. Husain went on to co-found Quilliam, a 'think-tank' which aims to promote moderate Islam, create environments in which converts to Global Salafi Jihad can be de-radicalized and rehabilitated, and raise public awareness of the radical incompatibility of Islam with Islamism.

It is revealing that in his account of his de-radicalization, Husain feels the need to deny the existence of an authentic tradition within Islam of global imperialism and militancy, treating Islamism as a form of Islam corrupted by the influence of Western ideology. His studies convinced him, for example, that the ideas of the Islamic state promoted by the ideologue who had most influenced him, Taqiuddin al-Nabhani, whose rejection of *kuffar* was second only to Qutb's in its vitriol, were 'formed by Western political discourse' dressed up in Muslim idioms.[59] Plans to Islamize the world thus owed more to Hegel, and Gramscian Marxism than Islam itself. It is an argument that has been adopted not just by moderate Muslims keen to dissociate themselves from terrorism but, as we have seen, by certain 'liberal' Western commentators on Islamism who seem reluctant to accept its globalizing agenda as an authentic face of Islam out of a fear of being tarred with the brush of Islamophobia.

The position adopted in this book is different. It refuses both to condemn religious belief as the raw material of fanaticism and celebrate secular humanism as the sole basis of social progress, and to defend 'real' religion as intrinsically moderate and compassionate, so that all religious extremism becomes a 'heresy' or a modern 'perversion'. Instead, it stresses the *ambivalence* of the world's major religions, and acknowledges both their potential for fuelling fanatical hatreds and for universal compassion. Indeed, scripture, theology, and (mythicized) history can be deployed as much for the sanctioning, or even sanctification, of hatred and violence as for combating it. Though it conflicts with Husain's own interpretation of his de-radicalization process, I would argue that he moved from one reading of Islam fuelling splitting, heroic doubling, and violence, to another celebrating moderation, pacifism, and pluralism. In other words he discovered within his faith not secular humanism but a *transcultural humanism*, a potential within both atheistic and most religions for acknowledging the humanity of 'the Other' which is the psychological antidote to fanaticism.

This line of thought suggests that the premise of counter-radicalization and de-radicalization programmes should be two-fold. First, every fanatic contains within him- or herself a suppressed, confused, anomic, prefanatical self who can possibly be awakened and converted to moderation as a source of community and nomos. This was the self that Husain rediscovered in himself, and it is worth recalling that even the 9/11 hijackers had to be *reminded* on the eve of their mission of the correct spirit in which to carry it out, showing that a residual element of their private, doubting self still remained. In the case of violent fanatics of a secular creed this is the only strategy available, but it is to be followed on the premise not that they are 'mad' or intrinsically 'evil', but rather that they crave a sense of certainty, empowerment, and transcendent meaning through terrorism denied them in 'ordinary life'.

In the case of 'religious fanatics' there is another factor to be borne in mind. Rather than attempt to de-radicalize them by converting them to secular liberalism, emphasis should be placed on rechannelling their hunger for truth and certainty, their flight from anomy, into growth towards a moderate, tolerant form of their faith which embraces transcultural humanism. It is the path which Husain followed spontaneously when he found a mystical form of Sufism compatible with humanism, though only at the cost of denying that fanatical hatred and fantasies of globalization have historically been intrinsic to Islam, even if they are not its only 'true face' as Islamists claim. In each case it is vital that moderation, pacifism, humility, the tolerance of ambivalence, pluralism, and doubt, whether based on secular or religious humanism, are understood to be a *courageous* response to modernity and the human dilemma of living in the world, a *strong* nomos, not the absence of a nomos, one that can be presented as satisfying existential needs for a sacred canopy whether or not there is God to keep it in its place.

As for those not directly charged with combating terrorism, they have a duty to themselves, faced with the global threat of terrorism – alongside myriad other more practical social, economic, political, demographic and ecological concerns – not to succumb to the temptation to let it engorge our black reservoir of liquid fears. We must resist the temptation to incorporate the terror emanating from the threat of terrorism into our subliminal, media-driven narrative of imminent catastrophe. Our mission instead should be to use the terrorist threat, and equivalent global dangers, as a stimulus to deepen our own faith, secular or religious, and enhance our capacity not for activist Gnosticism but activist humanism. This means humanizing it ever more profoundly, and doing whatever our life situation, skills, and values allow to counteract the forces of prejudice and paranoia which feed into fanaticism. De-radicalization is possible. Modern society can generate strong but moderate nomoi to live by, 'muscular' forms of transcultural humanism, able to fill, even if only partially, the expanding spiritual void excavated by modernity. Such an approach to life can draw not just on countless acts of selfless compassion that have transcended ethnic and religious barriers, but on the astonishing works of art, in music, dance, and poetry, literature, philosophy, and ethics which celebrate the human spirit in defiance of absurdity and nihilism without hatred or violence.

So the 'hidden agenda' of this book has now been brought to light. By analysing the role played by the human quest for a nomic home in generating terrorism though the ages, it has hoped, however utopianly, to contribute to the formulation of a humanistic, but not exclusively secular, basis on which to come to grips with and even counteract the deeper non-instrumental causes of terrorism. The Sufist philosopher, Rumi (1207–73), Ed Husain's favourite poet, asked 'If your heart is a volcano, how shall you expect flowers to bloom?' This what he said of anger:

> When you see the face of anger
> look behind it
> and you will see the face of pride.
> Bring anger and pride
> under your feet, turn them into a ladder
> and climb higher.
> There is no peace until you become
> their master.
> Let go of anger, it may taste sweet
> but it kills.
> Don't become its victim.
> You need humility to climb to freedom.

These lines have a particular meaning not just for would-be Islamists, but for all fanatics committed to a terroristic solution for an intolerable situation that fills them with a burning sense of outrage. However, a state's 'war on terrorism' also presupposes anger, and has led to 'collateral damage', which means killing, suffering, and atrocities, on a terrible scale in the last decade. In this book we have attempted to understand the dynamics of fanaticism from the perspective of social anthropology and an existentialist diagnosis of the 'human condition'. Perhaps compassionate humanism, blending knowledge with humility, could create a greater role for itself in combating terrorism alongside surveillance techniques and counter-terrorist measures. This means identifying potential terrorists through methodological empathy with the radicalizing pressures to which they are exposed. It also means introducing measures to humanize and 'renomize' where possible the alienating, anomic social and cultural conditions that can give rise to terrorism in so many places in the world. When fear and anger no longer cloud the understanding of fanatical violence, then perhaps terrorist studies will bloom as a branch of the human sciences. A branch of a tree, which may not be able to grow within the Gates of Eden evoked in Bob Dylan's epiphanic song, but at least has a canopy that stretches beyond its walls.

Notes

1 Forethoughts: The Liquid Fear of Terrorism

1. Guy Debord, *The Society of the Spectacle* (London: Rebel Press, 2004).
2. Buzzle (2006) Yankee Pitcher Cory Lidle's Plane Crashes into NYC Skyscraper, http://www.buzzle.com/articles/yankee-pitcher-cory-lidle-plane-crashes-nyc-skyscraper.html, date accessed 29 November 2011.
3. The New York Times (2009) White House Apologizes for Air Force Flyover, http://cityroom.blogs.nytimes.com/2009/04/27/air-force-one-backup-rattles-new-york-nerve/, date accessed 29 November 2011.
4. Of course this is a simplistically US and perhaps Anglo-centric view, since a string of countries had experienced the daily fear of terrorist attack long before 9/11, but it is arguably with the Al Qaeda attack on the WTC and the spate of Islamist attacks that followed elsewhere that at least for several years the fear of terrorism became a global phenomenon and launched 'terrorist studies' world-wide.
5. Isabelle Duyvesteyn, 'The Role of History and Continuity in Terrorism Research', in Magnus Ranstorp (ed.), *Mapping Terrorism Research. State of the Art, Gaps and Future Direction* (London: Routledge, 2007), 51.
6. Zygmunt Bauman, *Liquid Modernity* (Cambridge: Polity, 2000); *Liquid Love: On the Frailty of Human Bonds* (Cambridge: Polity, 2003): *Liquid Life* (Cambridge: Polity, 2005); *Liquid Fear* (Cambridge: Polity, 2006); *Liquid Times: Living in an Age of Uncertainty* (Cambridge: Polity, 2006).
7. Bauman, *Liquid Fear*, 17.
8. See, for example, Esquire (2009) The Falling Man, http://www.esquire.com/features/ESQ0903-SEP_FALLINGMAN, date accessed 29 November 2011.
9. Mark D. Thompson, 'Luther on Despair', in Brian Rosner (ed.), *The Consolations of Theology* (New York, NY: Wm. B. Eerdmans Publishing, 2008), 63.
10. Bauman, *Liquid Fear*, 17.
11. An allusion to Baudelaire's preface to *Les Fleurs du Mal* (1857).
12. Bauman, *Liquid Fear*, 122–3.
13. Alex Houen, *Terrorism and Modern Literature* (Oxford: Oxford University Press, 2002).
14. Robert Cettl, *Terrorism in American Cinema: An Analytical Filmography, 1960–2008* (Jefferson, NC: McFarland, 2009).
15. Roger Griffin, *Modernism and Fascism. The Sense of a Beginning under Mussolini and Hitler* (London: Palgrave Macmillan, 2007).
16. For a sophisticated account of Weber's theory see Thomas Burger, *Max Weber's Theory of Concept Formation, History, Laws, and Ideal Types* (North Carolina: Duke University Press, 1976).
17. John Gray, *Black Mass: Apocalyptic Religion and the Death of Utopia* (London: Allen Lane, 2007) 174.
18. Joshua Sinai, 'New Trends in Terrorism Studies: Strengths and Weaknesses', in Ranstorp, *Mapping Terrorism Research*, 36.
19. Albert Jongman and Alex Schmid, *Political Terrorism: A New Guide to Actors, Authors, Concepts, Data Bases, Theories and Literature* (New Brunswick: Transaction Books, 1988), 5–7.
20. Bruce Hoffman, *Inside Terrorism* (Columbia: Columbia University Press, 2006), 34.
21. Sinai, 'New Trends', in Ranstorp, *Mapping Terrorism Research*, 47.
22. Ibid., 33.

23. In 1942 Goebbels ordered the press to replace the term 'partisan' with 'terrorist' in reporting the war in the East and in 1944 General-lieutenant Blaskowitz was talking about his 'war on terrorism' in Russia, anticipating Bush's description of Iraq resistance as terrorism. During the Syrian crisis that started in 2011 President Bashar Al-Assad attributed state-sponsored atrocities to the work of the 'terrorists' fighting for the opposition. See Wolfgang Dressen, *Politische Prozesse ohne Verteidigung?* (Wagenbach: Berlin, 1976), 65.
24. India Today (2010) Maoism is Terrorism, http://indiatoday.intoday.in/site/story/ Maoism+is+terrorism/1/92085.html, date accessed 1 December 2011. For a conflicting analysis of the 'terrorism' of India's poor, see Arundhati Roy, *Broken Republic* (Harmondsworth: Penguin, 2011).
25. There have been occasions when 'terrorism' is used by perpetrators themselves as a badge of pride. The Russian nihilist anarchist, Sergey Nechayev, founder of People's Retribution in 1869, described himself as a 'terrorist', and Johann Most, a contemporary German anarchist published 'advice for terrorists' in the 1880s.
26. E.g. Jeffrey Sluka (ed.), *Death Squad: The Anthropology of State Terror* (Philadelphia: University of Pennsylvania Press, 2000); Mark Curtis, *Western State Terrorism* (Cambridge: Polity Press, 2004); Frederick Henry Gareau, *State Terrorism and the United States: From Counterinsurgency to the War on Terror* (London: Zed Books, 2004); James Ron, *Frontiers and Ghettos: State Violence in Serbia and Israel* (Berkeley: University of California Press, 2003).
27. Noam Chomsky and Edward Herman, *The Washington Connection and Third World Fascism: The Political Economy of Human Rights: Vol. 1* (Boston: South End Press, 1979). More recently, Mikkel Thorup in *An Intellectual History of Terror: War, Violence and the State* (New York, NY: Routledge, 2010) offers an illuminating history of the evolution of state terror. He shows how it came to be deployed as a morally legitimate instrument of aggression, coercion, or purification against those conceived for whatever reason as beyond the pale of humanity so that the moral laws of (Christian/rational) civilization did/do not apply.
28. See Victor Luneev (2002) 'High-Organized Crime and Terrorism': Proceedings of a Russian-American Workshop on 'High Impact Terrorism, http://www.nap.edu/ openbook.php?record_id=10301&page=37, date accessed 29 November 2011.
29. The *normality* of the moral evil involved in genocide and terrorism is one of the main themes of Steven Bartlett, *The Pathology of Man. A Study in Human Evil* (Springfield, IL: Charles C. Thomas, 2005), e.g. 313–15.
30. Jean Rosenfeld (2010) The Religion of Osama bin Laden: Terror in the Hand of God, http://www.publiceye.org/frontpage/911/Islam/rosenfeld-TOC.html, date accessed 30 November 2011.
31. Christopher Coker, *Waging War without Warriors? The Changing Culture of Military Conflict* (Boulder, CO: Lynne Rienner, 2002), 6.
32. Jeffrey Bale offers an important account of the 'expressive dimension' of terrorist violence in his chapter 'Jihadist Ideology and Strategy and the Possible Employment of WMD', in Gary Ackerman and Jeremy Tamsett (eds), *Jihadists and Weapons of Mass Destruction* (Boca Raton: CRC Press, 2009), 7. In this chapter he stresses that the frequent nebulousness and utopianism of terrorist goals does not preclude their ability to formulate and ruthlessly execute strategic plans for their attacks of a deadly pragmatism and effectiveness.
33. Bruce Hoffman, 'Foreword', in Andrew Silke (ed.), *Research on Terrorism: Trends, Achievements and Failures* (Portland, OR: Frank Cass, 2004), xviii.
34. Jeffrey Cozzens, 'Approaching al-Qaeda's Warfare: Function, Culture and Grand Strategy' in Ranstorp, *Mapping Terrorism Research*, 136.
35. Ibid., 146–7.
36. Ibid., 128–9.
37. Ibid.

38. Ibid., 130.
39. Ibid., 136.
40. Ibid., 130.
41. Sinai, 'New Trends', in Ranstorp, *Mapping Terrorism Research*, 40. My emphasis.
42. Bale, 'Jihadist Ideology and Strategy', 4.
43. Duyvesteyn, 'The Role of History and Continuity'.
44. Michael Ignatieff, 'It's War – But it Doesn't Have to be Dirty', *The Guardian*, 1 October 2001. The emphasis he places on the nihilist basis of terrorist morality is explored at length in 'The Temptations of Nihilism', Chapter Five of his *The Lesser Evil: Political Ethics in an Age of Terror* (Princeton, NJ: Princeton University Press, 2004), 112–44. For a trenchant critique of the overemphasis on the role played by metaphysics in the conceptualization of terrorism see Andreas Behnke, 'Terrorising the Political: 9/11 within the Context of the Globalisation of Violence', *Millennium: Journal of International Studies* 33, 2 (2004), 279–312.
45. E.g. Maxwell Taylor, *The Fanatics: A Behavioural Approach to Political Violence* (Princeton, NJ: Princeton University Press, 2007); cf. Bartlett, *The Pathology of Man*, 199–2, 293–303.
46. The word thus has similar connotations to the Greek 'enthusiasm', which according to some accounts denotes 'the awakening of the God [*theos*] within'.
47. Cozzens, 'Approaching', 128–9. Cf. Coker, *Waging War*.
48. John Horgan, 'Understanding Terrorist Motivation: A Socio-psychological Perspective' in Ranstorp, *Mapping Terrorism Research*, 119.
49. Magnus Ranstorp, 'Introduction: Mapping terrorism research – challenges and priorities', in Ranstorp, *Mapping Terrorism Research*, 20.
50. Cozzens, 'Approaching', in Ranstorp, *Mapping Terrorism Research*, 148.
51. Ronald D. Crelinsten, 'Counterterrorism as global governance: A research inventory', in Ranstorp, *Mapping Terrorism Research*, 211.
52. Alain Badiou, *Metapolitics* (London: Verso, 2005).
53. Pierre Krebs, *Die europäische Wiedergeburt* [The European rebirth] (Tübingen: Grabert, 1982), 82–6. See Pierre Krebs (2006) The Metapolitical Rebirth of Europe http://www.newrightausnz.com/2006/02/24/the-metapolitical-rebirth-of-europe-by-pierre-krebs/, date accessed 1 December 2011. See also Troy Southgate (ed.), *The Primordial Tradition: Philosophy, Metapolitics and the Conservative Revolution* (n.pl: Primordial Traditions, 2011) for an important exposition in English of the principles of metapolitics as the pursuit of a grand design beyond party politics.
54. The classic, robust, sometimes swashbuckling refutation of the attack of fundamentalist postmodernists on the objectivity of history is Richard Evans, *In Defence of History* (London: Granta, 1997), which also offers a refutation of the distortions of 'culturalism' in the reductive sense.
55. Cozzens, 'Approaching', 147.
56. Horgan, 'Understanding' and Michael Taarnby, 'Understanding Recruitment of Islamist Terrorists in Europe', in Ranstorp, *Mapping Terrorism Research*.
57. For convenience, the Gregorian calendar will be used in this book along with BC and AD, though I am fully aware that these are culture specific terms with connotations of the 'Christian West'. I hope those who live in a cultural world following a different calendar will excuse this convention.

2 Terrorism as Zealotry: Defending the Nomos

1. Peter Berger, *The Sacred Canopy. Elements of a Sociological Theory of Religion* (London: Doubleday, 1967). Berger has since revised the theory of secularization that underpinned this analysis, but the anthropological insights into the human need for 'nomos' are still

arguably valid, especially since he shows that it is this need that drives the process of *de*-secularization which he now acknowledges.

2. Theoi Greek Mythology (2011) Nomos, http://www.theoi.com/Daimon/Nomos.html, first accessed 1 December 2011.

3. Berger, *The Sacred Canopy*, 22.

5. Ibid., 22 (my emphasis).

6. Ibid.

7. The importance of the myth of a primordial metaphysical order which provides the 'firmament' of a culture is central to Mircea Eliadea's work on the universal cosmological patterns found in the world's religions, e.g. in *The Sacred and the Profane. The Nature of Religion. The Significance of Religious Myth, Symbolism, and Ritual within Life and Culture* (San Diego, CA: Harcourt Brace & Co, 1959) and *The Myth of the Eternal Return, or Cosmos and History* (Princeton, NJ: Princeton University Press, 1971).

8. Peter Berger, *The Desecularization of the World: The Resurgence of Religion in World Politics* (Michigan: Wm B. Eerdmans, 1999).

9. Ernest Becker, *The Denial of Death* (New York, NY: Simon & Schuster, 1997), 5.

10. Ibid., 12–13.

11. Ernest Becker, *Escape from Evil* (New York, NY: Free Press, 1975), 64.

12. Ibid., 149–50.

13. Tom Psyzcynski, Sheldon Solomon, and Jeff Greenberg, *In the Wake of 9/11. The Psychology of Terror* (Washington DC: American Psychological Association, 2003), 22.

14. John Gray, *Enlightenment's Wake: Politics and Culture at the Close of the Modern Age* (London: Routledge, 1995), 17.

15. Ibid., 16.

16. David Mclagan, *Creation Myths: Man's Introduction to the World* (New York, NY: Thames and Hudson, 1977), 27.

17. The Radical Truth (2011) Eros and Thanatos, http://www.theradicaltruth.com/Footnotes/wilber-atman-project-fn.htm, first accessed 12 December 2011.

18. Robert Roy Britt (2005) 'Forces of Creation: Black Holes Spark Star Formation', http://www.space.com/767-forces-creation-black-holes-spark-star-formation.html, first accessed 21 February 2011.

19. Charles Strozier in Charles Strozier, Michael Flynn, *The Year 2000: Essays on the End* (New York, NY: New York University Press, 1997), 2.

20. An extended hermeneutic account of the existential need for individuals to locate their lives within a coherent 'metanarrative' is offered in Paul Ricoeur's highly influential *Time and Narrative (Temps et Récit)*, 3 vols (Chicago: University of Chicago Press, 1984, 1985, 1988).

21. John Gray, *Black Mass*, 204.

22. Cozzens, 'Approaching Al-Qaeda's Warfare', 129.

23. Erich Fromm, *The Revolution of Hope: Toward a Humanized Technology* (New York, NY: Harper & Row, 1968), 61.

24. Paul Bowles, *The Sheltering Sky* (Harmondsworth: Penguin, 1990).

25. Blaise Pascal, *Pensées* (Harmondsworth: Penguin, 1966), no. 201, 95.

26. Émile Cioran, *A Short History of Decay* (Oxford, Basil Blackwell, 1975), 3.

27. Robert Robins and Jerrold Post, *Political Paranoia. The Psychopolitics of Hatred* (London: Yale University Press, 1997), 144.

28. BBC (1999) Tradition http://news.bbc.co.uk/hi/english/static/events/reith_99/week3/week3.htm, first accessed 1 December 2011.

29. Slavoj Žižek, *Violence: Six Sideways Reflections* (London: Profile Books, 2008), 70.

30. Luciano Pellicani, *Revolutionary Apocalypse. Ideological Roots of Terrorism* (Westport, CT: Praeger, 2003), 250–1.

31. Arnold Toynbee, *A Study of History. Heroic Ages, Volume 8: Contacts Between Civilizations in Space* (Oxford: Oxford University Press, 1963).

32. Ibid., 583.

33. Ibid., 592–5.
34. Ibid., 581.
35. Albert Baumgarten, *The Flourishing of Jewish Sects in the Maccabean Era: An Interpretation* (Leiden: E.J. Brill, 1997).
36. Wayne Meeks, *The First Urban Christians: The Social World of the Apostle Paul* (New Haven: Yale University Press, 1983) 173–4, cited in Baumgarten, *The Flourishing of Jewish Sects*, 164.
37. Ibid.
38. Baumgarten, *The Flourishing of Jewish Sects*, 165.
39. On the relationship between threats to cultural nomoi and millennarianism see particularly Catherine Wessinger (ed.) *Millennialism, Persecution and Violence: Historical Cases* (Syracuse, NY: Syracuse University, 2000). Millennarianism has for obscure reasons come to be spelt with a single n though it derives from 'annus' in Latin (and not 'anus'), so throughout this volume I have restored the missing 'n' in defiance of the lexicon.
40. Eschatology, from *eschatos*, the last (days), refers to the sense that one dispensation of history is ending and another about to begin.
41. Soteriology is the doctrine of salvation or its scholarly study and here refers to the belief that history is moving to a moment of collective redemption for the elect believers or people, a myth that has assumed secular forms in the modern era (as in Fascism and Nazism).
42. Ami Pedahzur and Arie Perliger, *Jewish Terrorism in Israel* (New York, NY: Columbia University Press, 2009), 6. Chapter one of this book, 'The Founding Myths' offers extensive corroboration of Toynbee's account of the relationship between Herodization and Zealotry as responses to Hellenization.
43. The article Answering Christianity (2011) Was Jesus Poisoned? http://www.answering-christianity.com/abdullah_smith/alleged_poisoning_of_prophet_muhammad_2.htm, first accessed 1 December 2011, claims the disciples James and John were also Zealots which are misleadingly conflated with the Sicarii who were their militant, 'paramilitary' wing.
44. Yael Zerubavel, *Recovered Roots: Collective Memory and the Making of Israeli National Tradition* (*Chicago: University of Chicago Press, 1995*).
45. Robert Eisenman, *James the Brother of Jesus: The Key to Unlocking the Secrets of Early Christianity and the Dead Sea Scrolls* (New York, NY: Viking, 1997), 180.
46. Ian Netton, *Muslim Neoplatonists: An Introduction to the Thought of the Brethren of Purity* (Edinburgh: Edinburgh University Press, 1991).
47. Farhad Daftary, *The Ismāʿīlīs: Their History and Doctrines* (Cambridge: Cambridge University Press, 1990), 368–75.
48. An obviously highly speculative but fascinating account of the structure and beliefs of this order is offered by Richard Shand, 'The Secret Doctrine of the Assassins', which perfectly captures the cultic, esoteric component of terrorist radicalization which arguably still plays such an important role even in the case of some secular initiation processes, even virtual, Web-based ones, allowing the anomic self to be 'doubled' so that it rapidly gives way to a heroic self prepared to kill and be killed. See Richard Shand (1998) The Secret Doctrine of the Assassins http://www.alamut.com/subj/ideologies/alamut/secDoctrines.html, first accessed 1 December 2011.
49. Dafarty, *The Ismāʿīlīs*, 392–96.
50. Amin Maalouf, *Samarkand* (New York, NY: Interlink Publishing Group, 1998).
51. E.g. Dan Ben-David (2007) The Sicarii of the Third Temple http://www.haaretz.com/print-edition/opinion/the-sicarii-of-the-third-temple-1.226260, first accessed 1 December 2011.
52. Particularly illuminating here is Thorup's analysis of the brutality with which the states that regard themselves as 'civilized' seek to exterminate cultures they regard as primitive or using 'uncivilized' forms of warfare that place themselves outside the orbit and

protection of 'civilization', and are thus 'legitimately' treated with barbarous cruelty in the interests of defending it. See Thorup, *History of Terror*.

53. See The Economist (2008) The wild south http://www.economist.com/node/12627992, first accessed 2 December 2011.

54. For the use of library burning as a weapon of deliberate culturecide see Rebecca Knuth, *Burning Books and Levelling Libraries. Extremist Violence and Cultural Destruction* (Westport, CT: Praeger, 2006).

55. Leon Aron (2003) Chechnya: New Dimensions of the Old Crisis, http://www.aei.org/article/foreign-and-defense-policy/regional/europe/chechnya-outlook/, first accessed 2 December 2011.

56. Aron emphasizes this point in 'Chechnya', ibid.

57. Statement issued in English by the Kavkaz Centre (2010) English Transcript, http://www.kavkazcenter.com/eng/content/2010/03/08/11569_print.html, first accessed 2 December 2011.

58. See the article by Rebecca Knuth (2006) Destroying a Symbol: Checkered History of Sri Lanka's Jaffna Public Library, http://archive.ifla.org/IV/ifla72/papers/119-Knuth-en.pdf, first accessed 27 June 2006.

59. George Michael, *The Enemy of my Enemy. The Alarming Convergence of Militant Extremism and the Extreme Right* (Lawrence, KS: University Press of Kansas, 2006), 24.

60. Channel 4 (2011) Sri Lanka's Killing Fields, http://www.channel4.com/programmes/sri-lankas-killing-fields, first accessed 1 December 2011.

61. Gloria Spitte (2010) Keeping the Cause Alive: The Post-LTTE Tamil Eelam Support Network, http://thuppahi.wordpress.com/2010/11/29/keeping-the-cause-alive-the-post-ltte-tamil-eelam-support-network/, first accessed 11 November 2011.

62. The effective use of female martyr bombers is a prominent feature of both Chechen and Tamil liberation movements, and is symptomatic of the way terrorism sets itself apart from conventional rules of military engagement, while also underlining the fact that the potential for fanatical commitment to a cause is in no way gender specific. See Rosemarie Skaine, *Female Suicide Bombers* (Jefferson, NC: McFarland, 2006).

63. Ami Pedahzur, *Suicide Terrorism* (Cambridge: Polity, 2005), 81.

64. Ibid., 70–86.

65. See SATP (2001) Suicide Killings – An Overview, http://www.satp.org/satporgtp/countries/shrilanka/database/suicide_killings.htm, first accessed 2 December 2011.

66. Quoted in Dagmar Hellmann-Rajanayagam, *The Tamil Tigers. Armed Struggle for Identity* (Stuttgart: Franz Steiner, 1994), 69. I say 'generally' because during the 1990s thousands of Muslims were forced out of their northern homeland by the LTTE, an intolerance officially ended in 2002.

67. International Socialism (2006) Marxism and terrorism, http://www.isj.org.uk/index.php4?id=182&issue=110, first accessed 3 December 2011.

68. For example, the many articles on the topic by Michael Roberts.

69. Hellmann-Rajanayagam, *The Tamil Tigers*, 67.

70. Ibid., 68.

71. Tamil Eelam (2011) Advancing the Independence of Tamil Eeelam, http://www.eelam.com, first accessed 3 November 2011.l

3 Modernist Terrorism: Creating the Nomos

1. Peter Berger, *The Sacred Canopy. Elements of a Sociological Theory of Religion* (London: Doubleday, 1967), 27.

2. On the concept 'temporalized utopia' see Roger Griffin, *Modernism and Fascism. The Sense of a Beginning under Mussolini and Hitler* (London: Palgrave Macmillan, 2007), 88–91. The concept was coined by Reinhardt Koselleck in *The Practice of Conceptual History. Timing History, Spacing Concepts* (Palo Alto, CA: Stanford University Press, 2002).

3. E.g. Michael Burleigh, *Earthly Powers: The Clash of Religion and Politics in Europe from the French Revolution to the Great War* (New York, NY: Harper Collins, 2005); *Sacred Causes: The Clash of Religion and Politics from the Great War to the War on Terror* (New York, NY: Harper Collins, 2007); Emilio Gentile, *Politics* as *Religion* (Princeton, NJ: Princeton University Press, 2006).

4. Among Turner's many seminal texts on the nomic and renomizing function of ritual note Victor Turner, *The Ritual Process. Structure and Anti-Structure* (Chicago, IL: Aldine, 1969); Victor Turner, 'Variations on a Theme of Liminality', in Sally Moore and Barbara Myerhoff (eds), *Secular Ritual. Forms and Meaning* (Assen, Netherlands: Van Gorcum, 1977). On the universality of millennarian, eschatological and apocalyptic fantasies see Jeffrey Kaplan (ed.), *Millennial Violence Past, Present, and Future* (London: Frank Cass and Company Limited, 2002); Charles Strozier, Michael Flynn, *The Year 2000: Essays on the End* (New York, NY: NYU Press, 1997).

5. Anthony Wallace, 'Revitalization Movements', *American Anthropologist*, 58, 2 (1956), 264–81. See also Robert Grumet (ed.), *Anthony Wallace. Revitalization & Mazeways. Essays on Cultural Change, Volume 1* (Lincoln, NE: University of Nebraska Press, 2003).

6. Cf. Russell Thornton, *We Shall Live Again: The 1870 and 1890 Ghost Dance Movements as Demographic Revitalization* (Cambridge: Cambridge University Press, 1986).

7. Hong Beom Rhee, *Asian Millenarianism: An Interdisciplinary Study of the Taiping and Tonghak in Global Context* (London: Cambria Press, 2007); Jonathan Spence, *God's Chinese Son* (New York, NY: W.W. Norton & Company, 1996); Thomas H. Reilly, *The Taiping Heavenly Kingdom: Rebellion and the Blasphemy of Empire* (Seattle: University of Washington Press, 2004); Frederic Wakeman Jr, *The Fall of Imperial China* (New York, NY: Free Press, 1975).

8. Colin Campbell, 'The Cult, the Cultic Milieu and Secularization', *A Sociological Yearbook of Religion in Britain*, 5, (1972): 119–36.

9. This description is taken from the publicity for Jeffrey Kaplan and Helene Loow (eds), *The Cultic Milieu: Oppositional Subcultures in an Age of Globalization* (eds) (Walnut Creek, CA: Altamira Press, 2002), which reprints Campbell's essay as chapter 2. The cultic milieu which bred pervasive Messianic longings in turn-of-the-millennium Biblical Jerusalem is evoked hilariously in Monty Python's *The Life of Brian* (1979).

10. See Heinz Bechert (ed.), *Buddhism in Ceylon and Studies on Religious Syncretism in Buddhist Countries: Report on a Symposium in Göttingen* (Göttingen: Vandenhoeck & Ruprecht, 1978).

11. Eric Maroney, *Religious Syncretism* (London: SCM Press, 2006).

12. *Linda Tuhiwai, Decolonizing Methodologies: Research and Indigenous Peoples* (New York, NY: St Martin's Press, 1999).

13. See in particular, Shmuel Eisenstadt, *Tradition, Change and Modernity* (New York, NY: Wiley, 1973); Shmuel Eisenstadt, 'Multiple Modernities', *Daedalus*, 129, 1 (2000): 1–29.

14. For a fuller account of the theory of modernity proposed here see Roger Griffin, *Modernism and Fascism*, chapter 2, 'Two Modes of Modernism', 43–69. The classic (but each highly original) exponents of the general approach to a sociological understanding of modernity as a radically 'denomizing' force are Friedrich Nietzsche, Ferdinand Tönnies, Max Weber, Émile Durkheim, Joseph Schumpeter, Frederic Jameson, Zygmunt Bauman and Anthony Giddens.

15. For the utopian nature of historical schemes such as Enlightenment progress, Marxism, Nazism, or Islamism see John Gray, *Black Mass*, which explores the way they all meet the human demand for meaning by supplying 'narratives in which each individual life is part of an all-encompassing story'. He observes in the same passage that 'if universal narratives create meaning for those who live by them, they also destroy it in the lives of others' (204–5).

16. Marshall Berman, *All that is Solid Melts into Air. The Experience of Modernity* (London: Verso, 1982).

17. Michael Mazarr, *Unmodern Men in the Modern World* (Cambridge: Cambridge University Press, 2007), 17. Using different premises about modernity (which lead him to categorize utopian and apocalyptic politics as 'anti-modern' rather than pursuing an *alternative* modernity), Mazarr's book also explores the way terrorism can arise either to defend a traditional culture or solve a nomic crisis.
18. Ibid., 47.
19. Ibid., 84.
20. Zygmunt Bauman, *Modernity and Ambivalence* (Cambridge: Polity Press, 1991).
21. Zygmunt Bauman, *Liquid Life*; *Liquid Fear*; *Culture in a Liquid World*.
22. Cf. Arpad Szakolczai, *Reflexive Historical Sociology* (London: Routledge, 2000), 218–19; here he uses the (anthropologically less precise but more familiar) term 'liminality' in a very similar sense to the way 'liminoidality' is used in this book.
23. Peter Osborne, *The Politics of Time. Modernity and the Avant-garde* (London: Verso, 1995).
24. See Robert Gooding-Williams, *Zarathustra's Dionysian Modernism* (Palo Alto, CA: Stanford University Press, 2001).
25. Peter Fritzsche, 'Nazi Modern', *Modernism/Modernity*, 3, 1 (1996), 12.
26. Osborne, *Politics*, 164: see also chapter 1 for his concept of modernity as the temporalization of history.
27. Christopher Wilk, 'Introduction: What was Modernism?', in Christopher Wilk (ed.), *Modernism 1914–1939. Designing a New World* (London: V&A Publications, 2006), 12–13.
28. Griffin, *Modernism and Fascism*, chapter 2, 'Two Modes of Modernism', 43–69.
29. Obvious examples of 'programmatic' forms of aesthetic modernism are the manifestos of Futurists, Dada, Constructivism, Vorticists, Surrealism, De Stijl, and the Bauhaus, as well as such 'programmatic' books as Wassily Kandinsky's *Concerning the Spiritual in Art* (1914) and Kasimir Edschmid's influential text on Expressionism as cultural revolt, *Über den Expressionismus in der Literatur und die neue Dichtung* [*Concerning Expressionism in Literature and the New Art*] (Berlin: Reiß, 1917).
30. In practice there are examples of modernists who display elements of both epiphanic and programmatic visions of their role: even Van Gogh, Picasso, and Kafka experienced moments when they were drawn to utopian movements for change, while Nietzsche had his 'epiphanic' moments.
31. Sergey Nechayev (1869) The Revolutionary Catechism, http://www.marxists.org/subject/anarchism/nechayev/catechism.htm, first accessed 3 December 2011.
32. Ibid.
33. For some classic essays on this intellectual milieu see Isaiah Berlin, *Russian Thinkers* (London: Hogarth Press, 1978). See also Aileen Kelly, *Toward Another Shore: Russian Thinkers Between Necessity and Chance* (New Haven, CT: Yale University Press, 1998).
34. Alex Danchev, *100 Artists' Manifestos: From the Futurists to the Stuckists* (Harmondsworth: Penguin, 2011).
35. Peter Osborne, *Philosophy in Cultural Theory* (London: Routledge, 2000), 63–77.
36. The relevant line from the play read: 'A nihilist is a person who does not bow down to any authority, who does not accept any principle on faith, however much that principle may be revered.' This emphasizes that the nihilism of the rebel exists only in the mind of those who continue to revere the traditional nomos, no matter how much under threat.'
37. Alfred B. Evans Jr (2011) Nihilism and Nihilists, http://www.answers.com/topic/nihilism-and-nihilists, first accessed 11 November 2011. My emphasis.
38. Shane Weller, *Modernism and Nihilism* (London: Routledge, 2010), 30–41.
39. Ibid., 94–5.
40. Mona Ozouf, *La Fête révolutionnaire 1789/1799* (Paris: Gallimard, 1989).
41. Weller, *Modernism*, 17–19.
42. Friedrich Nietzsche, *The Gay Science* (1882), Section 282.
43. David Ohana, *The Nihilist Order* (Eastbourne: Sussex Academic Press, 2008), Vol. 1, 1–2.
44. Alain Badiou, *The Century* (Cambridge: Polity Press, 2007), 31–2.

45. Ibid.
46. Gooding-Williams, *Zarathustra's Dionysian Modernism*.
47. Mikhail Bakunin (1842) The Reaction in Germany, http://www.marxists.org/reference/archive/bakunin/works/1842/reaction-germany.htm,first accessed 3 December 2011. My emphasis.
48. John Merriman, *The Dynamite Club. How a Bombing in Fin-de-Siècle Paris Ignited the Age of Modern Terror* (London: JR Books, 2009), 75.
49. Cited in Wendy McElroy, *The Debates of Liberty: An Overview of Individualist Anarchism, 1881–1908* (Lanham, MD: Rowman & Littlefield, 2003), 33.
50. Luciano Pellicani, *Revolutionary Apocalypse. Ideological Roots of Terrorism* (Westport, CT: Praeger, 2003), 62.
51. Max Horkheimer, *La nostalgia del totalmente Altro* (Brescia: Queriana, 1972) 15, translation of Max Horkheimer, *Die Sehnsucht nach dem ganz Anderen (*Hamburg: Furche-Verl., 1970).
52. Pellicani, *Revolutionary Apocalypse*, 63.
53. Ibid.
54. Aileen Kelly, 'Introduction' to Berlin, *Russian Thinkers*, xv–xvi.
55. For a case study in the sacralization of the people as a response to the anomy of modernity see George Mosse, *The Nationalization of the Masses* (New York, NY: Howard Fertig, 1975).
56. See Marius Turda, *Modernism and Eugenics* (Basingstoke: Palgrave Macmillan, 2010).
57. David Weir, *Anarchy & Culture. The Aesthetic Politics of Modernism* (Amherst, MA: University of Massachusetts Press, 1997), 158.
58. Richard Stites, *Revolutionary Dreams. Utopian Vision and Experimental Life in the Russian Revolution* (New York, NY: Oxford University Press, 1989).
59. On the mutual attraction between Fascism and modernist architects see Richard Etlin, *Modernism in Italian Architecture, 1890–1940* (London: MIT Press, 1991).
60. Eric Michaud, *The Cult of Art in Nazi Germany* (1996) (Palo Alto, CA: Stanford University Press, 2004).
61. Patricia Leighten, *Re-Ordering the Universe: Picasso and Anarchism, 1897–1914* (Princeton, NJ: Princeton University Press, 1989). For the interpretive problems involved in establishing the precise relationship of a modernist artist to anarchism see Robert Lubar's review of *Reordering the Universe* in *The Art Bulletin*, 72, 3, (1990): 505–10.
62. Marja Härmänmaa, 'Beyond Anarchism: Marinetti's Futurist (anti-)Utopia of Individualism and 'Artocracy', *The European Legacy: Toward New Paradigms*, 14 (2009), 857–71.
63. Richard D. Sonn, *Anarchism and Cultural Politics in Fin de Siècle France* (Lincoln, NE: University of Nebraska Press, *1989)*; Mark Antliff and Patricia Leighten, *The Liberation of Painting: Modernism and Anarchism in Avant-Guerre Paris* (Chicago, IL: University of Chicago Press, 2011).
64. Richard D. Sonn, *Sex, Violence, and the Avant-Garde: Anarchism in Interwar France* (University Park, PA: Pennsylvania State University Press, 2010).
65. See Deaglán Ó Donghaile, 'Anarchism, anti-imperialism and "The Doctrine of Dynamite"', *Journal of Postcolonial Writing*, 46, 3 (2010): 294–6; Weir, *Anarchy and Culture*, 101–9.
66. Paul Avrich, *The Modern School Movement: Anarchism and Education in the United States* (Princeton, NJ: Princeton University Press, 1980).
67. Allan Antliff, 'Carl Zigrosser and the Modern School: Nietzsche, Art and Anarchism', *Archives of American Art Journal*, 34, 4 (1994): 16–23. See also his *The Culture of Revolt: Art and Anarchism in America, 1908–1920* (Newark, DE: University of Delaware Press, 1998).
68. Mark Antliff, 'Henri Gaudier-Brzeska': Guerre sociale. Art, Anarchism and Anti-Militarism in Paris and London, 1910–1915', *Modernism/Modernity*, 17, 1 (2010): 135–69.

69. Eric Voegelin, *The Political Religions* (1938) (Lewiston, NY: E. Mellen Press, 1986).
70. Pellicani, *Revolutionary Apocalypse*, 151–3. Original emphasis.

4 The Metapolitics of Terrorism in Fiction

1. John Gray, *Black Mass*, 145.
2. Ibid., 143–4. For Brooks' original article see David Brooks (2004) The C.I.A.: Method and Madness, http://query.nytimes.com/gst/fullpage.html?res=9C03E6D9173BF930A35751 C0A9629C8B63, first accessed 4 November 2011.
3. Fyodor Dostoevsky, *The Devils* (Oxford: Oxford University Press, 1992), 18–19.
4. J.M. Coetzee, *The Master of Petersburg* (London: Vintage, 1999). For an MA thesis highly relevant to this topic see Marco Ceccarelli (2009) 'Revolutionary Self-fulfilment? Individual Radicalisation and Terrorism in Fyodor Dostoyevsky's *Notes from the Underground*, *Crime and Punishment* and *The Devils*', http://www.loganscentrostudi.org/public/pubblicazioni/Individual%20Radicalisation%20and%20Terrorism%20in%20Fyodor%20by%20Marco%20Ceccarelli.pdf, first accessed 13 November 2011.
5. Coetzee, *The Master of Petersburg*, 202.
6. Dostoevsky, *The Devils*, 447–8.
7. Ibid., 748–9.
8. James Wood (2005) 'Warning Notes from the Underground', http://www.guardian.co.uk/books/2005/feb/26/featuresreviews.guardianreview33, first accessed 4 November 2011.
9. E.g. Adam Kirsch (2008) 'Demons Inner and Outer', http://www.nysun.com/arts/demons-inner-and-outer/83262, first accessed 17 November 2011. Michael Ignatieff's 'metapolitical' interpretation of terrorism in terms of nihilism in the chapter 'The Temptations of Nihilism' in his *The Lesser Evil: Political Ethics in an Age of Terror* (Princeton, NJ: Princeton University Press, 2004), 112–44, also makes extensive reference to Dostoevsky's *The Devils* and Joseph Conrad's *The Secret Agent*.
10. Slavoj Žižek (2006) 'The Anatomies of Tolerant Reason: A Blood-dimmed Tide is Loosed', http://www.lacan.com/zizantinomies.htm, first accessed 16 November 2011.
11. André Glucksmann, *Dostoïevski à Manhattan* (Paris: Robert Laffont, 2002), 275. My emphasis.
12. C.G. Jung (1928) 'The Spiritual Problems of Modern Man' in *Modern Man in Search of a Soul* (London: Routledge, 2001), 201–2. My emphasis.
13. Fyodor Dostoevsky (2009) The Brothers Karamazov, http://www.gutenberg.org/files/28054/28054-pdf.pdf, Part One, Book One, Chapter 5, 'The Elders', 27, first accessed 13 November 2011.My emphasis. The Tower of Babel also figures in the Grand Inquisitor scene on p. 319 of this edition. See also Charles Moser (1986) '*The Brothers Karamazov* as a novel of the 1860s', http://www.utoronto.ca/tsq/DS/07/073.shtml, first accessed 6 July 2011.
14. An allusion to Fyodor Dostoevsky's novella *The Double. A Petersburg Poem* (1848).
15. Eleanor Marx (1883) 'Underground Russia', http://www.marxists.org/archive/eleanor-marx/1883/08/underground-russia.htm, first accessed 4 December 2011. Original emphasis.
16. Sergey Stepniak, *Underground Russia* (London: Smith, Elder and Co, 1883), 42–5. For more on the Nietzschean dimension of Bolshevism see Bernice Rosenthal, *New Myth, New Man. From Nietzsche to Stalin* (University Park, PA: Pennsylvania State University Press, 2002).
17. Alex Houen, *Terrorism and Modern Literature* (Oxford: Oxford University Press, 2002), 64.
18. Friedrich Nietzsche, *Ecce Homo* (Portland, ME: Smith and Sales, 1911), section 8, 'Why I am a Fatality', 58.
19. Ibid., section 4, 48.

20. Joseph Conrad, *Under Western Eyes* (Harmondsworth: Penguin, 1990), 67–8, cited in Houen, *Terrorism and Modern Literature*, 73.
21. Conrad, *Under Western Eyes*, 69–70, cited in Houen, *Terrorism and Modern Literature*, 73.
22. Houen, *Terrorism and Modern Literature*, 74.
23. Ibid.
24. Ibid., 36–7.
25. Walter Benjamin (1973) 'Theses on the Philosophy of History', in Hannah Arendt (ed.), *Illuminations. Walter Benjamin* (London: Fontana, 1973), 264.
26. Ibid., 263.
27. Ibid., 265.
28. David Caroll, *Albert Camus the Algerian: Colonialism, Terrorism, Justice* (New York, NY: Columbia University Press, 2007).
29. Derek Allan, 'The Psychology of a Terrorist: Tchen in *La Condition humaine*', *Nottingham French Studies*, 21, 1 (May 1982), 50–2.
30. André Malraux, *Man's Fate* (Harmondsworth: Penguin Classics, 2009), 4.
31. Ibid., 7.
32. Ibid., 192. My emphasis.
33. Ibid., 59.
34. Tom Robbins, *Still Life with Woodpecker* (New York, NY: Bantam, 1980), 3.
35. Ibid., 24.
36. Ibid., 94–5. For more on Robbins' novel see Stacey Suver (2008) 'Exploding Narrative: The Literature of Terrorism in Contemporary America', http://etd.lib.fsu.edu/theses/available/etd-07082008-182749/, first accessed 12 December 2011.
37. Robbins, *Still Life with Woodpecker*, 221–2.
38. André Breton (1929) Second Manifesto of Surrealism, http://alangullette.com/lit/surreal/, first accessed 13 December 2011.
39. Robbins, *Still Life with Woodpecker*, 221–2.
40. Ibid., 64–5.
41. Ibid., 150–1.
42. Ibid., 86.
43. Sunjeev Sahota, *Ours are the Streets* (London: Picador, 2011), 53.
44. Ibid., 137–8.
45. Ibid., 153.
46. Ibid., 117.
47. Ibid., 180.
48. Ibid., 132.
49. Ibid., 158.
50. Ibid., 211.
51. Ibid.
52. Ibid., 181–2.
53. Ibid., 183.
54. Ibid., 203.
55. Ibid., 29.
56. Ibid., 130.
57. Ibid., 164.
58. Ibid., 70.
59. Ibid., 115.
60. The emotional logic of espousing fundamentalism to resolve the conflict between total assimilation to an alien culture and a routinized, watered down, version of an ethnic culture which cannot satisfy an adolescent's intense craving for belonging, roots, and nomic certainty is explored presciently in a 'pre-terroristic' context by Hanif Kureishi in his novella (1994) – subsequently a film (1997) – *My Son the Fanatic* (first published as a novella in *The New Yorker* in 1994).

5 The Metapolitics of Terrorist Radicalization

1. Tom Psyzcynski, Sheldon Solomon, and Jeff Greenberg, *In the Wake of 9/11. The Psychology of Terror* (Washington, DC: American Psychological Association, 2003), 27.
2. Ibid., 149.
3. Jessica Stern, *Terror in the Name of God. Why Religious Militants Kill* (New York, NY: Ecco, 2004), xix.
4. Ibid., 69.
5. Ibid., 283.
6. James Jones, *Blood that Cries Out from the Earth* (Oxford: Oxford University Press, 2008), 40.
7. Ibid., 68.
8. Eric Hoffer, *The True Believer. Thoughts on Nature of Mass Movements* (New York: Harper Collins, 1966 (1951)), 13.
9. Dipak Gupta, ' "Selfish Altruist": Modelling the mind of a terrorist', in *Understanding Terrorism and Political Violence. The Life Cycle of Birth, Growth, Transformation and Demise* (London: Routledge, 2008).
10. Hoffer, *The True Believer*, 41.
11. Ibid., 16.
12. Arie Kruglanski (2002) 'Inside the Terrorist Mind', in Joshua Sinai, 'New Trends in Terrorism Studies: Strengths and Weaknesses', in Ranstorp, *Mapping Terrorism Research*, 37.
13. Arie Kruglanski, Xiaoyan Chen, Mark Dechesne, Shira Fishman, Edward Orehek, 'Fully Committed: Suicide Bombers' Motivation and the Quest for Personal Significance', *Political Psychology*, 30, 3 (May 2009); note the critique of this article for its reductionist stress on 'the quest for personal significance' in Mia Bloom, 'Chasing Butterflies and Rainbows: A Critique of Kruglanski et al.'s "Fully Committed: Suicide Bombers' Motivation and the Quest for Personal Significance" ', *Political Psychology* 30, 3 (May 2009), 387–95. I must stress once more that the generic model of radicalization which highlights the role of a 'nomic crisis' is neither monocausal, since it acknowledges a plurality of causes besides the need for a metapolitical creed, nor reductionist, since it anticipates myriad unique manifestations of this need and its nomic resolution in practice.
14. Janja Lalich, *Bounded Choice. True Believers and Charismatic Cults* (Berkeley, CA: University of California Press, 1988), 16.
15. Ibid., 15–18, 56–7.
16. See Luciano Pellicani, *Revolutionary Apocalypse. Ideological Roots of Terrorism* (Westport, CT: Praeger, 2003), 151–3.
17. Lalich, *Bounded Choice*, 35.
18. Ibid., 259.
19. Ibid., 137–40, 254–9.
20. Ibid., 169.
21. Ibid., 14–19.
22. See Bettina Muenster and David Lotto, 'The Social Psychology of Humiliation and Revenge. The Origin of the Fundamentalist Mindset', in Charles Strozier, David Terman, and James Jones (eds), *The Fundamentalist Mindset* (Oxford: Oxford University Press, 2010), 71–9.
23. Arie W. Kruglanski et al. 'Fully Committed'.
24. See Lalich, *Bounded Choice*, 17, 77–80.
25. Stern, *Terror in the Name of God*, 261.
26. Mohammed Hafez, 'Rationality, Culture, and Structure in the Making of Suicide Bombers', *Studies in Conflict and Terrorism*, 29, 2 (2006), 181.

27. Robert Robins and Jerrold Post, *Political Paranoia. The Psychopolitics of Hatred* (London: Yale University Press, 1997), 113. My emphasis.
28. For a sample of specialist literature on this topic see J.R. Gould, N.M. Prentice, N.M. and R.C. Ainslie, 'The splitting index: Construction of a scale measuring the defense mechanism of splitting, *Journal of Personality Assessment*, 66, 2 (1996), 414–30. On the importance of cosmic war in the imaginary universe of the religious terrorist see Mark Juergensmeyer, 'Cosmic War', *Terror in the Mind of God. The Global Rise of Religious Violence* (Berkeley, CA: University of California Press, 2003), 148–66.
29. The term alludes to the Zarathustrian cosmology of ancient Persia which polarized the spiritual world into the forces of light and dark.
30. See Juergensmeyer, 'Martyrs and Demons', *Terror in the Mind of God*, 167–89.
31. Ibid., 123.
32. Jones, *Blood that Cries*, 141. Cf. 128–37.
33. James Jones, 'Eternal Warfare: Violence on the Mind of American Apocalyptic Christianity', in Charles Strozier, David Terman, and James Jones (eds), *The Fundamentalist Mindset*, 103.
34. Mazarr, *Unmodern Men*, 85.
35. Daniel Hill, 'Fundamentalist Faith States: Regulation Theory as a Framework for the Psychology of Religious Fundamentalism', in Charles Strozier, David Terman, and James Jones (eds), *The Fundamentalist Mindset*, 84–5. Cf. Robins and Post, *Political Paranoia*, 141–3.
36. Jerrold Post, 'Terrorist psycho-logic: Terrorist behaviour as a product of psychological forces', in Walter Reich (ed.), *Origins of Terrorism: Psychologies Ideologies, Theologies, States of Mind* (Washington, DC: Woodrow Wilson Centre Press, 1998), 27. Post is a professor of 'psychiatry, political psychology, and international affairs'.
37. 'Grandiosity' is a technical term often used in the study of bipolar disorder and paranoia, where it refers to the manic, narcissistic distortions in self-perception, but it has an obvious relevance to the sense of 'mission' and of having the power to change history that accompanies some forms of 'paranoid' politics.
38. Robert Lifton, *The Protean Self* (Chicago, IL: University of Chicago Press, 1993), 1.
39. Ibid. Cf. 208.
40. Ibid., 172.
41. See Lalich, *Bounded Choice*, 224. For the importance of syncretism in resolving liminoid crises through a 'mazeway resynthesis' see Griffin, *Modernism and Fascism*, 104–7.
42. Lalich, *Bounded Choice*, 169.
43. Gregory Lande and David Armitage (eds), *Principles and Practice of Military Forensic Psychiatry* (Springfield, Il: Charles C. Thomas, 1997), 428.
44. Ibid., 417. For an account of terrorism's psychodynamics that covers similar ground to the one in this chapter, see the chapter 'The Psychology of Terrorism and Human Evil' in Steven Bartlett, *The Pathology of Man. A Study of Human Evil* (Springfield, Il: Charles Thomas, 2005), 189–208.
45. Charles Lindholm and José Zúquete, *The Struggle for the World. Liberation Movements for the 21st Century* (Palo Alto, CA: Stanford University Press, 2010), 3.
46. Mazarr, *Unmodern Men*, 87.
47. See Lalich, *Bounded Choice*, 184–8, 211–18 for fascinating testimony to this.
48. Ruth Stein, *For Love of the Father. A Psychoanalytical Study of Religious Terrorism* (Palo Alto, CA: Stanford University Press, 2010), 21. Stein's book is central to any attempt to produce a Freudian reading of the syndrome of 'God's orphans' emphasized by Pellicani.
49. Christopher Coker, *The Warrior Ethos. Military Culture and the War on Terror* (London: Routledge, 2007), 4–5. Cf. Juergensmeyer, 'Warrior's Power', *Terror in the Mind of God*, 190–218; Klaus Theweleit, *Male Fantasies* (Cambridge: Polity Press, 1989).

50. Tsunetomo Yamamoto, *Bushido. The Way of the Samurai* (New York: Square One, 2001), 73.
51. Ibid., 14.
52. The term was first expounded by Michel Foucault in the article 'Des Espaces Autres' published by the French journal *Architecture /Mouvement/ Continuité* in October, 1984.
53. Charles Strozier and Katherine Boyd, 'The Apocalyptic', in Charles Strozier and Katherine Boyd, 'The Apocalyptic', in Charles Strozier, David Terman, and James Jones (eds), *The Fundamentalist Mindset*, 37.
54. Jones, *Blood that Cries*, 144–5.
55. Ibid., 151–5.
56. Theweleit, *Male Fantasies* (Vol. 2), 'Male Bodies and the White Terror', 242–3. For a parallel theory of the development of the terrorist persona as the product of 'distorted individuation' in the context of Islamism, see Farhad Khosrokhavar, *Jihidist Ideology. The Anthropological Perspective* (Aarhus: CIR, 2011), 179–82.
57. For the concept of the 'true self' see Jones, *Blood that Cries*, 126–8.
58. Post, 'Terrorist Psycho-logic', 31.
59. It should be noted that abnormal psychology has studied the 'Alice in Wonderland Syndrome'(or 'Todd's Syndrome') and acute confusions of inner and outer reality in some detail in psychotic patients. See, for example, J. Kew, A. Wright, and P.W. Halligan (2010), 'Somesthetic aura: The experience of "Alice in Wonderland"', http://www.thelancet.com/journals/lancet/article/PIIS0140-6736%2805%2979301-6/fulltext, first accessed 5 December 2011. Here I am postulating a subjective confusion of demonized and utopian projections with objective reality and the power to change it through violence in those 'fanatically' committed to a cause without suffering from psychosis, unless their fanatical, emotionally locked-in state is considered a special form of self-induced psychosis.
60. Franco Ferracuti, 'Ideology and Repentance', in Walter Reich (ed.) *Origins of Terrorism: Psychologies Ideologies, Theologies, States of Mind* (Washington, DC: Woodrow Wilson Centre Press, 1998), 60–1.
61. Robins and Post, *Political Paranoia*. On the paranoia in cultic dynamics see Lalich, *Bounded Choice*, 225.
62. Yamamoto, *Bushido*, 60.
63. Mazarr, *Unmodern Men*, 88.
64. Hoffer, *The True Believer*, 11.
65. Pedahzur and Perliger, *Jewish Terrorism in Israel*, 165.
66. Günter Rohrmoser, 'Ideologien und Strategien, in Bundesminister des Innern (ed.), *Analysen zum Terrorismus* (Opladen: Westdeutscher Verlag, 1981–1984), Vol. 2, 87, in Konrad Kellen, 'Ideology and Rebellion: Terrorism in West Germany', in Reich, *Origins of Terrorism*, 43–58. James Jones also draws attention to the significance of this passage in *Blood that Cries*, 42.
67. Strozier and Boyd, 'The Apocalyptic', 30.
68. On the crucial role played by perceptions of 'running out of time' and the ensuing 'temporal panic' in revolutionary movements see Richard Fenn, *The End of Time. Religion, Ritual, and the Forging of the Soul* (Cleveland, OH: Pilgrim Press, 1997); and *Time Exposure. The Personal Experience of Time in Secular Societies* (Oxford: Oxford University Press, 2000).
69. Lalich, *Bounded Choice*, 140–1, 193–5.
70. Stern, *Terror in the Name of God*, xxviii.
71. Ibid., 280.
72. Stein, *For the Love of the Father*, 40.
73. Mazarr, *Unmodern Men*, 84.
74. Friedrich Nietzsche, *The Gay Science*, section 283.
75. Bale, 'Jihadist Ideology and Strategy' provides a convincing account of the relationship between these two spheres of terrorism.

76. The full script is available at Awesome Film (2011) Taxi Driver, http://www. awesomefilm.com/script/taxidriver.txt, first accessed 13 November 2011, where each citation can be searched.
77. Chuck Palahniuk, *Fight Club* (London: Vintage Books, 2006), 12.
78. Ibid., 13–14.
79. Jack's job is curiously reminiscent of Kafka's work as an accident claims assessor in the Habsburg civil service.
80. An allusion to Hermann Hesse's novel *Steppenwolf* (1927) which studies the ferocious 'wolf of the steppes' that lurks in the psyche of the extremely cultured Harry Haller whose life outwardly is one of self-restraint, moderation, and bourgeois culture.
81. Palahniuk, *Fight Club*, 54.
82. Ibid., 112.
83. Ibid., 146.
84. Ibid., 201.
85. The evil twin is an ancient mythological topos found, for example at the heart of Zoroastrianism, a form of metaphysical dualism which contributed to the genesis of the original Manichaeanism.
86. Palahniuk, *Fight Club*, 114.
87. A Jungian term for the dream image or persona of the initiator into higher mystic states.
88. Ibid., 123.
89. Ibid., 124.
90. Ibid., 73.
91. Ibid., 185. As we saw in the last chapter, Robbins' terrorist, the Woodpecker, also delights in concocting bomb recipes, but the ludic element in Palahniuk's novel is much darker and more psychotic.
92. Palahniuk, *Fight Club*, 149.
93. Ibid., 125.
94. Ibid., 122. Nadine Klemens is thus misleading when she asserts in her seminar paper that 'Jack' wants simply 'to destroy history', and takes insufficient account of the elements of 'positive' nihilism in Project Mayhem, however delusional. See Nadine Klemens, *IKEA Boys and Terrorists: Fight Club in the Light of 9/11* (Norderstedt: GRIN, 2002), 8. Perhaps she might have considered looking at 9/11 in the light of *Fight Club*.
95. Palahniuk, *Fight Club*, 141. This passage duplicates some of the logic of Baudelaire's concept of blasphemy, which can be seen as a 'phatic' way of invoking the divine. The reference to being abandoned by the father-God has obvious resonance both with the concept of 'God's orphans' and Stein's Oedipal reading of the terrorist need for total submission to the divine father.
96. Slavoj Žižek *Violence: Six Sideways Reflections* (London: Picador, 2008), 63–7.
97. Palahniuk, *Fight Club*, 54.
98. Ibid., 143.
99. Ibid., 53.
100. Ibid., 149.
101. Ibid., 204.
102. Ibid., 205–8.

6   Modern Zealots of the Sacred Homeland

1. This term (literally 'nomos-making') is used in distinction to 'idiographic' in the philosophy of history, but here it is given specific connotations of creating a new sacred canopy or total value-system.
2. Slavoj Žižek, *Violence: Six Sideways Reflections (London:* Picador, 2008), 66.

3. It is because the Thugees do not fit these criteria, and the motivation and responsibility for the Gunpowder Plot conspiracy against the English Monarchy and Parliament is still contested that they are not included in this book.

4. Cf. *Joshua Muravchik, Heaven on Earth: The Rise and Fall of Socialism* (New York, NY: Encounter Books, 2002), the basis of PBS TV mini-series of the same name.

5. See Steve Bruce, *Politics and Religion* (Oxford: Polity, 2003).

6. George Mosse, *The Crisis of German Ideology: Intellectual Origins of the Third Reich* (New York, NY: Howard Fertig, 1964); *The Nationalization of the Masses* (New York, NY: Howard Fertig, 1975).

7. Shmuel Eisenstadt, *Fundamentalism, Sectarianism, and Revolution: The Jacobin Dimension of Modernity* (Cambridge: Polity, 1999), 65.

8. Ibid., 72–3.

9. In the context of our conceptual framework it is significant that Eisenstadt independently refers (ibid., 90–3) to the tendency of modern fundamentalist and Jacobin movements to assume 'very strong eschatological components...with a message of messianic redemption' (i.e. 'millennarianism'), and to 'construct sharp boundaries between the "pure" inside and the "polluted" outside' based on their 'self-perception as the "elect"' charged with realizing a 'missionary vision' by bringing 'the Kingdom of God to Earth' (i.e. what we have referred to as 'splitting', 'Manichaeanism', 'heroic doubling', and the 'temporalization of utopia'). Such totalizing tendencies he attributes to 'a very low threshold of tolerance for ambiguity on both personal and collective levels' (90), an observation which resonates with one of the key premises of this book, the way modernity has created a state of permanent ambivalence (documented by Zygmunt Bauman), called here liminoidality, and that a broad category of individuals finds the resulting anomy intolerable, driving them to find a new or new-old nomos to shelter them from absurdity.

10. Eisenstadt, *Fundamentalism*, 82–118.

11. Ibid., 95.

12. Ibid., 184–95.

13. Ibid., 89.

14. In the case of some forms of fascism the fundamental secularity of such totalitarianisms is obscured by their readiness to harness the mass-mobilizing power of the national Church (e.g. Italy and Romania) or Churches (in Nazi Germany).

15. This thesis is applied to Fascism and Nazism at considerable length in Roger Griffin, *Modernism and Fascism*, (Part Two).

16. The categories of terrorism proposed here closely correlate to the four types identified by Jeffrey Bale in a paper on the definition of terrorism produced for the Monterey Terrorism & Research Education Program: 'religious terrorist groups'; 'ethno-nationalist separatist and irredentist groups'; 'secular left-wing groups'; 'secular right-wing groups'. As in this book, Bale subsumes 'single issue' terrorism under these four categories according to the type of goal it pursues, which also applies to my treatment of 'lone wolf' terrorism, so they are not treated as separate or 'extra' categories. See Jeffrey Bale (2011) What is Terrorism, http://www.miis.edu/academics/researchcenters/terrorism/about/Terrorism_Definition, first accessed 12 November 2011.

17. Jeffrey Bale, 'The Chechen Resistance and Radiological Terrorism', unpublished paper for Monterey Institute of International Studies. An updated version appears as a chapter in a new (2012) edition of Russell Howard and James J.F. Forest (eds), *Weapons of Mass Destruction and Terrorism* (New York, NY: McGraw Hill, 2007).

18. On this complex topic see also Julie Wilhelmsen, 'Between a Rock and a Hard Place: The Islamisation of the Chechen Separatist Movement', *Europe–Asia Studies* 57, 1 (2005), 38–46.

19. All the following quotes relating to Tamil nationalism are taken from the four-part article posted by Michael Roberts on the Groundview Website, see Michael Roberts

(2009) LTTE and Tamil People I: Preamble, http://groundviews.org/2009/04/21/ltte-and-tamil-people-i-preamble/, first accessed 13 December 2011, just as the conflict with the Sinhalese government entered its gruesomely exterminatory endgame.

20. Roberts comments that the *de facto* Tamil state created after 1990 assumed character-istics of 'a one-party totalitarian state of fascist character' with its own charismatic leader, but this authoritarianism was forced on it by the exigencies of the military cam-paign against a highly aggressive enemy, and was never integral to the vision of Tamil Eelam.

21. A reference to the theory of spectacularity of modern society pioneered by the French Situationist Guy Debord.

22. Timeless Myths (2006) Nibelungenlied, http://www.timelessmyths.com/norse/nibelungs.html, first accessed 12 December 2011.

23. Naravila Dhammaratana (2008) Buddhist Nationalism and Religious Violence in Sri Lanka, http://www.class.uidaho.edu/ngier/slrv.htm, first accessed 12 November 2011.

24. Subhash Gatade, *Godse's Children: Hindutva Terror in India* (New Delhi: Pharos Media & Publishing Pvt, 2011).

25. For more on this aspect of Hindutva see Meera Nanda, *Prophets Facing Backward: Postmodern Critiques of Science and Hindu Nationalism in India* (New Brunswick, NJ: Rutgers University Press, 2003); and also the Facebook campaign to oppose 'Hindutva/Hindu-Nazism' at http://www.facebook.com/group.php?gid=67355280352, first accessed 12 November 2011.

26. See Iftikhar Malik, 'Beyond Ayodhya: Hindutva and Implications for South East Asia', in *Jihad, Hindutva and the Taliban* (Oxford: Oxford University Press, 2005), 84–110.

27. For the problems of applying 'fundamentalism' uncritically to Sikh religious militancy see W.H. McLeod, 'Sikh Fundamentalism', *Journal of the American Oriental Society*, 118, 1 (Jan.–Mar., 1998), 15–27.

28. For the account of a fascinating interview with a religious Sikh separatist leader see Mark Juergensmeyer, 'The Sword of Sikhism', in *Terror in the Mind of God* (Berkeley, CA: University of California Press, 2003), 85–102.

29. Simrat Dhillon, (2007) The Sikh Diaspora and the Quest for Khalistan: A Search for State-hood or for Self-preservation?, http://www.ipcs.org/pdf_file/issue/1787132181IPCS-ResearchPaper12-SimratDhillon.pdf, first accessed 12 December 2007, 1–10.

30. Although, from a secular standpoint, they can be argued to have granted themselves this sense of ethnic superiority on the basis of their cosmology – itself 'objectively' yet another original product of syncretism and mazeway resynthesis.

31. Elizeir Schweid, *The Land of Israel: National Home or Land of Destiny* (Madison, NJ: Fairleigh Dickinson University Press, 1985), 56.

32. Todd Presner, *Muscular Judaism: The Jewish Body and the Politics of Regeneration* (London: Routledge, 2007).

33. Daniel L. Byman, 'The Logic of Ethnic Terrorism', *Studies in Conflict and Terrorism*, 21, 2 (April/June 1998), 150.

34. Nachman Ben-Yehuda, *Political Assassinations by Jews: A Rhetorical Device for Justice* (Albany, NY: SUNY Press, 1993), 95.

35. See E. Katz, *LECHI: Fighters for the Freedom of Israel* (Tel Aviv: Yair Publishers, 1987).

36. Anonymous 'Terror', *He Khazit*, Issue 2, (August 1943).

37. For a brief introduction to Gush Emunim see Ehud Sprinzak (1986) 'Fundamen-talism, Terrorism, and Democracy. The Case of the Gush Emunim Underground', http://members.tripod.com/alabasters_archive/gush_underground.html, first accessed 12 November 2011. Note the use of the term fundamentalism here.

38. The Walt Disney cartoon *Mulan* (1998) brings out this aspect of heroic self-sacrifice for the nation effectively for younger viewers.

39. See Denis Warner and Peggy Warner, *The Sacred Warriors: Japan's Suicide Legions* (New York, NY: Van Nostrand Reinhold, 1982).

40. 'The Power from Within', *Das Schwarze Korps*, 11, 4 (25 January 1945), in Roger Griffin (ed.), *Fascism* (Oxford: Oxford University Press, 1995), 163. My emphasis.
41. Ami Pedahzur and Arie Perliger, *Jewish Terrorism in Israel* (New York, NY: Columbia University Press, 2009), ix–xi.

7 Modernist Terrorism Red, Black, and White

1. See Yonah Alexander 'Contemporary Terrorism: An Overview' in Yonah Alexander and Dennis Pluchinsky, *Europe's Red Terrorists: The Fighting Communist Organizations* (London: Frank Cass, 1992).
2. For an articulate glimpse into the mindset of a terrorist whose world-view was a similar blend of ideological extremism and hedonism, passive and active nihilism, see the autobiography of Bommi Baumann, founder of the anarchist Movement 2 June terrorist group: Bommi Baumann, *How It All Began: Personal Account of a West German Urban Guerrilla* (Vancouver: Arsenal Pulp Press, 1981).
3. This dark period of West Germany's history is portrayed in the documentary film *Deutschland im Herbst* (1978).
4. The phrase was popularized by the documentary film *Anni di Piombo* (1981) by the German director Margherete von Trotta.
5. For a left-wing take on Black terrorism see the articles published by libcom.org (2011) Strategy of Tension, http://libcom.org/tags/strategy-of-tension, first accessed 12 December 2011.
6. Cited in Alston Chase, *A Mind for Murder. The Education of the Unabomber and the Origins of Modern Terrorism* (New York, NY: W.W. Norton, 2004), 334.
7. William McCloughlin, *Revivals, Awakenings, and Reform. An Essay on Religion and Social Change in America, 1607–1977* (Chicago, IL: University of Chicago Press, 1978), 199–211.
8. Janja Lalich, *Bounded Choice. True Believers and Charismatic Cults* (Berkeley, CA: University of California Press, 1988), 113–48.
9. McCloughlin, *Revivals*, 206–7.
10. Chase, *Mind for Murder*, 335. For a summary of the anxieties of the young see 333–4, and of the new intellectual influences on the disaffected see 307–26. Anyone who wants to read a detailed case study in the main stages of terrorist radicalization, from profound nomic crisis, to splitting and heroic doubling within an elaborated cosmology, to focusing and identifying a target (though never reaching the final stage of complete self-possession), is urged to read Chase's biography.
11. These traits are well brought out by the film on the RAF based on Stefan Aust, *The Baader–Meinhof Complex* (London: Bodley Head, 2008).
12. Jillian Becker, *Hitler's Children. The Story of the Baader–Meinhof Terrorist Gang* (London: Pickwick Books, 1989); Aust, *The Baader–Meinhof*.
13. An allusion to the deeply flawed attempt to do just this by T.W. Adorno (et al.) in the research that led to T.W. Adorno, Else Frenkel-Brunswik, Daniel J. Levinson and R. Nevitt Sanford, *The Authoritarian Personality* (Oxford: Harpers, 1950).
14. Karin Bauer 'In Search of Ulrike Meinhof', in Elfriede Jelinek (ed.), *Everybody Talks about the Weather...We Don't. The Writings of Ulrike Meinhof* (New York, NY: Seven Stories Press, 2008), 42–65.
15. Cited in Alan Nothnagel (2010) 'From Pastor's Daughter to Terrorist: Gudrun Ensslin at the Age of 70', http://open.salon.com/blog/lost_in_berlin/2010/08/16/from_pastors_daughter_to_terrorist_gudrun_ensslin_at_70, first accessed 12 December 2011.
16. Ibid. My emphasis.
17. The talk was published as an article and is available at Stefan Aust (2008) Terrorism in Germany: The Baader–Meinhof Phenomenon, http://www.ghi-dc.org/files/publications/bulletin/bu043/45.pdf, first accessed 12 December 2011. My emphasis.

18. Web-resource of the Red Army Faction (in German) rafinfo.de (1998) Homepage, http://www.rafinfo.de/archiv/raf/raf-20-4-98.php, first accessed 12 December 2011.

19. For perhaps the most authoritative account of both Red and Black terrorism during this period see Richard Drake, *The Revolutionary Mystique and Terrorism in Contemporary Italy* (Bloomington, IN: Indiana University Press, 1989).

20. This violent bombing was initially blamed on anarchists, leading to the suspicious suicide in custody which inspired Dario Fo's satirical play *Accidental Death of an Anarchist*.

21. Attributed to the Brigate Rosse, but plausible conspiracy theories about governmental complicity linger on.

22. See Anna Bull, *Italian Neofascism: The Strategy of Tension and the Politics of Nonreconciliation* (Oxford, Berghahn Books, 2007); see also Franco Ferraresi, *Threats to Democracy: The Radical Right in Italy after the War* (Princeton, NJ: Princeton University Press, 1996), 84–127.

23. For the seminal importance of Evola both to neo-fascist ideology and Black terrorism in Italy see Ferraresi, *Threats to Democracy*, 43–9, 57–8; Drake, *The Revolutionary Mystique*, 114–34. Other important publications on Evola are Franco Ferraresi, 'Julius Evola: Tradition, Reaction and the Radical Right', *Archives européennes de sociologie*, 28 (1987), 107–51; Richard Drake, 'Julius Evola and the Ideological Origins of the Radical Right in Contemporary Italy', in Peter H. Merkl (ed.) *Political Violence and Terror: Motifs and Motivations* (Berkeley, CA: University of California Press, 1986), 61–89.

24. Tolkien's *Lord of the Rings* is essential reading for the Evolian Right. For essays on Evola by a mixture of critics and admirers, one of which deals with his affinities with Tolkien, see Troy Southgate (2011) Evola. A Radical Traditionalist, http://ebookbrowse.com/southgate-julius-evola-a-radical-traditionalist-doc-d13275019, first accessed 12 December 2011.

25. Key publications on this topic are Thomas Sheehan, 'Myth and Violence: The Fascism of Julius Evola and Alain de Benoist', *Social Research*, 48 (1981), 45–73; Ferraresi, 'Julius Evola', 107–51; Drake, 'Julius Evola', 61–89.

26. Ferraresi, *Threats to Democracy*, Chapter 7, section 3 'Lo spontaneismo armato'.

27. Donatella Della Porta, *Il terrorismo di sinistra* (Bologna: Il Mulino, 1990), 182.

28. Ferraresi, *Threats to Democracy*, 179–5.

29. True to the original meaning of fanatic as someone acting in rapt religious fervour, secular fanatics such as Freda tend to imbue their causes with holy, sacral, and hence suprahistorical significance (in this case of Evola's 'Tradition'), even in a Godless universe. Elsewhere in the text Freda refers to the 'sacred' and 'divine' reality that must be the foundation of the 'true state', a concept again derived from Evola who developed his own metaphysical theory of the Tradition influenced by, among others, the occultist René Guénon.

30. Franco Freda, *La Disintegrazione del Sistema* (Padova: Edizioni del Ar, 1969). The e-version cited here was originally available from http://megaupload.com/?d=017ZIWSU, first accessed 10 August 2011, but the site has since been closed down.

31. Mark Juergensmeyer, *Terror in the Mind of God*, 32–3.

32. Charles Strozier and Michael Flynn (eds), *The Year 2000. Essays on the End* (New York, NY: New York University Press, 2000), 106.

33. Jessica Stern, *Terror in the Name of God* (New York, NY: HarperCollins, 2003), 17–18.

34. See Lewis Loflin (2001) The Tim McVeigh and the Christian Identity Connection, http://www.sullivan-county.com/identity/cal_shoot.htm, first accessed 12 December 2011.

35. James Jones, *Blood that Cries Out from the Earth* (Oxford: Oxford University Press, 2008), 88–114.

36. Cited ibid., 2004.

37. For the promiscuous relationships of neo-Nazis, CI, and KKK racists see James Ridgeway, *Blood in the Face* (New York, NY: Thunder Mouth Press, 1995).

38. Karl Poewe, *New Religions and the Nazis* (Oxford: Routledge, 2006).
39. Nicholas Goodrick-Clarke, *The Occult Roots of Nazism* (Wellingborough: Aquarian Press, 1985).
40. Jeffrey Kaplan, *Radical Religion in America. Millenarian Movements from the Far Right to the Children of Noah* (New York, NY: Syracuse University Press, 1997), 67.
41. The biography of David Copeland by Graeme McLagan and Nick Lowes, *Mr Evil. The Secret Life of Racist Bomber and Killer David Copeland* (London: John Blake, 2000), shows striking parallels both in the ideological influences and in the process leading from anomy, to splitting and heroic doubling, focusing the generic hatred on a mission, and coldly and numbly carrying out the plan in the full grip of the Alice Syndrome that can be observed in Timothy McVeigh.
42. Jeffrey Kaplan, *Encyclopedia of White Power: A Sourcebook on the Radical Racist Right* (Lanham, MD: Rowman & Littlefield, 2000), 216.
43. Jones, *Blood that Cries*, 148.
44. Robert Lifton, *Destroying the World to Save It. Aum Shinrikyō, Apocalyptic Violence, and the New Global Terrorism* (New York, NY: Holt, 1999), 328.
45. Lou Michel and Dan Herbeck, *American Terrorist. Timothy McVeigh and the Tragedy at Oklahoma City* (New York, NY: Harper Collins, 2001), 124–5.
46. Ibid., 113–38.
47. Ibid., 118.
48. A reference to how Travis Bickle describes himself in *Taxi Driver*.
49. An allusion both to a passage in Pellicani's *The Revolutionary Apocalypse* and a passage in *Fight Club* cited in Chapter 5.
50. For an assessment of the evidence that Nichols had links with Middle East terrorists, possibly sponsored by Saddam Hussein, see George Michael, *The Enemy of my Enemy. The Alarming Convergence of Militant Extremism and the Extreme Right* (Lawrence, KS: University Press of Kansas, 2006), 131–6. On McVeigh's debt to the far right milieu and other possible accomplices see Susie Skari (2011) The Secret Life of Timothy McVeigh: Contradictions, Collaborators, and Hidden Connections in the Field', http://ncp.pcaaca.org/presentation/secret-life-timothy-mcveigh-contradictions-collaborators-and-hidden-connections-field, first accessed 12 December 2011.
51. 19 April was also the 220th anniversary of the Battle of Lexington and Concord whose opening shots 'rang around the world' as the beginning of the American war of independence from Britain. See Juergensmeyer, 'The Theatre of Terror', *Terror in the Mind of God*, 121–7 for the phatic dimension of terrorism as a form of performance to an audience.
52. Ibid., 128–41.
53. Charles Strozier, 'Apocalyptic Violence and the Politics of Waco', in Charles Strozier, Michael Flynn, *The Year 2000: Essays on the End*, 109.
54. Peter Osborne. *The Politics of Time. Modernity and the Avant-garde* (London: Verso, 1995), 164. Original emphasis.
55. Ibid., 166. Original emphasis.
56. Michael Burleigh, *The Third Reich* (London: Pan Macmillan, 2000), 256.
57. Pádraic H. Pearse, 'The Coming Revolution', in Pádraic Pearse, *Political Writings and Speeches* (Dublin: Phoenix Publishing, 1924), 99.
58. Cited in Bob de Graaf, *History of Fanaticism: From Enlightenment to Jihad* (Aarhus: CIR, 2010), 15.
59. Cited in Malise Ruthven, *A Fury for God. The Islamist Attack on America* (London: Granta, 2002), 204.
60. See Chip Berlet, 'The United States: Messianism, Apocalypticism, and Political Religion', in Roger Griffin, Matthew Feldman, and John Tortice (eds), *The Sacred in Twentieth Century Politics: Essays in Honour of Professor Stanley G. Payne* (Basingstoke: Palgrave Macmillan, 2008), 221–57.

8　The Hybrid Metapolitics of Religious Terrorism

1. See the charts produced in Andrew Silk, 'The Impact of 9/11 on Research on Terrorism', in Magnus Ranstorp (ed.) *Mapping Terrorism Research. State of the Art, Gaps and Future Direction*, 76–93.
2. On the success of the attackers in spreading terror see Tom Psyzcynski, Sheldon Solomon, and Jeff Greenberg, *In the Wake of 9/11. The Psychology of Terror* (Washington, DC: American Psychological Association, 2003).
3. Jeremy Gunn, 'The Complexity of Religion and the Definition of "Religion" in International Law', *Harvard Human Rights Journal*, 16 (2003), 189–215.
4. James W. Dow (2007) A Scientific Definition of Religion, http://www.anpere.net/2007/2.pdf, first accessed 12 December 2011.
5. David Carrasco, *City of Sacrifice: The Aztec Empire and the Role of Violence in Civilization* (Boston, MA: Beacon Press, 1999).
6. Emilio Gentile, *Politics as Religion* (Princeton, NJ: Princeton University Press, 2006).
7. George Michael, *The Enemy of my Enemy. The Alarming Convergence of Militant Islam with the Extreme Right* (Lawrence, KS: University of Kansas Press, 2006), 283–94.
8. Kumar Ramakrishna, 'The (Psychic) Roots of Religious Violence in South and Southeast Asia', in Linnell Cady and Sheldon Simon (eds), *Religion and Conflict in South and Southeast Asia* (London: Routledge, 2007), 130–1.
9. Linell Cady and Sheldon Simon, 'Introduction', *Religion and Conflict in South and Southeast Asia* (London: Routledge, 2007), 26–7.
10. Vjekoslav Perika, *Balkan Idols: Religion and Nationalism in Yugoslav States* (Oxford: Oxford University Press, 2002).
11. Cathie Carmichael, *Ethnic Cleansing in the Balkans: Nationalism and the Destruction of Tradition* (London: Routledge, 2002).
12. Michael Doran, 'The Pragmatic Fanaticism of Al Qaeda: Statements and Evolving Ideology', *Congressional Research Service Report*, 15 Nov. (2005), 5.
13. See Time (1939) Church v. I.R.A., http://www.time.com/time/magazine/article/0,9171,761165,00.html, first accessed 12 December 2011.
14. Denis O'Hearn, *Nothing But an Unfinished Song. Bobby Sands, the Irish Hunger Striker who Ignited a Generation* (New York, NY: Nation Books, 2006).
15. See Bobby Sands Trust (2011) The Rhythm of Time, http://www.bobbysandstrust.com/writings/the-rhythm-of-time, first accessed 12 December 2011.
16. See the essays posted on the topic of religion and violence by the Centre for Public Christianity (2011) Violence, http://www.publicchristianity.com/library/topic/violence, first accessed 12 December 2011, and, for a contrasting indictment of religion as a source of violence, the chapter 'Religion Kills' in Christopher Hitchens, *God is Not Great: How Religion Poisons Everything* (London: Atlantic, 2007).
17. Between 1961 and 1990 the ANC's military wing, Umkhonto we Sizwe or MK ('Spear of the Nation'), co-founded by Mandela, committed numerous acts of terrorism in its guerrilla war against Apartheid South Africa – a campaign of violence whose eventual success, as well as the self-evident justice (from a humanist perspective) of its ultimate cause despite the atrocities caused to achieve it, might explain why the MK figures so little in surveys of the history of terrorism. By fighting for a democratic South Africa, the MK's cause was more Modernist than Zealotic, since, unlike the Irish homeland at the heart of the IRA struggle, there was no nomos or original African homeland to restore, but a new multiracial one to create on the territorial template of the colonial state.
18. Mohammed Hafez, 'Rationality, Culture and Structure in the Making of Suicide Bombers', *Studies in Conflict and Terrorism*, 29/2, (2006), 169.
19. Jeffrey Bale, 'Jihadist Ideology and Strategy and the Possible Employment of WMD', in Gary Ackerman and Jeremy Tamsett (eds) *Jihadists and Weapons of Mass Destruction* (Boca Raton: CRC Press, 2009).

20. Robert Lifton, *Destroying the World to Save It. Aum Shinkryo, Apocalyptic Violence and the New Global Terrorism* (New York, NY: Holt, 1999), 59–88.
21. Christopher Partridge (ed.), *Encyclopedia of New Religions: New Religious Movements, Sects and Alternative Spiritualities* (Oxford: Lion, 2004); Peter Clarke (ed.), *Encyclopedia of New Religious Movements* (London: Routledge, 2006).
22. Essential reading on this topic is the chapter 'A Japanese Phenomenon?' in Lifton, *Destroying the World*, 232–70. On the world of Japanese 'new new religions' see Peter Clarke, *Japanese New Religions in Global Perspective* (Richmond: Curzon Press, 2000). On the two waves of postwar NRMs which arose to solve the nomic crisis of postwar Japan see Mark Juergensmeyer, *Terror in the Mind of God. The Global Rise of Religious Violence*, 116–18.
23. Lifton, *Destroying the World*, 12.
24. See James Jones, *The Blood that Cries Out from the Earth*, 72–3.
25. Juergensmeyer, *Terror in the Mind of God*, 110; Lifton, *Destroying the World*, 44–58.
26. Lifton, *Destroying the World*, 257–8.
27. An illuminating book on the apocalyptic mindset as a human archetype is Charles Strozier and Michael Flynn (eds), *The Year 2000. Essays on the End*.
28. Ibid., 23–4.
29. Ibid., 89–114, 214–31.
30. Juergensmeyer, *Terror in the Mind of God*, 108–13.
31. See the important passages on doubling in Lifton, *Destroying the World*, 94–5, 156–7, 219–22.
32. Ibid., 118.
33. Lifton, *Destroying the World*, 113.
34. The best source on this episode is Norman Cohn, *The Pursuit of the Millennium* (London: Granada, 1970).
35. It is worth stressing that the psychosis, sociopathology, or psychopathology of terrorists is of a particular kind. Clark McCauley's 'Understanding the 9/11 Perpetrators: Crazy, Lost in Hate, or Martyred?', in N. Matuszak (ed.) *History Behind the Headlines: The Origins of Ethnic Conflicts Worldwide* (New York, NY: Gale, 2002), Vol. 5, 274–86, points out that the hallmark of these conditions is *selfishness* so that the terms lose their relevance. However, I would suggest that the selfishness/solipsism of the terrorist is not of the 'small self', but of his 'heroic double', a selfishness that is so total that it causes the complete breakdown of empathy with the victims of the terrorist act. In the case of martyrdom actions, the private self is 'sacrificed' to this infinitely aggrandized 'heroic double' so brilliantly evoked in *Fight Club* in the character of Tyler Durden.
36. Franco Ferracuti, 'Ideology and Repentance', in Walter Reich (ed.) *Origins of Terrorism: Psychologies Ideologies, Theologies, States of Mind* (Washington, DC: Woodrow Wilson Centre Press, 1998), 60–1.
37. Robert Lifton, 'Reflections on Aum Shinrikyo', in Strozier and Flynn, *The Year 2000*.
38. Lifton, *Destroying the World*, 201.

9   Islamism's Global War against Nomocide

1. It is a sign of our electronic times that, though clerics advise against reading Islamic scriptures too fast, there is now a 'Free speed reading Quran MP3 download': see software.informer (2012) Free speed reading Quran MP3 download, http://softwaretopic. informer.com/speed-reading-quran-mp3-download, first accessed 12 December 2011. As Bob Dylan once commented 'it's easy to see without looking too far that not much is really sacred' (in the song 'It's All Right Ma: I'm Only Bleeding').
2. Olivier Roy, *Globalised Islam. The Search for a New Ummah* (London: Hurst and Company, 2004), 6.

3. Bassam Tibi (2009) Ballot and Bullet. The Politicization of Islam to Islamism, http://cir.au.dk/fileadmin/site_files/filer_statskundskab/subsites/cir/pdf-filer/H%C3%A6fte_5_Tibi.pdf, first accessed 21 January 2012, 10.

4. Kai Hafez, *Radicalism and Political Reform in the Islamic and Western Worlds* (Cambridge: Cambridge University Press, 2010), 217.

5. For a useful introduction to the slippery terminology in this field see Mehdi Mozaffari, 'What is Islamism? History and Definition of a Concept', *Totalitarian Movements and Political Religions* 8, 1 (2007), 17–33. In his *Radicalism and Political Reform*, 192–3, Kai Hafez sums up the elaborate sub-divisions of Islamism proposed by the International Crisis Group, which significantly includes categories that are not violent.

6. E.g. in Jonathan Githens-Mazer, 'Islamic Radicalisation among North Africans in Britain', *British Journal of Politics and International Relations*, 10 (2008), 550–70.

7. Tibi, Ballot and Bullet, 12–13; Jeffrey Bale, 'Islamism and Totalitarianism', *Totalitarian Movements and Political Religions*, 10, 2 (2009), 73–96.

8. E.g. Mehdi Mozaffari, Bassam Tibi, Faisal Devij, Malise Ruthven, Jeffrey Bale, Kai Hafez, Peter Demant, Will McCants, Roel Meijer, Thomas Hegghammer, Joas Wagemakers.

9. Roy, *Globalised Islam*, is a penetrating study of the anomic experience of diaspora Muslims.

10. For a case study of the radicalization of one ethnic group see Githens-Mazer, 'Islamic Radicalisation among North Africans in Britain'.

11. Thomas Asbridge, *The Crusades: The War for the Holy Land* (London: Simon & Schuster, 2010), reveals that actually Islamic hatred of the West for launching the Crusades is an 'invented tradition' dating back to the nineteenth century.

12. The pathological social violence resulting from the nomic crisis is documented in such key books as Norman Cohn, *The Pursuit of the Millennium* (London: Oxford University Press, 1970), and Robert Kinsman (ed.), *The Darker Vision of the Renaissance* (Berkeley, CA: University of California Press, 1974).

13. A good introduction is Part One of Peter Demant, *Islam vs Islamism. The Dilemma of the Modern World* (London: Praeger, 2006), 3–88.

14. See Bassam Tibi, *Islam's Predicament with Modernity. Religious Reform and Cultural Change* (London: Routledge, 2009).

15. This process is discussed by José Casanova in *Public Religions in the Modern World* (Chicago, IL: University of Chicago Press, 1994).

16. Gabriel Warburg, 'Mahdism and Islamism in Sudan', *International Journal of Middle Eastern Studies*, 27, 2 (1995).

17. See Malise Ruthven, *A Fury for God. The Islamist Attack on America* (London: Granta, 2002), Ch. 5, 'Cultural Schizophrenia', 134–68.

18. See Hafez, *Radicalism and Political Reform*, 195–223.

19. One of the most vociferous and erudite advocates of a moderate and modern Islam (Euro-Islam) is Bassam Tibi in *Islam's Predicament with Modernity*. See too Omid Safi, *Progressive Muslims* (Oxford: One World, 2003), Angel Rabasa et al., *Building Moderate Muslim Networks* (Santa Monica, CA: RAND Corporation, 2007).

20. Raymond Ibrahim, (2012) 'Muslim Brotherhood Declares "Mastership of the World"', *Middle East Forum*, http://www.meforum.org/3151/muslim-brotherhood-world-mastership, first accessed 15 January 2012. My emphasis.

21. Forming electoral parties to overthrow parliamentary democracy was a tactic used both by fascists and communists in inter-war Europe in order to secure a power base.

22. Demant, *Islam vs. Islamism*, 97–176.

23. Bale, 'Islamism and Totalitarianism', 84.

24. Mehdi Mozaffari, 'The Rise of Islamism in the Light of European Totalitarianism', *Totalitarian Movements and Political Religions* 10, 1 (2009), 1–13.

25. Tibi, Ballot and Bullet, 11–13.
26. Abdul Maududi, *Jihad in Islam* (Lebanon: Holy Koran Publishing, 2006), 10. My emphasis.
27. Faisal Devji, *Landscapes of the Jihad. Militancy, Morality, Modernity* (London: Hurst, 2005), 27.
28. Maududi, *Jihad in Islam*, 5. My emphasis.
29. Sayydi Qutb, *Milestones* (New Delhi: Islamic Book Services, 2001), 80.
30. Ibid., 82.
31. Ibid., 11.
32. Ibid., 7.
33. Ibid., 12.
34. Ibid., 34–5.
35. Ibid., 75.
36. John Larsen, *A Western Source on Islamism. Soundings in the Influence of Alexis Carrell on Sayyid Qutb* (Aarhus: Centre for Studies in Islamism and Radicalisation, 2011).
37. The relation of the theme of purification to revolutionary apocalypse is treated in Luciano Pellicani, *Revolutionary Apocalypse. Ideological Roots of Terrorism* (Westport, CT: Praeger, 2003); and his essay '*I purificatori del mondo*', *Filosofia e questioni pubbliche* 13, 1 (2008), 107–34.
38. As example of the confusing terminology in this area, Olivier Roy sees the Taliban as an example of 'neo-fundamentalism' in *Globalized Islam*, 260–1. However, the prefix 'neo' points to the modernizing ('Jacobin') element added to traditionalist theological, which makes his use of the term the equivalent of Eisenstadt's 'fundamentalism, while his 'proto-fundamentalism equates to Roy's 'fundamentalism'.
39. Shmuel Eisenstadt, *Fundamentalism, Sectarianism, and Revolution. The Jacobin Dimension of Modernity* (Cambridge: Cambridge University, 1999), 96.
40. A detailed account of the context of Al Qaeda's formation is provided by Jason Burke, *Al-Qaeda* (London: Penguin, 2007), 2. See 1–21 for a discussion of the ambiguity of what is meant by 'Al Qaeda'.
41. Hafez, *Radicalism and Political Reform*, 42.
42. On the effectiveness of a network of leaderless groupuscules in maintaining ideological radicalism in contrast to traditional organizations see Roger Griffin, 'From slime mould to rhizome: An introduction to the groupuscular right', *Patterns of Prejudice*, 37, 1 (March, 2003), 27–50.
43. Qutb, *Milestones*, 131.
44. Raymond Ibrahim, *The Al Qaeda Reader* (New York, NY: Broadway Books, 2007), xxviii.
45. Roxanne Eugen, *Enemy in the Mirror: Islamic Fundamentalism and the Limits of Modern Rationalism – A Work of Comparative Political Theory* (Princeton, NJ: Princeton University Press, 1999), 15.
46. Marc Sageman, *Understanding Terror Networks* (Philadelphia, PA: University of Pennsylvania Press, 2004), 97.
47. Charles Lindholm and José Zúquete, *The Struggle for the World. Liberation Movements for the 21st Century* (Palo Alto, CA: Stanford University Press, 2010), 146.
48. It is perhaps worth pointing out that technically Islamism's vision of the globalized Islamic *umma* is not apocalyptic, because it foresees a new era of humanity rather than the messianic rule of the long-awaited Mahdi. See Devji, *Landscapes of the Jihad*, 149.
49. John Gray, *Black Mass. Apocalyptic Religion and the Death of Utopia*, 2.
50. Ibid., 177.
51. Qutb, *Milestones*, 145.
52. Ibid., 7–8.

53. It is significant that in 2006 the Global Islamic Media Front released the video game *Night of Bush Capturing* heavily indebted to standard fantasy war games such as *Call of Duty*. See Jihad Watch (2006) New "jihad" video game targets Bush, US Forces, Shi'ite leaders, http://www.jihadwatch.org/ 2006/09/new-jihad-video-game-targets-bush-us-forces-shiite-leaders.html, first accessed 18 January 2012.

54. Burke, *Al-Qaeda*, 295.

55. Hans Kippenberg, ' "Consider that it is a raid on the path of god": The spiritual manual of the attackers of 9/11', *Numen*, 52 (2005), 46.

56. See, for example, Saïd Arjoman, 'Islamic Apocalypticism in the Classical Period' in B. McGinn (ed.) *The Encyclopedia of Apocalypticism* (New York, NY: Continuum, 1998), Vol. 2, 238–83.

57. Laurent Murawiec, *The Mind of Islam* (Cambridge: Cambridge University Press, 2008).

58. Jean Rosenfeld (2001) 'The Religion of Osama bin Laden: Terror as the Hand of God', http://www.publiceye.org/frontpage/911/Islam/rosenfeld2001.html, first accessed 12 December 2011.

59. John Gray, *Al Qaeda and What it Means to be Modern* (London: Faber and Faber, 2003).

60. Ibid., 20–1.

61. John Gray, *Black Mass*, 177.

62. Ibid., 26–7. It should be noted that such a passage imparts an apocalyptic violence to 'Jacobinism' as a generic term that goes far beyond its connotations for Eisenstadt in its destructive intensity.

63. Demant, *Islam vs Islamism*, 90.

64. Jeffrey Bale, 'Jihadist Ideology and Strategy and the Possible Employment of WMD', in Gary Ackerman and Jeremy Tamsett (eds), *Jihadists and Weapons of Mass Destruction* (Boca Raton, FL: CRC Press, 2009), 19.

65. Ibrahim, *The Al Qaeda Reader*, 165.

66. Mohammed Ali Musawi, (2009) A Selected Translation of the LIFG Recantation Document, http://www.quilliamfoundation.org/images/a_selected_translation_of_the_lifg. pdf, first accessed 12 December 2011.

67. Tibi, Ballot and Bullet, 11–13.

68. Robert Brym, 'Religion, politics, and suicide bombing: An interpretive essay', *Canadian Journal of Sociology* 33, 1 (2008), 96.

69. Devji, *Landscapes of the Jihad*, 125.

70. Ibid., 149.

71. Ibid., 90–1.

72. Ruthven, *A Fury for God*, 244–5.

73. Ibid., 131–2.

74. Ibid., 127.

75. See Anti-Defamation League (2012) International Terrorism Database, http://www.adl. org/terrorism/symbols/, first accessed 12 December 2011.

76. Olivier, *Globalized Islam*, 272–75.

77. Faisal Devji, *The Terrorist in Search of Humanity. Militant Islam and Global Politics* (London: Hurst, 2008), 43–5.

78. Bruce Lawrence (ed.), *Messages to the World: The Statements of Osama Bin Laden* (New York, NY: Verso, 2005), 114.

79. Free Republic (2011) 'Sudanese Cleric Pays Homage to Bin Laden and Calls upon Muslims to Attack US Citizens Worldwide', http://www.freerepublic.com/focus/f-news/ 2742260/posts, first accessed 12 December 2011.

80. An allusion to Wilfred Owen's poem inspired by the futile slaughter of the First World War, 'The Parable of the Old Man and the Young'.

81. Abdullah Azzam, (2001) Martyrs: The Building Blocks of Nations, http://www. religioscope.com/info/doc/jihad/azzam_martyrs.htm, first accessed 12 December 2011.

82. Hassan Mneimneh, Kanan Makija (2002) 'Manual for a Raid', http://www.nybooks. com/articles/archives/2002/jan/17/manual-for-a-raid/, first accessed 12 December 2011.
83. Ibid.

10   Afterthoughts on the Nature of Terrorism

1. Roger Griffin, *Modernism and Fascism. The Sense of a Beginning under Mussolini and Hitler*.
2. From the Latin 'concipere', to take hold of, grasp. (Cf. the German Begriff, cognate with *'Griff*, a handle or grip').
3. See Close Protection (2011) Failed anti-terror campaigns 'waste of money', Prevent strategy admits, http://www.closeprotectionworld.com/security-news-uk/49262-failed-anti-terror-campaigns-waste-money-prevent-strategy-admits.html, first accessed 12 January 2012.
4. Gerry Gable and Paul Jackson, *Lone Wolves*: *Myth or Reality* (Searchlight: Islington, 2011).
5. Fox News (2008) FBI: Eco-terrorism remains the No. 1 Domestic Terror Threat, http://www.foxnews.com/story/0,2933,343768,00.html, first accessed 12 December 2011.
6. Stephanie Ernst (2009) On the FBI's 'Most Wanted' Vegan 'Terrorist', http://news.change.org/stories/on-the-fbis-most-wanted-vegan-terrorist, first accessed 12 June 2011.
7. The manifesto can be seen http://www.scribd.com/doc/36763699/Discovery-Channel-Hostage-Taker-s-Manifesto, accessed 12 December 2011.
8. SciDev.net (2011) Anti-nanotech group behind Mexican scientist bombings, http://www.scidev.net/en/new-technologies/nanotechnology/news/anti-nanotech-group-behind-mexican-scientist-bombings.html, first accessed 12 December 2011.
9. Theodore Kaczynski (2002) Industrial Society and Its Future, http://editions-hache.com/essais/pdf/kaczynski2.pdf, first accessed 20 December 2011.
10. E.g. Theodore Roszak, *Person/Planet: The Creative Disintegration of Industrial Society (New York, NY:* Anchor Press, 1978).
11. Alston Chase, *A Mind for Murder. The Education of the Unabomber and the Origins of Modern Terrorism* (New York, NY: W.W. Norton, 2004).
12. Jonathan Rosenbaum (1998) Yigal Amir: Religious fanatic or Zionist, http://www.jewishmediaresources.com/75/yigal-amir-religious-fanatic-or-zionist, first accessed 7 February 2012.
13. Such delusions played a key role in Jan Bockleson's leadership of the Münster Anabaptists in 1525. For a fascinating case study in religious delusion see M. Kalian et al., 'Spiritual Starvation in a holy space – a form of Jerusalem Syndrome', *Mental Health, Religion & Culture*, 11, 2 (2008), 161–72.
14. Jason Burke, *Al-Qaeda*, 310.
15. John Gray, *Black Mass. Apocalyptic Religion and the Death of Utopia*, 177–8.
16. The profound ambivalence of religion with respect to democratic, humanistic values is an under-researched area crucial to understanding genuinely 'religious terrorism', but useful introductions to the subject are Scott Appleby, *The Ambivalence of the Sacred: Religion, Violence, and Reconciliation* (Lanham, MD: Rowman & Littlefield, 2000); Daniel Philpott, 'Explaining the Political Ambivalence of Religion', *American Political Science Review*, 101, 3 (2007), 505–25.
17. Walter Skya, *Japan's Holy War*: *The Ideology of Radical Shinto Ultranationalism* (Durham, NC: Duke University Press, 2009).
18. Émile Cioran, *A Short History of Decay* (Oxford, Basil Blackwell, 1975) contains sustained diatribes against religion as a source of fanatical violence and persecution, even in secularized 'ideological form', including such memorable aphorisms as 'a jesting wisdom is gentler than an unbridled sanctity. In the fervent mind you always find the camouflaged beast of prey; no protection is adequate against the claws of a prophet.'

19. Richard Dawkins, *The God Delusion* (Boston, MA: Houghton Mifflin, 2006).
20. Ed Husain, *The Islamist* (London: Penguin, 2007), 144.
21. Burke, *Al-Qaeda*, 302.
22. The Washington Post (2011) Motive of shooter who targeted military sites is unclear, http://www.washingtonpost.com/local/crime/motive-of-shooter-who-targeted-military-sites-is-unclear/2012/01/26/gIQAoGj6TQ_story.html, first accessed 27 January 2012.
23. Kevin Slaughter (2011) Anders Behring Breivik: Is this the e-mail he sent to friends with 2083 Manifesto?, http://www.kevinislaughter.com/tag/2083-european-declaration-of-independence/, first accessed 12 November 2011, 4.
24. Ibid., 762.
25. Ibid., 240.
26. Ibid., 1307.
27. Ibid., 1162.
28. Ibid., 940.
29. Ibid.
30. Ibid., 339.
31. The Guardian (2011) Anders Behring Breivik may avoid jail after psychiatrists declare him insane, http://www.guardian.co.uk/world/2011/nov/29/anders-behring-breivik-avoid-jail-insane, first accessed 12 November 2011.
32. Reuters (2011) Norwegian mass killer ruled insane, likely to avoid jail, http://uk.reuters.com/article/2011/11/29/uk-norway-killer-idUKTRE7AS0PT20111129, first accessed 15 December 2011.
33. John B. Thompson, *Studies in the Theory of Ideology* (Cambridge: Polity Press, 1984), 6.
34. George Steiner, *Language and Silence* (New York, NY: Atheneum, 1967).
35. See 'Changing Perspectives: Reading *Mao II* after September 11', in Alex Houen, *Terrorism and Modern Literature* (Oxford: Oxford University Press, 2002).
36. Don DeLillo, *Mao II* (London: Vintage, 1992), 156–7. My emphasis.
37. See Christian Hänggi (2011) 'The greatest work of art', http://schuel.ch/tl_files/vortraege-kursunterlagen/interventions-stockhausen-lecture.pdf, first accessed 12 December 2011.
38. DeLillo, *Mao II*, 157.
39. Houen, *Terrorism and Modern Literature*, 12.
40. DeLillo, *Mao II*, 16.
41. Ibid., 72.
42. Today (30/01/12) the UK government website reassures me that 'The current threat level of an attack by international terrorists is *Substantial*', which means 'a terrorist attack is a strong possibility' See Home Office (2012) Current threat level, http://www.homeoffice.gov.uk/counter-terrorism/current-threat-level/, first accessed 30 January 2012. It might be worth checking how the reader's government assesses the threat now on its website.
43. DeLillo, *Mao II*, 6–9.
44. Ibid., 16.
45. Ibid., 16.
46. Ibid., 237.
47. Ibid., 200. My emphasis.
48. Husain, *The Islamist*, 147.
49. Ibid., 186.
50. Ibid., 36.
51. Ibid., 135.
52. Ibid., 138.
53. Ibid., 146.
54. Ibid., 153.

55. Ibid., 164.
56. Ibid., 156.
57. Ibid., 198.
58. Ibid., 215.
59. Ibid., 161.

Bibliography

Books

Adorno, T.W., Frenkel-Brunswik, Else, Levinson, Daniel J. and Sanford, R. Nevitt (1950) *The Authoritarian Personality*, Oxford: Harpers.

Alexander, Yonah (1992) 'Contemporary Terrorism: An Overview', in Yonah Alexander and Dennis Pluchinsky, *Europe's Red Terrorists: The Fighting Communist Organizations*, London: Frank Cass.

Antliff, Allan (1998) *The Culture of Revolt: Art and Anarchism in America, 1908–1920*, Newark, DE: University of Delaware Press.

Antliff, Mark and Leighten, Patricia (2011) *The Liberation of Painting: Modernism and Anarchism in Avant-Guerre Paris*, Chicago, IL: University of Chicago Press.

Appleby, Scott (2000) *The Ambivalence of the Sacred: Religion, Violence, and Reconciliation*, Lanham, MD: Rowman & Littlefield.

Arjoman, Saïd (1998) 'Islamic Apocalypticism in the Classical Period' in McGinn, B. (ed.), *The Encyclopedia of Apocalypticism*, New York, NY: Continuum.

Asbridge, Thomas (2010) *The Crusades: The War for the Holy Land*, London: Simon & Schuster.

Aust, Stefan (2008) *The Baader–Meinhof Complex*, London: Bodley Head.

Avrich, Paul (1980) *The Modern School Movement: Anarchism and Education in the United States*, Princeton, NJ: Princeton University Press.

Badiou, Alain (2005) *Metapolitics*, London: Verso.

Badiou, Alain (2007) *The Century*, Cambridge: Polity Press.

Bale, Jeffrey (2009) 'Jihadist Ideology and Strategy and the Possible Employment of WMD', in Gary Ackerman and Jeremy Tamsett (eds), *Jihadists and Weapons of Mass Destruction*, Boca Raton, FL: CRC Press.

Bartlett, Steven (2005) *The Pathology of Man. A Study in Human Evil*, Springfield, IL: Charles C. Thomas.

Baudelaire, Charles (1857) *Les Fleurs du Mal*, Paris: Poulet-Malassis et De Broisse.

Bauer, Karin (2008) 'In Search of Ulrike Meinhof', in Elfriede Jelinek (ed.), *Everybody Talks about the Weather...We Don't. The Writings of Ulrike Meinhof*, New York: Seven Stories Press.

Bauman, Zygmunt (1991) *Modernity and Ambivalence*, Cambridge: Polity Press.

Bauman, Zygmunt (2000) *Liquid Modernity*, Cambridge: Polity.

Bauman, Zygmunt (2003) *Liquid Love: On the Frailty of Human Bonds*, Cambridge: Polity.

Bauman, Zygmunt (2005) *Liquid Life*, Cambridge: Polity.

Bauman, Zygmunt (2006) *Liquid Fear*, Cambridge: Polity.

Bauman, Zygmunt (2006) *Liquid Times: Living in an Age of Uncertainty*, Cambridge: Polity.

Bauman, Zygmunt (2011) *Culture in a Liquid World*, Cambridge: Polity.

Baumann, Bommi (1981) *How It All Began: Personal Account of a West German Urban Guerrilla*, Vancouver: Arsenal Pulp Press.

Baumgarten, Albert (1997) *The Flourishing of Jewish Sects in the Maccabean Era: An Interpretation*, Leiden: E.J. Brill.

Bechert, Heinz (ed.) (1978) *Buddhism in Ceylon and Studies on Religious Syncretism in Buddhist countries: Report on a Symposium in Göttingen*, Göttingen: Vandenhoeck & Ruprecht.

Becker, Ernest (1975) *Escape from Evil*, New York, NY: Free Press.

Becker, Ernest (1997) *The Denial of Death*, New York, NY: Simon & Schuster.

Becker, Jillian (1989) *Hitler's Children. The Story of the Baader–Meinhof Terrorist Gang*, London: Pickwick Books.

Ben-Yehuda, Nachman (1993) *Political Assassinations by Jews: A Rhetorical Device for Justice*, Albany, NY: SUNY Press.

Berger, Peter (1967) *The Sacred Canopy. Elements of a Sociological Theory of Religion*, London: Doubleday.

Berger, Peter (1999) *The Desecularization of the World*: *The Resurgence of Religion in World Politics*, Michigan: Wm. B. Eerdmans.

Berlet, Chip (2008) 'The United States: Messianism, Apocalypticism, and Political Religion', in Matthew Feldman, Roger Griffin, and John Tortice (eds), *The Sacred in Twentieth Century Politics: Essays in Honour of Professor Stanley G. Payne*, London: Palgrave Macmillan.

Berlin, Isaiah (1978) *Russian Thinkers*, London: Hogarth Press.

Berman, Marshall (1982) *All that is Solid Melts into Air. The Experience of Modernity*, London: Verso.

Bowles, Paul (1990) *The Sheltering Sky*, Harmondsworth: Penguin.

Boyd, Katherine and Strozier, Charles (2010) 'The Apocalyptic', in James Jones, Charles Strozier, and David Terman (eds) *The Fundamentalist Mindset*, Oxford: Oxford University Press.

Bruce, Steve (2003) *Politics and Religion*, Oxford: Polity.

Bull, Anna (2007) *Italian Neofascism: The Strategy of Tension and the Politics of Nonreconciliation*, Oxford: Berghahn Books.

Burger, Thomas (1976) *Max Weber's Theory of Concept Formation, History, Laws, and Ideal Types*, North Carolina: Duke University Press.

Burke, Jason (2007) *Al-Qaeda*, London: Penguin.

Burleigh, Michael (2000) *The Third Reich*, London: Pan Macmillan.

Burleigh, Michael (2005) *Earthly Powers: The Clash of Religion and Politics in Europe from the French Revolution to the Great War*, New York, NY: Harper Collins.

Burleigh, Michael (2007) *Sacred Causes: The Clash of Religion and Politics from the Great War to the War on Terror*, New York, NY: Harper Collins.

Cady, Linnell and Simon, Sheldon (2007) 'Introduction', in Linnell Cady and Sheldon Simon (eds), *Religion and Conflict in South and Southeast Asia*, London: Routledge.

Carmichael, Cathie (2002) *Ethnic Cleansing in the Balkans: Nationalism and the Destruction of Tradition*, London: Routledge.

Caroll, David (2007) *Albert Camus the Algerian: Colonialism, Terrorism, Justice*, New York, NY: Columbia University Press.

Carrasco, David (1999) *City of Sacrifice: The Aztec Empire and the Role of Violence in Civilization*, Boston, MA: Beacon Press.

Casanova, José (1994) *Public Religions in the Modern World*, Chicago, IL: University of Chicago Press.

Cettl, Robert (2009) *Terrorism in American Cinema*: *An Analytical Filmography, 1960–2008*, Jefferson, NC: McFarland.

Chase, Alston (2004) *A Mind for Murder. The Education of the Unabomber and the Origins of Modern Terrorism*, New York, NY: W.W. Norton.

Chomsky, Noam and Herman, Edward (1979) *The Washington Connection and Third World Fascism: The Political Economy of Human Rights: Vol. 1*, Boston: South End Press.

Cioran, Émile (1975) *A Short History of Decay*, Oxford: Basil Blackwell.

Clarke, Peter (2000) *Japanese New Religions in Global Perspective*, Richmond: Curzon Press.

Clarke, Peter (ed.) (2006) *Encyclopedia of New Religious Movements*, London: Routledge.

Coetzee, J.M. (1999) *The Master of Petersburg*, London: Vintage.

Cohn, Norman (1970) *The Pursuit of the Millennium*, London: Granada.

Coker, Christopher (2002) *Waging War Without Warriors? The Changing Culture of Military Conflict*, Boulder, CO: Lynne Rienner.

Coker, Christopher (2007) *The Warrior Ethos. Military Culture and the War on Terror*, London: Routledge.

Conrad, Joseph (1990) *Under Western Eyes*, Harmondsworth: Penguin.

Cozzens, Jeffrey (2007) 'Approaching al-Qaeda's Warfare: Function, Culture and Grand Strategy', in Ranstorp, Magnus (ed.) *Mapping Terrorism Research. State of the Art, Gaps and Future Direction*, London: Routledge.

Crelinsten, Ronald D. (2007) 'Counterterrorism as global governance: A research inventory', in Magnus Ranstorp (ed.), *Mapping Terrorism Research. State of the Art, Gaps and Future Direction*, London: Routledge.

Curtis, Mark (2004) *Western State Terrorism*, Cambridge: Polity Press.

Daftary, Farhad (1990) *The Isma'ilis: their History and Doctrines*, Cambridge: Cambridge University Press.

Danchev, Alex (2011) *100 Artists' Manifestos: From the Futurists to the Stuckists*, Harmondsworth: Penguin.

Dawkins, Richard (2006) *The God Delusion*, Boston, MA: Houghton Mifflin.

Debord, Guy (2004) *The Society of the Spectacle*, London: Rebel Press.

DeLillo, Don (1992) *Mao II*, London: Vintage.

Della Porta, Donatella (1900) *Il terrorismo di sinistra*, Bologna: Il Mulino.

Demant, Peter (2006) *Islam vs Islamism. The Dilemma of the Modern World*, London: Praeger.

Devji, Faisal (2005) *Landscapes of the Jihad. Militancy, Morality, Modernity*, London: Hurst.

Devji, Faisal (2008) *The Terrorist in Search of Humanity. Militant Islam and Global Politics*, London: Hurst.

Dostoevsky, Fyodor (1848) *The Double. A Petersburg Poem*. First published in the almanac *Notes of the Fatherland* (Moscow).

Dostoevsky, Fyodor (1992) *The Devils*, Oxford: Oxford University Press.

Drake, Richard (1986) 'Julius Evola and the Ideological Origins of the Radical Right in Contemporary Italy', in Peter H.Merkl (ed.), *Political Violence and Terror: Motifs and Motivations*, Berkeley, CA: University of California Press.

Drake, Richard (1989) *The Revolutionary Mystique and Terrorism in Contemporary Italy*, Bloomington, IN: Indiana University Press.

Dressen, Wolfgang (1976) *Politische Prozesse ohne Verteidigung?*, Wagenbach: Berlin.

Duyvesteyn, Isabelle (2007) 'The Role of History and Continuity in Terrorism Research', in Magnus Ranstorp (ed.), *Mapping Terrorism Research. State of the Art, Gaps and Future Direction*, London: Routledge.

Edschmid, Kasimir (1919) *Über den Expressionismus in der Literatur und die neue Dichtung*, Berlin: Reiß.

Eisenman, Robert (1997) *James the Brother of Jesus: The Key to Unlocking the Secrets of Early Christianity and the Dead Sea Scrolls*, New York, NY: Viking.

Eisenstadt, Shmuel (1973) *Tradition, Change and Modernity*, New York, NY: Wiley.

Eisenstadt, Shmuel (1999) *Fundamentalism, Sectarianism, and Revolution: The Jacobin Dimension of Modernity*, Cambridge: Polity.

Eliadea, Mircea (1959) *The Sacred and the Profane. The Nature of Religion. The Significance of Religious Myth, Symbolism, and Ritual within Life and Culture*, San Diego, CA: Harcourt Brace & Co.

Eliadea, Mircea (1971) *The Myth of the Eternal Return, or Cosmos and History*, Princeton, NJ: Princeton University Press.

Etlin, Richard (1991) *Modernism in Italian Architecture, 1890–1940*, London: MIT Press.

Eugen, Roxanne (1999) *Enemy in the Mirror: Islamic Fundamentalism and the Limits of Modern Rationalism – A Work of Comparative Political Theory*, Princeton, NJ: Princeton University Press.

Evans, Richard (1997) *In Defence of History*, London: Granta.

Fenn, Richard (1997) *The End of Time. Religion, Ritual, and the Forging of the Soul*, Cleveland, OH: Pilgrim Press.

Fenn, Richard (2000) *Time Exposure. The Personal Experience of Time in Secular Societies*, Oxford: Oxford University Press.

Ferraresi, Franco (1996) *Threats to Democracy: The Radical Right in Italy after the War*, Princeton, NJ: Princeton University Press.

Flynn, Michael and Strozier, Charles (1997) *The Year 2000: Essays on the End*, New York, NY: New York University Press.

Forest, James J.F. and Howard, Russell (eds) (2007) *Weapons of Mass Destruction and Terrorism*, New York, NY: McGraw Hill.

Foucault, Michel (1984) 'Des Espaces Autres', *Architecture /Mouvement/ Continuité*, 5, (October) 46–9.

Fromm, Erich (1968) *The Revolution of Hope: Toward a Humanized Technology*, New York, NY: Harper & Row.

Gable, Gerry and Jackson, Paul (2011) *Lone Wolves: Myth or Reality*, Searchlight: Islington.

Gareau, Frederick Henry (2004) *State Terrorism and the United States: From Counterinsurgency to the War on Terror*, London: Zed Books.

Gatade, Subhash (2011) *Godse's Children: Hindutva Terror in India*, New Delhi: Pharos Media & Publishing Pvt.

Gentile, Emilio (2006) *Politics as Religion*, Princeton, NJ: Princeton University Press.

Glucksmann, André (2002) *Dostoïevski à Manhattan*, Paris: Robert Laffont.

Gooding-Williams, Robert (2001) *Zarathustra's Dionysian Modernism*, Palo Alto, CA: Stanford University Press.

Goodrick-Clarke, Nicholas (1985) *The Occult Roots of Nazism*, Wellingborough: Aquarian Press.

Graaf, Bob de (2010) *History of Fanaticism: From Enlightenment to Jihad*, Aarhus: CIR.

Gray, John (1995) *Enlightenment's Wake: Politics and Culture at the Close of the Modern Age*, London: Routledge.

Gray, John (2003) *Al Qaeda and What it Means to be Modern*, London: Faber and Faber.

Gray, John (2007) *Black Mass: Apocalyptic Religion and the Death of Utopia*, London: Allen Lane.

Greenberg, Jeff, Psyzcynski, Tom and Solomon, Sheldon (2003) *In the Wake of 9/11. The Psychology of Terror*, Washington DC: American Psychological Association.

Griffin, Roger (ed.) (1995) *Fascism*, Oxford: Oxford University Press.

Griffin, Roger (2007) *Modernism and Fascism. The Sense of a Beginning under Mussolini and Hitler*, London: Palgrave Macmillan.

Grumet, Robert (ed.) (2003) *Anthony Wallace. Revitalization & Mazeways. Essays on Cultural Change, Volume 1*, Lincoln, NE: University of Nebraska Press.

Gupta, Dipak (2008) *Understanding Terrorism and Political Violence. The Life Cycle of Birth, Growth, Transformation and Demise*, London: Routledge.

Hafez, Kai (2010) *Radicalism and Political Reform in the Islamic and Western Worlds*, Cambridge: Cambridge University Press.

Hellmann-Rajanayagam, Dagmar (1994) *The Tamil Tigers. Armed Struggle for Identity*, Stuttgart: Franz Steiner.

Herbeck, Dan and Michel, Lou (2001) *American Terrorist. Timothy McVeigh and the Tragedy at Oklahoma City*, New York, NY: Harper Collins.

Hesse, Hermann (1927) *Steppenwolf*, Berlin: S. Fischer.

Hill, Daniel (2010) 'Fundamentalist Faith States: Regulation Theory as a Framework for the Psychology of Religious Fundamentalism', in James Jones, Charles Strozier, and David Terman (eds), *The Fundamentalist Mindset*, Oxford: Oxford University Press.

Hitchens, Christopher (2007) *God is Not Great: How Religion Poisons Everything*, London: Atlantic.

Hoffer, Eric (1951, 1966) *The True Believer. Thoughts on Nature of Mass Movements*, New York, NY: Harper Collins.

Hoffman, Bruce (2004) 'Foreword', in Andrew Silke (ed.) *Research on Terrorism: Trends, Achievements and Failures*, Portland, OR: Frank Cass.

Hoffman, Bruce (2006) *Inside Terrorism*, Columbia, NY: Columbia University Press.

Horgan, John (2007) 'Understanding Terrorist Motivation: A Socio-psychological Perspective' in Magnus Ranstorp (ed.), *Mapping Terrorism Research. State of the Art, Gaps and Future Direction*, London: Routledge.

Horkheimer, Max (1972) *La nostalgia del totalmente Altro*, Brescia: Queriana.

Horkheimer, Max (1970) *Die Sehnsucht nach dem ganz Anderen*, Hamburg: Furche-Verl.

Houen, Alex (2002) *Terrorism and Modern Literature*, Oxford: Oxford University Press.

Husain, Ed (2007) *The Islamist*, London: Penguin.

Ibrahim, Raymond (2007) *The Al Qaeda Reader*, New York, NY: Broadway Books.

Ignatieff, Michael (2004) *The Lesser Evil: Political Ethics in an Age of Terror*, Princeton, NJ: Princeton University Press.

Jones, James (2008) *Blood that Cries Out from the Earth*, Oxford: Oxford University Press.

Jones, James, Strozier, Charles and Terman, David (eds), *The Fundamentalist Mindset*, Oxford: Oxford University Press.

Jones, James (2010) 'Eternal Warfare: Violence on the Mind of American Apocalyptic Christianity', in James Jones, Charles Strozier, and David Terman (eds), *The Fundamentalist Mindset*, Oxford: Oxford University Press.

Jongman, Albert and Schmid, Alex (1988) *Political Terrorism: A New Guide to Actors, Authors, Concepts, Data Bases, Theories and Literature*, New Brunswick: Transaction Books.

Juergensmeyer, Mark (2003) *Terror in the Mind of God. The Global Rise of Religious Violence*, Berkeley, CA: University of California Press.

Jung, Carl (1928) *Modern Man in Search of a Soul*, London: Routledge, 2001.

Kandinsky, Wassily (1914) *Concerning the Spiritual in Art*, New York: Dover Publications, 1977.

Kaplan, Jeffrey (1997) *Radical Religion in America. Millenarian Movements from the Far Right to the Children of Noah*, New York, NY: Syracuse University Press.

Kaplan, Jeffrey (2000) *Encyclopedia of White Power: A Sourcebook on the Radical Racist Right*, Lanham, MD: Rowman & Littlefield.

Kaplan, Jeffrey (ed.) (2002) *Millennial Violence Past, Present, and Future*, London: Frank Cass and Company Limited.

Kaplan, Jeffrey and Loow, Helene (eds) (2002) *The Cultic Milieu: Oppositional Subcultures in an Age of Globalization*, Walnut Creek, CA: Altamira Press.

Katz, E. (1987) *LECHI: Fighters for the freedom of Israel*, Tel Aviv: Yair Publishers.

Kelly, Aileen, Introduction to Berlin, Isaiah (1974) *Russian Thinkers*, Harmondsworth: Penguin Books.

Kelly, Aileen (1998) *Toward Another Shore: Russian Thinkers Between Necessity and Chance*, New Haven, CT: Yale University Press.

Khosrokhavar, Farhad (2011) *Jihidist Ideology. The Anthropological Perspective*, Aarhus: CIR.

Kinsman, Robert (ed.), *The Darker Vision of the Renaissance*, Berkeley, CA: University of California Press.

Klemens, Nadine (2002) *IKEA Boys and Terrorists: Fight Club in the Light of 9/11*, Norderstedt: GRIN.

Knuth, Rebecca (2006) *Burning Books and Levelling Libraries. Extremist Violence and Cultural Destruction*, Westport, CT: Praeger.

Koselleck, Reinhardt (2002) *The Practice of Conceptual History. Timing History, Spacing Concepts*, Palo Alto, CA: Stanford University Press.

Krebs, Pierre (1982) *Die europäische Wiedergeburt*, Tübingen: Grabert.

Kruglianski, Arie (2002) 'Inside the Terrorist Mind', in Joshua Sinai (2007) 'New Trends in Terrorism Studies: Strengths and Weaknesses', in Magnus Ranstorp (ed.), *Mapping Terrorism Research. State of the Art, Gaps and Future Direction*, London: Routledge.

Lalich, Janja (1988) *Bounded Choice. True Believers and Charismatic Cults*, Berkeley, CA: University of California Press.

Laren, John (2011) *A Western Source on Islamism. Soundings in the Influence of Alexis Carrell on Sayyid Qutb*, Aarhus: Centre for Studies in Islamism and Radicalisation.

Lawrence, Bruce (ed.) (2005) *Messages to the World: The Statements of Osama Bin Laden*, New York, NY: Verso.

Leighten, Patricia (1989) *Re-Ordering the Universe: Picasso and Anarchism, 1897–1914*, Princeton, NJ: Princeton University Press.

Lifton, Robert (1993) *The Protean Self* , Chicago, IL: University of Chicago Press.

Lifton, Robert (1999) *Destroying the World to Save It. Aum Shinrikyō, Apocalyptic Violence, and the New Global Terrorism*, New York, NY: Holt.

Lindholm, Charles and Zúquete, José (2010) *The Struggle for the World. Liberation Movements for the 21st Century*, Palo Alto, CA: Stanford University Press.

Lotto, David and Muenster, Bettina (2010) 'The Social Psychology of Humiliation and Revenge. The Origin of the Fundamentalist Mindset', in James Jones, Charles Strozier, and David Terman (eds), *The Fundamentalist Mindset*, Oxford: Oxford University Press.

Lowes, Nick and McLagan, Graeme (2000) *Mr Evil. The Secret Life of Racist Bomber and Killer David Copeland*, London: John Blake.

Maalouf, Amin (1998) *Samarkand*, New York, NY: Interlink Publishing Group.

Malik, Iftikhar (2005)'Beyond Ayodhya: Hindutva and Implications for South East Asia', in *Jihad, Hindutva and the Taliban*, Oxford: Oxford University Press.

Malraux, André (2009) *Man's Fate*, Harmondsworth: Penguin Classics.

Maroney, Eric (2006) *Religious Syncretism*, London: SCM Press.

Maududi, Abdul (2006) *Jihad in Islam*, Lebanon: Holy Koran Publishing.

Mazarr, Michael (2007) *Unmodern Men in the Modern World*, Cambridge: Cambridge University Press.

McElroy, Wendy (2003) *The Debates of Liberty: An Overview of Individualist Anarchism, 1881–1908*, Lanham, MD: Rowman & Littlefield.

McCloughlin, William (1978) *Revivals, Awakenings, and Reform. An Essay on Religion and Social Change in America, 1607–1977*, Chicago, IL: University of Chicago Press.

Mclagan, David (1977) *Creation Myths: Man's Introduction to the World*, New York, NY: Thames and Hudson.

Meeks, Wayne (1983) *The First Urban Christians: The Social World of the Apostle Paul*, New Haven: Yale University Press.

Merriman, John (2009) *The Dynamite Club. How a Bombing in Fin-de-Siècle Paris Ignited the Age of Modern Terror*, London: JR Books.

Michael, George (2006) *The Enemy of my Enemy. The Alarming Convergence of Militant Extremism and the Extreme Right*, Lawrence, KS: University Press of Kansas.

Michaud, Eric (2004) *The Cult of Art in Nazi Germany*, Palo Alto, CA: Stanford University Press.

Mosse, George (1964) *The Crisis of German Ideology: Intellectual Origins of the Third Reich*, New York, NY: Howard Fertig.

Mosse, George (1975) *The Nationalization of the Masses*, New York, NY: Howard Fertig.

Muravchik, Joshua (2002) *Heaven on Earth: The Rise and Fall of Socialism*, New York, NY: Encounter Books.

Murawiec, Laurent (2008) *The Mind of Islam*, Cambridge: Cambridge University Press.

Nanda, Meera (2003) *Prophets Facing Backward: Postmodern Critiques of Science and Hindu Nationalism in India*, New Brunswick, NJ: Rutgers University Press.

Netton, Ian (1991) *Muslim Neoplatonists: An Introduction to the Thought of the Brethren of Purity*, Edinburgh: Edinburgh University Press.

Nietzsche, Friedrich (1882), *The Gay Science*, New York, Random House, 1974.

Nietzsche, Friedrich (1911) *Ecce Homo*, Portland, ME: Smith and Sales.

Ohana, David (2008) *The Nihilist Order*, Eastbourne: Sussex Academic Press.

O'Hearn, Denis (2006) *Nothing But an Unfinished Song. Bobby Sands, the Irish Hunger Striker who Ignited a Generation*, New York, NY: Nation Books.

Osborne, Peter (1995) *The Politics of Time. Modernity and the Avant-garde*, London: Verso.

Osborne, Peter (2000) *Philosophy in Cultural Theory*, London: Routledge.

Ozouf, Mona (1989) *La Fête révolutionnaire 1789/1799*, Paris: Gallimard.

Palahniuk, Chuck (2006) *Fight Club*, London: Vintage Books.

Partridge, Christopher (ed.) (2004) *Encyclopedia of New Religions: New Religious Movements, Sects and Alternative Spiritualities*, Oxford: Lion.

Pascal, Blaise (1966) *Pensées*, Harmondsworth: Penguin.

Pearse, Pádraic H. (1924) *Political Writings and Speeches*, Dublin: Phoenix Publishing.

Pedahzur, Ami (2005) *Suicide Terrorism*, Cambridge: Polity.

Pedahzur, Ami and Perliger, Arie (2009) *Jewish Terrorism in Israel*, New York, NY: Columbia University Press.

Pellicani, Luciano (2003) *Revolutionary Apocalypse. Ideological Roots of Terrorism*, Westport, CT: Praeger.

Perika, Vjekoslav (2002) *Balkan Idols: Religion and Nationalism in Yugoslav States*, Oxford: Oxford University Press.

Poewe, Karl (2006) *New Religions and the Nazis*, Oxford: Routledge.

Post, Jerrold and Robins, Robert (1997) *Political Paranoia. The Psychopolitics of Hatred*, London: Yale University Press.

Post, Jerrold (1998) 'Terrorist psycho-logic: Terrorist behaviour as a product of psychological forces', in Walter Reich (ed.), *Origins of Terrorism: Psychologies Ideologies, Theologies, States of Mind*, Washington, DC: Woodrow Wilson Centre Press.

Presner, Todd (2007) *Muscular Judaism: the Jewish Body and the Politics of Regeneration*, London: Routledge.

Qutb, Sayydi (2001) *Milestones*, New Delhi: Islamic Book Services.

Rabasa, *Angel* et al. (2007) *Building Moderate Muslim Networks*, Santa Monica, CA: RAND Corporation.

Ramakrishna, Kumar (2007) 'The (Psychic) Roots of Religious Violence in South and Southeast Asia', in Linnell Cady and Sheldon Simon (eds), *Religion and Conflict in South and Southeast Asia*, London: Routledge.

Ranstorp, Magnus (2007) 'Introduction: mapping terrorism research – challenges and priorities', in Magnus Ranstorp (ed.), *Mapping Terrorism Research. State of the Art, Gaps and Future Direction*, London: Routledge.

Reilly, Thomas H. (2004) *The Taiping Heavenly Kingdom: Rebellion and the Blasphemy of Empire*, Seattle: University of Washington Press.

Rhee, Hong Beom (2007) *Asian Millenarianism: An Interdisciplinary Study of the Taiping and Tonghak in Global Context*, London: Cambria Press, 2007.

Ricoeur, Paul (1984, 1985, 1988) *Time and Narrative (Temps et Récit)*, Chicago, IL: University of Chicago Press.

Ridgeway, James (1995) *Blood in the Face*, New York, NY: Thunder Mouth Press.

Robbins, Tom (1980) *Still Life with Woodpecker*, New York, NY: Bantam.

Rohrmoser, Günter (1981–84) 'Ideologien und Strategien, in Bundesminister des Innern (ed.) *Analysen zum Terrorismus*, Opladen: Westdeutscher Verlag, Vol. 2, 87, in Konrad Kellen, 'Ideology and Rebellion: Terrorism in West Germany', in Walter Reich (ed.), *Origins of Terrorism: Psychologies Ideologies, Theologies, States of Mind*, Washington, DC: Woodrow Wilson Centre Press.

Ron, James (2003) *Frontiers and Ghettos: State Violence in Serbia and Israel*, Berkeley, CA: University of California Press.

Rosenthal, Bernice (2002) *New Myth, New Man. From Nietzsche to Stalin*, University Park, PA: Pennsylvania State University Press.

Roszak, Theodore (1978) *Person/Planet: The Creative Disintegration of Industrial Society, New York, NY:* Anchor Press.

Roy, Arundhati (2011) *Broken Republic*, Harmondsworth: Penguin.

Roy, Olivier (2004) *Globalised Islam. The Search for a New Ummah*, London: Hurst and Company.

Ruthven, Malise (2002) *A Fury for God. The Islamist Attack on America*, London: Granta.

Safi, Omid (2003) *Progressive Muslims*, Oxford: One World.

Sageman, Marc (2004) *Understanding Terror Networks*, Philadelphia, PA: University of Pennsylvania Press.

Sahota, Sunjeev (2011) *Ours are the Streets*, London: Picador.

Schweid, Elizeir (1985) *The Land of Israel: National Home or Land of Destiny*, Madison, NJ: Fairleigh Dickinson University Press.

Silk, Andrew (2007) 'The Impact of 9/11 on Research on Terrorism', in Magnus Ranstorp (ed.) *Mapping Terrorism Research. State of the Art, Gaps and Future Direction*, London: Routledge.

Sinai, Joshua (2007) 'New Trends in Terrorism Studies: Strengths and Weaknesses', in Magnus Ranstorp (ed.), *Mapping Terrorism Research. State of the Art, Gaps and Future Direction*, London: Routledge.

Skaine, Rosemarie (2006) *Female Suicide Bombers*, Jefferson, NC: McFarland.

Skya, Walter (2009) *Japan's Holy War: The Ideology of Radical Shinto Ultranationalism*, Durham, NC: Duke University Press.

Sluka, Jeffrey (ed.) (2000) *Death Squad: The Anthropology of State Terror*, Philadelphia: University of Pennsylvania Press.

Sonn, Richard D. (1989) *Anarchism and Cultural Politics in Fin de Siècle France*, Lincoln, NE: University of Nebraska Press.

Sonn, Richard D. (2010) *Sex, Violence, and the Avant-Garde: Anarchism in Interwar France*, University Park, PA: Pennsylvania State University Press.

Southgate, Troy (ed.) (2011) *The Primordial Tradition: Philosophy, Metapolitics and the Conservative Revolution*, n.pl: Primordial Traditions.

Spence, Jonathan (1996) *God's Chinese Son*, New York, NY: W.W. Norton & Company.

Steiner, George (1967) *Language and Silence*, New York, NY: Atheneum.

Stein, Ruth (2010) *For Love of the Father. A Psychoanalytical Study of Religious Terrorism*, Palo Alto, CA: Stanford University Press.

Stepniak, Sergey (1883) *Underground Russia*, London: Smith, Elder and Co.

Stern, Jessica (2004) *Terror in the Name of God. Why Religious Militants Kill*, New York, NY: Ecco.

Stites, Richard (1989) *Revolutionary Dreams. Utopian Vision and Experimental Life in the Russian Revolution*, New York, NY: Oxford University Press.

Strozier, Charles (1997)'Apocalyptic Violence and the Politics of Waco', in Michael Flynn and Charles *Strozier, The Year 2000: Essays on the End*, New York, NY: New York University Press.

Szakolczai, Arpad (2000) *Reflexive Historical Sociology*, London: Routledge.

Taarnby, Michael (2007) 'Understanding Recruitment of Islamist Terrorists in Europe', in Magnus Ranstorp (ed.), *Mapping Terrorism Research. State of the Art, Gaps and Future Direction*, London: Routledge.

Taylor, Maxwell (2007) *The Fanatics: A Behavioural Approach to Political Violence*, Princeton, NJ: Princeton University Press.

Theweleit, Klaus (1989) *Male Fantasies*, Cambridge: Polity Press, 1989.

Thompson, John B. (1984) *Studies in the Theory of Ideology*, Cambridge: Polity Press.

Thompson, Mark D. (2008) 'Luther on Despair', in Rosner, Brian (ed.) *The Consolations of Theology*, New York, NY: Wm. B. Eerdmans Publishing.

Thornton, Russell (1986) *We Shall Live Again: The 1870 and 1890 Ghost Dance Movements as Demographic Revitalization*, Cambridge: Cambridge University Press.

Thorup, Mikkel (2010) *An Intellectual History of Terror: War, Violence and the State*, New York, NY: Routledge.

Tibi, Bassam (2009) *Islam's Predicament with Modernity. Religious Reform and Cultural Change*, London: Routledge.

Toynbee, Arnold (1963) *A Study of History. Heroic Ages, Volume 8: Contacts Between Civilizations in Space*, Oxford: Oxford University Press.

Tuhiwai, Linda (1999) *Decolonizing Methodologies: Research and Indigenous Peoples*, New York, NY: St Martin's Press.

Turda, Marias (2010) *Modernism and Eugenics*, Basingstoke: Palgrave Macmillan.

Turner, Victor (1969) *The Ritual Process. Structure and Anti-Structure*, Chicago, IL: Aldine.

Turner, Victor (1977) 'Variations on a Theme of Liminality', in Sally Moore and Barbara Myerhoff (eds), *Secular Ritual. Forms and Meaning*, Assen, Netherlands: Van Gorcum.

Voegelin, Eric (1986) *The Political Religions*, Lewiston, NY: E. Mellen Press.

Wakeman Jr, Frederic (1975) *The Fall of Imperial China*, New York, NY: Free Press.

Warner, Denis and Warner, Peggy (1982) *The Sacred Warriors: Japan's Suicide Legions*, New York, NY: Van Nostrand Reinhold.

Weir, David (1997) *Anarchy & Culture. The Aesthetic Politics of Modernism*, Amherst, MA: University of Massachusetts Press.

Weller, Shane (2010) *Modernism and Nihilism*, London: Routledge.

Wessinger, Catherine (ed.) (2000) *Millennialism, Persecution and Violence: Historical Cases*, Syracuse, NY: Syracuse University.

Wilk, Christopher (2006) 'Introduction: What was Modernism?', in Wilk, Christopher (ed.) *Modernism 1914–1939. Designing a New World*, London: V&A Publications.

Yamamoto, Tsunetomo (2001) *Bushido. The Way of the Samurai*. New York: Square One.

Zerubavel, Yael (1995) *Recovered Roots: Collective Memory and the Making of Israeli National Tradition*, Chicago, IL: University of Chicago Press.

Žižek, Slavoj (2008) *Violence: Six Sideways Reflections*, London: Profile Books.

Articles

Ainslie, R.C., Gould, J.R., and Prentice, N.M. (1996) 'The splitting index: Construction of a scale measuring the defense mechanism of splitting', *Journal of Personality Assessment*, 66, 2, 414–30.

Allan, Derek (1982) 'The Psychology of a Terrorist: Tchen in *La Condition humaine*', *Nottingham French Studies*, 21, 1, 50–2.

Anonymous (1943) 'Terror', *He Khazit*, Issue 2, August.

Antliff, Allan (1994) 'Carl Zigrosser and the Modern School: Nietzsche, Art and Anarchism', *Archives of American Art Journal*, 34, 4, 16–23.

Antliff, Mark (2010) 'Henri Gaudier-Brzeska': Guerre sociale. Art, Anarchism and Anti-Militarism in Paris and London, 1910–1915', *Modernism/Modernity*, 17, 1, 135–69.

Bale, Jeffrey (2009) 'Islamism and Totalitarianism', *Totalitarian Movements and Political Religions*, 10, 2, 73–96.

Behnke, Andreas (2004) 'Terrorising the Political: 9/11 within the Context of the Globalisation of Violence', *Millennium: Journal of International Studies* 33, 2, 279–312.

Bloom, Mia (June 2009) 'Chasing Butterflies and Rainbows: A Critique of Kruglanski et al.'s "Fully Committed: Suicide Bombers' Motivation and the Quest for Personal Significance"', *Political Psychology* 30, 3 (June 2009), 387–95.

Brym, Robert (2008) 'Religion, politics, and suicide bombing: An interpretive essay', *Canadian Journal of Sociology* 33, 1, 96.

Byman, Daniel L. (1998) 'The Logic of Ethnic Terrorism', *Studies in Conflict and Terrorism*, 21, 2, 150.

Campbell, Colin (1972) 'The Cult, the Cultic Milieu and Secularization', *A Sociological Yearbook of Religion in Britain*, 5, 119–36.

Chen, Xiaoyan, Dechesne, Mark, Fishman, Shira, Kruglanski, Arie, and Orehek, Edward (May 2009) 'Fully Committed: Suicide Bombers' Motivation and the Quest for Personal Significance', *Political Psychology*, 30, 3.

Doran, Michael (2005) 'The Pragmatic Fanaticism of Al Qaeda: Statements and Evolving Ideology', *Congressional Research Service Report*, Nov. 15, 5.

Eisenstadt, Shmuel (2000) 'Multiple Modernities', *Daedalus*, 129, 1, 1–29.

Ferraresi, Franco (1987) 'Julius Evola: Tradition, Reaction and the Radical Right', *Archives européennes de sociologie*, 28, 107–51.

Fritzsche, Peter (1996) 'Nazi Modern', *Modernism/Modernity*, 3, 1.

Githens-Mazer, Jonathan (2008) 'Islamic Radicalisation among North Africans in Britain', *British Journal of Politics and International Relations*, 10, 550–70.

Griffin, Roger (2003) 'From slime mould to rhizome: An introduction to the groupuscular right', *Patterns of Prejudice*, 37, 1, 27–50.

Gunn, Jeremy (2003) '*The Complexity of Religion and the Definition of "Religion" in International Law*', *Harvard Human Rights Journal*, 16, 189–215.

Hafez, Mohammed (2006) 'Rationality, Culture, and Structure in the Making of Suicide Bombers', *Studies in Conflict and Terrorism*, 29, 2, 181.

Härmänmaa, Marja (2009) 'Beyond Anarchism: Marinetti's Futurist (anti-)Utopia of Individualism and 'Artocracy', *The European Legacy: Toward New Paradigms*, 14, 857–71.

Ignatieff, Michael (2001) 'It's War – But it Doesn't Have to be Dirty', *The Guardian*, 1 October 2001.

Kalian, M. et al. (2008) 'Spiritual Starvation in a holy space – a form of Jerusalem Syndrome', *Mental Health, Religion & Culture*, 11, 2, 161–72.

Kippenberg, Hans (2005) 'Consider that it is a raid on the path of god': The spiritual manual of the attackers of 9/11', *Numen*, 52, 46.

Lubar, Robert (1990) *The Art Bulletin*, 72, 3, 505–10.

McLeod, W.H. (1998) 'Sikh Fundamentalism', *Journal of the American Oriental Society*, 118, 1, 15–27.

Mozaffari, Mehdi (2007) '*What is Islamism?* History and Definition of a Concept', *Totalitarian Movements and Political Religions*, 8, 1, 17–33.

Mozaffari, Mehdi (2009) 'The Rise of Islamism in the Light of European Totalitarianism', *Totalitarian Movements and Political Religions* 10, 1, 1–13.

Ó Donghaile, Deaglán (2010) 'Anarchism, anti-imperialism and "The Doctrine of Dynamite" ', *Journal of Postcolonial Writing*, 46, 3, 294–6.

Pellicani, Luciano (2008) 'I purificatori del mondo', *Filosofia e questioni pubbliche* 13, 1 (2008), 107–34.

Philpott, Daniel (2007) 'Explaining the Political Ambivalence of Religion', *American Political Science Review*, 101, 3, 505–25.

Sheehan, Thomas (1981) 'Myth and Violence: The Fascism of Julius Evola and Alain de Benoist', *Social Research*, 48, 45–73.

Wallace, Anthony (1956) 'Revitalization Movements', *American Anthropologist*, 58, 2, 264–81.

Warburg, Gabriel (1995) 'Mahdism and Islamism in Sudan', *International Journal of Middle Eastern Studies*, 27, 2.

Wilhelmsen, Julie (2005) 'Between a Rock and a Hard Place: The Islamisation of the Chechen Separatist Movement', *Europe–Asia Studies* 57, 1, 38–46.

Websites

Answering Christianity (2011) Was Jesus Poisoned?, http://www.answering-christianity.com/abdullah_smith/alleged_poisoning_of_prophet_muhammad_2.htm, 1 December 2011.

Anti-Defamation League (2012) International Terrorism Database, http://www.adl.org/terrorism/symbols/, 12 December 2011.

Aron, Leon (2003) Chechnya: New Dimensions of the Old Crisis, http://www.aei.org/article/foreign-and-defense-policy/regional/europe/chechnya-outlook/, 2 December 2011.

Aust, Stefan (2008) Terrorism in Germany: The Baader–Meinhof Phenomenon, http://www.ghi-dc.org/files/publications/bulletin/bu043/45.pdf, 12 December 2011.

Awesome Film (2011) Taxi Driver, http://www.awesomefilm.com/script/taxidriver.txt, 13 November 2011.

Azzam, Abdullah (2001) Martyrs: The Building Blocks of Nations, http://www.religioscope.com/info/doc/jihad/azzam_martyrs.htm, 12 December 2011.

Bakunin, Mikhail (1842) The Reaction in Germany, http://www.marxists.org/reference/archive/bakunin/works/1842/reaction-germany.htm, 3 December 2011.

Bale, Jeffrey (2011) What is Terrorism, http://www.miis.edu/academics/researchcenters/terrorism/about/Terrorism_Definition, 12 November 2011.

BBC (1999) Tradition, http://news.bbc.co.uk/hi/english/static/events/reith_99/week3/week3.htm, 1 December 2011.

Ben-David, Dan (2007) The Sicarii of the Third Temple, http://www.haaretz.com/print-edition/opinion/the-sicarii-of-the-third-temple-1.226260, 1 December 2011.

Breton, André (1929) Second Manifesto of Surrealism, http://alangullette.com/lit/surreal/, 13 December 2011.

Britt, Robert Roy (2005) Forces of Creation: Black Holes Spark Star Formation, http://www.space.com/767-forces-creation-black-holes-spark-star-formation.html, 21 February 2011.

Brooks, David (2004) The C.I.A.: Method and Madness, http://query.nytimes.com/gst/fullpage.html?res=9C03E6D9173BF930A35751C0A9629C8B63, 4 November 2011.

Buzzle (2006) Yankee Pitcher Cory Lidle's Plane Crashes into NYC Skyscraper, http://www.buzzle.com/articles/yankee-pitcher-cory-lidle-plane-crashes-nyc-skyscraper.html, 29 November 2011.

Ceccarelli, Marco (2009) Revolutionary Self-fulfilment? Individual Radicalisation and Terrorism in Fyodor Dostoyevsky's *Notes from the Underground*, *Crime and Punishment* and *The Devils*, http://www.loganscentrostudi.org/public/pubblicazioni/Individual%20Radicalisation%20and%20Terrorism%20in%20Fyodor%20by%20Marco%20Ceccarelli.pdf, 13 November 2011.

Channel 4 (2011) Sri Lanka's Killing Fields, http://www.channel4.com/programmes/sri-lankas-killing-fields, 1 December 2011.

Close Protection (2011) Failed anti-terror campaigns 'waste of money', Prevent strategy admits, http://www.closeprotectionworld.com/security-news-uk/49262-failed-anti-terror-campaigns-waste-money-prevent-strategy-admits.html, 12 January 2012.

Dhammaratana, Naravila (2008) Buddhist Nationalism and Religious Violence in Sri Lanka, http://www.class.uidaho.edu/ngier/slrv.htm, 12 November 2011.

Dhillon, Simrat (2007) The Sikh Diaspora and the Quest for Khalistan: A Search for Statehood or for Self-preservation?, http://www.ipcs.org/pdf_file/issue/1787132181IPCS-ResearchPaper12-SimratDhillon.pdf, 12 December 2007.

Dostoevsky, Fyodor (2009) The Brothers Karamazov, http://www.gutenberg.org/files/28054/28054-pdf.pdf, 13 November 2011.

Dow, James W. (2007) A Scientific Definition of Religion, http://www.anpere.net/2007/2.pdf, first accessed 12 December 2011.

Ernst, Stephanie (2009) On the FBI's 'Most Wanted' Vegan 'Terrorist', http://news.change.org/stories/on-the-fbis-most-wanted-vegan-terrorist, 12 June 2011.

Esquire (2009) The Falling Man, http://www.esquire.com/features/ESQ0903-SEP_FALLINGMAN, 29 November 2011.

Evans Jr, Alfred B. (2011) Nihilism and Nihilists, http://www.answers.com/topic/nihilism-and-nihilists, 11 November 2011.

Fox News (2008) FBI: Eco-terrorism remains the No. 1 Domestic Terror Threat, http://www.foxnews.com/story/0,2933,343768,00.html, 12 December 2011.

Freda, Franco (1969) La Disintegrazione del Sistema, http://megaupload.com/?d=017ZIWSU, 10 August 2011 (no longer available).

Free Republic (2011) Sudanese Cleric Pays Homage to Bin Laden and Calls upon Muslims to Attack US Citizens Worldwide, http://www.freerepublic.com/focus/f-news/2742260/posts, 12 December 2011.

Halligan, P.W., Kew, J., and Wright, A. (2010) Somesthetic aura: The experience of 'Alice in Wonderland', http://www.thelancet.com/journals/lancet/article/PIIS0140-6736%2805%2979301-6/fulltext, 5 December 2011.

Hänggi, Christian (2011) The greatest work of art, http://schuel.ch/tl_files/vortraege-kursunterlagen/interventions-stockhausen-lecture.pdf, 12 December 2011.

Home Office (2012) Current threat level, http://www.homeoffice.gov.uk/counter-terrorism/current-threat-level/, 30 January 2012.

Ibrahim, Raymond (2012) Muslim Brotherhood Declares 'Mastership of the World', *Middle East Forum*, http://www.meforum.org/3151/muslim-brotherhood-world-mastership, 15 January 2012.

India Today (2010) Maoism is Terrorism, http://indiatoday.intoday.in/site/story/Maoism+is+terrorism/1/92085.html, 1 December 2011.

International Socialism (2006) Marxism and terrorism, http://www.isj.org.uk/index.php4?id=182&issue=110, first accessed 3 December 2011.

Jihad Watch (2006) New 'jihad' video game targets Bush, US Forces, Shi'ite leaders, http://www.jihadwatch.org/2006/09/new-jihad-video-game-targets-bush-us-forces-shiite-leaders.html, 18 January 2012.

Kaczynski, Theodore (2002) Industrial Society and Its Future, http://editions-hache.com/essais/pdf/kaczynski2.pdf, 20 December 2011.

Kavkaz Centre (2010) English Transcript, http://www.kavkazcenter.com/eng/content/2010/03/08/11569_print.html, 2 December 2011.

Kirsch, Adam (2008) Demons Inner and Outer, http://www.nysun.com/arts/demons-inner-and-outer/83262, 17 November 2011.

Knuth, Rebecca (2006) Destroying a Symbol: Checkered History of Sri Lanka's Jaffna Public Library, http://archive.ifla.org/IV/ifla72/papers/119-Knuth-en.pdf, 27 June 2006.

Krebs, Pierre (2006) The Metapolitical Rebirth of Europe, http://www.newrightausnz.com/2006/02/24/the-metapolitical-rebirth-of-europe-by-pierre-krebs/, 1 December 2011.

libcom.org (2011) Strategy of Tension, http://libcom.org/tags/strategy-of-tension, 12 December 2011.

Loflin, Lewis (2001) The Tim McVeigh and the Christian Identity Connection, http://www.sullivan-county.com/identity/cal_shoot.htm, 12 December 2011.

Luneev, Victor (2002) High-Organized Crime and Terrorism: Proceedings of a Russian-American Workshop on 'High Impact Terrorism', http://www.nap.edu/openbook.php?record_id=10301&page=37, 29 November 2011.

Makija, Kanan and Mneimneh, Hassan (2002) Manual for a Raid, http://www.nybooks.com/articles/archives/2002/jan/17/manual-for-a-raid/, 12 December 2011.

Marx, Eleanor (1883) Underground Russia, http://www.marxists.org/archive/eleanor-marx/1883/08/underground-russia.htm, first accessed 4 December 2011.

Moser, Charles (1986) *The Brothers Karamazov* as a novel of the 1860s, http://www.utoronto.ca/tsq/DS/07/073.shtml, 6 July 2011.

Musawi, Mohammed Ali (2009) A Selected Translation of the LIFG Recantation Document, http://www.quilliamfoundation.org/images/a_selected_translation_of_the_lifg.pdf, 12 December 2011.

Nechayev, Sergey (1869) The Revolutionary Catechism, http://www.marxists.org/subject/anarchism/nechayev/catechism.htm, 3 December 2011.

Nothnagel, Alan (2010) From Pastor's Daughter to Terrorist: Gudrun Ensslin at the Age of 70, http://open.salon.com/blog/lost_in_berlin/2010/08/16/from_pastors_daughter_to_terrorist_gudrun_ensslin_at_70, 12 December 2011.

rafinfo.de (1998) Homepage, http://www.rafinfo.de/archiv/raf/raf-20-4-98.php, 12 December 2011.

Reuters (2011) Norwegian mass killer ruled insane, likely to avoid jail, http://uk.reuters.com/article/2011/11/29/uk-norway-killer-idUKTRE7AS0PT20111129, 15 December 2011.

Roberts, Michael (2009) LTTE and Tamil People I: Preamble, http://groundviews.org/2009/04/21/ltte-and-tamil-people-i-preamble/, 13 December 2011.

Rosenbaum, Jonathan (1998) Yigal Amir: Religious fanatic or Zionist, http://www.jewishmediaresources.com/75/yigal-amir-religious-fanatic-or-zionist, 7 February 2012.

Rosenfeld, Jean (2010) The Religion of Osama bin Laden: Terror in the Hand of God, http://www.publiceye.org/frontpage/911/Islam/rosenfeld-TOC.html, 30 November 2011.

SATP (2001) Suicide Killings- An Overview, http://www.satp.org/satporgtp/countries/shrilanka/database/suicide_killings.htm, 2 December 2011.

SciDev.net (2011) Anti-nanotech group behind Mexican scientist bombings, http://www.scidev.net/en/new-technologies/nanotechnology/news/anti-nanotech-group-behind-mexican-scientist-bombings.html, 12 December 2011.

Scribd (2011) Discovery Channel Hostage Taker's Manifesto, http://www.scribd.com/doc/36763699/Discovery-Channel-Hostage-Taker-s-Manifesto, 12 December 2011.

Shand, Richard (1998) The Secret Doctrine of the Assassins, http://www.alamut.com/subj/ideologies/alamut/secDoctrines.html, 1 December 2011.

Skari, Susie (2011) The Secret Life of Timothy McVeigh: Contradictions, Collaborators, and Hidden Connections in the Field, http://ncp.pcaaca.org/presentation/secret-life-timothy-mcveigh-contradictions-collaborators-and-hidden-connections-field, 12 December 2011.

Slaughter, Kevin (2011) Anders Behring Breivik: Is this the e-mail he sent to friends with 2083 Manifesto?, http://www.kevinislaughter.com/tag/2083-european-declaration-of-independence/, 12 November 2011.

software.informer (2012) Free speed reading Quran MP3 download, http://softwaretopic.informer.com/speed-reading-quran-mp3-download, 12 December 2011.

Southgate, Troy (2011) Evola. A Radical Traditionalist, http://ebookbrowse.com/southgate-julius-evola-a-radical-traditionalist-doc-d13275019, 12 December 2011.

Spittel, Gloria (2010) Keeping the Cause Alive: The Post-LTTE Tamil Eelam Support Network, http://thuppahi.wordpress.com/2010/11/29/keeping-the-cause-alive-the-post-ltte-tamil-eelam-support-network/, 11 November 2011.

Suver, Stacey (2008) Exploding Narrative: The Literature of Terrorism in Contemporary America, http://etd.lib.fsu.edu/theses/available/etd-07082008-182749/, 12 December 2011.

Tamil Eelam (2011) Advancing the Independence of Tamil Eeelam, http://www.eelam.com, first accessed 3 November 2011.

The Centre for Public Christianity (2011) Violence, http://www.publicchristianity.com/library/topic/violence, 12 December 2011.

The Economist (2008) The wild south, http://www.economist.com/node/12627992, 2 December 2011.

The Guardian (2011) Anders Behring Breivik may avoid jail after psychiatrists declare him insane, http://www.guardian.co.uk/world/2011/nov/29/anders-behring-breivik-avoid-jail-insane, 12 November 2011.

The New York Times (2009) White House Apologizes for Air Force Flyover, http://cityroom.blogs.nytimes.com/2009/04/27/air-force-one-backup-rattles-new-york-nerve/, 29 November 2011.

The Washington Post (2011) Motive of shooter who targeted military sites is unclear, http://www.washingtonpost.com/local/crime/motive-of-shooter-who-targeted-military-sites-is-unclear/2012/01/26/gIQAoGj6TQ_story.html, 27 January 2012.

Tibi, Bassam (2009) Ballot and Bullet. The Politicization of Islam to Islamism, http://cir.au.dk/fileadmin/site_files/filer_statskundskab/subsites/cir/pdf-filer/H%C3%A6fte_5_Tibi.pdf, 21 January 2012.

Time (1939) Church v. I.R.A., http://www.time.com/time/magazine/article/0,9171,761165,00.html, 12 December 2011.

Theoi Greek Mythology (2011) Nomos, http://www.theoi.com/Daimon/Nomos.html, 1 December 2011.

The Radical Truth (2011) Eros and Thanatos, http://www.theradicaltruth.com/Footnotes/wilber-atman-project-fn.htm, 12 December 2011.

Wood, James (2005) Warning Notes from the Underground, http://www.guardian.co.uk/books/2005/feb/26/featuresreviews.guardianreview33, 4 November 2011.

Žižek, Slavoj (2006) The Anatomies of Tolerant Reason: A Blood-dimmed Tide is Loosed, http://www.lacan.com/zizantinomies.htm, 16 November 2011.

Index

Only individuals and titles directly related to terrorism and the most salient passages of the book relating to its key themes have been included. Page references **in bold** indicate the principal passages in which the topics are discussed.